QUIET

.... Time

1-YEAR DAILY DEVOTIONAL WITH COMMENTARY

Quiet Time
One year devotional with Commentary

Word of Life Local Church Ministries
A division of Word of Life Fellowship, Inc.
Joe Jordan – Executive Director
Jack Wyrtzen & Harry Bollback - Founders
Mike Calhoun – VP of Local Church Ministries

USA
P.O. Box 600
Schroon Lake, NY 12870
talk@wol.org
1-888-932-5827

Web Address: www.wol.org

Canada
RR#8/Owen Sound
ON, Canada N4K 5W4
LCM@wol.ca
1-800-461-3503 or
(519) 376-3516

Publisher's Acknowledgements
Writers and Contributors:

Bill Boulet	Proverbs, 1 Corinthians
Dr. Tom Davis	Esther, Song of Solomon, Lamentations, Nahum, Malachi, Revelation
Jeff Farris	John
Don Kelso	Psalms, Hebrews
Dr. Chuck Scheide	Ephesians, 2 Timothy, Titus & Philemon
Dr. Charles Wagner	1 Kings, 2 Kings

Editor: Dr. Tom Davis
Curriculum Manager: Don Reichard
Cover and page design: Adam Rushlow

ISBN - 978-1-931235-52-5
Printed in the United States of America

Helpful Hints For a Daily Quiet Time

The purpose of this Quiet Time is to meet the needs of spiritual growth in the life of the Christian in such a way that they learn the art of conducting their own personal investigation into the Bible. Consider the following helpful hints:

1 Give priority in choosing your quiet time. This will vary with each individual in accordance with his own circumstances. The time you choose must:

- have top priority over everything else
- be the quietest time possible.
- be a convenient time of the day or night.
- be consistently observed each day.

2 Give attention to the procedure suggested for you to follow. Include the following items.

- Read God's Word.
- Mark your Bible as you read. Here are some suggestions that might be helpful:
  a. After you read the passage put an exclamation mark next to the verses you completely understand.
  b. Put a question mark next to verses you do not understand.
  c. Put an arrow pointing upward next to encouraging verses.
  d. Put an arrow pointing downward next to verses which weigh us down in our spiritual race.
  e. Put a star next to verses containing important truths or major points.
- Meditate on what you have read (In one sentence, write the main thought). Here are some suggestions as guidelines for meditating on God's Word:

a. Look at the selected passage from God's point of view.

b. Though we encourage quiet time in the morning, some people arrange to have their quiet time at the end of their day. God emphasizes that we need to go to sleep meditating on His Word. "My soul shall be satisfied and my mouth shall praise thee with joyful lips: when I remember thee upon my bed, and meditating on thee in the night watches" (Psalm 63:5,6).

c. Deuteronomy 6:7 lists routine things you do each day during which you should concentrate on the portion of Scripture for that day:

> — when you sit in your house (meals and relaxation)
> — when you walk in the way (to and from school or work)
> — when you lie down (before going to sleep at night)
> — when you rise up (getting ready for the day)

■ Apply some truth to your life. (Use first person pronouns I, me, my, mine). If you have difficulty in finding an application for your life, think of yourself as a Bible SPECTator and ask yourself the following questions.

> **S** – is there any sin for me to forsake?
>
> **P** – is there any promise for me to claim?
>
> **E** – is there any example for me to follow?
>
> **C** – is there any command for me to obey?
>
> **T** – is there anything to be thankful for today?

■ Pray for specific things (Use the prayer sheets found in the Personal Prayer Diary section).

3 Be sure to fill out your quiet time sheets. This will really help you remember the things the Lord brings to your mind.

4 Purpose to share with someone else each day something you gained from your quiet time. This can be a real blessing for them as well as for you.

my personal
prayer journal

daily prayer list

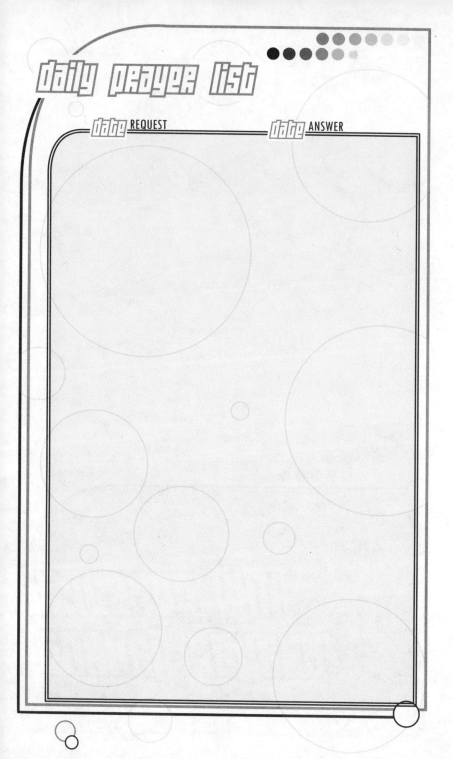

date REQUEST date ANSWER

daily prayer list

date REQUEST   **date** ANSWER

daily prayer list

date REQUEST   date ANSWER

daily prayer list

date REQUEST   **date** ANSWER

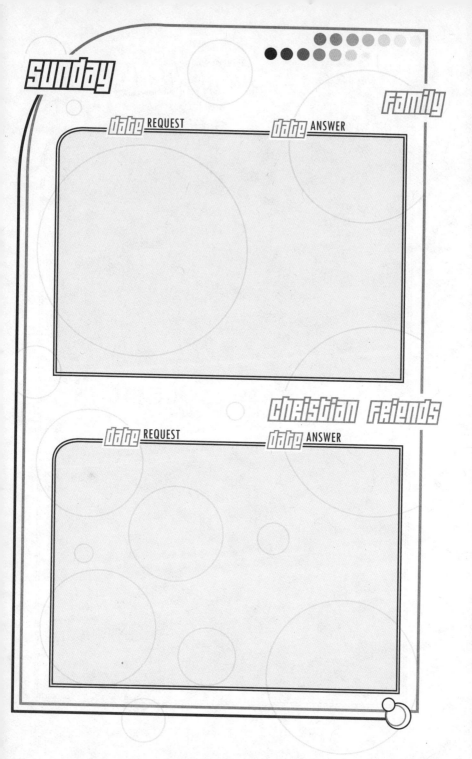

Sunday

Family

date REQUEST date ANSWER

Christian Friends

date REQUEST date ANSWER

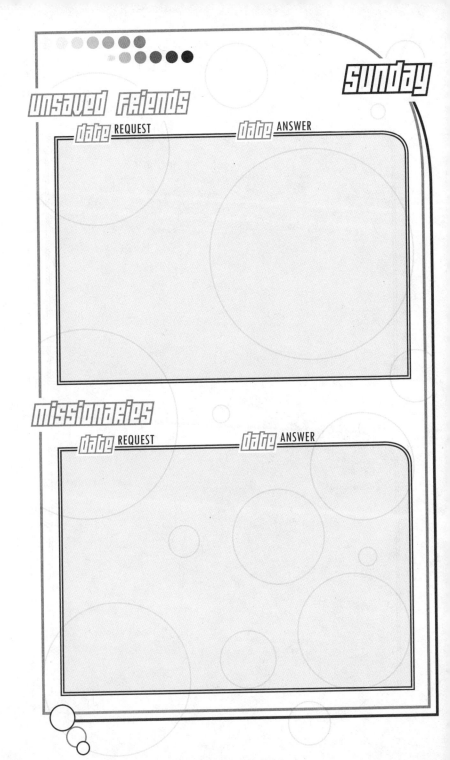

unsaved friends

date REQUEST   date ANSWER

missionaries

date REQUEST   date ANSWER

monday

Family

date	REQUEST	date	ANSWER

christian friends

date	REQUEST	date	ANSWER

unsaved friends

date REQUEST   date ANSWER

missionaries

date REQUEST   date ANSWER

tuesday

Family

date REQUEST   date ANSWER

christian friends

date REQUEST   date ANSWER

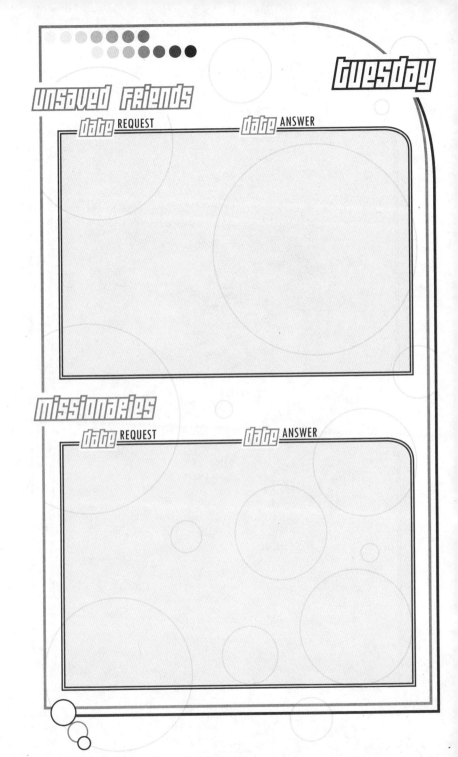

unsaved friends

date REQUEST   *date* ANSWER

missionaries

date REQUEST   *date* ANSWER

wednesday

Family

date REQUEST   *date* ANSWER

christian friends

date REQUEST   *date* ANSWER

wednesday

unsaved friends

date REQUEST   *date* ANSWER

missionaries

date REQUEST   *date* ANSWER

thursday

Family

date REQUEST date ANSWER

christian friends

date REQUEST date ANSWER

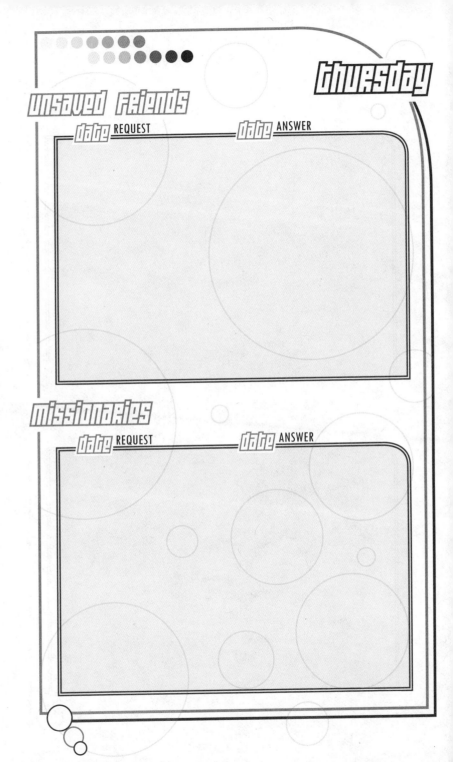

thursday

unsaved friends

date REQUEST   **date** ANSWER

missionaries

date REQUEST   **date** ANSWER

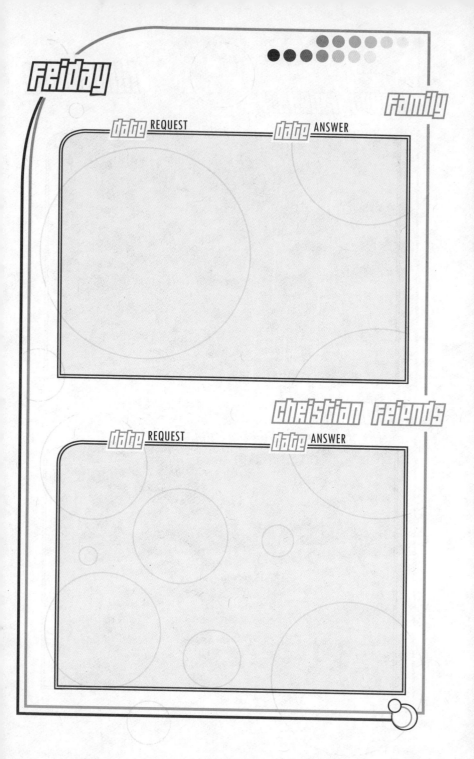

Friday

Family

date REQUEST   **date** ANSWER

christian Friends

date REQUEST   **date** ANSWER

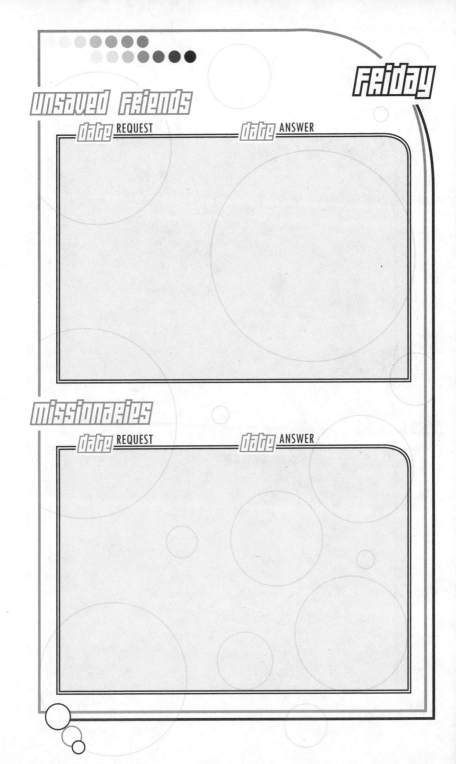

FRIDAY

UNSAVED FRIENDS

date REQUEST   **date** ANSWER

MISSIONARIES

date REQUEST   **date** ANSWER

saturday

family

date REQUEST   date ANSWER

christian friends

date REQUEST   date ANSWER

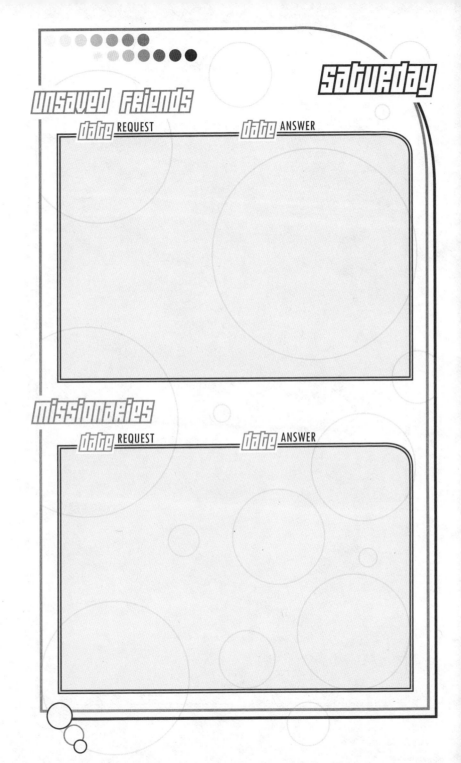

unsaved friends

date REQUEST   *date* ANSWER

missionaries

date REQUEST   *date* ANSWER

daily praise list

date I AM PRAISING GOD FOR...

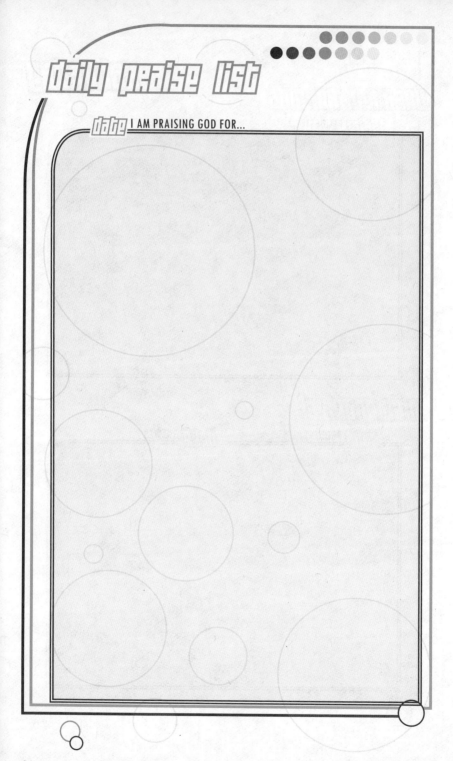

daily praise list

date I AM PRAISING GOD FOR...

daily praise list

date I AM PRAISING GOD FOR...

daily praise list

date I AM PRAISING GOD FOR...

daily praise list

I AM PRAISING GOD FOR...

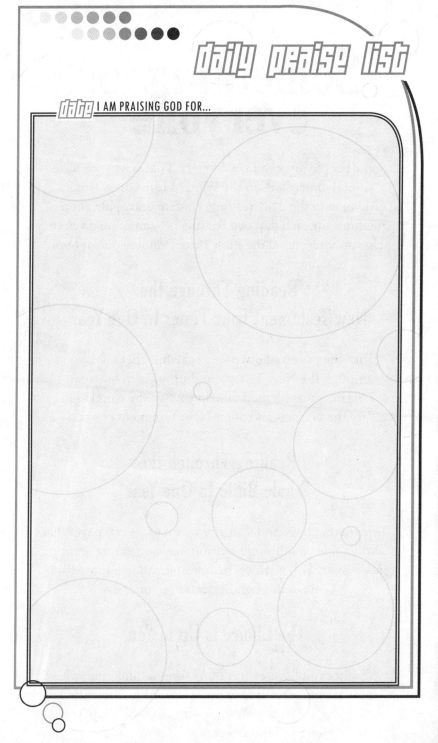

daily praise list

date I AM PRAISING GOD FOR...

Something for everyone

Some people just can't get enough! That is why we have several dimensions in the Word of Life Quiet Time. Along with the daily reading, content and application questions for each day, two reading programs are given to help you understand the Bible better. Choose one or both.

Reading Through the New Testament Four Times In One Year

Turn the page and discover a schedule that takes you through the New Testament four times in one year. This is a great method to help you see the correlation of the Gospels and other New Testament books.

Reading Through the Whole Bible In One Year

Turn another page and find a program of several pages that will guide you through a chronological reading of the entire Bible. Follow this schedule and you will move from Genesis through Revelation in one year.

The Choice is Up to You

Whether you have a short quiet time, a quiet time with more scripture reading or one with a mini-Bible study each day, we trust your time with God will draw you closer to Him in every area of your life.

Read through the new testament

Weeks 1-13		Weeks 14-26	
☐ Matthew 1-3	☐ Romans 4-6	☐ Matthew 1-3	☐ Romans 4-6
☐ Matthew 4-6	☐ Romans 7-9	☐ Matthew 4-6	☐ Romans 7-9
☐ Matthew 7-9	☐ Rom. 10-12	☐ Matthew 7-9	☐ Rom. 10-12
☐ Matt. 10-12	☐ Rom. 13-16	☐ Matt. 10-12	☐ Rom. 13-16
☐ Matt. 13-15	☐ 1 Cor. 1-4	☐ Matt. 13-15	☐ 1 Cor. 1-4
☐ Matt. 16-18	☐ 1 Cor. 5-9	☐ Matt. 16-18	☐ 1 Cor. 5-9
☐ Matt. 19-21	☐ 1 Cor. 10-12	☐ Matt. 19-21	☐ 1 Cor. 10-12
☐ Matt. 22-24	☐ 1 Cor. 13-16	☐ Matt. 22-24	☐ 1 Cor. 13-16
☐ Matt. 25-26	☐ 2 Cor. 1-4	☐ Matt. 25-26	☐ 2 Cor. 1-4
☐ Matt. 27-28	☐ 2 Cor. 5-8	☐ Matt. 27-28	☐ 2 Cor. 5-8
☐ Mark 1-3	☐ 2 Cor. 9-13	☐ Mark 1-3	☐ 2 Cor. 9-13
☐ Mark 4-5	☐ Galatians 1-3	☐ Mark 4-5	☐ Galatians 1-3
☐ Mark 6-8	☐ Galatians 4-6	☐ Mark 6-8	☐ Galatians 4-6
☐ Mark 9-11	☐ Ephesians 1-3	☐ Mark 9-11	☐ Ephesians 1-3
☐ Mark 12-14	☐ Ephesians 4-6	☐ Mark 12-14	☐ Ephesians 4-6
☐ Mark 15-16	☐ Philippians 1-4	☐ Mark 15-16	☐ Philippians 1-4
☐ Luke 1-2	☐ Colossians 1-4	☐ Luke 1-2	☐ Colossians 1-4
☐ Luke 3-5	☐ 1 Thes. 1-3	☐ Luke 3-5	☐ 1 Thes. 1-3
☐ Luke 6-7	☐ 1 Thes. 4-5	☐ Luke 6-7	☐ 1 Thes. 4-5
☐ Luke 8-9	☐ 2 Thes. 1-3	☐ Luke 8-9	☐ 2 Thes. 1-3
☐ Luke 10-11	☐ 1 Timothy 1-3	☐ Luke 10-11	☐ 1 Timothy 1-3
☐ Luke 12-14	☐ 1 Timothy 4-6	☐ Luke 12-14	☐ 1 Timothy 4-6
☐ Luke 15-17	☐ 2 Timothy 1-4	☐ Luke 15-17	☐ 2 Timothy 1-4
☐ Luke 18-20	☐ Titus 1-3	☐ Luke 18-20	☐ Titus 1-3
☐ Luke 21-22	☐ Philemon	☐ Luke 21-22	☐ Philemon
☐ Luke 23-24	☐ Hebrews 1	☐ Luke 23-24	☐ Hebrews 1
☐ John 1-3	☐ Hebrews 2-4	☐ John 1-3	☐ Hebrews 2-4
☐ John 4-5	☐ Hebrews 5-7	☐ John 4-5	☐ Hebrews 5-7
☐ John 6-7	☐ Hebrews 8-10	☐ John 6-7	☐ Hebrews 8-10
☐ John 8-10	☐ Hebrews 11-13	☐ John 8-10	☐ Hebrews 11-13
☐ John 11-12	☐ James 1-3	☐ John 11-12	☐ James 1-3
☐ John 13-15	☐ James 4-5	☐ John 13-15	☐ James 4-5
☐ John 16-18	☐ 1 Peter 1-3	☐ John 16-18	☐ 1 Peter 1-3
☐ John 19-21	☐ 1 Peter 4-5	☐ John 19-21	☐ 1 Peter 4-5
☐ Acts 1-3	☐ 2 Peter 1-3	☐ Acts 1-3	☐ 2 Peter 1-3
☐ Acts 4-6	☐ 1 John 1-3	☐ Acts 4-6	☐ 1 John 1-3
☐ Acts 7-8	☐ 1 John 4-5	☐ Acts 7-8	☐ 1 John 4-5
☐ Acts 9-11	☐ 2 Jn, 3 Jn, Jude	☐ Acts 9-11	☐ 2 Jn, 3 Jn, Jude
☐ Acts 12-15	☐ Rev. 1-3	☐ Acts 12-15	☐ Rev. 1-3
☐ Acts 16-18	☐ Rev. 4-6	☐ Acts 16-18	☐ Rev. 4-6
☐ Acts 19-21	☐ Rev. 7-9	☐ Acts 19-21	☐ Rev. 7-9
☐ Acts 22-24	☐ Rev. 10-12	☐ Acts 22-24	☐ Rev. 10-12
☐ Acts 25-26	☐ Rev. 13-15	☐ Acts 25-26	☐ Rev. 13-15
☐ Acts 27-28	☐ Rev. 16-18	☐ Acts 27-28	☐ Rev. 16-18
☐ Romans 1-3	☐ Rev. 19-22	☐ Romans 1-3	☐ Rev. 19-22

four times in one year

Read through the new testament

Weeks 27-39		Weeks 40-52	
☐ Matthew 1-3	☐ Romans 4-6	☐ Matthew 1-3	☐ Romans 4-6
☐ Matthew 4-6	☐ Romans 7-9	☐ Matthew 4-6	☐ Romans 7-9
☐ Matthew 7-9	☐ Romans 10-12	☐ Matthew 7-9	☐ Romans 10-12
☐ Matt. 10-12	☐ Romans 13-16	☐ Matt. 10-12	☐ Romans 13-16
☐ Matt. 13-15	☐ 1 Cor. 1-4	☐ Matt. 13-15	☐ 1 Cor. 1-4
☐ Matt. 16-18	☐ 1 Cor. 5-9	☐ Matt. 16-18	☐ 1 Cor. 5-9
☐ Matt. 19-21	☐ 1 Cor. 10-12	☐ Matt. 19-21	☐ 1 Cor. 10-12
☐ Matt. 22-24	☐ 1 Cor. 13-16	☐ Matt. 22-24	☐ 1 Cor. 13-16
☐ Matt. 25-26	☐ 2 Cor. 1-4	☐ Matt. 25-26	☐ 2 Cor. 1-4
☐ Matt. 27-28	☐ 2 Cor. 5-8	☐ Matt. 27-28	☐ 2 Cor. 5-8
☐ Mark 1-3	☐ 2 Cor. 9-13	☐ Mark 1-3	☐ 2 Cor. 9-13
☐ Mark 4-5	☐ Galatians 1-3	☐ Mark 4-5	☐ Galatians 1-3
☐ Mark 6-8	☐ Galatians 4-6	☐ Mark 6-8	☐ Galatians 4-6
☐ Mark 9-11	☐ Ephesians 1-3	☐ Mark 9-11	☐ Ephesians 1-3
☐ Mark 12-14	☐ Ephesians 4-6	☐ Mark 12-14	☐ Ephesians 4-6
☐ Mark 15-16	☐ Philippians 1-4	☐ Mark 15-16	☐ Philippians 1-4
☐ Luke 1-2	☐ Colossians 1-4	☐ Luke 1-2	☐ Colossians 1-4
☐ Luke 3-5	☐ 1 Thes. 1-3	☐ Luke 3-5	☐ 1 Thes. 1-3
☐ Luke 6-7	☐ 1 Thes. 4-5	☐ Luke 6-7	☐ 1 Thes. 4-5
☐ Luke 8-9	☐ 2 Thes. 1-3	☐ Luke 8-9	☐ 2 Thes. 1-3
☐ Luke 10-11	☐ 1 Timothy 1-3	☐ Luke 10-11	☐ 1 Timothy 1-3
☐ Luke 12-14	☐ 1 Timothy 4-6	☐ Luke 12-14	☐ 1 Timothy 4-6
☐ Luke 15-17	☐ 2 Timothy 1-4	☐ Luke 15-17	☐ 2 Timothy 1-4
☐ Luke 18-20	☐ Titus 1-3	☐ Luke 18-20	☐ Titus 1-3
☐ Luke 21-22	☐ Philemon	☐ Luke 21-22	☐ Philemon
☐ Luke 23-24	☐ Hebrews 1	☐ Luke 23-24	☐ Hebrews 1
☐ John 1-3	☐ Hebrews 2-4	☐ John 1-3	☐ Hebrews 2-4
☐ John 4-5	☐ Hebrews 5-7	☐ John 4-5	☐ Hebrews 5-7
☐ John 6-7	☐ Hebrews 8-10	☐ John 6-7	☐ Hebrews 8-10
☐ John 8-10	☐ Hebrews 11-13	☐ John 8-10	☐ Hebrews 11-13
☐ John 11-12	☐ James 1-3	☐ John 11-12	☐ James 1-3
☐ John 13-15	☐ James 4-5	☐ John 13-15	☐ James 4-5
☐ John 16-18	☐ 1 Peter 1-3	☐ John 16-18	☐ 1 Peter 1-3
☐ John 19-21	☐ 1 Peter 4-5	☐ John 19-21	☐ 1 Peter 4-5
☐ Acts 1-3	☐ 2 Peter 1-3	☐ Acts 1-3	☐ 2 Peter 1-3
☐ Acts 4-6	☐ 1 John 1-3	☐ Acts 4-6	☐ 1 John 1-3
☐ Acts 7-8	☐ 1 John 4-5	☐ Acts 7-8	☐ 1 John 4-5
☐ Acts 9-11	☐ 2 Jn, 3 Jn, Jude	☐ Acts 9-11	☐ 2 Jn, 3 Jn, Jude
☐ Acts 12-15	☐ Revelation 1-3	☐ Acts 12-15	☐ Revelation 1-3
☐ Acts 16-18	☐ Revelation 4-6	☐ Acts 16-18	☐ Revelation 4-6
☐ Acts 19-21	☐ Revelation 7-9	☐ Acts 19-21	☐ Revelation 7-9
☐ Acts 22-24	☐ Rev. 10-12	☐ Acts 22-24	☐ Rev. 10-12
☐ Acts 25-26	☐ Rev. 13-15	☐ Acts 25-26	☐ Rev. 13-15
☐ Acts 27-28	☐ Rev. 16-18	☐ Acts 27-28	☐ Rev. 16-18
☐ Romans 1-3	☐ Rev. 19-22	☐ Romans 1-3	☐ Rev. 19-22

four times in one year

Bible reading schedule

Read through the Bible in one year! As you complete each daily
reading, simply place a check in the appropriate box.

☐ 1 Genesis 1-3
☐ 2 Genesis 4:1-6:8
☐ 3 Genesis 6:9-9:29
☐ 4 Genesis 10-11
☐ 5 Genesis 12-14
☐ 6 Genesis 15-17
☐ 7 Genesis 18-19
☐ 8 Genesis 20-22
☐ 9 Genesis 23-24
☐ 10 Genesis 25-26
☐ 11 Genesis 27-28
☐ 12 Genesis 29-30
☐ 13 Genesis 31-32
☐ 14 Genesis 33-35
☐ 15 Genesis 36-37
☐ 16 Genesis 38-40
☐ 17 Genesis 41-42
☐ 18 Genesis 43-45
☐ 19 Genesis 46-47
☐ 20 Genesis 48-50
☐ 21 Job 1-3
☐ 22 Job 4-7
☐ 23 Job 8-11
☐ 24 Job 12-15
☐ 25 Job 16-19
☐ 26 Job 20-22
☐ 27 Job 23-28
☐ 28 Job 29-31
☐ 29 Job 32-34
☐ 30 Job 35-37
☐ 31 Job 38-42
☐ 32 Exodus 1-4
☐ 33 Exodus 5-8
☐ 34 Exodus 9-11
☐ 35 Exodus 12-13
☐ 36 Exodus 14-15
☐ 37 Exodus 16-18
☐ 38 Exodus 19-21
☐ 39 Exodus 22-24
☐ 40 Exodus 25-27
☐ 41 Exodus 28-29
☐ 42 Exodus 30-31
☐ 43 Exodus 32-34
☐ 44 Exodus 35-36
☐ 45 Exodus 37-38
☐ 46 Exodus 39-40
☐ 47 Leviticus 1:1-5:13
☐ 48 Leviticus 5:14-7:38
☐ 49 Leviticus 8-10
☐ 50 Leviticus 11-12
☐ 51 Leviticus 13-14
☐ 52 Leviticus 15-17

☐ 53 Leviticus 18-20
☐ 54 Leviticus 21-23
☐ 55 Leviticus 24-25
☐ 56 Leviticus 26-27
☐ 57 Numbers 1-2
☐ 58 Numbers 3-4
☐ 59 Numbers 5-6
☐ 60 Numbers 7
☐ 61 Numbers 8-10
☐ 62 Numbers 11-13
☐ 63 Numbers 14-15
☐ 64 Numbers 16-18
☐ 65 Numbers 19-21
☐ 66 Numbers 22-24
☐ 67 Numbers 25-26
☐ 68 Numbers 27-29
☐ 69 Numbers 30-31
☐ 70 Numbers 32-33
☐ 71 Numbers 34-36
☐ 72 Deuteronomy 1-2
☐ 73 Deuteronomy 3-4
☐ 74 Deuteronomy 5-7
☐ 75 Deuteronomy 8-10
☐ 76 Deuteronomy 11-13
☐ 77 Deuteronomy 14-17
☐ 78 Deuteronomy 18-21
☐ 79 Deuteronomy 22-25
☐ 80 Deuteronomy 26-28
☐ 81 Deuteronomy 29:1-31:29
☐ 82 Deuteronomy 31:30-34:12
☐ 83 Joshua 1-4
☐ 84 Joshua 5-8
☐ 85 Joshua 9-11
☐ 86 Joshua 12-14
☐ 87 Joshua 15-17
☐ 88 Joshua 18-19
☐ 89 Joshua 20-22
☐ 90 Joshua 23 - Judges 1
☐ 91 Judges 2-5
☐ 92 Judges 6-8
☐ 93 Judges 9
☐ 94 Judges 10-12
☐ 95 Judges 13-16
☐ 96 Judges 17-19
☐ 97 Judges 20-21
☐ 98 Ruth
☐ 99 1 Samuel 1-3
☐ 100 1 Samuel 4-7
☐ 101 1 Samuel 8-10
☐ 102 1 Samuel 11-13
☐ 103 1 Samuel 14-15
☐ 104 1 Samuel 16-17

Bible reading schedule
Day 105-199

- [ ] 105 1 Samuel 18-19; Psalm 59
- [ ] 106 1 Samuel 20-21; Psalm 56; 34
- [ ] 107 1 Samuel 22-23; 1 Chronicles 12:8-18; Psalm 52; 54; 63; 142
- [ ] 108 1 Samuel 24; Psalm 57; 1 Samuel 25
- [ ] 109 1 Sam. 26-29; 1 Chronicles 12:1-7, 19-22
- [ ] 110 1 Samuel 30-31; 1 Chronicles 10; 2 Sam. 1
- [ ] 111 2 Samuel 2-4
- [ ] 112 2 Samuel 5:1-6:11; 1 Chronicles 11:1-9; 2:23-40; 13:1-14:17
- [ ] 113 2 Samuel 22; Psalm 18
- [ ] 114 1 Chron. 15-16; 2 Sam. 6:12-23; Psalm 96
- [ ] 115 Psalm 105; 2 Sam. 7; 1 Chronicles 17
- [ ] 116 2 Sam. 8-10; 1 Chronicles 18-19; Psalm 60
- [ ] 117 2 Sam. 11-12; 1 Chron. 20:1-3; Psalm 51
- [ ] 118 2 Samuel 13-14
- [ ] 119 2 Samuel 15-17
- [ ] 120 Psalm 3; 2 Samuel 18-19
- [ ] 121 2 Samuel 20-21; 23:8-23; 1 Chronicles 20:4-8; 11:10-25
- [ ] 122 2 Samuel 23:24-24:25;
- [ ] 123 1 Chronicles 11:26-47; 21:1-30, 1 Chronicles 22-24
- [ ] 124 Psalm 30; 1 Chronicles 25-26
- [ ] 125 1 Chronicles 27-29
- [ ] 126 Psalms 5-7; 10; 11; 13; 17
- [ ] 127 Psalms 23; 26; 28; 31; 35
- [ ] 128 Psalms 41; 43; 46; 55; 61; 62; 64
- [ ] 129 Psalms 69-71; 77
- [ ] 130 Psalms 83; 86; 88; 91; 95
- [ ] 131 Psalms 108-9; 120-21; 140; 143-44
- [ ] 132 Psalms 1; 14-15; 36-37; 39
- [ ] 133 Psalms 40; 49-50; 73
- [ ] 134 Psalms 76; 82; 84; 90; 92; 112; 115
- [ ] 135 Psalms 8-9; 16; 19; 21; 24; 29
- [ ] 136 Psalms 33; 65-68
- [ ] 137 Psalms 75; 93-94; 97-100
- [ ] 138 Psalms 103-4; 113-14; 117
- [ ] 139 Psalm 119:1-88
- [ ] 140 Psalm 119:89-176
- [ ] 141 Psalms 122; 124; 133-36
- [ ] 142 Psalms 138-39; 145; 148; 150
- [ ] 143 Psalms 4; 12; 20; 25; 32; 38
- [ ] 144 Psalms 42; 53; 58; 81; 101; 111; 130-31; 141; 146
- [ ] 145 Psalms 2; 22; 27
- [ ] 146 Psalms 45; 47-48; 87; 110
- [ ] 147 1 Kings 1:1-2:12; 2 Samuel 23:1-7
- [ ] 148 1 Kings 2:13-3:28; 2 Chron. 1:1-13
- [ ] 149 1 Kings 5-6; 2 Chronicles 2-3
- [ ] 150 1 Kings 7; 2 Chronicles 4
- [ ] 151 1 Kings 8; 2 Chronicles 5:1-7:10
- [ ] 152 1 Kings 9:1-10:13; 2 Chron. 7:11-9:12
- [ ] 153 1 Kings 4; 10:14-29; 2 Chronicles 1:14-17; 9:13-28; Psalm 72
- [ ] 154 Proverbs 1-3
- [ ] 155 Proverbs 4-6
- [ ] 156 Proverbs 7-9
- [ ] 157 Proverbs 10-12
- [ ] 158 Proverbs 13-15
- [ ] 159 Proverbs 16-18
- [ ] 160 Proverbs 19-21
- [ ] 161 Proverbs 22-24
- [ ] 162 Proverbs 25-27
- [ ] 163 Proverbs 28-29
- [ ] 164 Proverbs 30-31; Psalm 127
- [ ] 165 Song of Solomon
- [ ] 166 1 Kings 11:1-40; Ecclesiastes 1-2
- [ ] 167 Ecclesiastes 3-7
- [ ] 168 Ecclesiastes 8-12; 1 Kings 11:41-43; 2 Chronicles 9:29-31
- [ ] 169 1 Kings 12; 2 Chronicles 10:1-11:17
- [ ] 170 1 Kings 13-14; 2 Chron. 11:18-12:16
- [ ] 171 1 Kings 15:1-24; 2 Chronicles 13-16
- [ ] 172 1 Kings 15:25-16:34; 2 Chronicles 17; 1 Kings 17
- [ ] 173 1 Kings 18-19
- [ ] 174 1 Kings 20-21
- [ ] 175 1 Kings 22:1-40; 2 Chronicles 18
- [ ] 176 1 Kings 22:41-53; 2 Kings 1; 2 Chronicles 19:1-21:3
- [ ] 177 2 Kings 2-4
- [ ] 178 2 Kings 5-7
- [ ] 179 2 Kings 8-9; 2 Chronicles 21:4-22:9
- [ ] 180 2 Kings 10-11; 2 Chron. 22:10-23:21
- [ ] 181 Joel
- [ ] 182 2 Kings 12-13; 2 Chronicles 24
- [ ] 183 2 Kings 14; 2 Chronicles 25; Jonah
- [ ] 184 Hosea 1-7
- [ ] 185 Hosea 8-14
- [ ] 186 2 Kings 15:1-7; 2 Chron. 26; Amos 1-4
- [ ] 187 Amos 5-9; 2 Kings 15:8-18
- [ ] 188 Isaiah 1-4
- [ ] 189 2 Kings 15:19-38; 2 Chronicles 27; Isaiah 5-6
- [ ] 190 Micah
- [ ] 191 2 Kings 16; 2 Chron. 28; Isaiah 7-8
- [ ] 192 Isaiah 9-12
- [ ] 193 Isaiah 13-16
- [ ] 194 Isaiah 17-22
- [ ] 195 Isaiah 23-27
- [ ] 196 Isaiah 28-30
- [ ] 197 Isaiah 31-35
- [ ] 198 2 Kings 18:1-8; 2 Chronicles 29-31
- [ ] 199 2 Kings 17; 18:9-37; 2 Chronicles 32:1-19; Isaiah 36

Bible reading schedule
Day 200-288

- [ ] 200 2 Kings 19; 2 Chron. 32:20-23; Isaiah 37
- [ ] 201 2 Kings 20; 2 Chron. 32:24-33; Isaiah 38-39
- [ ] 202 2 Kings 21:1-18; 2 Chronicles 33:1-20; Isaiah 40
- [ ] 203 Isaiah 41-43
- [ ] 204 Isaiah 44-47
- [ ] 205 Isaiah 48-51
- [ ] 206 Isaiah 52-57
- [ ] 207 Isaiah 58-62
- [ ] 208 Isaiah 63-66
- [ ] 209 2 Kings 21:19-26; 2 Chronicles 33:21-34:7; Zephaniah
- [ ] 210 Jeremiah 1-3
- [ ] 211 Jeremiah 4-6
- [ ] 212 Jeremiah 7-9
- [ ] 213 Jeremiah 10-13
- [ ] 214 Jeremiah 14-16
- [ ] 215 Jeremiah 17-20
- [ ] 216 2 Kings 22:1-23:28; 2 Chron. 34:8-35:19
- [ ] 217 Nahum; 2 Kings 23:29-37; 2 Chron. 35:20-36:5; Jeremiah 22:10-17
- [ ] 218 Jeremiah 26; Habakkuk
- [ ] 219 Jeremiah 46-47; 2 Kings 24:1-4, 7; 2 Chronicles 36:6-7; Jeremiah 25, 35
- [ ] 220 Jeremiah 36, 45, 48
- [ ] 221 Jeremiah 49:1-33; Daniel 1-2
- [ ] 222 Jeremiah 22:18-30; 2 Kings 24:5-20; 2 Chron. 36:8-12; Jeremiah 37:1-2; 52:1-3; 24; 29
- [ ] 223 Jeremiah 27-28, 23
- [ ] 224 Jeremiah 50-51
- [ ] 225 Jer. 49:34-39; 34:1-22; Ezekiel 1-3
- [ ] 226 Ezekiel 4-7
- [ ] 227 Ezekiel 8-11
- [ ] 228 Ezekiel 12-14
- [ ] 229 Ezekiel 15-17
- [ ] 230 Ezekiel 18-20
- [ ] 231 Ezekiel 21-23
- [ ] 232 2 Kings 25:1; 2 Chronicles 36:13-16; Jer. 39:1; 52:4; Ezekiel 24; Jer. 21:1-22:9; 32:1-44
- [ ] 233 Jeremiah 30-31, 33
- [ ] 234 Ezekiel 25; 29:1-16; 30; 31
- [ ] 235 Ezekiel 26-28
- [ ] 236 Jeremiah 37:3-39:10; 52:5-30; 2 Kings 25:2-21; 2 Chronicles 36:17-21
- [ ] 237 2 Kings 25:22; Jeremiah 39:11-40:6; Lamentations 1-3
- [ ] 238 Lamentations 4-5; Obadiah
- [ ] 239 Jer. 40:7-44:30; 2 Kings 25:23-26
- [ ] 240 Ezekiel 33:21-36:38
- [ ] 241 Ezekiel 37-39
- [ ] 242 Ezekiel 32:1-33:20; Daniel 3
- [ ] 243 Ezekiel 40-42
- [ ] 244 Ezekiel 43-45
- [ ] 245 Ezekiel 46-48
- [ ] 246 Ezekiel 29:17-21; Daniel 4; Jeremiah 52:31-34; 2 Kings 25:27-30; Psalm 44
- [ ] 247 Psalms 74; 79-80; 89
- [ ] 248 Psalms 85; 102; 106; 123; 137
- [ ] 249 Daniel 7-8; 5
- [ ] 250 Daniel 9; 6
- [ ] 251 2 Chronicles 36:22-23; Ezra 1:1-4:5
- [ ] 252 Daniel 10-12
- [ ] 253 Ezra 4:6-6:13; Haggai
- [ ] 254 Zechariah 1-6
- [ ] 255 Zech. 7-8; Ezra 6:14-22; Psalm 78
- [ ] 256 Psalms 107; 116; 118
- [ ] 257 Psalms 125-26; 128-29; 132; 147; 149
- [ ] 258 Zechariah 9-14
- [ ] 259 Esther 1-4
- [ ] 260 Esther 5-10
- [ ] 261 Ezra 7-8
- [ ] 262 Ezra 9-10
- [ ] 263 Nehemiah 1-5
- [ ] 264 Nehemiah 6-7
- [ ] 265 Nehemiah 8-10
- [ ] 266 Nehemiah 11-13
- [ ] 267 Malachi
- [ ] 268 1 Chronicles 1-2
- [ ] 269 1 Chronicles 3-5
- [ ] 270 1 Chronicles 6
- [ ] 271 1 Chronicles 7:1-8:27
- [ ] 272 1 Chronicles 8:28-9:44
- [ ] 273 John 1:1-18; Mark 1:1; Luke 1:1-4; 3:23-38; Matthew 1:1-17
- [ ] 274 Luke 1:5-80
- [ ] 275 Matthew 1:18-2:23; Luke 2
- [ ] 276 Matthew 3:1-4:11; Mark 1:2-13; Luke 3:1-23; 4:1-13; John 1:19-34
- [ ] 277 John 1:35-3:36
- [ ] 278 John 4; Matthew 4:12-17; Mark 1:14-15; Luke 4:14-30
- [ ] 279 Mark 1:16-45; Matthew 4:18-25; 8:2-4, 14-17; Luke 4:31-5:16
- [ ] 280 Matthew 9:1-17; Mark 2:1-22; Luke 5:17-39
- [ ] 281 John 5; Matthew 12:1-21; Mark 2:23-3:12; Luke 6:1-11
- [ ] 282 Matt. 5; Mark 3:13-19; Luke 6:12-36
- [ ] 283 Matthew 6-7; Luke 6:37-49
- [ ] 284 Luke 7; Matthew 8:1, 5-13; 11:2-30
- [ ] 285 Matt. 12:22-50; Mark 3:20-35; Luke 8:1-21
- [ ] 286 Mark 4:1-34; Matthew 13:1-53
- [ ] 287 Mark 4:35-5:43; Matthew 8:18, 23-34; 9:18-34; Luke 8:22-56
- [ ] 288 Mark 6:1-30; Matthew 13:54-58; 9:35-11:1; 14:1-12; Luke 9:1-10

Bible reading schedule ● ● ● ●
Day 289-365

- [ ] 289 Matthew 14:13-36; Mark 6:31-56; Luke 9:11-17; John 6:1-21
- [ ] 290 John 6:22-7:1; Matthew 15:1-20; Mark 7:1-23
- [ ] 291 Matthew 15:21-16:20; Mark 7:24-8:30; Luke 9:18-21
- [ ] 292 Matthew 16:21-17:27; Mark 8:31-9:32; Luke 9:22-45
- [ ] 293 Matthew 18; 8:19-22; Mark 9:33-50; Luke 9:46-62; John 7:2-10
- [ ] 294 John 7:11-8:59
- [ ] 295 Luke 10:1-11:36
- [ ] 296 Luke 11:37-13:21
- [ ] 297 John 9-10
- [ ] 298 Luke 13:22-15:32
- [ ] 299 Luke 16:1-17:10; John 11:1-54
- [ ] 300 Luke 17:11-18:17; Matthew 19:1-15; Mark 10:1-16
- [ ] 301 Matthew 19:16-20:28; Mark 10:17-45; Luke 18:18-34
- [ ] 302 Matthew 20:29-34; 26:6-13; Mark 10:46-52; 14:3-9; Luke 18:35-19:28; John 11:55-12:11
- [ ] 303 Matthew 21:1-22; Mark 11:1-26; Luke 19:29-48; John 12:12-50
- [ ] 304 Matthew 21:23-22:14; Mark 11:27-12:12; Luke 20:1-19
- [ ] 305 Matthew 22:15-46; Mark 12:13-37; Luke 20:20-44
- [ ] 306 Matthew 23; Mark 12:38-44; Luke 20:45-21:4
- [ ] 307 Matthew 24:1-31; Mark 13:1-27; Luke 21:5-27
- [ ] 308 Matthew 24:32-26:5, 14-16; Mark 13:28-14:2, 10-11; Luke 21:28-22:6
- [ ] 309 Matthew 26:17-29; Mark 14:12-25; Luke 22:7-38; John 13
- [ ] 310 John 14-16
- [ ] 311 John 17:1-18:1; Matthew 26:30-46; Mark 14:26-42; Luke 22:39-46
- [ ] 312 Matthew 26:47-75; Mark 14:43-72; Luke 22:47-65; John 18:2-27
- [ ] 313 Matthew 27:1-26; Mark 15:1-15; Luke 22:66-23:25; John 18:28-19:16
- [ ] 314 Matthew 27:27-56; Mark 15:16-41; Luke 23:26-49; John 19:17-30
- [ ] 315 Matthew 27:57-28:8; Mark 15:42-16:8; Luke 23:50-24:12; John 19:31-20:10
- [ ] 316 Matthew 28:9-20; Mark 16:9-20; Luke 24:13-53; John 20:11-21:25
- [ ] 317 Acts 1-2
- [ ] 318 Acts 3-5
- [ ] 319 Acts 6:1-8:1
- [ ] 320 Acts 8:2-9:43
- [ ] 321 Acts 10-11
- [ ] 322 Acts 12-13
- [ ] 323 Acts 14-15
- [ ] 324 Galatians 1-3
- [ ] 325 Galatians 4-6
- [ ] 326 James
- [ ] 327 Acts 16:1-18:11
- [ ] 328 1 Thessalonians
- [ ] 329 2 Thessalonians; Acts 18:12-19:22
- [ ] 330 1 Corinthians 1-4
- [ ] 331 1 Corinthians 5-8
- [ ] 332 1 Corinthians 9-11
- [ ] 333 1 Corinthians 12-14
- [ ] 334 1 Corinthians 15-16
- [ ] 335 Acts 19:23-20:1; 2 Corinthians 1-4
- [ ] 336 2 Corinthians 5-9
- [ ] 337 2 Corinthians 10-13
- [ ] 338 Romans 1-3
- [ ] 339 Romans 4-6
- [ ] 340 Romans 7-8
- [ ] 341 Romans 9-11
- [ ] 342 Romans 12-15
- [ ] 343 Romans 16; Acts 20:2-21:16
- [ ] 344 Acts 21:17-23:35
- [ ] 345 Acts 24-26
- [ ] 346 Acts 27-28
- [ ] 347 Ephesians 1-3
- [ ] 348 Ephesians 4-6
- [ ] 349 Colossians
- [ ] 350 Philippians
- [ ] 351 Philemon; 1 Timothy 1-3
- [ ] 352 1 Timothy 4-6; Titus
- [ ] 353 2 Timothy
- [ ] 354 1 Peter
- [ ] 355 Jude; 2 Peter
- [ ] 356 Hebrews 1:1-5:10
- [ ] 357 Hebrews 5:11-9:28
- [ ] 358 Hebrews 10-11
- [ ] 359 Hebrews 12-13; 2 John; 3 John
- [ ] 360 1 John
- [ ] 361 Revelation 1-3
- [ ] 362 Revelation 4-9
- [ ] 363 Revelation 10-14
- [ ] 364 Revelation 15-18
- [ ] 365 Revelation 19-22

Our English word "Psalms" derives from a Greek word denoting "poems sung to the accompaniment of string instruments." The English translation of the Hebrew title is "Book of Praises." Actually Psalms consist of five books – each ending with a doxology. The superscriptions in the Hebrew text ascribe authorship of 73 Psalms to David and 27 to various other writers. 50 Psalms are anonymous. However, New Testament references and textual content indicate Davidic authorship of some of the 50. Truly, David the son of Jesse was "raised up on high and anointed of God" not only to be king, but also as "the Sweet Psalmist of Israel" (2 Samual 23:1).

The Psalms contain praise, petition, prophecy, and perspective on the past history of God's people. A number of them are songs about the creation, glorifying the Creator. Others extol the veracity and the power of God's word. The prophetic Psalms are especially intriguing. Sixteen of these are designated "Messianic" because, in whole or in part, they foretell events concerning either the first of the second Coming of Christ. The words of the risen Christ Himself in Luke 24:27 and 24:44 should alert us to search for our Lord in every Psalm.

Several Scriptures let us know that the human authors were aware that they were writing under the power and in the wisdom of a Divine Author. See 2 Samuel 23:2, Psalm 102:18-19 and I Peter: 10:12.

If you'll find time to meditate on the words of the Psalms, here are some promises for you. You will be fruitful and prosperous in all that you do (Psalm 1:2-3). You will sleep well (Psalm 4:4, 8). Your soul will be satisfied (Psalm 63:5-6). You will be glad in the Lord (Psalm 104:34). You will not sin against your God (Psalm 119:11), but will have respect unto His ways (Psalm 119:15). You will be wiser than your enemies and understand more than your teachers and your elders (Psalm 119:97-100).

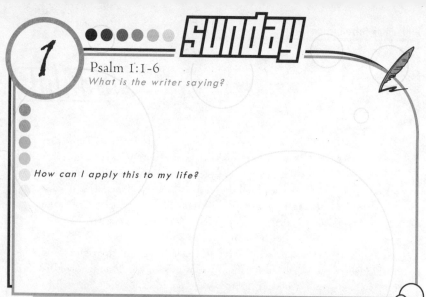

Psalm 1:1-6

What is the writer saying?

How can I apply this to my life?

Thailand — Fruit from the circulation of Christian cassettes recorded in more than 64 languages.

Our very first Psalm tells of two persons, two ways, and two destinies. The first individual is described as "blessed." His way is called righteous and he is destined to "prosper." The second is called ungodly in his way and "shall perish."

Notice there are three pursuits from which the blessed man refrains that have to do with his walk, where he stands, and with whom he sits. Rather, he engages himself in pursuits, which cause whatsoever he does to prosper.

How does a tree prosper — by engaging in frantic activity? Does it wave its branches forcefully to bear much fruit? It prospers by situating itself correctly and receiving the God-given provision. Likewise, the godly person earnestly desires the fruit producing water of life and the fruit comes forth!

The blessed person is situated "in Christ" (Ephesians 1:3) and is walking "in the Spirit" (Galatians 5:16). He is righteous because he is one with Christ who is the way (Psalm 1:1), the truth (Psalm 1:2) and the life (Psalm 1:3). The ungodly is "in Adam" (1 Corinthians 15:22) and his walk is "according to the course of this world" (Ephesians 2:2). Therefore, he shall perish!

Life stEP

If I delight in the Word of God, I will meditate in the Word of God. If I don't meditate, it is evident that I am not delighted in His Word, and therefore should not expect to qualify for the promise — "whatsoever he doeth shall prosper."

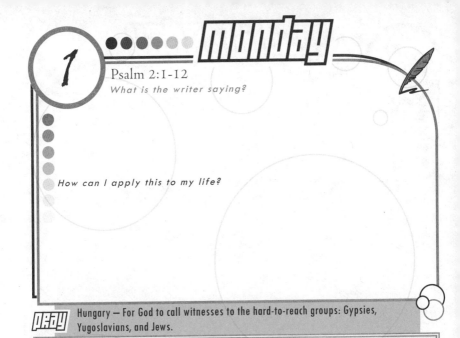

Psalm 2:1-12

What is the writer saying?

How can I apply this to my life?

PRAY Hungary — For God to call witnesses to the hard-to-reach groups: Gypsies, Yugoslavians, and Jews.

Sixteen Psalms are designated as "Messianic." These, in whole or in part, contain prophetic reference to the first or the second coming of Christ. In addition, there is New Testament documentation of the Messianic portion. Psalm 2 is quoted in Acts, Hebrews, and Revelation for a total of seven times. Acts 4:25-28 quotes, then applies, Psalm 2:1,2 to events surrounding the crucifixion of Christ as recorded in Matthew 26:3,4; Mark 3:6; and Luke 23:12,13.

Consider Psalm 2 as a drama on the world stage. In verses 1 and 2, the political and religious leaders are under the spotlight. In effect they say (verse 3): "We will not be controlled by God." They are swept off the stage in verse 4 by God the Father, who announces in verse 6 that He has determined who will be King on Earth. In verse seven, God the Son takes center stage and gives forth a royal decree under the authority given by the Father. His total decree is a promise from the Father! In verse ten, while the spotlight remains on the Son, God the Holy Spirit sounds out advice and warning and offers salvation.

Life **stEP**

According to the last words of Psalm 2, who will be blessed? If you have already trusted Him as Savior, do you now trust Him as absolute King of your life (Colossians 2:6)?

tuesday

1

Psalm 3:1-8

What is the writer saying?

How can I apply this to my life?

pray Fiji — For the success of church planting ministries, as Mormons and Jehovah's Witnesses grow in numbers.

Many of the Psalms of David arose from his experiences. Psalms 3 was probably written on the first or second morning after his nighttime flight across the Jordan River when he was pursued by the armies of his son Absalom (see 2 Samuel 17).

As David was reflecting upon the events of the previous night, he recorded the progress of his outlook from troubled (verses 1 and 2) to trusting (verses 3 and 4) to tranquil (verse 5). He awakened triumphant (verses 6-8)! His recipe for transforming a troubled soul into a trusting soul was to turn his thoughts from "the many against me" to "the LORD my shield, my glory, and the lifter up of my head."

The result is a tranquil soul that is able to lie down and sleep, and then awake with confidence restored. Although the battle lay ahead, the victory was already claimed.

The little Hebrew word "selah" is found in the Bible only in the Psalms (71 times) and Habakkuk (3 times). Most Bible scholars see the word as a directive to the instrumental musicians accompanying the singing of the Psalm. This would mean the word was not in the original composition. Other scholars say the root meaning is "always and forever." One commentator believes the thought conveyed to the reader is: "You have just read eternal truth; pause and reflect upon it."

Life stEP

How often have troubles arisen in your life that robbed you of sleep and tranquility? Not many of us have been in circumstances so dire as David's. Yet he testifies that this recipe worked for him!

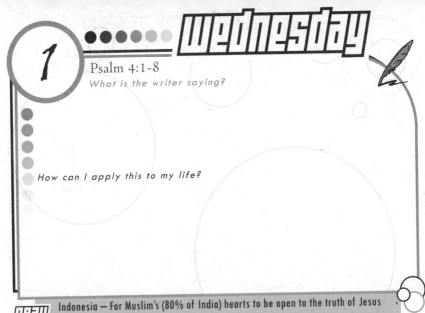

1

Psalm 4:1-8

What is the writer saying?

How can I apply this to my life?

PRAY Indonesia – For Muslim's (80% of India) hearts to be open to the truth of Jesus Christ.

Since ancient times, Psalm 3 has been entitled "a morning Psalm" and Psalm 4 "an evening Psalm." Psalm 4 was probably penned as a result of the victory recorded in 2 Samuel 18:1-8 and before David learned of the death of Absalom (2 Samuel 18:9).

"O God of my righteousness" – David knew that he possessed no righteousness of his own and that a right relationship with God depended upon appropriating for himself God's righteousness. When one is walking in divinely supplied righteousness, he has God's special attentiveness because "the LORD hath set him apart" (v.3). Absalom offered a vain sacrifice unacceptable to God (2 Samuel 15:12), whereas David understood the true significance of animal sacrifice. Compare Psalm 50:8-15 with Psalm 51:16-19.

When a person receives material gain such as a bountiful harvest (v. 7), there is gladness of heart. David wants us to know that there is available from the Lord an inner gladness of heart that transcends any elation obtained from material gain. The evidence of such gladness is peace and security and a good night's sleep! Our God supplies the best brand of sleeping pills!

Life **stEP** "The work of righteousness shall be peace; and the effect of righteousness, quietness and assurance forever" (Isaiah 32:17). Whether peace among nations, peace within the family circle or peace within the heart, there is no peace apart from righteousness, because peace is a product of righteousness.

1 thursday

Psalm 5:1-12
What is the writer saying?

How can I apply this to my life?

PRAY New Zealand — For the continued transformation of lives through effective prison ministry.

Our Psalm for today is a morning prayer for guidance through the day while living in a godless, hostile world. It has been suggested that it will be of particular relevance to the Jewish remnant during the Great Tribulation (Romans 9:27). Certainly it is a good prayer for anyone of any age desiring to follow the right path in an adverse environment.

The foolish in verse 5 are not those who are simpletons or clowns but persons who possess an arrogant denial of God's right to exercise authority over His creatures (Psalm 14:1). Such are described in detail in Romans 3:10-18. There the apostle uses quotations from four Psalms, including this one (v. 9), and also several passages from Isaiah, to uncover the depth of human depravity.

The temple mentioned in verse 7 does not refer to the temple at Jerusalem, which was built after David's death, but to God's heavenly dwelling place. See Psalm 11:4 and Psalm 18:6.

The answer to the prayer in verse 10 will have final culmination at Armageddon as described in Revelation 19:11-21.

Notice in verse 11 that rejoicing doesn't arise from present favorable circumstances but from absolute trust in the defender and a love for His name (Luke 6:22-23; 1 Peter 1:6).

Life stEP "Thou wilt bless and compass with a shield" (v. 12). What type of blessings do you want from God? According to Ephesians 1:3-7, we have already been blessed through being chosen (v. 4), accepted (v. 6), redeemed (v. 7) and forgiven (v. 7). Your sealing by the Holy Spirit (Ephesians 1:13) is your "compassing as with a shield." Do you require material blessings also?

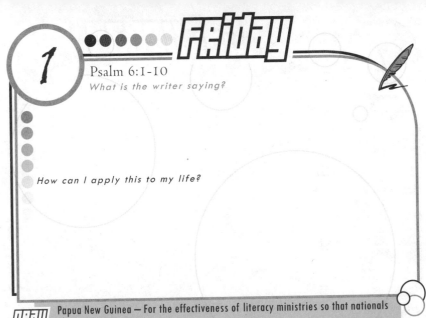

FRIDAY

1

Psalm 6:1-10

What is the writer saying?

How can I apply this to my life?

PRAY Papua New Guinea — For the effectiveness of literacy ministries so that nationals can study God's Word.

From ancient times, seven of the Psalms have been classified as "penitential." These seven express confession and sorrow for sins committed. Six of the seven are attributed to David and at least four are considered to have arisen from David's act of adultery with Bathsheba and his murder of Uriah (2 Samuel Chapter 11). The prophet Nathan confronted David with his sins and he confessed (2 Samuel 12:10-14). The fulfillment of these prophesied consequences are recorded in 2 Samuel 12:15-20:13. In 2 Samuel 12:14, Nathan prophesied, "by this deed, thou hast given great occasion to the enemies of the LORD to blaspheme." This is the consequence that gave David grief of spirit and soul for the rest of his life.

David's penitential Psalms can best be understood if read in the following sequence: First 38, then 6, next 51 and finally 32. This is likely the order in which they were penned over a period of weeks as he progressed from overwhelming remorse to a joyful realization of the blessedness of divine forgiveness. You will then understand why the Lord could call such a gross sinner as David "a man after mine own heart" (Acts 13:22).

Life stEP Every faithful servant of God will likely encounter a fellow Christian in deep remorse, existing day to day with head bowed in shame and disgrace for sins already confessed and forgiven. Someone needs to show such a one how to get the "accuser of the brethren" off his back. What better way than to show him the pathway trod by King David as recorded in God's book!

43

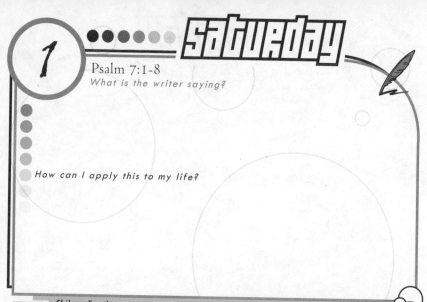

Psalm 7:1-8

What is the writer saying?

How can I apply this to my life?

pray Chile — For the perseverance of the Chilean saints as only 38% attend church regularly.

For a number of years between the anointing of David by Samuel (1 Samuel 16:13), and the death of King Saul (1 Samuel 31:6), David was relentlessly pursued, persecuted and falsely accused by Saul and his armies. Saul knew that David was the LORD's choice for king (1 Samuel 24:20); but he coveted the crown for his own son. During these years David penned several psalms. The likely historical background for Psalm 7 is in 1 Samuel chapters 23 through 26.

Notice the superscription above the psalm. Since the translators didn't know the meaning of "Siggaion," they left it untranslated. Respected Hebrew scholars vary in opinions about the meaning. The historical text doesn't mention a Benjamite named "Cush." The reference is probably to Saul who was the Benjamite who persecuted (v. 1), pursued (v. 2) and falsely accused (v. 3) David.

In verses 3-5, David declares his innocence before the LORD. In verse 6, he pleads with the LORD to awaken unto His office of Judge and take action against David's enemies. In verse 7, he points out that his request is on behalf of the LORD's people. In verse 8 he quotes from Deuteronomy 32:36 in order to give a scriptural basis for his plea.

Verse 2 reminds us that David's real enemy (and ours) is the Devil who "like a roaring lion walketh about seeking who he may devour" (1 Peter 5:8). In His own time, the Judge of the whole earth will rise up and judge both Satan and those who do his work (Matthew 25:41, Revelation 20:10). Just as Satan uses humans to do his work, so will the LORD use us in bringing Satan to judgment (Romans 16:20).

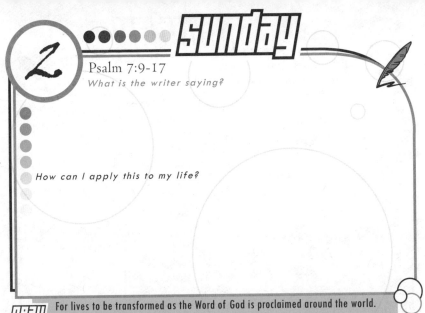

Psalm 7:9-17

What is the writer saying?

How can I apply this to my life?

PRAY For lives to be transformed as the Word of God is proclaimed around the world.

David longs for a time when wickedness will cease and righteousness will prevail. He also knows that only his God can accomplish this result. He expresses his confidence that the LORD has both the will and the ability to make things right.

When David is given the opportunity to avenge himself, he refuses to do so (1 Samuel 26:8-11). He knows that vengeance belongs to God alone (Deuteronomy 32:35, Hebrews 10:30). Therefore he appeals to God for vindication.

Having declared his confidence in God (v. 10), David uses this psalm to council others about God's attitude and actions concerning the righteous versus the wicked. Let the wicked be informed that "the righteous God" is fully aware of the thoughts and deeds of the wicked. He is angry at their wickedness and is fully prepared to take appropriate action in His time.

In verse 14, David describes his adversary. In verse 15, he likens him to a huntsman who digs a camouflaged pit to catch prey and then falls into his own trap.

See also Psalm 57:6, Proverbs 26:27 and Ecclesiastes 10:8. The fate of Haman (Esther 7:10) is a good scriptural example of a wicked man destroyed by his own evil devices (Psalm 10:2).

Notice in verse 17 of our psalm how David ends by offering praise and adoration to his God. He knows how to get God's ear, so that God has a basis for preserving David in order to use him to perform God's purposes on Earth. David exalts the LORD regardless of his circumstances. This is why God is pleased to call David, "a man after His own heart."

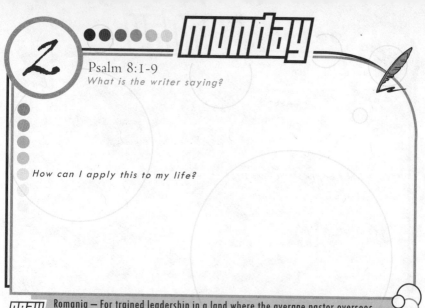

monday

2

Psalm 8:1-9

What is the writer saying?

How can I apply this to my life?

pray Romania — For trained leadership in a land where the average pastor oversees five churches.

Has God indeed crowned man with glory and honor above all created things, including the angels? It is true that God has ordained that man shall have dominion "over all the earth" (Genesis 1:26; Psalm 8:6; Hebrews 2:8). He has not retracted nor will He retract that ordinance. However, the human race, in Adam, forfeited dominion to Satan. When the Son of Man, Christ Jesus, has all things "put under His feet" (Psalm 8:6; I Corinthians 15:25; Ephesians 1:22), the dominion by man will far surpass that which was lost in Adam! The Man Christ Jesus shall be exalted "far above all principality, and power and might, and dominion" (Ephesians 1:21). We who are "joint heirs with Christ" shall be "glorified together" with Him (Romans 8:17).

Psalm 8 is the second of the Messianic Psalms. (See commentary on Psalm 2). Messianic Psalms can be fully appreciated only when Jesus Christ is the focal point. Christ quoted verse 2 on the day of the "triumphal entry" (Matthew 21:16). Verses 4 and 6 are quoted in Hebrews 2:6-8, with Hebrews 2:9 explaining that the reference is to Jesus. Above we pointed to the quotations from verse 6 in I Corinthians and Ephesians. "O LORD (Yahweh), our Lord (Adonai) how excellent is thy name in all the earth!" The first and last lines of Psalm 8 are the same for emphasis. Yahweh (Jehovah) is God as He deigns to reach down to man. Adonai is God as man responds. Jesus is our access to God, reaching down to us.

Life stEP "—we would see Jesus" (John 12:21). Let us look for the person and ministry of Christ in every Psalm — especially in the Messianic Psalms. Read what Jesus himself said on His resurrection day concerning His presence in the Psalms (Luke 24:44).

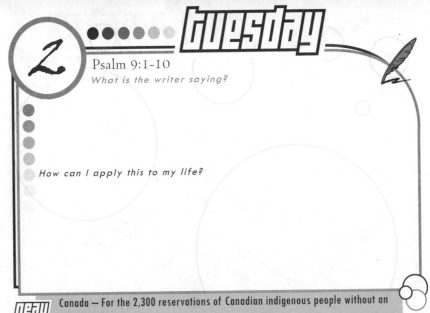

2

Psalm 9:1-10

What is the writer saying?

How can I apply this to my life?

PRAY Canada — For the 2,300 reservations of Canadian indigenous people without an ongoing witness.

Because of structure and content, scholars have long deduced that Psalms 9 and 10 were originally one acrostic poem of 22 four-line stanzas. Each line of the first stanza began with "Aleph," the first letter, and so on through the 22 letters of the Hebrew alphabet. When the psalm was divided, probably for liturgical purposes, the stanzas for some Hebrew letters were omitted. However, we can be certain that the Holy Spirit has preserved for us that which is needful. His faithfulness is to all generations (Psalms 33:11; 100:5; 119:89,90).

King David declares his determination to render whole-hearted praise to the LORD and to yield body, soul and spirit for the LORD's marvelous works (v. 1). He will joyfully praise the Most High (v. 2) because of past victories (v.v. 3-6). In verse 7, he acknowledges that the LORD has heard and will continue to hear the plea he made in Psalm 7:6. In verses 8 and 9 David looks forward to the time, later prophesied in Isaiah 11:1-5, when the righteous Judge shall sit upon His throne at Jerusalem.

Meanwhile, God's people from David's day until our day rested and continue to rest in the promises of verses 9 and 10. Think of the comfort this psalm will be to the oppressed people waiting for Messiah's deliverance during the Great Tribulation!

Notice the order of the four "I wills" in the first two verses of Psalm 9. A singing heart comes from one who is glad and rejoicing. There is nothing in this world that gladdens a heart more than the realization that God is using one's life to show forth His marvelous works. This privilege is reserved for those who are "whole hearted" in their praise to the Lord.

WEDNESDAY

2

Psalm 9:11-20

What is the writer saying?

How can I apply this to my life?

PRAY Jamaica — For Jamaican churches to have a hunger for God's Word and a passion for missions.

The name Zion is found 37 times in the Psalms. One cannot understand the full significance of some Psalms without knowing the significance of Zion. It is named at least 150 times in the Old Testament and seven times in the New. Historically, it was that particular fortress hill on which King David built his palace. After the Temple was built, it became a designation for the city of Jerusalem, particularly as that city was the place of gathering for the faithful who came to observe the feasts three times each year. Figuratively, Zion is that place from which God's true government emanates.

Psalm nine declares at least five awesome truths about the LORD (Yahweh). 1. He shall endure forever (v. 7). 2. He has prepared a throne for judgment (v. 7). 3. He shall judge the world in righteousness (v. 8). 4. He will be a refuge for the oppressed in times of trouble (v. 9). 5. He is known by the judgment he executes (v. 16).

As a result of the five truths above, what will happen to the wicked enemies of God's people? 1. They shall fall and perish (v. 3). 2. Their names shall be blotted out forever (v. 5). 3. They shall sink in the pit that they made (v. 15). 4. They shall be snared in the work of their own hands (v. 16). 5. They shall know themselves to be but men (v. 20).

Therefore, what should Jehovah's people do? 1. Put their trust in Him (v. 10). 2. Seek Him (v. 10). 3. Sing His praises (v. 11). 4. Declare His doings (v. 11). 5. Rejoice in His salvation (v. 14).

Life stEP

"For whatsoever things were written aforetimes were written for our learning, that we, through patience and comfort of the scriptures, might have hope" (Romans 15:4). To what extent do you think God may have had you in mind when He had the above truths put in writing thousands of years ago?

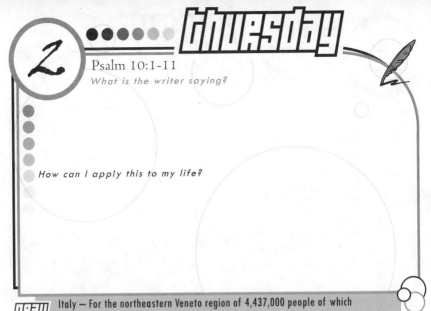

thursday

2

Psalm 10:1-11

What is the writer saying?

How can I apply this to my life?

PRAY Italy — For the northeastern Veneto region of 4,437,000 people of which approximately 2,000 are believers.

In both Psalm 9 and Psalm 10, the psalmist is observing the wicked and God's judgment of wickedness. Why is it then that in Psalm 9 there is singing, praising and rejoicing while in Psalm 10 there is somber consternation? In Psalm 9, although the psalmist observes the wicked, his eyes are focused upon the Judge of all the earth. In Psalm 10, although he is aware of the Judge, his eyes are focused upon the wicked. That's the difference between singing and somberness whether one is living in David's day or ours. On the one hand, God seems to be "dwelling in Zion" (9:11); on the other hand, He seems to be "hiding afar off" (10:1).

A fuller explanation involves the identity of the wicked ones under King David's observation. Those in Psalm 9 are inhabitants of the surrounding heathen nations. David's armies are being used by God to bring judgment upon the wickedness of those nations (9:15). In Psalm 10 it appears that David's concern is about the proud oppressors of the poor within his own realm. He is puzzled as to why God is bringing judgment to the wicked ones without and appears to be unconcerned about the wickedness within. "God is not in all his thoughts" (Psalm 10:4). "The LORD knows the thoughts of man" (Psalm 94:11). "They know not the thoughts of the LORD" (Micah 4:12). Though man may not want to think about God, that doesn't keep God from knowing the thoughts of man. It just bars man from knowing how God thinks. How comforting for the believer to know that His thoughts are "us-ward" (Psalm 40:5).

Life stEP

The Bible is clear concerning the fact that God knows our thoughts (Psalm 139:2; Luke 9:47). The unspiritual person resents this as an invasion of his privacy. The spiritual person is comforted that God knows and still cares. I wonder how pleased God is with my thought life!

49

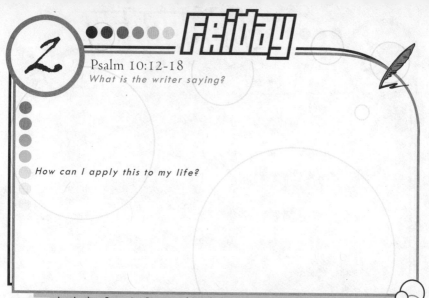

Psalm 10:12-18

What is the writer saying?

How can I apply this to my life?

pray Joe Jordan, Executive Director of Word of Life, for wisdom and discernment in making decisions for the ministry of Word of Life.

We learned in chapter 9 that the psalmist is certain that God will judge wickedness. However, in 10:1 he expresses impatience with God's timing. In verses 2 through 11, he rehearses to God all the reasons why it is time for God to act. In verses 12-15 he is saying, "God, you are forgetting that the lowly ones are counting on you, so please get busy with your judging!" The psalmist knows that God is omniscient (v. 14). He knows that God is able (v. 15). So why is God waiting to act?

The psalmist's problem is the same as our problem concerning many of our petitions. We are looking at circumstances from our perspective instead of God's perspective. The root problem is that we have not spent enough time meditating upon God's Word. That's where we'll find God's viewpoint. It is interesting to note that the first three recorded prayers in the Bible are all petitions by Abraham, "the Friend of God." In each case the answer was "no!" (Genesis 15:3; 17:18; 18:23) Abraham didn't know God's viewpoint.

Thankfully, David ended his prayer well (vs. 16-18). He simply recounted to God that which he knew to be true about God concerning the problem. As a result, God measured to him enough faith to be at rest (Psalm 37:5-7).

Life stEP

Is God causing you to wait concerning some of your anxious petitions? You know that God is omniscient. Therefore, He knows the correct timing. You know that He is omnipotent. Therefore, He is able to do it when the time is right. Rest and rejoice in that knowledge!

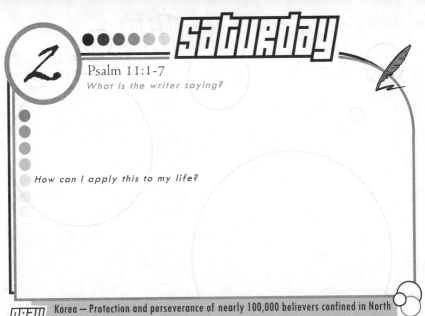

Psalm 11:1-7

What is the writer saying?

How can I apply this to my life?

Psalm 11 likely arises from the historical events recorded in 1 Samuel 15-17. Against God's known will, the people of Israel had insisted on having a king "that we also may be like all the nations" (1 Samuel 8:20). Now the harvest had failed and the people were hiding in caves, thickets, rocks, holes and pits for fear of the invading Philistines (1 Samuel 13:6). God rejected the king because of disobedience (13:13; 15:19; 16:14). King Saul had become a sniveling coward and the army had fled before the Philistines (17:24). The King and the people were "dismayed and greatly afraid" (17:11).

In Psalm 11, David hears, "flee to the mountains! Wickedness is winning over righteousness! The foundations of the nation are destroyed! What is there to do but flee?" David's reaction: My trust is in the LORD. He is on the throne in a place where the enemy cannot reach. He is intently watching the scene concerning His people on earth. He is holy, and looks upon His people as holy because He has set them apart for His purposes. He is in control and is testing His people. He will care for them and will rain destruction upon the wicked that He hates.

Life stEP

If you are a realist, you recognize that the foundations of the social order in which you live are crumbling. The Bible predicts that the political, religious, military, educational and cultural orders of this present world will surely be destroyed. So "what can the righteous do?" Answer: place complete reliance upon the all-sufficient God of the Universe personified in the Lord Jesus Christ who loves you and gave Himself for you. "I have overcome the world" (John 16:33).

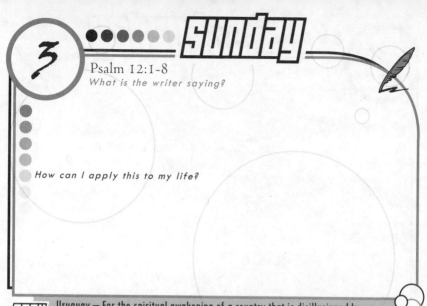

Psalm 12:1-8

What is the writer saying?

How can I apply this to my life?

pray Uruguay — For the spiritual awakening of a country that is disillusioned by secularism.

Psalm 12 consists of four, two-verse stanzas. The first two stanzas tell how sinful man uses words to oppress others and defy the LORD. In answer to the plea in verse 1, God promises what He will ultimately do about the situation. In verses 5-8 He gives words of assurance to the oppressed, poor and needy. For all generations, the LORD will preserve both His Words and the oppressed. This promise is true even though "the wicked walk on every side" and "the vilest men are exalted"!

To flatter is to praise or compliment in order to receive a favorable reaction and without regard for veracity. Most of us are given to flattery to some degree. It may not be for socially evil motives such as occupational advancement, political support or sexual favor. Maybe it's just because we want to be considered a "a nice person." If you want to know what God thinks of flattery for any purpose look up the word in its noun, verb and adjective forms in a good concordance.

Many numbers such as "seven" (v. 6) are often used in a figurative sense in Scriptures. The figurative meaning for the number "seven" is "complete" or "to the fullest extent" (Daniel 3:19). Sometimes the number is to be taken literally, but there is a figurative connotation (2 Kings 5:14; 8:1). The discerning reader will understand by the context.

Only by diligent study of the Bible can we know how to use words in a way pleasing to the Lord (2 Timothy 2:15-17). If we rely upon our society's educational process we will surely use words to our temporal and eternal detriment (1 Timothy 6:20,21).

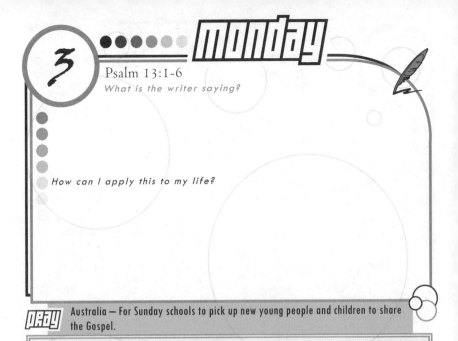

3

Psalm 13:1-6

What is the writer saying?

How can I apply this to my life?

PRAY Australia — For Sunday schools to pick up new young people and children to share the Gospel.

From the time that Samuel anointed David king (1 Samuel 16:13) until the time he began to reign at age 30 (2 Samuel 5:4) was about twelve to fourteen years. After slaying Goliath, David was a part of King Saul's court for several years. When Saul saw that David was more popular than he was, Saul tried in several ways to kill David. David escaped and was a fugitive for a number of years. Several times he despaired of his life until he recalled God's promise to make him king. When his trust overcame his fear, he would write a Psalm. This is one that arose from that experience. It was probably penned during the late years of his flight after he had tried several devious devises to survive (1 Samuel 21:10-15; 27:5-12).

At times it really seemed to David that his LORD had forgotten him (v. 1). During those times he would council with himself and try to use his own ingenuity to solve his problems. This brought nothing but sorrow (v. 2), so he pled with God, using both of the most prevalent names for God (Elohim and Yahweh). He begged for enlightenment (v. 3). Then he reasoned with God, saying how the enemy would be the one to benefit by David's death (v. 4). The LORD answered by measuring to David sufficient faith to trust (v. 5; Romans 12:3). In spite of dire circumstances, David was able to rejoice in the salvation God had promised. His faith produced singing for David and this Psalm for us.

Life **stEP**

Think of all the occasions throughout history when God's people have needed and used this Psalm of David's faith for strength in their times of weakness. Think of all the people that have sunk in the mire of despondency because they haven't spent enough time in the Word to know this Psalm is available.

tuesday

3

Psalm 14:1-7

What is the writer saying?

How can I apply this to my life?

Kenya — Protection for Christian leaders speaking out against corruption and social sins.

Psalm 14 is repeated as Psalm 53 with some variation and is quoted in Romans 3:10-12 to show the condition of the unregenerate human heart.

Psalm 53 (v.1) says, "The fool hath said in his heart, There is no God." In Bible terminology sins of thought and conduct are "heart errors." Israel wandered in the desert instead of possessing the land of abundance because they "erred in their hearts" (Psalm 95:10; Hebrews 3:10). Jesus said of all the gross sins listed in Mark 7:21, out of the heart come 11 of them. Pharaoh (Exodus 9:34), Ananias (Acts 5:4), and Simon the Sorcerer (Acts 8:21) all had "heart" problems.

Often in Scripture, the LORD looked and came down from heaven to bring judgment upon sinful man — the flood (Genesis 6:5), the confusion of languages (Genesis 11:5), the destruction of Sodom and Gomorrah (Genesis 18:21). Also the LORD comes down from heaven to show mercy and bring deliverance. See Exodus 3:8, 19:20, 20:20, 34:5 and John 6:33, 38, 51. Also note Acts 7:34.

Verse 7 looks forward to the Millennium when God's people Israel will live in blessedness under the rule of their Messiah. God changed Jacob's name to Israel in Genesis 32:28. Jacob is used to designate all of the literal descendants of the patriarch Jacob, son of Isaac, son of Abraham. Israel (Prince of God or God's ruler) designates the nation of people that derived from Jacob's 12 sons, so in a sense, the terms can be anonymous.

Life sTEP

One day we will rejoice and be glad along with God's special nation as we join in the benefits of the reign of Jesus Christ on earth. Looking forward in joyous anticipation, let us not be weary in well doing (Galatians 6:9).

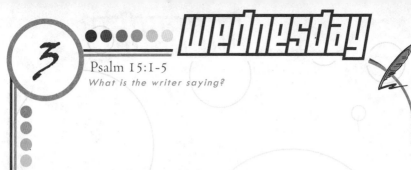

wednesday

3

Psalm 15:1-5

What is the writer saying?

How can I apply this to my life?

PRAY Bulgaria — That Christians would be protected from the violent attacks of neo-Nazi groups.

The subject matter of Psalm 14 involves the conduct of those who have no "heart for God." In contrast, Psalm 15 tells how one lives who has a genuine "heart for God."

The question in the first verse of Psalm 15 is not asking what is required to attain a place in heaven. It is asking how one conducts himself here on earth as a proper member of the household of God. In order to have moment-by-moment fellowship with a holy God, one needs an upright walk, righteous works, and truthful words (v. 2). Verses 3 through 5 expand upon the walk, works, and words theme but in inverse order. There are eight practical examples.

The surest way to do evil to a neighbor or reproach a friend is to use the tongue against him. The result is not only the loss of a good neighbor but also broken fellowship with God. Good works and a proper walk involve keeping promises regardless of cost (v. 4).

Disunity and discord within the household of faith frequently involves financial matters (v. 5). According to 1 Corinthians 6:7, we should be willing to be defrauded financially by a brother in Christ rather than to seek legal remedies (Ephesians 4:2,3).

The last line of verse 5 is a promise from God that one who lives by these principles will not be toppled from his foundation of faith in God's Word.

Life **stEP**

It is amazing that words written 3,000 years ago could be completely applicable in the modern Hi-Tech world. It should cause the person who has "a heart for God" to cry from within, "surely these are God-words and not man-words." Only an eternal omniscient God could see my time and know how to meet my needs.

thursday

3

Psalm 16:1-11

What is the writer saying?

How can I apply this to my life?

David introduces this Messianic Psalm by invoking the 3 most frequent Old Testament names for God — Elohim (God), Yahweh or Jehovah (LORD), and Adonai (Lord).

For those who enjoy alliteration, here is an outline for verses 1 through 7:

v. 1 Secure in the Lord

v. 2 Surrendered to the Lord

v. 3 Separated unto the Lord's people

v. 4 Separated from the world's people

v. 5 Sustained by the Lord

v. 6 Satisfied in the Lord

v. 7 Supported by the Lord. Verses 8 through 11 comprise the Messianic portion of the Psalm. In the first sermon preached after the birth of the church on the day of Pentecost, the Apostle Peter used this Psalm to prove that the resurrection of Jesus Christ, as well as His death on the cross, was "according to the Scriptures" (I Corinthians 15:4). Verses 8-11 are quoted in Acts 2:25-28. The Spirit's own interpretation follows in Acts 2:29-31. In view of the results of the preaching of this sermon (Acts 2:41), we will do well to study it for an understanding of the Messianic portion of the Psalm.

In Acts 13:35 the Apostle Paul quotes Psalm 16:10 to prove that Jesus conquered death and was alive on the resurrection side of death in His resurrected body. Read Paul's exposition of verse 10 in Acts 13:36-39.

Life **stEP**

Count the number of verses in Peter's sermon (Acts 2:22-36) to discover how effectively the saving gospel message can be presented in a few words. He didn't try to explain the gospel; he simply proclaimed the gospel. The power of God unto salvation is in the message — not in the explanation of the message (Romans 1:16; I Corinthians 15:1).

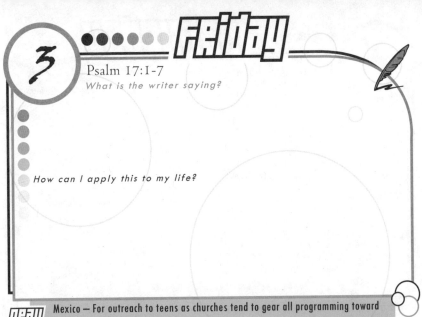

3

Psalm 17:1-7

What is the writer saying?

How can I apply this to my life?

Pray Mexico — For outreach to teens as churches tend to gear all programming toward adults.

Many of the psalms, or portions thereof, are in the form of prayers. Psalm 17 is one of five that are specifically entitled "a prayer." A probable historical setting for this psalm involves David's perilous situation as recorded in 1 Samuel 23:25, 26.

At that time, through depending upon the LORD during his many trials and tests, David had come to know his God intimately. He knew that the LORD hears the cry of one calling from a sincere heart having a just cause (v. 1). He knew God vindicates the innocent and makes right things that are uneven (v. 2). David was confident that he was not undergoing punishment by God for sinful words and conduct (v. 3). He had avoided association with men of evil purposes by heeding God's Word (v. 4). He was looking to God for direction that he would not slip in his walk (v. 5).

David was having difficulty reconciling his dire situation with that which he knew to be true concerning the character and purposes of his God. He had experienced miraculous deliverance in past perils. In verses 6 and 7, he is earnestly pleading with God to demonstrate His power and His loving-kindness. The basis of his plea is that his heart attitude, and his conduct entitle him to God's action on his behalf.

Life stEP

There comes into the life of every dedicated believer those times when our situation doesn't appear to mesh with our understanding of God's love for us and His watch-care over us. Applying Scriptures like Psalm 139:23,24 and studying Psalm 17 should be helpful in building a firm confidence as we trust our God.

saturday

3

Psalm 17:8-15

What is the writer saying?

How can I apply this to my life?

Portugal — For the churches to raise up full-time workers of the Gospel.

"The apple of the eye" is figurative for that which is dearest and most needful of safeguarding (Deuteronomy 32:10, Proverbs 7:2, Lamentations 2:18, Zechariah 2:8). "Under the shadow of Thy wings" denotes the place of optimum safety (Psalms 36:7, 57:1, 61:4, 63:7, 91:1-4).

David's enemies are described as wicked, oppressive and deadly. They have fleshly appetites and speak boastfully. They are like a crouching lion greedy for prey (9-12).

In verse 13, David calls upon the LORD to deprive the lion of his prey. In verse 14, the wicked are said to live only for this life, gathering treasures in order to accumulate wealth for their children.

Verse 15 gives us insight into that which Old Testament saints understood concerning life beyond the grave. This verse, along with Job 19:25-27 and Isaiah 26:19, verifies that they looked for bodily resurrection, which would bring ultimate satisfaction in the presence of the LORD. Parallel New Testament passages include 1 Corinthians 13:12 and 1 John 3:2.

Trust in an eternal God gave David an eternal perspective on life in contrast to the temporal perspective of his enemies. The extent to which we live day to day with an eternal perspective is the extent to which we will experience moment-by-moment victory over circumstances.

Life stEP

Looking back over the psalm we see that the LORD searches the heart (v. 3), saves the trusting (v. 7), shelters His dear ones (v. 8), shields from the adversary (v. 9) and satisfies forever (v. 15). We should keep in mind that the Spirit had in view the requirements of all who would need David's words throughout the centuries.

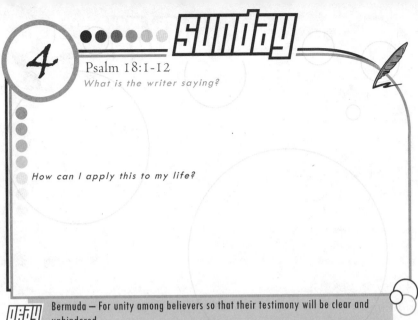

SUNDAY

4

Psalm 18:1-12

What is the writer saying?

How can I apply this to my life?

PRAY Bermuda — For unity among believers so that their testimony will be clear and unhindered.

Psalm 18 is also recorded in 2 Samuel as chapter 22 with a few variations. For instance, the superscription of Psalm 18 is verse 1 of 2 Samuel 22. The historical setting for the Psalm is at the height of David's kingdom. Verses 1-12 involve praise and thanksgiving to God for the extent to which He will go to deliver His own. It is in recognition by David that all of the glory and honor for his success belongs to his God.

In verse 2, the Psalmist proclaims His LORD by using 2 of His names, 2 descriptive nouns and 5 metaphors. Because of the widespread use in Scripture of the word "horn" in an obviously figurative manner, it particularly catches our attention here being used as a metaphor for God.

In Deuteronomy 33:17, the descendants of Joseph are said to have horns like the horns of a wild ox with which they will push other people. In her prayer, of praise and adoration, Hannah thanks the LORD for giving her a horn to use against her adversary (1 Samuel 2:1). At the end of her prayer, Hannah prophesies that the Messiah will possess an exalted horn. In Luke 1:69, Zechariah calls the coming Messiah Israel's Horn of Salvation. That prophecy will ultimately be fulfilled at Armageddon. Even though Antichrist will be the most powerful ruler in human history, God calls him a "little horn" (Daniel 7:8). That's what he will be compared to--the "Horn of our Salvation." In Scripture, when one is said to have a horn or to be a horn, he has a usable advantage over his adversary such as a horned animal has over a hornless one.

Life stEP

"All the horns of the wicked also will I cut off; but the horns of the righteous shall be exalted." (Psalm 75:10). You may have never thanked God for giving you "horns" of righteousness!

monday

4

Psalm 18:13-24

What is the writer saying?

How can I apply this to my life?

PRAY — France — For godly elected officials who will provide leadership to a government and a country at an important crossroads.

"The LORD also thundered" – Yahweh manifested Himself in judgment. "The Highest (usually translated Most High) gave voice" (Psalm 29:3-5). "The Most High God, possessor of Heaven and Earth" (Genesis 14:22) is the LORD's title as the Supreme Ruler of the Universe.

The many waters of verse 16 are the "strong enemy" and "those who hate me" of verse 17 (Psalms 93:4, 144:7). Do you think there might be also a prophetic implication in regards to the nation of Israel? Did God also have the "flood" of Revelation 12:15 and the "many waters" of Revelation 17:1,15 in view? This could explain some of the language of verses 7-15, which appears to be more applicable to end times than to David's time. Keep in mind the following: 1. Prophets knew they were saying much that was for future hearers (Psalm 102:18; 1 Peter 1:11,12). 2. Much prophecy is written in the past tense. From God's point of view future events are as certain as if they had already transpired.

What David experienced in verses 16-19, could also apply to your own salvation. Notice God's salvation is not only for the purpose of saving from Hell. When He delivers "out of" it is to take "into" (Exodus 3:8). Also, as you read verses 20-24, think in terms of your own Christian walk in relationship to the judgment seat of Christ (2 Corinthians 5:10).

The practical value of Bible study comes from applying the passage under consideration to our daily conduct. In a manner of speaking, we must learn to place ourselves into the situation presented and find a way of applying the words to our hour-by-hour Christian walk. Can you do this with verse 24?

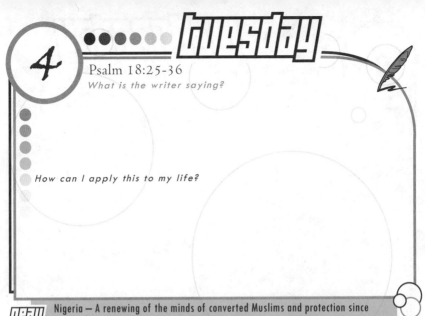

Psalm 18:25-36

What is the writer saying?

How can I apply this to my life?

David's desire was to be merciful and upright (v. 25) as well as pure (v. 26) and humble (v. 27). Therefore, the LORD delighted in him and brought deliverance from his enemies (v. 19). God was pleased to give him the light of the LORD for his walk in a world of darkness (v. 28). David gave all the credit for his victories to his God (v. 29), and never missed an opportunity to extol God and His Word (v. 30).

The word "rock" is the translation of two Hebrew words. Both are used as metaphors for God in Psalm 18. "Sela" in verse 2 means a rocky protrusion like a crag. "Tsoor" in verse 31 means a rocky mass like a boulder. Both words are used in Deuteronomy 32:13.

The verb "gird" (vv. 32 and 39) and the corresponding noun "girdle" are used both literally and figuratively in both Testaments of older English versions. Modern versions experience difficulty finding suitable synonyms for these archaic words (Psalm 109:18, Ephesians 6:14, 1 Peter 1:13), and still preserve the figure. In Bible times a girdle was a necessary adjunct to male apparel. It was similar to a sash worn around the waist. When at rest, a man loosed his girdle. In order to work, run or fight he tied the girdle tightly around his waist. Figuratively, to gird oneself is to prepare for action! See 1 Kings 18:46 and Luke 12:35-37.

In verses 30 and 31 David exalts His God and the in verses 32-36, he recounts what God has accomplished for him and in him.

Life stEP

Because the way of God is perfect, and the word of God is proven, we can trust in Him (v. 30). If we are fearful in any circumstance of life, it is because we are deficient in trust, not because the provision is insufficient! How do we correct our deficiency? Simply by recounting His faithfulness in past experiences.

How can I apply this to my life?

The historical background for Psalm 18:37-42 may be found in 1 Chronicles 18 and 19 as well as in the parallel passages of 2 Samuel. These verses rehearse the conquest of the enemies of David's conquering armies. In verse 43 David gives to God credit to the end to years of strife within his own country and his exaltation as ruler over the surrounding nations. In verses 44 and 45 he tells of the submission of other peoples and of their obeisance to him.

One wonders to what extent David presently has knowledge of the thousands of believers who today sing the words of verse 46 as a praise chorus to the LORD whom he served 3,000 years ago! Maybe such singing and praising is the beginning of what was on the mind of Jesus as he faced the cross (Hebrews 12:2).

When King Saul was pursuing David, he had two clear opportunities to slay his persecutor, but he chose to let God be his avenger. Now he is praising God not only for deliverance but also for his exaltation (vv. 47-48).

In Romans 15:4, the Apostle Paul assures us that the Old Testament was written for us. Then in Romans 15:9-12, the apostle uses five Old Testament passages to prove that the Holy Spirit not only had Gentiles in mind when He authored the Scriptures, but that they have always been included in God's plans. Verse 49 is the first of those five passages.

Verse 50 looks forward to the greater David, Messiah, and points out the eternality of God's plans concerning David.

Look carefully at Romans 15:4 and then consider how you can derive learning, patience, comfort and hope from the truths in Psalm 18.

thursday

4

Psalm 19:1-14

What is the writer saying?

How can I apply this to my life?

PRAY Peru – Outreach among the 7,400,000 people of Lima, of whom 60% live in abject poverty.

We might paraphrase verses 1-6 in this manner: God, through His creation, has, without words, spoken to every human being that has ever lived in such a way that a response is required. The divine interpretation is found in Romans 1:18-20.

In verses 7 and 8, the Word of God is designated in four different terms. His law in this context is His instruction in regard to sin and righteousness. His testimony is what He has to say about His own nature and purposes. His statutes are rules of conduct. His commandments are authoritative directives. Notice the four adjectives by which His Word is described – perfect, sure, right and pure. In the same two verses He tells us what His Word will do – convert the soul, make wise the simple, rejoice the heart and enlighten the eyes.

Fear and love are two necessary and complimentary attitudes toward God. Love prevents fear from becoming paralyzing inactivity. Fear keeps love from becoming silly or showy familiarity. The relationship should be like that of a child toward a tender, loving parent who is also a consistent and effective disciplinarian.

When the Bible speaks of rewards it uses superlatives (v. 11). See Genesis 15:1 and Luke 6:23,35. God's system of testing and rewards is very important to Him. Christians in general know far too little about the subject.

In the Old Testament there were no sacrifices for presumptuous sins – only judgment (Numbers 15:30, Deuteronomy 17:12). In the New Testament they are called willful sins (Hebrews 10:26) and sin unto death (1 John 5:16).

This world desperately needs something perfect, something sure, something right and something pure. The people of this world need someone willing to dedicate a life for the task of delivering the above!

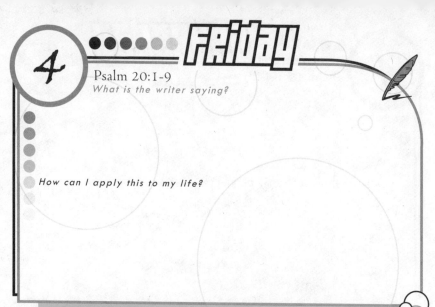

4

FRIDAY

Psalm 20:1-9
What is the writer saying?

How can I apply this to my life?

PRAY Bahamas — For committed Christians to stand up and do the Lord's work.

The scene for Psalm 20 is in Jerusalem as King David and his general, Joab are preparing to face superior enemy forces in battle. The occasion is thought to be as recorded in 2 Samuel 10 and 1 Chronicles 19. The Ammonites had joined with the Syrians to overthrow David's rule. They hired thousands of chariots and foot soldiers against David. As was his custom, before going into battle David called his people to worship and sacrifice.

The petition of verses 1-5 was probably sung by Levites responsible for worship procedures. "The God of Jacob defend Thee"– the words of Jacob in Genesis 35:3 were no doubt the inspiration for their prayer. This petition exudes an aura of faith and anticipation. They are confident that the LORD will perform for them as He did for their patriarch. In verses 6-8, the king himself or someone on his behalf responds in faith to the petition. "Now I know – He will hear –." There is total reliance – no shadow of doubt – no wavering (James 1:6).

"Some trust in chariots –." Pharaoh trusted in his 600 chariots (Exodus 14:7). Moses had no chariots, but trusted solely in the LORD (Exodus 14:13). "So the LORD saved Israel that day out of the hand of the Egyptians – " (Exodus 14:30).

Notice in verse 8 victory is appropriated before the battle begins.

Life stEP

The petitions recorded in the Bible are short and to the point. Look at the first two Bible prayers that received affirmative answers – the prayer by Abraham's servant (Genesis 24:12-14) and the prayer by Jacob (Genesis 32:9-12). Both received immediate and precise answers! What can we learn from those two prayers?

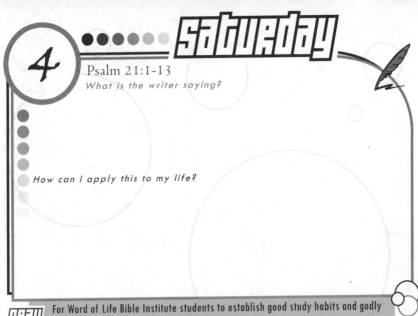

4

Psalm 21:1-13

What is the writer saying?

How can I apply this to my life?

PRAY For Word of Life Bible Institute students to establish good study habits and godly friendships as they begin a new year.

Students of the Psalms have long noted the connection between Psalms 20 and 21. Psalm 20 is a confident petition in anticipation of victory. Compare 20:2 with 21:6; 20:4 with 21:2 and 20:7 with 21:7.

The old English word "preventest" (v. 3) is from two Latin words meaning, "come before." The word now has a different connotation than it did when the King James Version was produced. See Psalm 88:13; 119:147 and I Thessalonians 4:15.

By way of application we read this—"a crown of pure gold"— in anticipation of the crown of victory awaiting us (2 Timothy 4:8) at the Lord's return (Revelation 22:12). Our desire for crowns is not for wearing but for having

our part in the wondrous celebration of Revelation 4:9-11.

From our study of Psalm 17, we know that David looked forward to eternal life in a resurrected body. He would be the recipient of his LORD's blessings forever! Notice that his sole ground for receiving God's blessings, both temporal and eternal is: "the king trusteth in the LORD."

Verses 8-12 look forward to future battles and future victories. David's confidence for success is based on the knowledge that his enemies are the LORD's enemies and his battles are therefore the LORD's battles.

This Psalm begins and ends with rejoicing in the Lord's strength. Are you aware of the difference between attempting to attain joy in your own strength and manifesting joy through singing and praising in the strength and power of the Lord? The one leads to frustration. The other exalts the Lord and delights the soul.

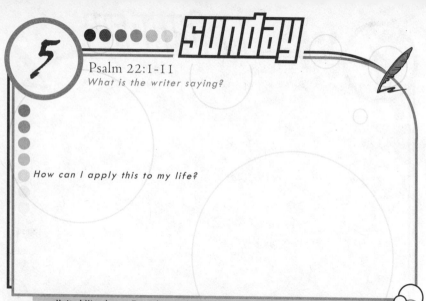

sunday

5

Psalm 22:1-11

What is the writer saying?

How can I apply this to my life?

PRAY United Kingdom — To exchange their passion for political correctness for one of biblical correctness.

"Christ died for our sins according to the scriptures (1 Corinthians 15:3). Certainly, today's reading consists of scriptures according to which Christ died! The Holy Spirit is the author (2 Samuel 23:2). David is the prophet (Acts 4:25). The precise fulfillment is recorded in Matthew 27:39-49 and to a lesser extent in the other three Gospels. David is speaking. Perhaps he has some of his own enemies in mind. However, it is clear that the Holy Spirit is looking beyond David to the "Greater Son of David" who would experience these events 1000 years later at the crucifixion. Specifically, He is revealing the heart sufferings that our Savior endured while hanging on the cross. Verses 1-5 speak of His heart sufferings due to His abandonment by God. We are not being informed that the Father and Son relationship was severed. We know this was not the case because of the first (Luke 23:34) and the seventh (Luke 23:46) utterances by Christ from the cross. The answer to the question in verse 1 is found in verse 3. The human sin-bearer was forsaken by a Holy God who could not look upon the exceeding sinfulness of the sins laid upon the sinless offering (2 Corinthians 5:21). The daytime and night of verse 2 correspond to the three hours of light and three hours of darkness during the crucifixion. Verses 6-11 describe the heart sufferings of Christ due to spurning by His fellow man. The emphasis is upon Christ's human characteristics.

If you really want to think about what transpired in the mind of your own Savior as He bore your sins on the cross, meditate long and diligently upon today's scripture portion. As you indicate a genuine interest, the indwelling Holy Spirit will awaken your understanding of that which is here written.

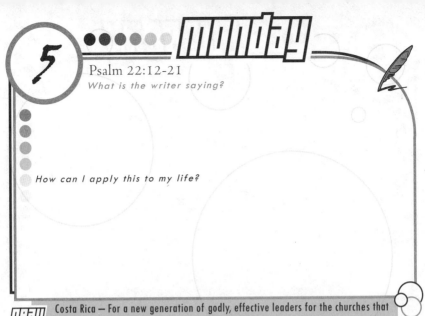

monday

5

Psalm 22:12-21

What is the writer saying?

How can I apply this to my life?

Pray — Costa Rica — For a new generation of godly, effective leaders for the churches that will commend the Gospel.

Ferocious bulls, predatory lions and scavenger dogs figuratively describe the spectators at our Lord's crucifixion. Perhaps the bulls represent the Roman military presence. The Lion (v. 21) could be Satan and his agents (v. 13). The unicorn (wild ox) may illustrate the political and religious powers that counseled together to put Christ on the cross. The dogs illustrate the basest elements of human society who came to gawk and mock. Notice that the "sword" and animals appear a second time in reverse order in verses 20 & 21. Verses 14-17 graphically describe the suffering of a human body dying while nailed to a cross. This is particularly striking when we understand that the detailed account of Christ's physical suffering is told hundreds of years before death by crucifixion was ever practiced. Matthew 27:35 records the precise fulfillment of verse 18. Any possibility that the crucifixion of Christ was staged by his followers in order to conform to scriptures is precluded by this incident. Verses 19-21 prophesy a petition, which will be honored as described in the rest of the Psalm. Actually, the Psalm should be read at one sitting because God is careful to proclaim of the victorious resurrection after the horrors of the crucifixion (as He does in Isaiah 53 as well).

Life stEP

Never leave Christ on the cross! That is a grave fault of false religionists. "Death is swallowed up in victory" (1 Corinthians 15:54)! The cross and the tomb are empty! Christ is raised and glorified! Proclaim it loudly and frequently!

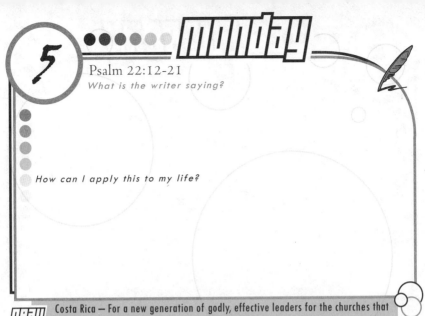

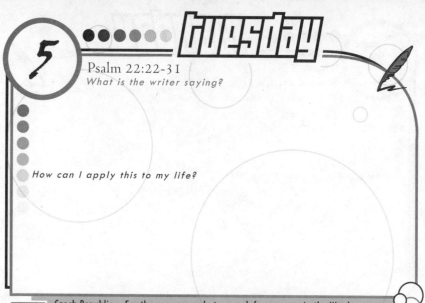

Psalm 22:22-31

What is the writer saying?

How can I apply this to my life?

At verse 22 the Psalm proceeds from the crucifixion to the resurrection. The words of this verse are attributed to the risen Jesus in Hebrews 2:12. The Holy Spirit used David as a prophet to tell what Jesus would say a thousand years in the future concerning His relationship to His followers. Notice how the relationship develops in the Gospel of John from Master to Friend to Brother. When we yield our lives to His call, the relationship is Master and servant (John 13:13-16). When we show forth our love for Him as He has shown His love for us, we become His friends (John 15:12-15). The ultimate relationship is brotherhood in the family of His Father (John 20:17; Hebrews 2:11-12).

The principal theme of today's scripture is "praise to the LORD in the coming kingdom." The king will praise Him (v. 22). The descendants of Jacob will praise and glorify Him (v. 23). The Psalmist will praise Him (v. 25). The lowly will praise Him (v. 26). All individuals and all nations shall worship Him (vv. 27-29). Verse 30 says, "A seed shall serve Him". In order to understand the impact of this prophecy, read Isaiah 53:8-10. In His crucifixion He was cut off without physical descendants. In His resurrection His progeny cannot be numbered for multitude (John 12:24).

Life stEP

Psalm 22:31 reminds us that we are like the second runner in a four-man relay race. We are responsible for the truths that were brought to us by the preceding generation. We must relay them to the next generation of believers in such a forceful manner that they will not fail to effectually pass them on to a generation not yet born. God has something to say on this subject in Psalm 78:3-6 and 2 Timothy 2:2.

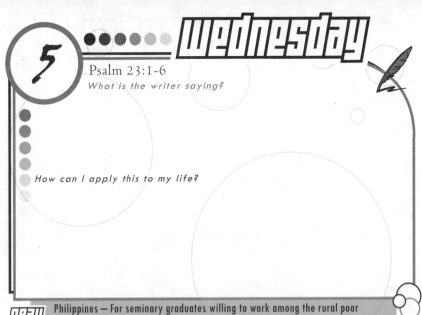

WEDNESDAY

5

Psalm 23:1-6

What is the writer saying?

How can I apply this to my life?

PRAY Philippines — For seminary graduates willing to work among the rural poor

"I have gone astray like a lost sheep—" (Psalm 119:176). (See also Isaiah 53:6). Whereas Psalm 22 presents the Good Shepherd who gave His life for the sheep (John 10:11), Psalm 23 is a song about the living Great Shepherd who currently oversees His sheep (Hebrews 13:20, 21; 1 Peter 2:25). Our earthly pastors might be desirous of giving their lives in shepherding their flocks. They might even be willing to die for their flocks if necessary. But only Jesus could provide for me my total need – a shepherd that could live for me after He died for me. None of the world's religions can provide such a shepherd! After providing the needed sacrifice for my sins (Psalm 22), He now provides my total needs (Psalm 23) for my walk.

My Shepherd attends to my needs day by day (v. 1). I have the "peace of God" (Philippians 4:7) as He leads me because He has provided "peace with God" (Romans 5:1) through His perfect sacrifice (v. 2). Since I am incapable of directing my own steps (Jeremiah 10:23), my Shepherd guides me along the correct pathway in my daily walk (v. 3). Since the day I was born, I have lived in the shadow of death. But my Shepherd is the conqueror of death (1 Corinthians 15:54-57) (v. 4). I banquet peacefully in the presence of the enemy of my soul; Why shouldn't my cup of joy overflow? (v. 5). My enemy cannot pursue me because my Shepherd's goodness and mercy pursue me every day all the way to my eternal abode!

Life stEP The only barrier to the enjoyment of the blessings of Psalm 23 is a lack of trust in the Shepherd. If a sheep were in a desert surrounded by predatory animals could it enjoy life without complete reliance upon its shepherd?

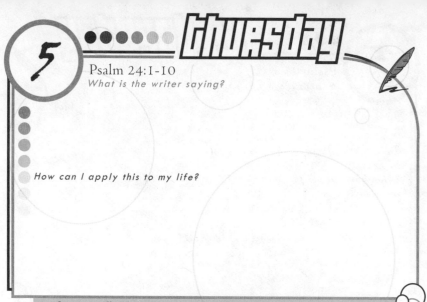

5

Psalm 24:1-10

What is the writer saying?

How can I apply this to my life?

Historians find the setting for this Psalm in the bringing of the Ark of God into the City of David (2 Samuel 6:12-19). Tradition says it was later arranged for antiphonal singing. It was sung as the worshipers ascended to the Holy Hill of Zion for the Feasts of Jehovah. The section from verses 7 to 10 was reserved for the triumphal entry through the gates. Church fathers entitled the Psalm "The ascension to the throne by the King of Glory." Many see it as the third Psalm of a trilogy about the Good Shepherd (Psalm 22), the Great Shepherd (Psalm 23), and the Chief Shepherd (Psalm 24). The good Shepherd died for us to pay the penalty for sin (John 10:11, 1 Peter 2:24). The Great Shepherd lives in us to protect from the power of sin (Hebrews 13:20, 21; 1 Peter 2:25). The Chief Shepherd comes for us to part us from the presence of sin (1 Peter 5:4).

The Earth and all that pertains to it, including its inhabitants belong to the LORD (v. 1) because He created all (v. 2). Therefore, He has the right to determine who controls the government and worship (v. 3). The prime requirements are righteousness for the King and His subjects (vv. 4-6).

Open the gates of Zion! The LORD has appointed His King to sit upon the throne (v. 7). He has conquered every opponent (v. 8) and is ready to enter (v. 9). The King of Glory and the LORD of Hosts are one and the same (v. 10). Be still and meditate upon that!

Life stEP

"Lift up your heads"! If you have received that which was done in the past for you by the Good Shepherd, and you are not now rejoicing in that which the Great Shepherd is doing in and through you; lift up your head! Look toward that which the Chief Shepherd will do in the future with you! (Hebrews 12:1-3)

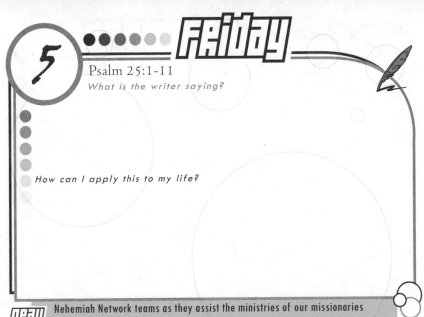

Psalm 25:1-11

What is the writer saying?

How can I apply this to my life?

PRAY Nehemiah Network teams as they assist the ministries of our missionaries around the world.

There are nine alphabetical psalms. Originally this one was structured so that the 22 verses each began with the next succeeding letter of the Hebrew alphabet, — ALEPH through TAV. Apparently, this and some other psalms, were somewhat rearranged in form for liturgical purposes. Most of the acrostic structure has been preserved in Hebrew manuscripts.

"Let none that wait on Thee be ashamed" — David is not speaking of feelings of guilt, disgrace or embarrassment. "Ashamed" here means being let down or disappointed because of misplaced trust. He was never in danger of being "ashamed" because his trust was in the LORD! (v. 20)

In verses 4 and 5, David petitions for guidance and instruction in knowing and following God's ways. He bases his request upon that which he already knows about the LORD's character and past performance (vv. 6-8). His God is, and always has been, loving, kind, good and upright. He forgives and teaches sinful ones who confess before Him.

Both Moses (Numbers 12:3) and Jesus (Matthew 11:29) were declared to be meek (v. 9). The word here means compliant and supple (it does not mean that he was deficient in spirit or courage).

Life stEP

When we bring our petitions before the Lord, we should verbalize to Him that which we know about Him from His word and from our past experiences with Him. We also confess what we are in His presence. We present a basis for why He should grant our requests. If our petitions are according to His promise and character, He will surely grant them "for His name's sake." He is both merciful and true!

Psalm 25:12-22

What is the writer saying?

How can I apply this to my life?

PRAY Honduras — For God to provide the teaching staff and funding needed to keep Bible schools operating.

Psalm 25 consists of a collection of petitions by David. These are interspersed with instructions by David concerning his knowledge and experiences of how God deals with people (vv. 8-10 and 12-15).

No doubt the petition in verses 16-21 was prayed during a time in the past when David was in deep distress. David, under the inspiration of the Holy Spirit (2 Samuel 23:1,2), may also have recorded it here for future distresses that would be experienced by the nation of Israel (v. 22). See Psalm 102:18.

Jeremiah's designation for the Great Tribulation (Matthew 24:21) is "the time of Jacob's trouble" (Jeremiah 30:7). Jeremiah adds "but he shall be saved out of it." Certainly, the words of verses 16-22 would be a proper prayer for Israel during that time.

There are three great prayers of national confession in the Old Testament. In Ezra 9, that great leader identifies with his nation in confession as though he were chief among the sinners. In Nehemiah 9, while confessing on behalf of the nation the petitioners say, "we have done wickedly" (Nehemiah 9:33). In his great prayer of national confession, Daniel says, "confessing my sin and the sin of my people, Israel" (Daniel 9:20). Here, the psalmist may be identifying prophetically with the nation's future distress.

Life stEP

Did you know that the LORD makes known his secrets only to those who qualify (v. 14)? These qualify — His friends (Genesis 18:17, John 15:15), the righteous (Proverbs 3:32), His prophets (Daniel 2:19, Amos 3:7), those who will to do His will (John 7:17), and he that is spiritual (1 Corinthians 2:10-16). Do you qualify? How much do you really desire to qualify?

ephesians

The book of Acts is the history of the early church. Primarily Jewish in character, it remained in Jerusalem after the resurrection and ascension of the Lord with its adherents continuing to worship in the temple and synagogue as well as in their own assemblies. These early believers were not yet fully aware that in Christ all those Old Testament practices were done away with. Their belief in Christ as the Messiah, however, was sufficient to bring persecution that was so intense (Acts 8:4) that the believers fled Jerusalem and went everywhere preaching the Word.

Paul's part in the persecution of the church, as well as his conversion, are both recorded in Acts 9 along with his commission to preach the Gospel to both Jew and Gentile. The church confirmed his testimony and ministry and he made three notable missionary journeys. The first (Acts 13-15:35) is to Asia Minor accompanied by Barnabas and John Mark. The second (Acts 15:36-18:22) finds Paul and Silas crossing over into Europe after a brief visit to Syria. Timothy (at Derbe) and Luke (at Troas) join the team. In Greece, they visit Athens and Corinth where Paul meets Aquila and Priscilla. He then visits Ephesus (Acts 18) and after a brief time of reasoning in the synagogue leaves Aquila and Priscilla and continues his journey. The third journey (Acts 18:23-21:14) finds Paul returning to Ephesus (Acts 19), where he remains for nearly three years in a teaching ministry. He finally departs to visit Macedonia and Greece planning to return to Jerusalem for Pentecost (Acts 20:16). A very touching scene is given to us in Acts 20 as he stops off at Miletus, some 40 miles south, and calls for the elders of the Ephesian church. His visit to Jerusalem ends in his being arrested and finally brought to Rome as a prisoner in bonds. It is from Rome, a prisoner under house arrest, that he writes the Ephesian epistle, and has it delivered by Tychicus, a "beloved brother" (Ephesians 6:21).

Why The Epistle Was Written
The early church was not only persecuted (Acts 8:4), but was threatened by doctrinal heresies, including that of Gnosticism, which presumed to "know" and sought to thrust between the soul and God all sorts of human and celestial mediators. Paul's letter to the Colossians deals with this heresy and emphasizes the pre-eminence of Christ. In Him alone dwells all the fullness of the Godhead bodily. He

Ephesians

sends that later letter by Tychicus and Onesimus, a fugitive slave from Colosse who was converted under Paul's ministry in Rome and is now sent back to his master Philemon with the letter that bears his name. What Paul has to say to this church is appropriate for all churches, both then and now. In fact, numerous scholars are of the opinion that Ephesians was "a circular letter," a doctrinal treatise in the form of a letter, to the churches in Asia Minor. Some good Greek manuscripts omit the words "at Ephesus" in 1:1. Since Paul had worked at Ephesus for about three years, and since he normally mentioned many friends in the churches to whom he wrote, the absence of personal names in this letter strongly supports the idea of its encyclical character. It was likely sent first to Ephesus by Tychicus (Ephesians 6:21:22; Colossians 4:7-8) and is probably the same letter that is called "my letter… from Laodicea" in Colossians 4:16 (Ryrie).

Harry Ironside offers this note that "there are very remarkable correspondences between certain Old Testament books and New Testament epistles. The Epistle to the Romans, for instance, answers to Exodus; the letter to the Hebrews is the counterpart of Leviticus; and this Epistle to the Ephesians is the New Testament parallel to Joshua. In Joshua we have the people of Israel entering upon the possession of their inheritance. In Ephesians believers are called upon to enter by faith now into the possession of that inheritance which we shall enjoy in all its fullness by-and-by. We are far richer than we realize. All things are ours, and yet how little we appropriate."

The Content Of The Epistle

Some have called this epistle the "profoundest book in existence." The epistle is divided into two sections, the first doctrinal and the second practical, each taking three chapters. The church is viewed as the body of Christ in which God unites Jew and Gentile through whom He will manifest His purposes to the universe. The epistle stresses the unity of the church, the unity of Jew and Gentile in Christ and the unity of its members within the body. The key words in the epistle are "in" (93 times); "grace" (13 times); "spiritual" (13 times); "heavenlies" (5 times). Accompanying Paul's great emphasis upon unity, you will find him placing a heavy stress upon love in this letter. He uses the verb form of "love" (agapa) nine times,

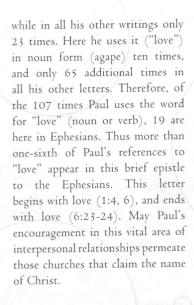

ephesians

while in all his other writings only 23 times. Here he uses it ("love") in noun form (agape) ten times, and only 65 additional times in all his other letters. Therefore, of the 107 times Paul uses the word for "love" (noun or verb), 19 are here in Ephesians. Thus more than one-sixth of Paul's references to "love" appear in this brief epistle to the Ephesians. This letter begins with love (1:4, 6), and ends with love (6:23-24). May Paul's encouragement in this vital area of interpersonal relationships permeate those churches that claim the name of Christ.

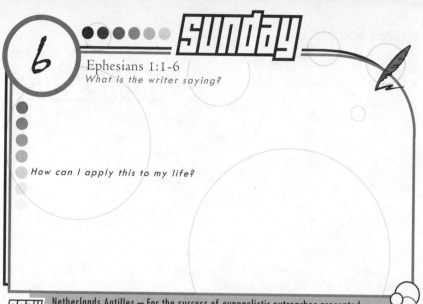

sunday

6

Ephesians 1:1-6

What is the writer saying?

How can I apply this to my life?

Paul's opening words are magnificent. He introduces himself as Paul (using his Gentile name: "small") not Saul (his Hebrew name: "to ask or pray"), and identifies himself as an apostle (one sent on a mission), in this case as an official ambassador of Christ. He uses his position to give the letter official character, for his apostolic appointment was "by the will of God" (v. 1).

He writes to "saints" ("set-apart ones" – Greek = "Hagios"); "set apart for God." From the same word comes the great doctrinal word, "sanctification." At salvation the new believer becomes a "saint." This is positional sanctification to be followed by progressive sanctification, which is to be a life-long process until ultimate sanctification takes place in glory. Paul describes these "saints" as "the faithful in Christ Jesus." Here the term "faithful" does not refer to lifestyle (though a saint should be faithful), but to the fact that they had placed their faith in Christ. Others (pagans) were set apart to their gods; Paul's readers were set apart to Christ.

Other words of import in this passage: "grace" and "peace" (v. 2). The former: God's steadfast love toward man; the latter: the relational state as a result of that grace. Verses 3-14 give us quite possibly "the longest sentence of connected discourse in existence" (Wuest). When Paul writes, "Blessed be the God," he uses the word "eulogetos," the Greek word, which gives us eulogize: "Let our God be well-spoken of." Other words to examine: "chosen," "predestinated" and "adoption." Nor should one overlook the truth that all of the "spiritual blessings" the believer receives are found "in Christ," (a phrase or its equivalent used ten times in verses 3-13).

Let us endeavor to live our lives in such a way that God is eulogized through them, and that our gratefulness for His grace and peace is obvious.

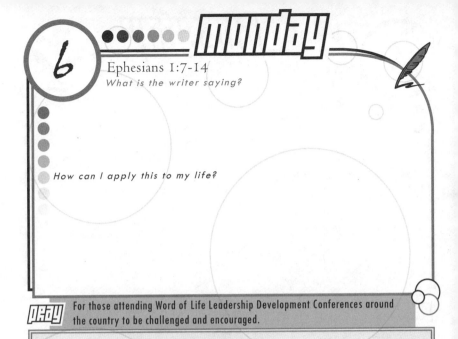

Ephesians 1:7-14

What is the writer saying?

How can I apply this to my life?

PRAY For those attending Word of Life Leadership Development Conferences around the country to be challenged and encouraged.

Paul's long sentence (vv. 3-14 comprise one long and magnificent sentence in the original Greek text) continues as does his doctrinal dissertation of God's work on man's behalf. He directs our attention to our redemption (vv. 7, 14), "to deliver by paying a price" and "the forgiveness of (our) sins," (Matthew 26:28), both secured "through His (Christ's) blood" cp. Ephesians 2:13; I Peter 1:19 and was "according to the riches of his grace," cp. Ephesians 1:6; 2:7.

In verses 8-10 we find that in God's grace the believer has the resources necessary to comprehend and understand God's will and purposes throughout the ages. Without God's gracious revelational input, all of this would have remained a "mystery" (v. 9, cp 3:3,4,9; 5:32), i.e., not something mysterious, but rather a secret hidden with God and held in reserve for its proper time of revealing. That mystery, relative to this book, is that of the New Testament Church as one body composed of both Jews and Gentiles (3:1-12); and the Church as the bride of Christ (5:23-32).

The phrase beginning verse 11 can be read two ways: "we have obtained an inheritance," or "we were made His inheritance." Both ideas are true: we, who were outcasts, are "heirs of God and joint-heirs with Christ" (Romans 8:17). And also, Christ, for the joy that was set before Him (that's us: we're His inheritance) endured the cross (Hebrews 12:2). Then, to ensure that this would take place, Paul tells his readers that God's will cannot be frustrated, nor will His purposes for His people be thwarted. Why not? Because once salvation has taken place, the believer is "sealed with the Holy Spirit" (v. 13), a mark of ownership and a pledge that our promised redemption will be completed.

What a great salvation we have! Now redeemed by the blood of the Lamb (purchased from the bondage of sin into the freedom of grace), let us commit ourselves to the task of telling other slaves how to be set free.

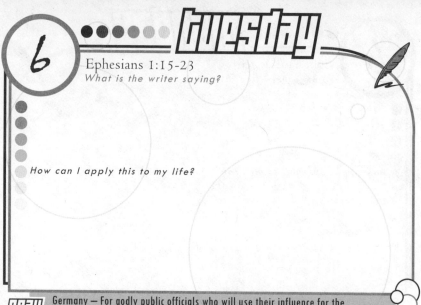

tuesday

6

Ephesians 1:15-23

What is the writer saying?

How can I apply this to my life?

pray Germany — For godly public officials who will use their influence for the furtherance of the Gospel.

Paul follows the normal custom in writing letters that include early on a word of thanksgiving. Here his "thank you" is to God for the Ephesian saints' "faith in the Lord Jesus" (a vertical relationship), and their "love unto all the saints" (a horizontal relationship). The former is to lead to the latter, and in this case it did, hence Paul's word of thanksgiving, which he follows with prayer. He was concerned that his readers would fully comprehend what they had received in Christ . . . that God would continue to bestow upon them "the spirit of wisdom and revelation in the knowledge of him (v. 17)." Only with the help of the Holy Spirit would that take place (cp. I Corinthians 2:14).

Three areas of desired knowledge are addressed: The Past (18b), "The hope of His calling" (vv. 3-6), with the follow-up of 4:1 . . . "walk worthy of the vocation to which ye are called." The Future (v. 18c), "The riches of the glory of His inheritance in the saints." Here we see God's inheritance – the believers He purchased at great price (v. 7); earlier it was the believer's inheritance: final redemption from sin's presence. The Present (vv. 19-23), "The exceeding greatness of His power toward us who believe." This power makes continued growth in the Lord possible. Four words in the final verses of the chapter explain how much power is available to the believer: "power" (dunamis), inherent power; "working" (energeia), operative power; "mighty" (krator), demonstrated strength; "power" (ischus), the possession of power. That power, available to the believer, was manifested in Christ's case through His resurrection (v. 20a), exaltation (v. 20b) and currently in His present position of absolute, universal authority and head of the church, His body (vv. 21-23).

Redeemed from the bondage of sin, the believer has the potential to fully understand, under the direction of the Spirit of God, the Word and will of God. May we echo Paul's prayer for the Ephesians that we too, may have enlightened eyes of understanding.

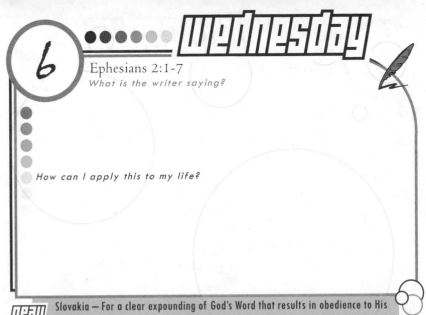
Ephesians 2:1-7

What is the writer saying?

How can I apply this to my life?

pray Slovakia — For a clear expounding of God's Word that results in obedience to His authority.

Chapter 2 gives to us a spiritual "before and after" picture. It shows some of the changes the Gospel makes in men, not the least of which is a death to life experience. That death ("in trespasses and sins," verse 1) is spiritual death, separation from God. In that state the unsaved man (1) walks according to the world, his external enemy, (v. 2a); (2) is controlled by Satan, his infernal enemy, (v. 2b); and (3) dominated by the desires of the flesh, his internal enemy, (v. 3). The result: as unbelievers we are the children of disobedience (v. 2a), and wrath, (v. 3b). God, however, has not left the believer at the mercy of these enemies. The same power that in chapter 1 was manifest in Christ's resurrection and exaltation brings about new life in the one who trusts Christ for salvation (v. 1). Because that is true, no longer does one have to live defeated in a devil-dominated world system, but can live victoriously. God, in His "great love" (v. 4), intervened in His mercy, and (1) implanted in all who believe, spiritual life, meaning no longer separated from God; (2) elevated them to a new level of life; and (3) permits them to enjoy a continuous relationship with Christ in this present earthly life (v. 5). All of this takes place through the instrumentality of the grace of God (v. 7), (i.e., unmerited favor extended where wrath was deserved).

In verse 6 we see the marked contrast between the former lost condition of believers and their present situation in Christ. Though still in human bodies on earth, they also participate in the resurrection life of Christ, being seated with Him in heavenly places (1:3). The emphasis here is on the believer's identification with Christ in His death (v. 5), resurrection (v. 6) and ascension (v. 6). Verse 7 shows the purpose behind God's actions in verses 4-6: that throughout all eternity believers will be a trophy of God's grace.

WOW! That's what these verses scream out. They talk of His great love, grace and mercy, bestowed on undeserving sinners like us. Take the time to thank Him. Rereading the passage will provide inspiration.

thursday

6

Ephesians 2:8-13

What is the writer saying?

How can I apply this to my life?

pray El Salvador – For effective discipling and motivation of believers for service, witness, and missions.

In verses 1-10, Paul gives three reasons behind God's desire to save people. First, to show His love (vv. 1-6); second, to show His grace; and third, to show His workmanship by our doing good works. The salvation His love provides is "by grace . . . through faith." That is spelled out in verse 5: "By grace ye are saved"; and amplified in verse 8: "For by grace are ye saved through faith." Furthermore, "it is the gift of God." Three key words to be noted: "grace" – the cause behind the plan of salvation; "faith" – the instrument by which it is received; and "gift" – the source of this grace is God Himself, and He gives it with no strings attached.

Noting the freeness of the "gift," and its inability to be earned, Paul makes it clear that boasting is eliminated (v. 9). However, even though salvation is not able to be earned, and while works cannot save, good works always follow salvation. Believers are God's "workmanship," His "work of art" that began at salvation and is to continue for a lifetime. "Ordained" to "good works," we are "to walk in them." In fact, believers were "created in Christ Jesus" for that purpose. While works cannot bring salvation to a person, they are to always accompany salvation (cp. James 2:17).

Verses 1-10 have application to both Jews and Gentiles before conversion; verse 11 ff has special reference to Gentiles. Jews referred to them as the uncircumcision, those without the veil, with no part in the Old Covenant. Even some Jewish believers were hesitant to treat them as equals in the faith. But now, says Paul, that great gulf that separated Jew and Gentile has been removed, and those Gentiles who were "once far off" and "without hope" have been "made nigh" (brought near) "by the blood of Christ."

Life **stEP**

This would be a good time to thank the Lord for His wonderful free gift of salvation and then to review one's life to see if the verbal thanks are followed up by a life of "good works."

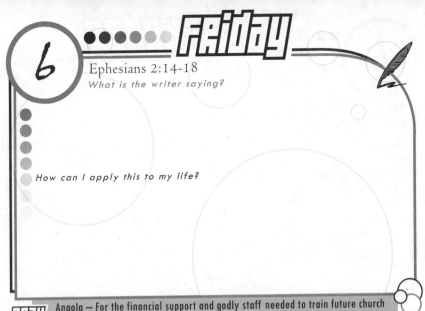

Ephesians 2:14-18

What is the writer saying?

How can I apply this to my life?

PRAY Angola — For the financial support and godly staff needed to train future church leadership.

Paul has noted that Jew and Gentile, once alienated, are now one in Christ (v. 13). He now goes on to state what is involved. First, the wall of enmity that once existed has been broken down (v. 14). The animosity that existed, which centered in the advantages God has given the Jew (and which the Gentiles resented, verse 15), was done away with in Christ. Now reconciled, the two have been made "one new man" (a ref. to the church, the body of Christ; i.e., 1 Corinthians 12:12-13; Ephesians 1:22-23).

That reconciliation (removal of enmity) was brought about by the death of Christ, for in His work on the cross, He rendered the Law inoperative, tearing it down, so that it is no longer a separator. Wiersbe states the tearing down was three-fold: Physically, for in Christ we are all one (Galatians 3:28-29); Spiritually, the "far off" Gentiles were brought "nigh" (v. 13); and Legally, Christ fulfilling the Law in Himself (by meeting all of its requirements and ending its reign at the cross).

Not only is there peace between Jew and Gentile (v. 14), but also between God and those who place their faith in Him (v. 16). (Paul writes of this latter reconciliation in Romans 5:10; 2 Corinthians 5:18-20; Colossians 1:20 and elsewhere.) The bottom line is this: whether Jew or Gentile all believers have a common denominator: their new life in Christ. In it they find oneness that does away with that which had kept them apart. They have lost their separate identities in the church. Through His death on the cross (v. 16), Christ proclaims peace to all mankind (v. 17), and He IS peace; for through Him all men have access to God by way of the

Life **stEP** Why not make your time in the Word today one of thanking the Lord for removing the barrier between Himself and you? Only His cross made the difference. Take time to reflect on, and enjoy, the peace that comes by faith.

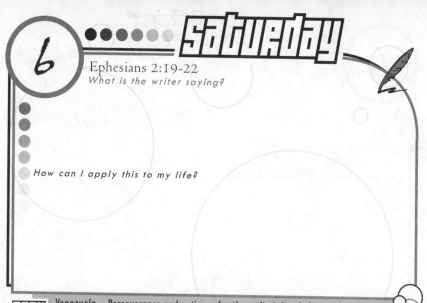

saturday

6

Ephesians 2:19-22
What is the writer saying?

How can I apply this to my life?

pray Venezuela — Perseverance and patience for those discipling believers from dysfunctional backgrounds.

With these verses, Paul changes the imagery from that of a body to that of a temple. These are climactic verses because in them we find a graphic picture (v. 21) of what the work of Christ will result in; a living temple built out of people who are called "living stones" (1 Peter 2:4-8). This would be appropriate imagery for both Jew (they greatly revered their temple in Jerusalem) and Gentile (for here in Ephesus was the great Temple of Diana).

Paul begins (v. 18) by making it clear that Gentiles in Christ (just like Jews in Christ) are secure, no longer strangers to God as outsiders. They are now fellow citizens, along with Jewish believers by birth, set apart as members of the household of God. Both Jew and Gentile are on equal footing in the Church of Jesus Christ, which began at Pentecost and will continue on earth until the Rapture.

Besides being a secure structure, this temple is also solidly built (v. 20). The laying of the foundation was the responsibility of the New Testament apostles and prophets. The foundation is Christ (1 Corinthians 3:11), not the apostles or prophets. Placing them there would destroy the imagery of the context. Like all other believers, they are parts of the temple building. Christ is also the cornerstone, because every line in the temple building is justified only when aligned with Him.

This "building" (v. 21), this "habitation of God" (v. 22), is the place where God dwells while the church is in this world. In the Old Testament God dwelt first in the Tabernacle (Exodus 40:34), and then in Solomon's temple (2 Chronicles 7:1); in the Gospels in Christ Himself (John 1:14); and today in individuals (1 Corinthians 6:19-20) and the church (Ephesians 2:21). Exodus 25:8 reads: "Let them make me a sanctuary; that I may dwell among them." Today, He Himself is building that sanctuary. It is called the church.

What a privilege to be the habitation of God. How important it is that our lives, individually and corporately, demonstrate that indwelling relationship. May that be true of all of us, and our churches.

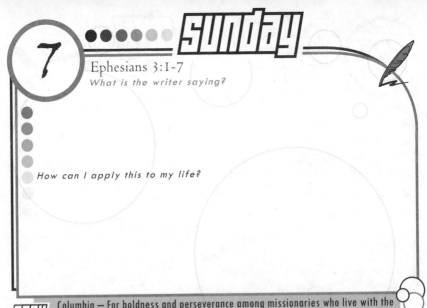

SUNDAY

Ephesians 3:1-7

What is the writer saying?

How can I apply this to my life?

PRAY Columbia — For boldness and perseverance among missionaries who live with the threat of violence.

In the verses immediately preceding this passage (2:11-21), Paul briefly discussed the union of Jews and Gentiles in one body (v. 16), called the church. Now, as he was about to offer a prayer for these united believers, he stopped right in the middle of a sentence (end of 3:1), and then returns to his prayer in verse 14. In between, Paul inserts one long sentence in which he felt compelled by the Holy Spirit to explain in some depth the equality of position that Jew and Gentiles have in the church. Prior to his interruption he reminds his readers who he is: "the prisoner of Jesus Christ" (not of Rome, though detained by them), and was such "for you Gentiles." Then he begins to develop for them the ministry to which he has been called, that of "the dispensation of the grace of God" (v. 2). He was to make known to the world the meaning of the mystery God had revealed to him (vv. 3-4): the no-distinction union of Jew and Gentile in the New Testament Church. "Mystery" here is not something mystical, but incomprehensible until God chooses to reveal it, first to and through Paul, and then others: "Holy (set apart) apostles and prophets" (v. 5).

In verse 6 Paul makes clear the meaning of the mystery in this context. It is not that Gentiles finally could be saved, for elsewhere Paul quotes Old Testament passages demonstrating God's past redemptive work among the Gentiles (Romans 9:24-33; 10:19-21; 15:9-12). It is that Gentile believers and Jewish believers are together (1) "fellow heirs," (2) of the "same body" and (3) "partakers of His promise" (a messianic promise) found "in Christ (cp. 2:12, Galatians 3:29) by the Gospel" (and that's good news). This joining together of Jew and Gentile into one was a revolutionary concept to both parties.

In verse 7ff, Paul shows clearly his attitude toward this great responsibility (of taking this mystery to the world) God had given him. He recognized that his position as a "minister," i.e., servant of God, was a "gift of the grace of God," and only through "His power" would he be able to fulfill his ministry.

Life stEP

God has been gracious to us as well, gifting us in many different ways to take the good news of the Gospel to a lost world. Let us live in such a way, that we don't thwart the power He has made available to fulfill our personal ministries.

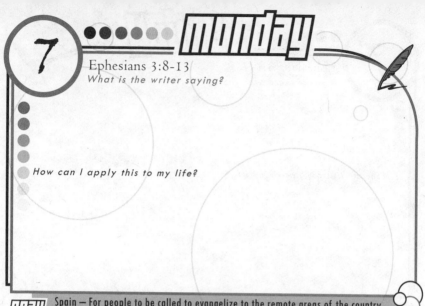

Ephesians 3:8-13
What is the writer saying?

How can I apply this to my life?

In verse 7 Paul noted his responsibility to God as a "minister" (servant) "of the gospel" (v. 6), a task given to him by God's grace, and made effective by God's power. Here (v. 8) he articulates his personal feeling of unworthiness for such a task, saying he is "less than the least of all saints." No doubt his background of persecuting the church (Acts 9:5; I Timothy 1:13 etc.) contributed to that assessment, hence his genuine humility in being given the assignment of proclaiming to the world the "mystery" of the church.

He was to "preach among the Gentiles the unsearchable riches of Christ," riches "past finding out," or "untraceable" (perhaps like an airplane in the air); "not capable of being tracked by footprints." Reason: it had, "from the beginning of the world...been hid in God" (v. 9). While just now being revealed, it had always been a part of God's eternal plan (cp. 1:4, 11). Paul's task was "to make all men see what is the fellowship of the mystery;" he is to "turn on the light" (from a word translated "photo" in English). He is to see to it that the entire world "gets the picture," i.e., that because of the grace of God, Jew and Gentile are now one body in Christ, called the church and through whom, of course, the world is to learn of the glories of the Gospel. But the Lord will also use the church to reveal the wisdom of God to angelic beings ("principalities and powers," c. 6:12). Comparing v. 10 with I Peter 1:12 we find that even angels did not previously know what God had planned for the Church Age, and only learned it when God chose to reveal it through Paul. As these angelic witnesses view the church, they must admit that having Jew and Gentile in one body is evidence of the "manifold wisdom of God" (v. 10).

Paul closes his interruption (begun in v. 1) by exhorting his readers to "faint not at (his) tribulations" incurred on their behalf. Instead, feel honored that in God's plan, their salvation was important enough for His servant to undergo such difficulties. While not glad he had to suffer, they could rejoice in its purpose and accomplishment.

Life stEP   Paul was goal-oriented in his service for Christ. Neither his past life nor his current suffering took the goal out of focus. May we learn from, and follow, his example.

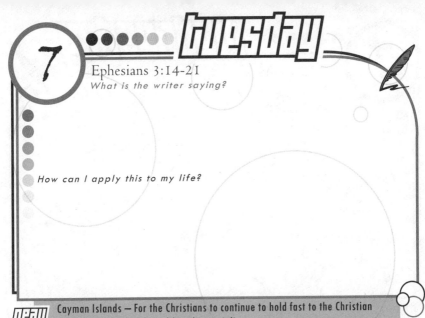

tuesday

7

Ephesians 3:14-21

What is the writer saying?

How can I apply this to my life?

PRAY Cayman Islands — For the Christians to continue to hold fast to the Christian values in the midst of wealth and materialism.

Paul's digression ends and he returns to the thought he had in mind as he began this chapter. "For this cause",…i.e., God's wonderful work of bringing Jew and Gentile together as one body in Christ, the apostle humbles himself before God in a great prayer for the church. This is the second of Paul's two prayers in this letter. The first (1:15-23) emphasized knowledge, this second prayer lifestyle. Paul wanted them to understand what they had and put it into practice. He prays for God's "whole family in heaven and earth" (v. 15). This verse is not teaching "the fatherhood of God," relative to salvation…that is based upon the crosswork of Christ…instead, it is relative to creation, for all families of men and angels find their origin in God. He then enumerates his requests for God's people. (1) That they would be "strengthened in the inner man" by the power of the Holy Spirit. (v. 16) (2) That Christ may dwell (feel at home) in your hearts by faith – He would have "the run of the house." (v. 17) (3) That they "may be able to comprehend…and know the love of Christ, which passeth knowledge" – an appeal to an experiential knowledge of Christ's love which exceeds all theoretical and intellectual knowledge (for Christianity is far more than a series of doctrines, it is a life to be experienced). (vv. 18-19) (4) That believers "might be filled with all the fullness of God," or better: "with respect to all the fullness of God." No believer could possibly contain all the fullness of God, but He is the unlimited source from which we draw for all of our needed spiritual resources.

Verses 20-21 form a doxology or praise, to God in which Paul notes that God can do "exceedingly abundantly (double compound word: "superabundantly") above anything we ask or think." And He does it through the power that works in us: The Holy Spirit.

 Life STEP

Does Christ really have "the run of the house" as it relates to your life? If He doesn't, why not stop right now and make plans to "clean house." Only then will He feel at home.

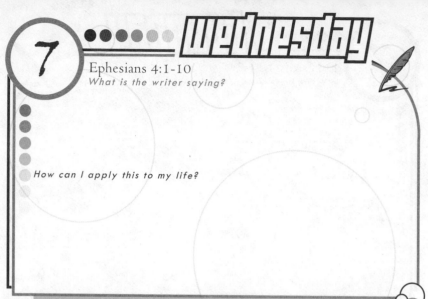

Ephesians 4:1-10
What is the writer saying?

How can I apply this to my life?

pray Praise God that He supplies all our needs according to His riches in glory by Christ Jesus (Philippians 4:19).

Ephesians follows Paul's practice of beginning with doctrine and following with practice. Chapters 1-3 are doctrinal and 4-6 are practical. Following his doctrinal dissertation, Paul now tells the Ephesians to "walk worthy of the vocation wherewith ye are called," i.e., the calling every believer has received and which brings to them the designation: "saint;" one set apart to God (Romans 1:6-7).

This profession of sainthood will be marked by three qualities: (1) "lowliness" – true, not false, humility: in Greek culture thought of as a vice to be practiced only by slaves. Christ demonstrated genuine humility. (Philippians 2: 6-8); (2) "meekness" – gentleness: not weakness, but ability to control one's emotions. Christ was meek (Matthew 11:29), but drove out the moneychangers from the temple. (Matthew 21:12-13); (3) "forbearing," or forbearance: the ability to be patient with the weakness of others (all 3 in verse 2). Unity will not take place without these three qualities.

Paul lists (vv. 4-6) the seven-fold oneness believers share, and the impetus behind a unified walk. (1) One body – all believers from Pentecost to the Rapture, 1:23; 2:16; 3:6; (2) One Spirit – the indwelling Holy Spirit, 2:22; (3) One hope – an expectant attitude toward Christ's return and their personal future, 1 Peter 1:3; 3:15; (4) One Lord – Christ, the head of the church, 1:22-23; Colossians 1:18; (5) One Faith – demonstrated by trusting Christ for salvation and life, Colossians 2:7; (6) One baptism – that of the Holy Spirit which all believers experience at salvation making them one, 1 Corinthians 12:13; (7) One God and Father: the relationship established when one trusts Christ, John 1:13; Galatians 3:26.

To accomplish the goal of walking in unity, God sovereignly bestows (spiritual) gifts upon all believers by the ascended Christ (vv. 7-9). How each believer uses these gifts will determine one's place of service during Christ's messianic, millennial reign.

Life **stEP** You are a gifted believer. Do you know what your gifts are? Paul lists some in this chapter, others in Romans 12 and 1 Corinthians 12. Know what they are and use them for Him.

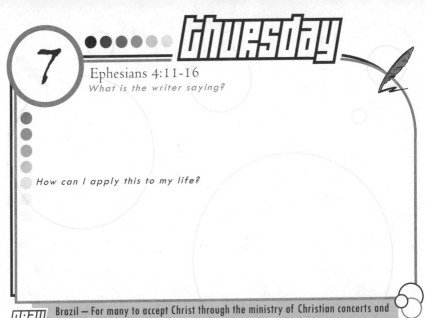

7

thursday

Ephesians 4:11-16

What is the writer saying?

How can I apply this to my life?

pray Brazil — For many to accept Christ through the ministry of Christian concerts and musical dramas.

To serve Christ every believer has been spiritually gifted (1 Corinthians 12; Romans 12). For the church to accomplish its purposes, the Lord provides gifted men and places them providentially (Acts 11:23-26) or through His Spirit (Acts 13:1-2). He does so based on their gifting and upon the need of the church. Verse 11 lists four or perhaps five, such men.

The first two, apostles and prophets, mentioned earlier (2:20; 3:5) are foundational gifts to the church. The former would include the Twelve Apostles, Paul and a handful of others, commissioned by the Lord to represent Him and deliver His message. The latter, strictly speaking, were those who were given direct revelation by God before the New Testament was written, to communicate to man. Being foundational in nature, neither has existed since the first generation of believers. Evangelists: preachers of the Gospel, helping to bring the lost into the body of Christ, while pastors and teachers (linked here, separate elsewhere,

Romans 12:7; 1 Peter 5:2) are those who shepherd the flock and instruct them in their ministries.

The goal of the church is outlined in verses 12-16. These gifted men are to (a) perfect (mature, prepare) the saints (by using their gifts) (b) so they (since all believers are gifted, all are to be involved) in turn will be able to accomplish the work of the ministry, (c) with the result of edifying – building up – the body of Christ (v. 12). Verse 13 makes it plain: spiritual unity and spiritual maturity are closely linked. The purpose of this linkage is described in verse 14, where the term "children" is applied to some believers. Spiritual children are often doctrinally insecure and can be "tossed to and fro," like a small boat in a storm, when false teaching comes along (v. 14). But when the "truth" is spoken in love (v. 15), "the whole body (no insignificant parts – 1 Corinthians 12:14-17) is joined together" (v. 16), resulting in an edified body, united to its head (Christ); one that functions as designed.

Life **stEP** A reminder: every believer is gifted; hence every believer is to be involved in Christian service, using one's gifts for Christ. Is that true in your life?

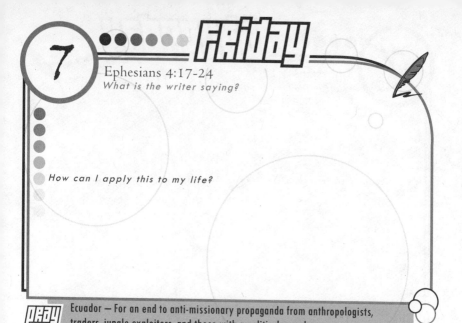

How can I apply this to my life?

PRAY — Ecuador — For an end to anti-missionary propaganda from anthropologists, traders, jungle exploiters, and those with a political agenda.

Paul begins a long passage (ending at 6:9) in which he draws the logical conclusion in terms of life and morals that follow membership in the body of Christ. He challenges believers to "walk not as other (unsaved) Gentiles walk, in the vanity of their mind." The challenge suggests two things: one, they could walk that way; two, they did not have to. Though one's fallen nature is not eradicated at salvation, the believer, by receiving a new nature and the indwelling Spirit, no longer needs to be governed by it, though internal warfare between the two will be constant (Romans 7; Galatians 2:20; 5:13-26 etc.).

Those "other Gentiles" have had their "understanding darkened" (v. 18) and are "past feeling" (v. 19). They have no sense of shame, the result of years of sin and debauchery, and "have given themselves over unto lasciviousness" (sensuality), which leads to all types of "uncleanness" that goes deeper and deeper because it is never satisfied. Three times in Romans

1 Paul says that God gave them over to something: first, to sinful desires (1:24); second, to shameful lusts (1:26); third, to a depraved mind (1:28). Result: (1) live right, (2) love right or (3) think right. "But ye have not so learned Christ." These Ephesians no longer existed in this state of ignorance and separation from God. Paul knew that – having been their teacher. They were taught the truth about Jesus and salvation took place, yet even with that great event in their past, they still had the responsibility of discarding their old way of life ("put off" – verse 22), denying the appetite of their old sinful nature (Romans 6:13; Galatians 2:20; 5:13). The way that is done is by being "renewed in the spirit of your mind" ("continuously yielding to the Holy Spirit" verse 23) while at the same time "putting on" (v. 24) the "new man"…allowing the Holy Spirit to be the controlling force in one's life. Doing so manifests itself in "righteousness and true holiness" (v. 24).

Life stEP

The Christian's life is like stripping off the dirty clothes of a sinful past and putting on the snowy white robes of Christ's righteousness. Be sure to do it daily.

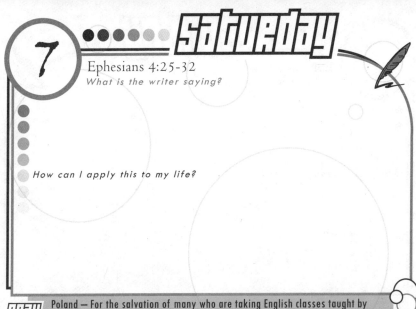

Ephesians 4:25-32

What is the writer saying?

How can I apply this to my life?

pray Poland — For the salvation of many who are taking English classes taught by missionaries.

In Matthew 7:20, speaking of true and false teachers, Christ said: "by their fruits ye shall know them." A similar application may be made relative to believers, for the fruit that comes from a person's life, his actions, will prove whether the individual is yielding to his old sinful nature or to the Holy Spirit. To illustrate, Paul uses four representative examples of problems present in his day and in ours. He underscores them all with a stern command: "grieve not the holy Spirit of God," (v. 30).

1. Lack of Truthfulness (v. 25). This was common among the heathen, but because Christians are "members one of another," lying among them is unthinkable. Would one's foot lie to one's hand?

2. Anger (v. 26), which is sometimes justified by its cause, must not be permitted to stay and fester and give the devil an opportunity to gain a foothold in one's life.

3. Stealing (v. 28), of course, is wrong but was apparently being practiced by some believers who carried some of their old ways into their new lives, so Paul says: Stop! He then provides them with a practical antidote: Work! That will not only meet their needs but also provide relief for others.

4. Corrupt Communication (foul speech) (v. 29), Another "unthinkable" for the believer. The remedy is more positive than negative: speak only "that which is good to the use of edifying." Let your language always build up, ministering "grace unto the hearers."

Finally, Christians are not to "grieve the Holy Spirit," remembering that the Spirit is a person, not an influence, and can be hurt when the believer turns away from His leading and follows the promptings of his flesh (some mentioned in verse 31). Paul closes this chapter with a number of positive characteristics that should mark all believers: kindness, a tender heart and forgiveness (v. 32).

Life **stEP** Years ago, a song contained these words: "Eliminate the negative, accentuate the positive." These would be good words to apply to this chapter. Put into practice they will keep you from grieving the Holy Spirit.

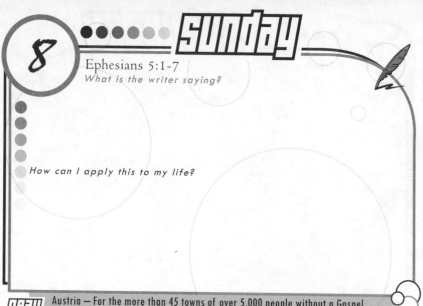

Ephesians 5:1-7

What is the writer saying?

How can I apply this to my life?

pray Austria — For the more than 45 towns of over 5,000 people without a Gospel witness.

The word "therefore" (or "wherefore") usually refers one back to the previous passage. Not so here. Instead it is referring, as do other "therefores" (4:1,17,25; 5:14,17) in this second half of the book (chapters 4-5) to the first half of the book (chapters 1-3). In other words, the "practical" follows the "doctrinal." Aware of whom we are doctrinally (the church, the body of Christ), there is to be a lifestyle worthy of that relationship. "Therefore," in these final three chapters we see Paul exhorting his readers to live a life that differentiates them from their pagan world. In Ephesus was the Temple to Diana, where all sorts of vile sexual immorality, in the name of religion, took place. Paul warns the believers to avoid the pitfalls of the pagans, including "fornication" (sexual immorality); "uncleanness" (any kind of impurity); "covetousness" (greed), (v. 3); "filthiness" (shameless, immoral conduct); "foolish talking" (characteristic of an empty head); "jesting" (words with double meaning),

(v. 4); for those who practice such things give evidence of an unchanged life and will have no place in God's kingdom, (v .5). Positively, however: "Be followers (imitators) of God" (v. 1). No other New Testament passage gives such instruction directly (to imitate God). Believers are told to imitate good (1 Peter 3:13); Paul (1 Corinthians 4:16; 11:1); godly men (Hebrews 6:11-12); and Christ (by implication, 1 Corinthians 11:1). To do so may not be as unrealistic as supposed, for we are His "dear children" (v. 1), partakers of His nature (2 Peter 1:4); have access to Him (Romans 5:2); and fellowship with Him (1 John 1:3). Such a relationship makes possible a higher kind of life than the unsaved can know, a life whose behavior is ordered by "love" (agape); and because "God is love" (1 John 4:8, 16), believers imitating Him will live a life that manifests that same love (1 Corinthians 13). The motivation for such a life is found in the sacrificial actions of Christ on the cross "for us" (for our benefit) (v. 2).

Life stEP

In Paul's words: "therefore, brothers and sisters in Christ," let us live a life that so imitates God that others desire the same relationship. A life so lived will be "sweet-smelling" to the nostrils of God.

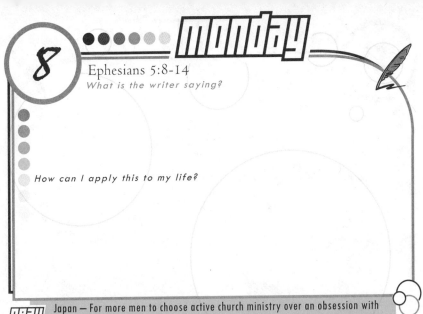

How can I apply this to my life?

PRAY Japan — For more men to choose active church ministry over an obsession with career advancement.

Paul again points out some contrasts between the conditions of the unbeliever with that of the believer. An unbeliever is dead; a believer has a new life (v. 14). An unbeliever is asleep; the believer is awake to reality and truth (v. 14). An unbeliever is darkness (note: not in darkness, but darkness itself) while the believer is light. That darkness was once true of the believer (v. 5); now he is numbered among those who are lights in the world (Matthew 5:14), and as such are to "walk as children of light" (keep their lights on), living lives reflective of their new life.

The parenthetical ninth verse explains that "the fruit of the light" (not Spirit according to most scholars), is "goodness and righteousness and truth," all desperately needed in a world of sensuality, sin and evil (vv. 3-5). "Light" comes from the Greek "photos" from which we get photography, etc. It is a common biblical expression, normally depicting the drastic difference between "what is acceptable unto the Lord" (v. 10), and that which is characteristic of a sinful life.

Verse 11 places upon the believer two responsibilities with respect to sin. First, no way is he to have "fellowship" or "to become a partaker with others" in the "unfruitful works of darkness." The second is to reprove such behavior by letting his life "show by contrast how dreary and futile these things are" (Phillips). By proper conduct, the believer living as a "child of light" will expose the deeds of other believers (not unbelievers – that is God's work – 1 Corinthians 5:12-13) who are not walking in the light. Their deeds were so vile that Paul hesitated to even mention them (v. 12), but "are made manifest" when "reproved by the light" (v. 13). Paul then appeals to the believer who is living inconsistently with his light position: "Be waking up the one who is sleeping, and arise from the dead, and there shall shine upon you Christ" (Wuest).

Life stEP

Little amplification is needed. You are a child of light. Keep on walking in it. And if you stumbled out of it, confess it. God does forgive and restore (1 John 1:9).

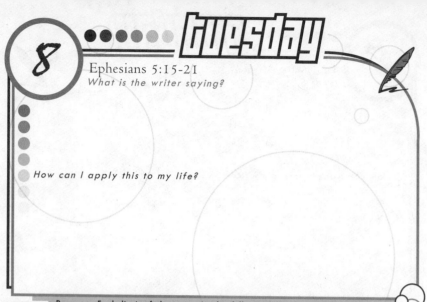

tuesday

8

Ephesians 5:15-21

What is the writer saying?

How can I apply this to my life?

The issue is still Christian conduct. Paul urges the Ephesian believers to pay careful attention to their behavior, walking "circumspectly" (v. 15) or accurately. The path has been marked out (Psalm 37:23) and the believer is not to wander off course, being careful where he "walks." He is to walk "wisely," "redeeming" (buying up) the time for "the days are evil" (v. 16) or morally corrupt. In a once-born world, the twice – born Christian is to take every opportunity to shed light on an ever-darkening world.

"Wherefore" (noting the commands to "walk in light," verse 8 and in "wisdom," v. 15), "be ye not unwise" (senseless), but conduct oneself in a manner demonstrating an "understanding" of "the will of the Lord" (v. 17). The pagan cannot do so (1 Corinthians 2:14); believers can. They possess in Scripture the objective revelation of His will and the indwelling Holy Spirit to interpret it. And once He is known, (for the Christian faith is not devoid of intellectual content), the Spirit will aid the believer in its application.

"Be not drunk with wine" (v. 18), a common sin among unbelievers in Paul's day, one that Paul, quoting from Proverbs 23:29-32, warns against. It has no place among believers. Instead, the believer is to "be filled with the Spirit." Paul has already taught that all believers are sealed, once for all, at the point of salvation (1:13-14; 4:30), but not all believers are filled. Filling is commanded in Scripture and is dependent upon one's yieldingness to God's will (v. 17), thus differing from God's instantaneous act of sealing. It can be repeated according to Acts 2:4 and 4:31. All believers have the Spirit; the command here is that the Spirit is to have the entire believer. Only then, will the wise walk with a verse 15 result.

Verses 19-21 advise as to how to carry out the command; First, through music (a) with other believers and (b) in your heart to the Lord (v. 19). Secondly, through constant thanksgiving to God for all things (v. 20), and Thirdly, through voluntary and willing submission to one another.

Life stEP

The successful Christian life is dependent upon the filling of the Spirit. Evaluate your life; is it measuring up to the command of verse 18?

WEDNESDAY

8

Ephesians 5:22-33

What is the writer saying?

How can I apply this to my life?

PRAY — Uganda — For God to call witnesses to the Karamojong, Pokot, and Jie, nomadic people.

The key word is "submit" (v. 22), from a Greek word of military origin, emphasizing the act of voluntary (not forced) submission to a proper authority. Paul uses it as a basis for the relationships between husbands–wives, parents–children and masters–servants.

He deals first with the husband-wife relationship, it being the most fundamental. "Wives, submit… unto your own husbands," for that is your service "to the Lord"(cp. Colossians 3:18). God has made the husband the family's spiritual leader. His position is compared to Christ's headship over His church; Christ is the Savior of the body, the husband the protector of his wife. For her to fail in voluntary submission would be like the church usurping Christ's headship. She is to respond to his assigned position of authority. This is not a picture of superiority vs. inferiority, but simply a role assignment. "Husbands, love your wives," doing so as "Christ… loved the church and gave Himself for it" (v. 25). This is self-sacrificial love… giving of oneself for another person. When the husband practices such Christ-like love, willing submission on the part of the wife should not be difficult. Christ's death (v. 26) was to "set-apart" His bride (the church) for Himself, forever (cp. Hebrews 10:10, 14). He did so by cleansing her "with the washing of water by the word" (v. 26), especially the preached word (Ephesians 6:17; Romans 10:8; 1 Peter 1:25) in order to "present it to himself" (v. 27) in faultless condition.

Verses 28-30 apply the truths of verses 25-27. The church is the body of Christ, united to Him, its head. The wife is united to her husband, they become "one flesh" (v. 31), and men are to love their wives as their own bodies, a manner that precludes anything but the exceptional care Christ displayed for His body, the church.

Life stEP

God's Word is a marriage manual, provided for family use. When the directions (such as above) are followed, so does blessing. Failure in following will negate the blessing. Don't let that happen to you.

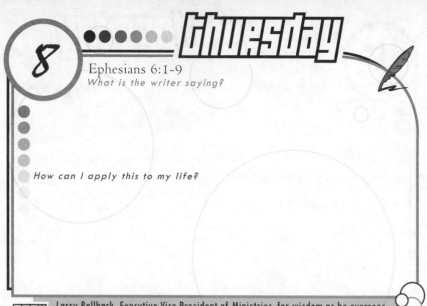

thursday

8

Ephesians 6:1-9

What is the writer saying?

How can I apply this to my life?

pray Larry Bollback, Executive Vice President of Ministries, for wisdom as he oversees all areas of ministry outreach.

Paul's discussion of personal relationships began in Ephesians 5:22 with husbands-wives. Now it continues with parents-children and slaves-masters. All three relationships require Spirit controlled lives (5:18), hence the instruction here is pointedly to believers.

Children and Parents: (vv. 1-4). Even as wives are to be subject to their husbands, so children are to "obey" their parents, doing so "in the Lord." Such behavior "is well pleasing to the Lord" (Colossians 3:20), and is "right." The "submit" of wives implies voluntary action, but "obey" is much stronger, implying that parental direction is to be carried out regardless of the children's wishes. "Honor" goes beyond obedience itself to the heart attitude. Obedience is the duty (external); honor the disposition (internal). Attached to such positive behavior is a promise (v. 2), "...that you may prosper and live a long life on earth" (Williams Translation). (See the fourth commandment – Exodus 20:12

– the only one of the ten with a promise.) As for the parents, they are to earn such obedience and honor, hence the instruction: "Do not provoke (exasperate) to wrath, but bring them (the children) up in the nurture (training) and admonition (instruction) of the Lord," i.e., not being unreasonable in their expectations of their children. They are to practice neither unlimited permissiveness nor spirit-breaking discipline (Colossians 3:21). Balance is the goal.

Slaves and Masters: (vv. 5-9). These instructions apply today to employee-employer relationships. Employees are to carry out the orders of their employers (v. 5), understanding that no matter whom they serve in "the flesh," they are really serving Christ (v. 6), and their ultimate reward comes from Him (v. 8). Employers are to have similar attitudes, treating their employees fairly, for their ultimate responsibility is also to Christ. Both are to understand that God is impartial… both are equal in His sight.

Once again the directions are clear. In which category do you find yourself? And are you meeting your responsibilities?

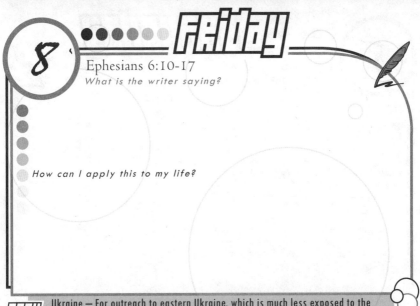

Ephesians 6:10-17

What is the writer saying?

How can I apply this to my life?

pray Ukraine – For outreach to eastern Ukraine, which is much less exposed to the Gospel than western Ukraine.

Paul now addresses the believer's warfare. Battlefield language is not uncommon to Paul, speaking often of the Christian life in military terms. This is more, however, than analogous language. The battle is real and no true soldier (cp. 2 Timothy 2:3) of Jesus Christ can expect to be immune from enemy attacks. And so, Paul exhorts the believers to "be strong in the Lord and in the power of His might" (v. 10). Victory will not be achieved on one's own; the believer needs the strength only the Lord can supply.

The "whole armor of God" is to be "put on" (v. 11). Paul is writing from prison. In full view would be fully armored Roman soldiers. That physical armor provides a picture of the spiritual battle facing the believer, a battle "not against flesh and blood, "but against Satan, his strategies and his cohorts ("principalities... powers... etc." v. 12). In God's armor, victory is assured (v. 13), for it meets every need. Briefly, here is what he is to put on (all of which are found in Christ): (1) The Girdle of Truth – tightened up it keeps everything else in place. Integrity is vital; union with the truth makes it possible (John 14:6); (2) The Breastplate of Righteousness – to protect the heart, imputed to the believer (2 Corinthians 5:21), demonstrated in life; (3) The Shoes of Peace – feet carry the soldier to battle, and the good news of salvation provides "peace with God" (Romans 5:1), and calmness for the conflict; (4) The Shield of Faith – to ward off the weapons of the enemy rendering them ineffective (1 John 5:4); (5) The Helmet of Salvation – to protect one's head (intellect) – "take it" says Paul; this salvation (all three tenses: past, from the penalty of sin; future, from the presence of sin; and present, from the power of sin) is a free gift. With it God provides victory. Finally, (6) The Sword of the Spirit – God's Word, to defend oneself against the thrusts of the enemy and attack his false teachings.

Life stEP Step in front of God's spiritual mirror (His Word) and see what you look like. You're a soldier in His army. Is the armor in place?

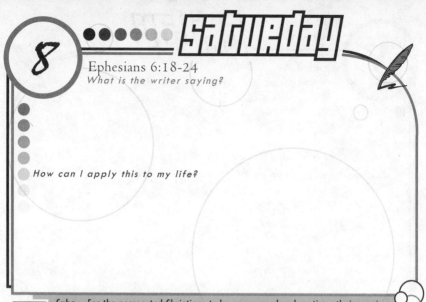

saturday

8

Ephesians 6:18-24

What is the writer saying?

How can I apply this to my life?

pray Cuba – For the persecuted Christians to be encouraged and continue their service for the Lord.

Having dealt with the proper equipment for the battle (vv. 10-17), Paul now deals with the equally important proper attitude, one of prayerfulness and watchfulness in this spiritual conflict. As to prayer, two different words are used: "prayer" (prayers in general – the necessity of a consistent prayer life) and "supplication" (special requests), both to be offered "in the Spirit." "Watching," to be sleepless, always awake, characteristic of a reliable soldier. Having the proper attitude in spiritual warfare cannot be overemphasized. The conflict is real, the enemies spiritual, but a proper attitude will avail itself of that which God has provided and is necessary for victory. Prayer is to be constant ("always") and for "all saints," for they are all in the same battle (v. 18).

Paul's request for himself was more ministerial than personal. Even in prison his request was not for ease or prosperity, but that God would give him the ability to preach the Gospel with boldness (v. 19). That was always Paul's chief aim in life. He considered himself an "ambassador in bonds," representing his Lord at all times.

Verses 21 and 22 are similar to Colossians 4:7-9. Recognizing that Paul's readers would want to know how he and his associates were doing ("our affairs," v. 22), Paul sends them this letter by the hand of Tychicus to provide that information and to "comfort" their "hearts" (v. 22). He doesn't name his associates, perhaps indicating that this letter was to be circular in nature, one intended for a number of churches around Ephesus.

Paul's closing benediction utilizes some of the same terms he used in beginning this letter, including "peace," "love" and "grace," all of which find their source in God, and which he desired for his brothers (and sisters) in Christ, for they are all "members one of another" (4:25).

It is checkup time. In this book the doctrinal (chapters 1-3) are followed by the practical (chapters 4-6). Belief is to dictate practice. You know what you believe. Does your practice demonstrate it? That should be your goal.

Esther is a fascinating book of the Bible. It is masterfully written in story form. Unlike the other 65 books of the Bible, no name for God appears in the story. There is no mention of prayer, the Law of Moses or worship. The closest example of any religious sentiment is Esther's mention of "fasting" before her dangerous visit with the king. Even though Mordecai and Esther are heroes in the story, their personal morality and the lifestyle of their fellow Jewish citizens are suspect. Esther's name means "star" and is related to "Ishtar," the fertility goddess represented by the planet Venus. Mordecai's name means, "Worshipper of Marduk." The Jewish people should have gone back to Israel by this time, but were enjoying a relatively comfortable life in Persia. No author is mentioned. Possibilities would include Ezra, Nehemiah and Malachi. The story can be accurately dated to 483-473 B.C. based on the Persian king in the story.

Despite the rather carnal nature of the book, it has been accepted as inspired by Jewish and Christian scholars since it is a classic example of the sovereignty of God over the affairs of men, especially in God's protection of the biological line of the Messiah. While God's name is absent overtly, in acrostic form it appears covertly in several places. Outline for the book:

Esther Becomes Queen   1-2
Haman Plots against the Jews   3
Israel is Delivered   4-10

Esther tells the story behind the Feast of Purim, which comes in February or March in our calendar. The word "purim" (pronounced "poorim") means "lots" in Hebrew. It refers to the "lots" that wicked Haman cast to determine the best day to go to the king with his suggestion to kill all the Jews in the kingdom of Persia. (Mordecai, the Jew would not bow to Haman in his presence. This enraged Haman, so he sought the extinction of all Jews. God used the strategic placement of the Jewish girl, Esther, as the new queen to short circuit Haman's treachery and win a great victory for her fellow people.

Theologically, there is debate within Judaism today as to whether it is proper to "gloat" over the defeat of an enemy. In the Middle Ages, Jewish communities sometimes got into trouble for hitting effigies of Haman. Since Purim falls close to Easter, Christians misinterpreted this violence and lashed out against Jews as both "Christ killers" and "Christian killers."

Significantly, the Book of Esther is the favorite book of Judaism after the Law of Moses. It is a good reminder that "Israel is the apple of God's eye." "Hamans" come and go, but the Jewish people remain.

There is a story (most likely apocryphal) about a man apprehended at one of Hitler's early rallies. He proudly stated that he was a Jew. When asked if he wasn't afraid of Hitler's plans he replied, "Once Pharaoh wanted us slain and now every year at Passover we eat matzos. Later Haman tried to destroy us; now each year we eat the delicious hamantaschens. I couldn't help wondering, Herr Hitler, while I listened to your ranting, what delicacy we will eat and what holiday we will celebrate to commemorate your downfall!"

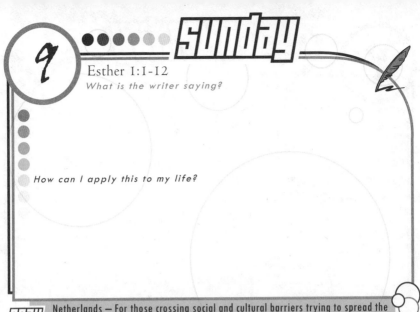

SUNDAY

9

Esther 1:1-12

What is the writer saying?

How can I apply this to my life?

PRAY Netherlands — For those crossing social and cultural barriers trying to spread the Gospel to the lesser-reached people.

The King of Persia in the Book of Esther was Xerxes I (486-465 B.C.). The author is impressed with the size of his empire. In the book of Daniel, the Persian Empire is pictured by a large ponderous bear (chapter 7). In 539 B.C. the Persians and the Medes joined to conquer Babylon. The Medes were centered in the mountainous region of northern Mesopotamia while Persia controlled the southern plain of what today is Iran. Shushan was east of Babylon, about 150 miles north of the Persian Gulf. The word means "lilies" which grew there in abundance. The Greek equivalent, which appears in our English Bible on occasion, is Susa. Daniel spent some time there under the Babylonian Empire. Later, Nehemiah also served in Shushan. The Persian palace located there was known as the "winter" palace since it was warmer there during the wintertime. Ecbatana was another Persian royal city in this period. Verse 3 mentions that it was the third year of his reign. The story picks up again in the seventh year of his reign (v. 2:16). The author does not tell us what the king was doing in the intervening four years, but secular history does. The Greek historian Herodotus says that Xerxes spent four years attacking Greece. Therefore, the banquet in chapter 1 was none other but the war counsel for this great undertaking. The initial 180-day meeting (v. 4) was capped-off with a seven-day feast. Xerxes gave himself the title "Ahasuerus" which means "king of kings." In his lifetime he fielded the largest army in ancient history: 2.5 million men. In an attack against Greece he built a "bridge" across the Dardanelles (from Asia Minor to Greece) by tying 674 ships side by side and constructing a roadway on top of them.

Life **stEP** God's name does not appear once in the book of Esther, but the theme is clearly that God, and not proud Xerxes, is the real "King of kings"!

99

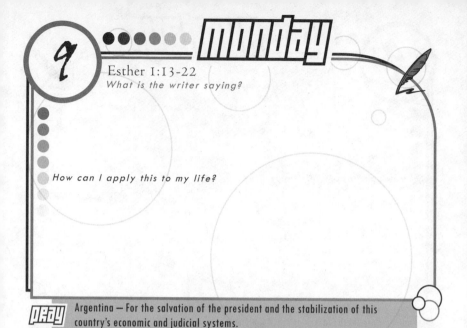

Esther 1:13-22

What is the writer saying?

How can I apply this to my life?

pray Argentina — For the salvation of the president and the stabilization of this country's economic and judicial systems.

In the midst of his drunken party, Ahasuerus commanded his wife, Vashti, to appear before the men. Apparently Vashti felt that the men would not respect her in their drunken condition, so she refused. Her name means, "beautiful woman." It is not clear how she thought she would get away with this disobedience. Amazingly, while she lost her position, it seems that she was allowed to live. Verses 8, 13, 15 and 19 indicate that there was a moral and binding aspect to Persian law (even though the society in general could be very violent and cruel).

It is significant that archaeologists in Shushan discovered one of the earliest law codes known to secular history, the Code of Hammurabi. Note also the detail contained in the story. This is a strong indicator of a true story, not fiction. The author gives all seven of the names of the chamberlains and then all seven of the names of the princes. One of the literary features of the whole story is that many items appear twice in the story (two groups of seven; later on there will be two groups of ten, two banquets, etc.). Not only is the king perturbed by the embarrassing disobedience in front of his men, but also one of his advisors takes a worst-case scenario.

Memucan is fearful that Vashti's poor example would spread throughout the kingdom and all wives would feel free to disobey their husbands. To ward off that potentiality, the king agrees to publish a decree throughout his kingdom, in all the languages of his kingdom that men were to rule their households unquestioned by their wives. Vashti was to lose her position in the kingdom.

Life stEP

When humans separate themselves from the wisdom of God and His Word, they can construct the most bizarre systems of acceptable social behavior. Where the Gospel goes, there too goes the betterment of human society.

9

Esther 2:1-11

What is the writer saying?

How can I apply this to my life?

According to verse 16, this chapter begins four years after the events of chapter 1. The Greek historian Herodotus tells us that despite Ahasuerus' planning, massive army and great potential, the Greeks beat him soundly. Herodotus reports that he returned to his palace and "was comforted by his harem." The court officials wanted to get Ahasuerus' mind off of his defeat. A massive beauty pageant was developed with the goal of finding a suitable replacement for Queen Vashti. "Hegai" is the name given to the keeper of the harem. It may be a name, but it means "eunuch" and describes the type of man that was placed in this kind of position.

Chapter two introduces us to Mordecai ("Worshipper of Marduk"). That he bore a pagan name does not necessarily mean that he was a carnal Jewish person. For instance, Shadrach, Meshach and Abed-nego (Daniel 1:7) were all pagan names, but the men were godly.

The statement that he was in "the palace" (v. 5) means that he was a high official. It is possible that he had been commissioned to lobby for the people of Jerusalem as they sought permission from the Persian government to rebuild the walls of the city. This suggestion arises from the fact the villain in the story, Haman, is called an "Agagite" (Esther 3:1). If this is a reference to King Agag of 1 Samuel 15, then Haman was an Amalekite.

The Amalekites would have been opposed to any Jewish revival in Judea. Making the tensions even greater, King Saul, who defeated the Amalekites, was from the tribe of Benjamin as was Mordecai (v. 5). Mordecai was the guardian of his younger cousin, Esther. Perhaps he saw an opportunity to advance the Jewish cause within the Persian government as Esther joins the beauty pageant. He asked her to hide her Jewish identity.

Life stEP

It is never right to do wrong to do right!

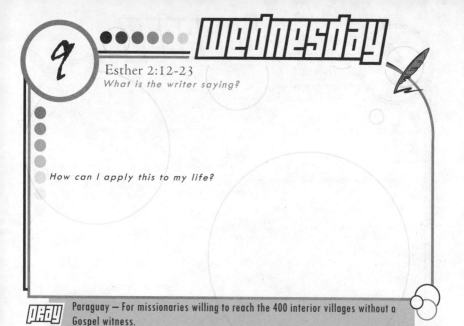

WEDNESDAY

9

Esther 2:12-23
What is the writer saying?

How can I apply this to my life?

Esther's Hebrew name was Hadassah (v. 7). It means "myrtle tree." The myrtle tree was a pleasant bush with white flowers, edible berries and flat evergreen leaves. It becomes a symbol for the nation of Israel in the Old Testament, while the Gentile nations are the "mighty oaks" that tower over little Hadassah (Zechariah 1). In the story we have noted spiritual deficiencies in Mordecai and Esther. Both bore names honoring pagan gods. They and their fellow Jewish countrymen still living in Persia, failed to return to Judea as Zerubbabel and the 50,000 did in the book of Ezra.

Now we see the young Jewish virgin sleeping with a pagan king and then becoming his wife, with no protest from her guardian, Mordecai. Now, it can be argued that they had no choice in the matter, that they would have been killed if they resisted. Esther and Mordecai then become heroes in the many tellings of this story.

This is somewhat illogical because both Christian and Jewish commentators honor those real heroes of the Old Testament era who would rather die than compromise their convictions. This would include the three Hebrew youths who were cast into the fiery furnace (Daniel 3). Mordecai and Esther do eventually take courageous steps, but it is very difficult to see them as "godly" and "holy" in their behavior. The story then becomes an illustration of how God continues to work with and protect the Jewish people even if they are carnal. It would seem to perfectly parallel the modern state of Israel. The Jewish people who have returned to Israel over the last 150 years are mostly non-believers in Jesus of Nazareth. God has brought them back to their ancestral homeland in unbelief for His own purposes.

God is the hand in the glove of history. We see the glove, but the hand is there.

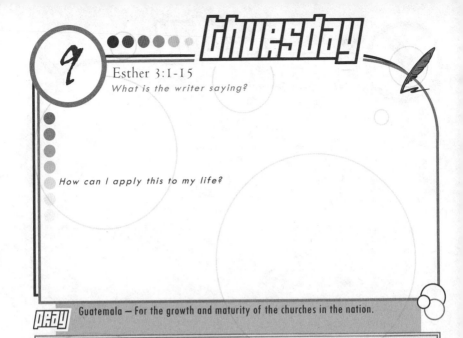

Esther 3:1-15

What is the writer saying?

How can I apply this to my life?

Guatemala — For the growth and maturity of the churches in the nation.

Mordecai overhears a plot to assassinate the king (vv. 2:21-23). Esther tells the king. The matter is recorded and seemingly forgotten. Chapter 3 introduces wicked Haman. It is five years after chapter 2 (v. 7). Mordecai refuses to bow when Haman passes by, even though the king had commanded this expression of respect (v. 2). Some have argued that this behavior was motivated by Mordecai's religious belief that only God was worthy of worship. That Mordecai told those who challenged him that he refused because he was a Jew (v. 4) implies a noble witness. This is probably not the case. Mordecai's refusal was probably not on religious grounds, but rather political. As a descendant of Agag, Haman the Amalekite was a bitter enemy and was in a position to oppose the work done on the city of Jerusalem. As the court spies reported Mordecai's heritage to Haman, Haman conceived a plot to take care of the "Jewish problem" once and for all. God saw to it that Esther's heritage was still a secret. Haman called in his pagan priests and he had his "pagan quiet time" over a calendar. They were seeking the "lucky day" to plan for the extermination of all the Jews in the Persian Empire. "Lots" were cast. They worked like dice with a "lucky number" predetermined. God controls even the throw of the lot (Proverbs 16:33). In this case, He made it so the "lucky day" was 11 months away. This gave Mordecai and Esther a chance to intervene. Amazingly, when Haman proposed that all the Jews be killed on a particular day, the king asked no questions. He allowed Haman to do as he wished. Fortunately, at least some of the people were puzzled by the strange decree (v. 15).

Life stEP

How big is your God? If He controls the outcome of the betting of wicked men in the casino, can't He control the details of your life as well?

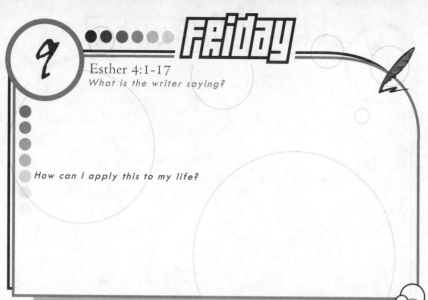

Friday

9

Esther 4:1-17

What is the writer saying?

How can I apply this to my life?

PRAY Dominican Republic — For the Holy Spirit to break the bondage of occultism, pervasive in this society.

Since we suppose that Mordecai has been carnally motivated, it is fair to wonder if he at all blamed himself for his arrogant treatment of Haman that led to this disaster. Regardless of the human actions, it is clear that God is working out all things for His own purposes. The crisis was as great as could be imagined. Not only would millions of innocent Jews die, but the very line of the Messiah and all the prophecies of salvation and blessing through Him were at stake. "Sackcloth and ashes" are a typical expression of extreme sorrow. Notice that at no time does it say that Mordecai or his fellow Jews prayed.

Now, it certainly could be that the story was written to minimize any religious offense to Persian readers or that as a literary device God is missing from the story to underscore that only He could have produced the results. While these are possible explanations, the sad conclusion is that these people were so spiritually dead that they move through the ancient trappings of intercessory prayer without really praying. The only ray of hope for Mordecai's spiritual discernment is that he does evidence a conviction that "fate" would protect the Jews from annihilation (v. 14). Esther was ignorant of the decree until Mordecai explained it through the intermediary, Hatach. Esther initially refuses to talk to the king because even as his wife and the queen of the kingdom, she was not allowed to approach the king unbidden. To make matters worse, she had not been called for a whole month. Mordecai pronounces the powerful challenge, "And who knoweth whether thou art come to the kingdom for such a time as this?" (v. 14) Esther responds equally dramatically, "If I perish, I perish" (v. 16).

Life stEP

Even unsaved people can act nobly, unfortunately sometimes more nobly than believers! Do you view every occasion as a divine appointment?

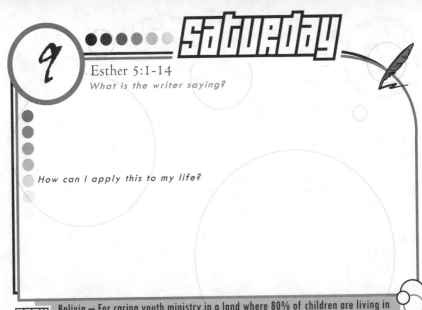

saturday

9

Esther 5:1-14

What is the writer saying?

How can I apply this to my life?

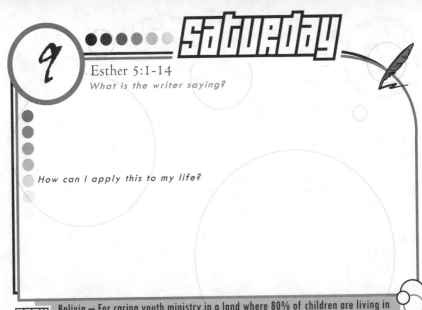

PRAY Bolivia — For caring youth ministry in a land where 80% of children are living in extreme poverty.

In 4:16 Esther asked that Mordecai not eat for three days, "night or day." This phrase reminds us of Christ's burial for "three days and three nights" (Matthew 12:40). Some have argued that Christ must have been crucified on a Thursday to have three complete days and three complete nights in the grave. Esther 5:1 indicates that in Hebrew, the phrase "day and night" does not necessarily mean, "24 hours" but rather is the equivalent of the more general English word "day." Therefore, just as Esther asked for three days and nights of fasting, but went into the king "on the third day" Christ could also have died on Friday and resurrected on Sunday, the "third day."

Certainly Esther was brave and bold to go to the king unasked. However, we can also imagine God encouraging her heart with her feminine charms. God worked it out that the king's heart leapt at the sight of his beloved and quickly any sense of impending doom fled from Esther's heart. Esther requested that the king and Haman join her in a banquet. Once again, the king is amazingly naïve. Why would Esther want Haman present? It is not clear if Esther had planned to expose Haman in the first banquet. If she had, God overruled to allow all the pieces of the story to be in place for the final conflict. Haman is obviously flattered and is enraged when Mordecai still refuses to bow. In typical ancient Mideastern fashion he regales his household with his successes and frustrations. His wife, Zeresh (the Persian word for "golden") tells him to kill his problem and enjoy life. The gallows she envisioned would flatter his ego, 50 cubits would be 75 feet high!

Life stEP

We are expected to use our minds in making decisions. However, we can be confident that God can override our decisions for His greater good.

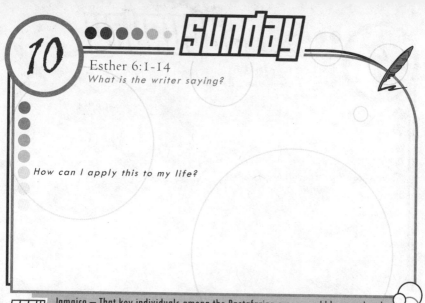

SUNDAY

Esther 6:1-14

What is the writer saying?

How can I apply this to my life?

PRAY Jamaica — That key individuals among the Rastafarian group would be saved and become witnesses.

In the sovereign plan of God, He uses the sleepless night of the king to enhance the story of His protection of the Jews. To counteract his insomnia, the king asks that the historical record be read to him. God also providentially has them read from the location five years earlier that described Mordecai's role in uncovering the assassination plot against the king. The king asks if Mordecai has ever been rewarded. Amazingly, the answer is "no." As the king ponders this embarrassing oversight, he hears someone in the outer court. It is Haman who has arrived early to ask the king permission to execute Mordecai. The king (typically) never thinks to ask why Haman was there. He simply asks him what should be done for the person the king wished to honor. Haman had good reason to think that "the person" must be him, so he lays it on thick.

The king should ask a trusted representative to put that person on the king's own horse, wearing the king's robe and crown and lead him through the streets announcing, "Thus shall it be done for the man whom the king delighteth to honor." The only possible addition to the scene would have been to have the king himself do the honors! You can imagine Haman's eyes gleaming as he anticipated the king proclaiming such for him. Can you imagine what Haman thought when the king said, "Good! Do it for Mordecai!" Notice that the king knew that Mordecai was "the Jew." Does that mean that the king knew that the people Haman planned to destroy were Jewish? Maybe not, since he was too quick to agree to even check who these people were. Haman was at home licking his wounds and hearing his advisors and wife predict his ultimate defeat at the hand of Mordecai when the summons came for him to go to the banquet.

God skewers man's sinful pride. Do we need a "pride adjustment?"

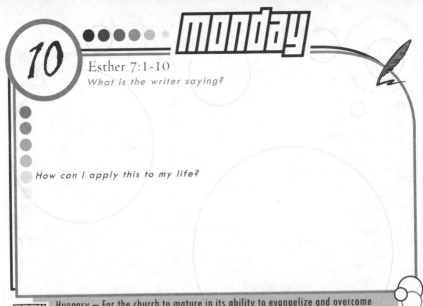

Esther 7:1-10

What is the writer saying?

How can I apply this to my life?

Hungary — For the church to mature in its ability to evangelize and overcome feelings of inferiority that restrain boldness in its witness.

The second banquet is called a "banquet of wine." It is not clear if this was a different type of banquet from the first one. We do know that the story began with the problem with Vashti at a banquet of wine. It should have been a happy occasion. The king asks Esther what she wants, and with oriental bravado promises anything up to half of his kingdom. At what point in the next several sentences did Haman realize that he was in big trouble? Notice that Esther drags the explanation out and includes the interesting argument that to kill or even just to enslave all the Jews in the kingdom would cost more money than the enemy could pay the king. Amazingly, even though Haman had already discussed this matter with the king (both of whom at the time did not know that Esther was Jewish), the king did not make the connection and had to ask whom the wicked man was. As Esther identifies Haman, the king leaves the room in anger and goes to think in the palace garden. That was also the place where the story began in chapter one (vv. 5-6).

There is no indication as to how long the king was gone, but Haman immediately began to plead for his life. In the ancient world, wealthy people reclined at their fancy meals on pillows or low couches. By the time the king came back, Haman in his desperation had fallen on Esther's couch (probably kneeling in a beseeching posture). The king puts the worst possible interpretation on Haman's behavior and asks in effect, "Will he assault my wife as well?" The servants did not need any instructions. They simply put a burial shroud over his face. His fate was sealed. Harbonah ("the bald man"), who also appears in chapter one, volunteers the information about the gallows and Haman is hung thereon.

God is not mocked. "For whatsoever a man soweth, that shall he also reap" Galatians 6:7

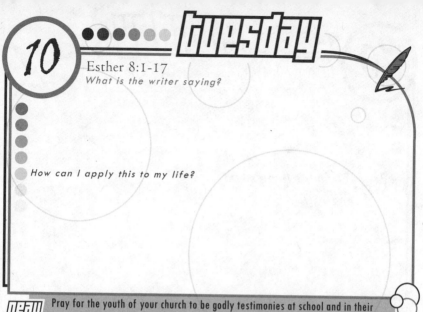

How can I apply this to my life?

PRAY Pray for the youth of your church to be godly testimonies at school and in their communities.

The prophecy of Haman's wife and his advisors (v. 5:14) comes to pass. Not only was Haman killed on the gallows he had prepared for Mordecai, but the king takes Haman's ring and gives it to Mordecai, elevating Mordecai to Haman's position of prime minister and giving him legal control of Haman's estate. Esther is obviously confident but boldly pursues the matter with her husband. The king shows official pleasure by extending his scepter to her. She stands freely in his presence and speaks her heart. She eloquently and respectfully pleads for a reversal of the decree to destroy the Jews.

In Persia at that time, the king was not above the law and in fact he could not reverse a law previously established (this was the case with Daniel and the lions den as well in Daniel 6). He could, however

issue another decree to encourage the Jewish people to prepare to protect themselves on that fateful day.

The events of chapter 8 take place in the third month so there were nine more months until the Jews would have to protect themselves. The king allows Mordecai to word the letter and the details are gruesome, including the death of women and babies. In the ensuing nine months, not only would the decree make it to every corner of the Persian Empire, but also the people would have had plenty of time to contemplate whose side the king most likely was on. The king gave Mordecai rich gifts and the Jews everywhere rejoiced. In fact, it was even an evangelistic tool as some Gentiles converted to Judaism as they contemplated the changing loyalties in the kingdom.

Life stEP The Lord will make even our enemies to be at peace with us. Evil men will triumph temporarily, but in the final accounting, the people of God will be infinitely more blessed than the doers of evil.

Esther 9:1-17

What is the writer saying?

How can I apply this to my life?

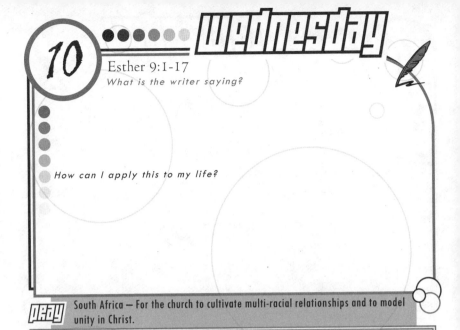

pray South Africa — For the church to cultivate multi-racial relationships and to model unity in Christ.

The fateful day arrived and amazingly, there were still men willing to touch the apple of God's eye and the blood relatives of the queen of the kingdom. This demonstrates the hardness of the human heart and how sin blinds the rational mind. In the capital, 500 men are killed on the first day. Haman's ten sons had lived for the previous nine months with the shadow of their father's actions hovering over their heads and now they are also killed. This was typical of ancient opinions of revenge.

There are warnings in Scripture that a man's sin will affect his children, although in many cases we assume that the family members participated in the father's sin for them to also receive a harsh punishment (such as Achan and his family who were destroyed for taking spoil from Jericho in Joshua 7). The king comes to Esther (now he seeks her out, not Esther seeking the king). He asks if there is anything else she would like and this time does not qualify the offer with "even to the half of the kingdom." Esther betrays a character flaw in requesting another day's worth of bloodshed. It might be argued that she knew of dangerous enemies who would be a threat if not neutralized, but the only apparent motivation was revenge.

There might have been some legitimate warning value in hanging Haman's ten dead sons, but this also seems to be a carnal request. The king grants the requests, which led to several days of rejoicing. The Jews in the capital fought for day 13 and 14 in the twelfth month and celebrated on the 15th. The Jews elsewhere fought on the 13th and celebrated on the 14th.

Life stEP The human heart is deceitful and desperately wicked. God gave Esther a stunning victory, but she was not satisfied and demanded more. When we have success we need to guard our hearts against greed and pride.

10

Esther 9:18-10:3

What is the writer saying?

How can I apply this to my life?

pray   Australia — For believers to reach out to the rapidly growing population of immigrants.

The word "Purim" (pronounced "Poorim") means "lots" in Hebrew. To this day, Jewish people fast on the 13th day of the 12th month in the Jewish calendar. On the evening of the 13th the entire book of Esther is read in the synagogue. It is read in a dramatic/comic fashion with different voices speaking the dialogue. Verses 1:7, 3:15 and 7:4 are sung and 2:5, 8:16 are recited by the congregation. When the name "Haman" is read, the congregation cries, "Let his name be blotted out" and "The wicked shall rot." Children make noise with a noisemaker ("grager"), boo and stamp their feet. The Rabbi reads the names of Haman's ten sons with one breath to symbolize their simultaneous hanging. Purim is primarily a joyous holiday. In fact, a later Rabbinic injunction stated that on Purim enough wine should be drunk that the individual cannot tell the difference between, "Curse Haman" and "Bless Mordecai." (This is a rarity in Judaism, Jewish people normally being very circumspect in relation to alcohol.) On the 14th day of the month, there is another religious gathering followed by a time of mirth. A "half shekel" (50 cents) is collected from each adult to be given to the needy. This is in remembrance of the ancient temple tax. The wealthy give gifts to the poor. Esther is read again. Rabbinic comedians do "celebrity roasts" on fellow rabbis. There is a festive dinner. Children wear costumes and some communities have a carnival. A special Purim treat is a cookie/pastry called "Hamantaschens," (German for "Haman [Poppy Seed] Pockets") or "Haman Hats." It is a triangular pastry filled with poppy seeds, prunes or other fillings.

Life **stEP**   Esther is the favorite book of Judaism after the Law of Moses. "Hamans" come and go, but with God's providential care, the Jewish people remain.

Song of Solomon

The title can also be "Song of Songs" which means, "the greatest song." The author is the famous, wise King Solomon who reigned from 970 to 930 B.C. Since he only has 140 wives in this book (6:8) it is dated to 960 B.C. The theme is "love," primarily human marital love. An outline for the book:

Courtship	1-3
Marriage	4-8

The content is frank enough that at certain times in Jewish history, men were not to read the book until they were married. There are childish thinkers in our society who argue against any form of censorship of reading materials in public libraries based on the frank nature of the Song of Solomon.

It is tempting to see the book as an allegory of God's love for Israel or Christ's love for the church, but the New Testament does not quote Song of Solomon nor does it apply the book to the church! Jewish people read it at Passover as a celebration of God's love for Israel as He redeemed them from their bondage in Egypt.

It is ironic that Solomon would write about selective love. Perhaps it was the only true romance that Solomon ever had as his other marriages were political alliances. The book mentions 21 varieties of plant life and 15 species of animals indicating Solomon's keen interest in nature and knowledge. The woman in the story is called a "Shulamite" which probably refers to the town of "Shunem" in northern Israel. The Hebrew text, accordingly, uses certain terms that are known to be unique to northern Israel. A popular theory claims that there is actually a love triangle in the story with the noble King Solomon losing the Shulamite woman to a rustic shepherd. It is also popular to try to find other hidden meanings behind the text, but the simplest explanation seems to be the best; this is a romantic love story concerning the developing relationship between a man and a woman.

Song of Solomon 2:1-17

What is the writer saying?

How can I apply this to my life?

pray Italy — For more believers to attend Bible schools and seminaries before entering the ministry.

Notice the romantic setting established with references to nature (such as in our modern idea that in the spring time, a young man's fancy turns to love.). First the woman speaks, calling herself the rose of Sharon. Sharon was a swampy plain along the coast of Israel just south of Mount Carmel. In the wet, rich soil beautiful wild flowers thrived. The "rose" here was probably like our crocus. The lily was a hyacinth or Easter lily with its main attribute the beautiful smell. The man lauds her beauty above other women who were "thorns" in comparison (v. 2). The woman speaks again in verses 3-7. An apple tree (v. 3) was an unusual and pleasant surprise in the forest. The banner in verse 4 refers to a military banner that goes in front of the troops and is visible by all. Raisin cakes (v. 4) were a common treat mentioned elsewhere as gifts for idols. Verse 7 does not say, "until he pleases" but "until it pleases." This is probably a reference to love itself and the teaching is that we should not rush love.

Couples need to let love have time to develop and mature. Verses 8-17 take place on another occasion. It is a visit by the man to the woman's family's house ("our wall" v. 9). She delights in his voice, his athleticism and his bodily form. In verses 10-15 she reports what he said to her. It is springtime (v. 11). Flowers and birds singing set the stage (v. 12). He entices her with endearing words to come with him (v. 13). "Stairs" speak of access. He desires a private, face-to-face encounter with his beloved. He also realistically acknowledges that there are issues that could harm their love relationship, like foxes spoil ripening grapes (v. 15). Their visit lasted all day until the day "broke" in nightfall (v. 17).

Some of us, by our behavior and attitudes, would better be addressed as "turkey buzzards." Let's be doves to our loved ones!

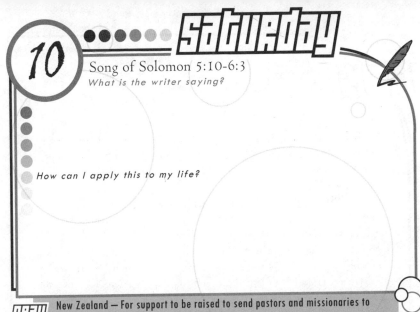

Song of Solomon 5:10-6:3

What is the writer saying?

How can I apply this to my life?

PRAY New Zealand — For support to be raised to send pastors and missionaries to Bible schools.

Verses 10-16 describe the beauty of the man in the woman's eyes. "White," especially as associated with "ruddy" would imply "dazzling." His complexion, though on the dark side, nevertheless shone. He was "one in a million" as we might say (v. 10). She comments on his complexion, head, hair, eyes, cheeks, lips, breath and body odor (v. 13). Beautiful gemstones describe his body. "Beryl" represents a golden brown stone and could be topaz, chalcedon, chrysolite or carbuncle. Ivory is glistening white and sapphires are blue. The Hebrew word translated "marble" actually refers to "alabaster" which is beautiful like marble, but not as hard. It is easy to carve into semi-translucent artwork. Gold in antiquity was the favorite metal for artwork. It was both beautiful and easily worked due to its relative softness. "Lebanon" means "white mountains" referring to the fact that they were so high that they were snow-capped most of the year. Lebanon was known for its majestic cedars. They were a type of evergreen. They grew asymmetrically which made them very exotic in appearance (somewhat like a bonsai tree). They had a beautiful rosy-red grain and due to the strong sap were impervious to insect blight, rotting and decay. The trees were big enough to provide timbers and paneling for large public buildings such as Solomon's Palace and Temple.

Life stEP

The family is the foundation of a stable society. The family is only stable if the husband and wife have a solid relationship. "Romance" is the strong attraction that God has designed to pull two individuals together for life. The nature of the romance will change with the stages of the couple's life, but it is crucial in all stages to take exquisite delight in each other for the sake of the children, grandchildren and society.

Titus

The book of Titus, along with Paul's two letters to Timothy, make up that section of New Testament books known as the Pastoral Epistles. Separated from his two young protégés, the older mentor, Paul, provides them with written information, "how-to" books, if you will, to use in their respective ministries (Timothy in Ephesus; Titus on the island of Crete). The key verse for all three books is found in I Timothy 3:15, where Paul says, in effect, since he cannot at the present time be with them, here is how they are "to behave" themselves "in the house of God… the church of the living God, the pillar and ground of the truth." It was a letter written shortly after I Timothy, approximately 63 A.D., during that period of time between Paul's two imprisonments.

Helpful to the understanding of the books individually is to take them collectively. Three themes seem to resonate throughout all three letters: (1) church organization; (2) sound doctrine and (3) consistent Christian living. While all three books touch on all three themes, each book has its particular emphasis, and those three themes follow the order in which they have been placed in most Bibles (thought not written in that order). I Timothy emphasizes church organization; 2 Timothy, sound doctrine; and Titus, consistent Christian living. Charles Erdman, in writing of these three books early in the twentieth century, offered this summation of these three themes this way: "Church government is not an end in itself; it is of value only as it secures sound doctrine, and doctrine is of value only as it issues in life." The point is this: you organize (that's I Timothy) so that you can teach sound doctrine (that's 2 Timothy), and you teach sound doctrine so that consistent Christian living (that's Titus) can result.

As to Titus himself, our knowledge concerning him is somewhat limited (in comparison to Timothy, for example). We meet him first in Galatians where we learn that he was a Gentile (Galatians 2:3) who had been with Paul as early as, or even prior to the time when Barnabas went to Tarsus to bring Paul back to Antioch (Galatians 2:1; cp. Acts 11:25-30). Paul's reference to him as "my true son" or "mine own son after the common faith" (Titus 1:4) is an indication that Titus had come to Christ through Paul's ministry. Some scholars have speculated that

Titus may have been the younger brother of Luke; and to avoid charges of nepotism, Luke never mentioned him when he authored the book of Acts. That he was a very capable and gifted young man can be deduced from the assignments that Paul gave him. He had been given the responsibility of reporting to Paul on the sad spiritual condition of the Corinthian Church (2 Corinthians 2:12-13; 7:2-16). He then returned to Corinth to deliver Paul's second letter to that church, a letter designed to correct the problems there. He also represented Paul in the matter of the collection for the saints in Jerusalem (2 Corinthians 2:3-4; 13; 7:6-16; 8:16-24). In light of his success in these assignments it is no surprise that Paul left him on the island of Crete to strengthen, organize and correct the churches there. Paul offers a great compliment when he calls him his "partner and fellow-helper" (2 Corinthians 8:23).

As to the place of his assignment: Crete... we do know it was not an easy assignment as our studies will show. The people of Crete, by their own admission, were "liars, evil beasts, slow bellies" (Titus 1:12). Paul confirmed that evaluation (Titus 1:13). Crete itself is a rather large island, approximately 160 miles long and 35 miles wide. It is in the Mediterranean Sea, and located 100 miles southeast of Greece. As to when the church began, we can only surmise. It could have been the result of a missionary journey that Paul took between his imprisonments, or it may go all the way back to the Day of Pentecost, some 30 years earlier. (Acts 2:11 indicates Cretians were there.) If the latter is the case, it is no wonder Paul placed him there to "set in order the things that are wanting," (v.5) for a church with apparently minimal direction for such an extended period of time would have many things wanting.

The purpose(s) of the book can be summed up as follows:

(1) To remind Titus of his work of reorganizing the church and appointing elders.
(2) To warn him about false teachers.
(3) To encourage him in pastoring the different kinds of people in the church.
(4) To emphasize the true meaning of grace in the life of the Christian.
(5) To explain how to deal with church troublemakers.

(Expanding on the above: it is likely that the Cretian church suffered from two sources: (a) visiting Judaizers, who mixed law and grace; and (b) ignorant Christians who abused the grace of God, and turned their liberty into license.)

A major emphasis in the book is consistent Christian living. Paul wanted the Cretians to be both hearers and doers of the Word (James 1:22), hence there is a constant emphasis upon "good works" (1:16; 2:7,14; 3:1,5,8,14).

Those "good works" ought to be the natural result of one's salvation, something Paul made very clear in Ephesians 2:8,9 and 10. A key verse for the book would be Titus 3:8: "...that they which have believed in God might be careful to maintain good works..."

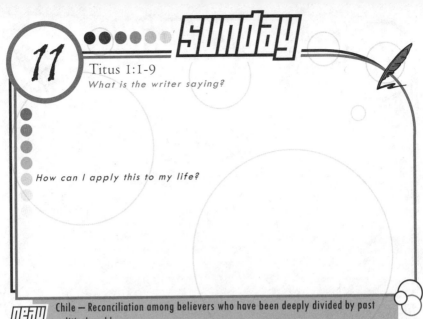

Titus 1:1-9

What is the writer saying?

How can I apply this to my life?

PRAY Chile — Reconciliation among believers who have been deeply divided by past political problems.

Paul introduces himself as a "servant of God" (doulos — one born into slavery, whose will is swallowed up in the will of another — this should be true of all believers) "and an apostle of Jesus Christ" (apostolos — one sent with proper credentials to represent someone else). His commission was to further "the faith of God's elect" leading to "godliness" (v. 1), a word introducing the theme of: "good works" (1:16; 2:7, 14; 3:1, 5, 8, 14). The addressee is Titus, though it is clear that like 1 and 2 Timothy, the letter was to be widely read. He is referred to as Paul's "own son after the common faith," similar to Timothy (1 Timothy 1:2), an indication both of these young men were products of Paul's ministry. Titus' assignment was two-fold: First, he was to preach the Word (v. 3). Second (v. 5) he was to organize the church and "set in order" (like setting a broken bone) the church's deficiencies. The state of disorganization may have been because

of minimal apostolic instruction since its inception, which may have been a result of Pentecost some 30 years earlier (Acts 2:11). Titus' task would involve dealing with false teachers (v. 9).

To correct the problems, he was to "ordain elders in every city" (v. 5); an ordination based on proper qualifications, some of which are listed in verses 6-9, and similar to I Timothy 3:1-7. Those qualifications fit into numerous categories, such as (1) General, verses 6-7; (2) Family, verse 6; (3) Personal, verses 7-8a; (4) Mental, verse 8b; and (5) Spiritual, verses 8c-9 (H. Kent). Without biblically qualified leadership a church courts disaster, for leadership sets the pace and establishes the standards. The leader ("elder" in verse 5, "bishop" in verse 7 — the terms are interchangeable, Acts 20:17, 28; I Peter 5:1-2) is "to hold fast the faithful word" so that by "sound doctrine" (healthy teaching) he can both exhort believers and rebuke opposers.

Life stEP A church's success, in God's eyes, is tied to its commitment to the Word of God. Is your church's ministry biblically-saturated, or simply biblically-scented? It does make a difference.

Titus 1:10-16

What is the writer saying?

How can I apply this to my life?

pray Mike Bush, Vice President of Inn Ministries, as he meets guests' needs, selects speakers, and encourages the staff.

After mentioning the elders' responsibility to refute the false teachings of "gainsayers" (KJV), or opposers, Paul discusses their characteristics and how to deal with them. They are just the opposite of the prescribed elder: "unruly" (demonstrated by a rebelliousness against both God's Word and God's messengers); "vain talkers" (their talk is useless, accomplishing nothing); and are intentionally "deceptive." This was especially true of those "of the circumcision" (Galatians 2:12); Jewish believers in the Cretian congregation who mistakenly taught that adherence to circumcision and Jewish ceremonial laws were necessary for salvation.

The description continues: they had an inordinate interest in money (v. 11), and held to unscriptural "Jewish fables" (legalism), and "commandments of men" (traditionalism) (v. 14). They were ascetics (practicing extreme self-denial for supposed spiritual value), labeling certain foods and practices as defiled, even that which God considered good (vv. 14-15; 1 Timothy 4:3-5; Acts 10:15). They did not understand that the blood of Christ sounded the death knell of legalism.

To effectively describe Cretian character, Paul quotes a sixth century Cretian poet – a philosopher named Epimenedes. His description is unbelievably harsh (v. 12), but accurate (v. 13). "To Cretianize" in Greek literature meant "to lie and cheat." To deal with such erroneous teaching, Paul told Titus to do the following: (1) "Stop their mouths" – silence them, for in failing to do so, "whole (church) houses" would be subverted, or upset (v. 11); (2) "Rebuke them sharply." Rebuke – here means to convict, convince or point out. The goal: "that they may be sound in the faith" (v. 13). Correction and restoration are to be Titus' goals.

Life stEP Never compromise the truth. False doctrine (unhealthy teaching) will lead to sickness in the body of Christ. The emphasis must always be on "sound doctrine" (v. 9) and "sound faith" (v. 13).

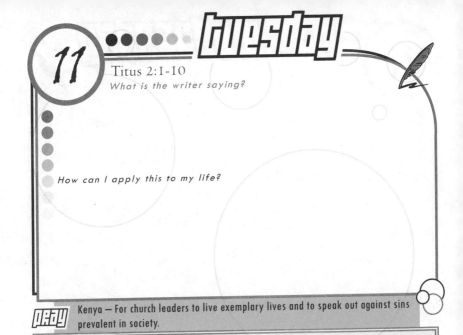

Titus 2:1-10

What is the writer saying?

How can I apply this to my life?

pray Kenya — For church leaders to live exemplary lives and to speak out against sins prevalent in society.

Paul now moves to positive exhortation. Certainly error must be dealt with, but there must be balance: truth must be taught and exhortations given. Unless they are, negativity will permeate a ministry. So Paul instructs Titus to "speak thou the things which become sound (healthy) doctrine" (v. 1) – a phrase familiar in all three pastoral epistles. Out of such teaching good works, such as faith, love and patience (v. 2) are produced. He then addresses three categories of church members:

1. The Aged Saints (or at least older, more mature) (vv. 1-3). First the men, then the women. The point behind the instruction: both are to serve as spiritual examples to all. While all believers should possess the virtues noted, they should to an eminent degree be manifested by those of advancing years. And to older women a very pointed assignment: pass on their insight as wives and mothers to the next generation of women. If those lessons are not taught and practiced, God's Word will be blasphemed.

2. The Younger Saints (vv. 4-8). They were to listen to the older saints, and pursue the character qualities that were to be already present in their parent's generation. As for Titus (vv. 7-8), he is to set the pattern. One's actions often speak louder than one's words, but both ("good works" – v. 7, "sound speech" – v. 8) are necessary.

3. Servants/Slaves (vv. 9-10) Upwards of 25% of the Roman Empire were slaves. Those who were believers, as with all other categories of believers, were to voluntarily submit to their masters in such a way that they beautified ("adorn the doctrine of God") their beliefs by their behavior. Paul's advice to slaves and masters, which he amplifies in other passages (see Ephesians 6:5-9; Colossians 3:22-4:1; 1 Timothy 6:1-2), would be good advice to employees and employers today.

Life stEP

There's a saying that matches today's passage: "Your talk talks, and your walk talks; but your walk talks louder than your talk talks." Read it again, and be sure to practice it. A consistent life gains a responsive audience.

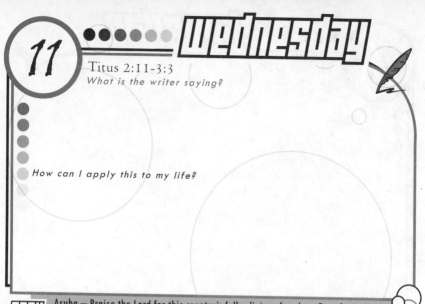

Titus 2:11-3:3

What is the writer saying?

How can I apply this to my life?

PRAY   Aruba — Praise the Lord for this country's full religious freedom. Pray for a harvest of souls.

In verses 11-14 we have the first of two major doctrinal portions in the book. The second will follow a chapter later (vv. 3:4-7). These verses provide a perfect balance of doctrine with Christian living. They follow Paul's instruction (v. 10) to "adorn the doctrine of God" with a lifestyle that pictures a transformed life. This passage begins with the incarnation ("the grace of God hath appeared," v. 11), and then relates that doctrine to a life that: (a) negatively, denies "ungodliness and worldly lusts" and (b) positively, lives "soberly, righteously and godly" in the here and now: "this present age" (v. 12). It continues by seeing in the return of Christ the incentive for Christ-honoring conduct ("looking for that blessed hope..." v. 13), and that ultimately expresses itself in personal holiness, i.e., purified "unto Himself (Christ)...zealous of good works" (v. 14). This passage, much like Ephesians 2:8-10 teaches us that God's purpose in redeeming us is not only to save us from hell; He also wants to free us so that we can produce good works that glorify Him. Certainly these two appearances of the grace of God, the first of which (the incarnation) provided redemption, and the second of which (Christ's return) will result in rewards, should provide much motivation for consistent Christian living (a key theme in this book).

In the early verses of chapter 3 Paul addresses the Christian's obligation to earthly government (subjection to their authority), not a particularly positive trait among the Cretians (remember the description of them in verse 1:12), so Paul reminds them to be good citizens ("ready to every good work," v.1). In doing so they would reflect positively on the power of the Gospel and bring glory to God. An additional motive for good works would be to remember that but for the grace of God (v. 2:11) they would still be lost in their sins, no different than the pagans they lived with (v. 3).

Life Step

Look back: Christ came with redemption in mind. Look ahead: He will return with rewards in hand. Look within: Does your life demonstrate gratefulness for those two appearances of the grace of God?

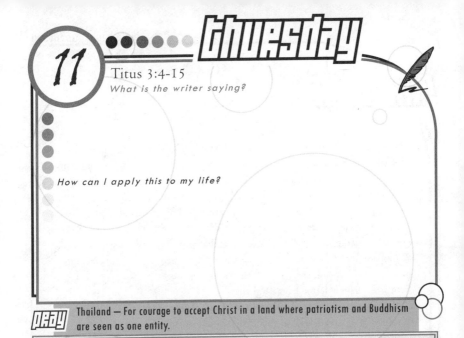

Titus 3:4-15

What is the writer saying?

How can I apply this to my life?

This section begins with "But" indicating a contrast, which is drawn between that which has gone before (verse 3 – a description of man's degenerative nature), and God's "kindness and love" (v. 4). In verses 4-7, we have the book's second major doctrinal portion. Paul writes that salvation is God's work, not the result of our own righteousness or works (v. 5), though good works result. The two agents of our new birth ("regeneration") are (1) The Word of God – pictured by "water for washing" – (John 15:3; Psalm 119:9; Ephesians 5:26, and (2) The Spirit of God – (John 3:5; 1 Peter 1:23; James 1:18). The latter has been "shed" (poured out) upon believers from Pentecost (Acts 2) to the present, and the mediator of this wonderful outpouring is "Jesus Christ our Savior" (v. 6).

Paul then moves from the overall doctrine of salvation to two of its aspects. The first is justification (God's declaration that the believer has been vindicated in His sight by the crosswork of Christ – cp. Romans 3:24-25; 5:9); hence all charges have been dropped (Romans 8:1, 31-34). The second is adoption. Once justified, adoption takes place (Galatians 4:5) and the believers' lives are "hidden with Christ in God" (Colossians 3:3), and they become heirs "according to the hope (utmost confidence) of eternal life" (v. 7).

Verse 8 is transitional, with the "faithful saying" referring to the doctrinal statement of verses 4-7. Titus is to keep on affirming "these things." Doing so is to result in continued "good works." Verses 9-11 admonish Titus to avoid anything that would cause unacceptable behavior in the assembly, and to cut off ("reject," v. 10) divisive people after two warnings (2 Thessalonians 3:14-15). In the remaining verses (12-15) greetings are given, as well as a challenge to "maintain good works." As in his other letters Paul closes with his favorite benediction: "Grace be with you all."

We are saved to serve a holy God with a holy life. How are you doing?

philemon

The Apostle Paul wrote four letters, which are referred to as his Prison Epistles, so named since he wrote them while he was under house arrest in Rome (see Acts 28:16-31). Three of those letters are somewhat normal in nature and style: Ephesians, Philippians and Colossians. One, however, is very unusual. It is this little one chapter letter from Paul to Philemon, a letter from one friend to another. Paul, we are well acquainted with; Philemon, however, is another story. He was a close friend of Paul's and had probably come to know Christ through Paul's ministry (vv. 19-20).

The story line is this: at the time of the writing, Philemon was a very wealthy Christian living in Colossae, and in keeping with the culture and economy of that day, was a slave owner. One of his slaves, a man by the name of Onesimus (v. 10), had run away and in the process had stolen some money from Philemon. Under Roman law, this immediately placed him under the possible penalty of execution to be done at the discretion of the owner. In running away he wound up in Rome when he came in contact with Paul and came to know Christ as his Savior. Paul then mentored him in his early days as a believer, and an obviously strong bond was forged between the two men. Now that he is a believer,

however, Onesimus was faced with a difficult problem. He had wronged his master and confession was necessary. Proper restitution required that he return to Philemon and place himself back under Philemon's mastership and accept whatever consequences his master deemed appropriate (including execution).

This letter from Paul, however, accompanied Onesimus' return to Philemon; a letter in which Paul would be Onesimus' intercessor and defender. In it he asks Philemon to receive Onesimus as himself (v. 17), and should any stolen funds need to be replaced, Paul said to place them on his account (v. 18). What happened when Onesimus returned is not recorded in Scripture, but church history does provide us with some hints.

Some 40 years after the sending of this letter, a well-known early church leader by the name of Ignatius, arrested for his belief in Christ and sent to Rome to be executed, wrote a number of letters to various groups of believers to encourage them to stand firm in their faith. One was sent to the believers of Ephesus, and in it he sent a personal greeting to the bishop (or pastor) of the church in that city. His name was Onesimus. It is quite

possible that this is the same man; and if so, what a wonderful testimony to the saving grace of Jesus Christ and the power of the Gospel - to take a slave, free him and place him in the Gospel ministry.

This brief letter is a wonderful example of that which Jesus Christ has done for those who place their faith in Him. Onesimus had the death penalty hanging over his head and needed someone to plead his cause. That someone would have to be familiar with both parties, in this case Philemon and Onesimus. Furthermore, the only way that Onesimus could be justly restored would be for the debt to be paid. Paul stepped into the breech and did all of this and more. This is exactly what Christ has done for the condemned sinner (Romans 6:23), separated from God by sin and a fugitive on the run.

Just as Paul intervened to restore Onesimus to Philemon, Jesus intervened to restore us to God. He took the sinner's deserved penalty on the cross of Calvary, and reconciliation (returning man to the place of perfect fellowship in which he was originally placed) becomes the sinner's lot once he accepts the gift offered in Christ (Acts 16:31). Paul says it this way in 2 Corinthians 5:21 "For he (God) hath made him (Christ) to be sin for us, who knew no sin; that we might be made the righteousness of God in Him."

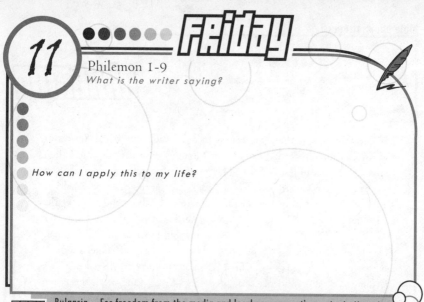

FRIDAY

Philemon 1-9

What is the writer saying?

How can I apply this to my life?

pray Bulgaria — For freedom from the media and local government's constant attempts to obstruct any form of evangelical outreach or growth.

Paul begins this letter as he normally does by introducing himself, but his attached appellation is unique to this book. He calls himself "a prisoner of Jesus Christ" (not of Rome, though in their custody). He alludes to that status often (vv. 9-10, 13, 22-23). He forgoes the use of his official title of apostle since this was to be a letter of request, not command. He wanted Philemon's response to be love-generated and not a response to authority. He adds Timothy as his associate in ministry (as he often did).

The addressee is Philemon, Paul's "dearly beloved ... fellow laborer." Apphia may have been Philemon's wife and Archippus, his son, perhaps an elder in the Colossian Church (see Colossians 4:17). He also addresses "the church" that meets "in thy house" (v. 2). (Until the third century, churches met in private homes and not separate buildings.) His greeting closes with his usual combination of the Greek idea of "grace" (favor displayed where

wrath is deserved), and the Hebrew concept of "peace" (internal, not based on circumstances, a result of grace) (v. 3).

He continues (v. 4) with words of thanksgiving, and notes the reasoning behind them: Philemon's faith in Christ and his love for the saints (v. 5). He prays that Philemon's faith would continue to be an "effectual" (effective) faith, one that has already brought great refreshment in the "bowels (the innermost part of one's being — as deep as you can go) of the saints" (v. 7). (Sometimes translated "heart," but this is not "kardia," it is "splancha.") Philemon was obviously an encouragement to others. Paul wanted that to continue.

In verses 8-9 Paul gets to the point: a passionate appeal to Philemon to accept his runaway slave, Onesimus, back into his household. His appeal was based upon matters about to be addressed, and not on "bold" authority (which he could have used as an apostle), but on the mutual love that they (Paul and Philemon) shared (v. 9).

Fellowship based on love is far better than fellowship based on some misplaced form of authoritarianism.

Philemon 10-25

What is the writer saying?

How can I apply this to my life?

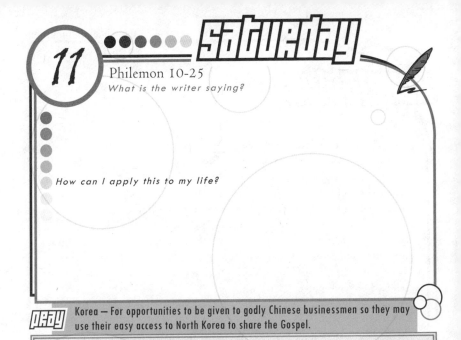

Paul's appeal to accept Onesimus back into his household picks up steam. Having referred (v. 9) to himself as "aged," he pleads for his "son Onesimus," the picture of a father-son relationship, one Paul used when speaking of his converts (1 Timothy 1:2; Titus 1:4). "My son" literally means "my child," and looks back to when Onesimus, under Paul's ministry (Acts 28:30-31), came to know Christ (v. 10).

Salvation changed Onesimus' life. He who was once "unprofitable" (useless) to Philemon, but was now "profitable" (useful) to both Philemon and Paul (v. 11). Understanding that restitution was required for past behavior, Paul tells Philemon he is sending Onesimus back, though he would have preferred to keep him (v. 13). He uses the term "bowels" once again (v. 7) to express the positive emotional connection that existed between he and Onesimus (v. 12), and which had been cultivated as Onesimus ministered to Paul in prison. In fact, he had served Paul in Philemon's "stead," and Paul would like him to continue, but only with Philemon's consent (v. 14).

Verses 15-16 (and reading between the lines) indicate that Onesimus' departure was for a "season" (short time). While not for positive reasons, there were positive results, i.e., his salvation and service on Paul's behalf (Romans 8:28). When Onesimus comes, "receive him not as a servant but above a servant, a brother beloved," for now a spiritual bond exists between all three: they are partners (v. 17). "If he... oweth thee ought (anything)," put that on "mine account" (v. 18). To support his commitment legally, Paul notes he had used his own hand (not that of an amanuensis) to write the letter. He expresses "confidence" that Philemon will respond positively (v. 21), and in doing so refresh Paul's "bowels (that word again) in the Lord" (v. 20). He closes with the anticipation of a soon release, a request for lodging and greetings from some friends (vv. 22-24).

Life stEP

Paul begins (v. 3), and ends (v. 25) with grace. Grace sent Christ to Calvary, compelled Paul to serve and is to motivate our lives. Thank God for its provision.

Revelation

John the Apostle wrote the book of Revelation around A.D. 95 during the reign of the Roman emperor Domitian (A.D. 81-96). John was in exile on the Isle of Patmos (a four by eight mile island that served as a penal mining colony located 60 miles southwest of Ephesus). Tradition states that John was released under Emperor Nerva who reigned A.D. 96-98.

In harmony with Christ's statement to Peter in John 21 and according to church history, John was the only apostle to live to old age (although he also died a martyr's death). It is believed that the Gospel of John and the epistles of 1, 2, and 3 John were also written in the A.D. 90's so we can't say dogmatically that Revelation was the last book written, but certainly it logically concludes the information given in both testaments. John was the "beloved disciple." He was a member of Jesus' inner circle of disciples along with Peter and James. He was with Christ on the Mount of Transfiguration. He took Peter to the high priest's home for Christ's first trial, as apparently John knew that influential family. He alone of all the disciples is mentioned at the crucifixion, as Christ asked him from the cross to take care of Mary. By A.D. 95 he would have been serving Jesus for almost 70 years. What memories would have enriched his mind as he received the amazing information contained in the Book of Revelation. Of all the New Testament authors, only Luke and Paul provide more written Scripture.

"Revelation" is the translation of the Greek word "apocalypse." Both refer to an "unveiling." While we normally associate the "unveiling" of future events (prophecy) with the book, actually the word is referring to the revelation of the person of Jesus Christ who is both the main subject and the "spirit" of future events. Revelation 1:19 provides a nice outline of the book in three tenses. John was told to write the things which "thou hast seen" (past tense – chapter 1), "the things which are" (present tense – chapters 2, 3), and "the things which shall be hereafter" (future tense – chapters 4-22). We could also consider the way in which the book presents Jesus. In chapters 1-3, He is pictured as the "Lord over the churches." In chapters 4-20, He is presented as the "lion over the nations." In chapters 21-22, He is viewed as the "lamb of eternity." The book is highly symbolic. Some

Revelation

of the symbols are explained in context. Most of the symbols have precedents in the Old Testament. We must be careful not to force statements introduced by "like" or "as." They indicate comparison, not identification.

Historically, there have been four ways to approach the book. In the "Preterist Theory," the predictions are thought to apply to events surrounding the A.D. 70 destruction of Jerusalem by the Romans. In the "Historical Theory," the predictions are thought to cover all of world history from John's day until the end of time. In the "Idealist Theory," it is thought that the book teaches principles, not specific events. The fourth view, which is the view affirmed in this commentary, is the "Futurist Theory." It holds that chapters 4–22 still lie in the future.

There is an amazing use of numbers in the book ("seven" appears 50 times!). Scholars have noted over 550 allusions to the Old Testament with 278 of the 404 verses containing references to Old Testament ideas. Daniel 2 is alluded to ten times and Daniel 7 has 30 parallels. The Greek text contains many irregularities in grammar that can only be explained by John's

intense excitement as he received and recorded the information.

The book presents the final struggle of God the Father, Son, and Holy Spirit against Satan, the father, son (Antichrist), and unholy spirit (false prophet). Revelation concludes with "newness": the new heaven and earth, new people, a new bride, a new home, a new temple, and a new light. It is the answer to the tragedy of Genesis 1-3 with paradise regained for redeemed humanity. Revelation is the only book in the Bible that promises a blessing for those who read it. (Yet for most of church history it has been ignored as being too hard to understand. Perhaps Daniel 12:4 indicates that in the end times, Christians would become knowledgeable in prophecy ("But thou, O Daniel, shut up the words, and seal the book, even to the time of the end: many shall run to and fro, and knowledge shall be increased.").

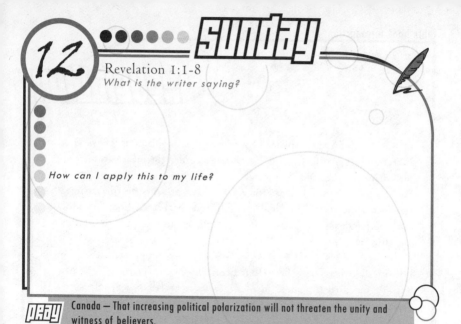

Revelation 1:1-8
What is the writer saying?

How can I apply this to my life?

pray   Canada — That increasing political polarization will not threaten the unity and witness of believers.

"Revelation" means "unveiling." It is an unveiling of future events and also the unveiling of a person, the person of Jesus Christ. Note the route of this revelation. It came from God the Father, to God the Son, to an angel, to John who then wrote it down for the rest of us. Angels ("messengers") appear in the chain of revelation over 70 times in the Bible.

God "signified" (v. 1) the information, which not only means "to indicate," but also "to put into signs." There are many signs and symbols in this book. The word "shortly" (v. 1) does not mean "soon" but rather that the events described can happen at any time (i.e., "imminent"). Later in the book there will be another word used for "soon." God has both a living Word (Jesus Christ) and a written Word (the Bible). Both "he that readeth" and "they that hear" (v. 3) will be blessed, indicating a public reading of the material with many listeners. The three tenses of "to be" in verse 4 reminds us of the meaning of "Jehovah" as explained in Exodus 3:13-14. The number seven is often associated with God, perhaps denoting completion and perfection. The seven "Spirits" (v. 4) may be seven angels or more likely, a reference to the fullness of the Holy Spirit (i.e., the sevenfold Spirit). The Greek word for "witness" (v. 5) is the word "martyr." So many of the early Christian witnesses lost their lives for the faith that we associate "death" with the word "martyr." "First begotten" (v. 5) refers to Christ's resurrection. The descriptive phrases concerning Christ in verse 5 are alluded to in Psalm 89, which is a commentary on the Davidic Covenant in 2 Samuel 7:1-16. "Amen" (v. 6) comes from the Hebrew word for "to believe" or "be firm." Christ's return in the clouds is mentioned in Daniel 7:13 and every eye seeing Him in Zechariah 12:10. Both ideas are included in Matthew 24:30. Behold (v. 7) occurs 25 times in this book.

Even so come Lord Jesus. Even so come today!

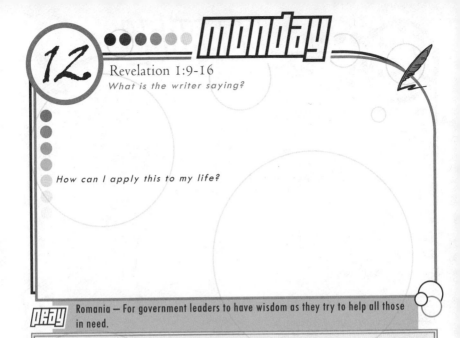

monday

12

Revelation 1:9-16

What is the writer saying?

How can I apply this to my life?

PRAY Romania — For government leaders to have wisdom as they try to help all those in need.

John was exiled to the Isle of Patmos. It was the first day of the week, "Resurrection Day" as it is still called in the Russian language. As John meditated, a commanding voice ("trumpet") interrupted his thoughts. "Alpha" is the first letter in the Greek alphabet and "Omega" is the last. Since "books" as we know them were not invented yet, John would have recorded this information on a scroll that would have been about 15 feet long unrolled. Apparently each of the seven churches would have then copied the information to keep for their use.

John saw Jesus walking among seven separate lamp stands (not the seven-branched Menorah of the Old Testament holy place). During the Church Age we do not have one place of religious observance (Jerusalem), but because of the indwelling Spirit of God we have worship centers around the globe. One day apostasy will extinguish the light of the churches and God will re-ignite Israel as His nation of priests. Of all the titles that Jesus could use to describe Himself, He preferred "Son of Man" since it associates Him with us.

The golden girdle was part of the high priest's garments (Exodus 28:8). "White" was the color of God's hair in Daniel 7:9-10, speaking of holiness. "Brass" should be "bronze" since that is the modern technical name for what the ancients used (an alloy of copper and tin). Since the altar in the temple was covered with bronze, we associate judgment with that metal. "Waters" convey power and tranquility. In Daniel 10:5-6, a supernatural being has a similar appearance and there his voice is described as the "voice of a multitude." The "right hand" is the place of power, privilege or protection. "Stars" represent either the guardian angels of the seven churches or more likely the human pastors. The sword signifies the on-going power of Christ's Word.

Can you imagine the awe John felt as he viewed the resurrected, glorified, ascended Lord!

Revelation 1:17-20
What is the writer saying?

How can I apply this to my life?

pray Uruguay — Bookmobile ministry that makes Christian books accessible to believers around the country.

"Fear not" is a trademark saying of Christ from the Gospels. If John didn't already recognize who He was, this phrase should have alerted him. "First and last" parallels the illustration of "Alpha and Omega." In the Book of Revelation, these designations are used of both God the Father and Jesus, implying their equality as deity. Christ's death, burial, and resurrection are the heart of the Gospel (1 Corinthians 15:3-5). It is because of His victory over death that we have the promise of our own salvation and the assurance that He (and not Satan) controls the after-life.

Verse 19 provides the past, present and future outline for the whole book. Chapter 1 represents the past tense ("things which thou hast seen"). Chapters 2 and 3 provide the present tense ("the things which are now"). "Now" refers to John's day of A.D. 95. In chapters 2-3 Christ has words for the seven churches of Asia Minor. These were real, historic churches about 50 miles apart in a circle around Ephesus. We will discover that the Lord criticizes five of the seven churches and that the two not criticized are the only cities remaining today (Smyrna and Philadelphia). Laodicea is the only church of the seven with no commendation.

Some commentators feel that the seven churches represent successive ages of church history. While God certainly could encode such symbolism into His Scriptures, it is of little value since the saints of the first century could not have understood the material as prophetic and we cannot prove it even with hindsight. It is more important to understand that these churches are representative of seven types of churches found in any age or locality. As chapter 1 comes to a close, we can say that it functions as the "signature" of the author to the letter to the seven churches and to us as well.

Life **stEP**

Jesus is the Lord over the churches, the lion over the nations, and the lamb of eternity.

Revelation 2:1-7

What is the writer saying?

How can I apply this to my life?

PRAY Harry Bollback, Co-founder of Word of Life, as he and his wife Millie travel and minister.

Ephesus means "desirable." It was the mother church of the region. Paul spent three years, his longest stay, at Ephesus (Acts 19). Aquila and Priscilla were there (Acts 18:26). Timothy eventually became the pastor of the church where he received the challenge from Paul not to be timid. By tradition, John lived at Ephesus starting in A.D. 68. With all of these significant early church leaders, the church received a firm foundation in doctrine. The following letters were written to the church at Ephesus: Ephesians, 1 and 2 Timothy, and Revelation. While Paul ministered in Ephesus, he wrote 1 Corinthians. John probably wrote the Gospel of John and 1, 2, 3 John from there. Ephesus was important even later as in A.D. 431 the Third General Church Council was held there.

In the first century, the city was prominent because it was a port city and controlled a major route through Asia Minor. One of the seven wonders of the ancient world was there, the Temple of Diana, which was three times as big as the Parthenon with 120 columns 60' high plated with gold. The ancients also hosted famous athletic games there.

"Says this" is a phrase that Persian kings used to introduce decrees. Seven of the eight times that this phrase occurs in the New Testament are here in Revelation. By A.D. 95, the church would have been over 40 years old. Despite their spiritual heritage, not all the members were truly saved as Christ anticipates that some might not be overcomers (the normal activity of saved individuals, Romans 8:37). The Nicolaitans excused immorality and compromise with pagans. The "deeds" of the Nicolaitans of 2:6 become the "doctrine" by 2:15. Perhaps this group was started by the Nicolas of Acts 6:5 and had Hymenaeus and Philetus of 2 Timothy 2:17 as members.

How sad when the thrill of new love weakens into careless presumption. Make it a point to fall in love all over again every morning in your meditations on the Lord over the churches.

thursday

12

Revelation 2:8-11
What is the writer saying?

How can I apply this to my life?

PRAY Papua New Guinea — For the unity found in Christ to transcend ethnic differences among believers.

Smyrna comes from the word "myrrh." Myrrh was highly valued in the ancient world as an aromatic plant. It was used for burial and interestingly enough, only released its odor when crushed. Myrrh was one of the gifts presented to baby Jesus by the wise men and would have been used for His burial as well. Smyrna was famous for its natural beauty, famous as the birthplace of Homer, and was the Asian center for emperor worship. This would explain the tribulation that the believers faced. Later, around A.D. 150, the great church leader Polycarp was there.

The word for "tribulation" is used elsewhere to refer to the pressure involved in the crushing of grapes. The word for "poverty" refers to abject poverty, probably produced by the persecution. Their enemies are Jewish, although Christ is careful to explain that such "Jews" are not true followers of Jehovah. "Blasphemy" refers to "injurious speech." It probably refers to the slander leveled against Christians such as cannibalism (because they ate the "body" of Jesus in communion) or immorality (because they practiced the holy kiss) or atheism (because they rejected the pagan gods) or subversion (because they refused to worship Caesar). In the Roman Empire prior to A.D. 325, Judaism was the only legal monotheistic religion. The "ten days" probably indicates that the persecution would be short-lived.

Notice that for each of these seven letters, Christ goes back to chapter 1 and picks one descriptive phrase to introduce Himself to that church. These are not random selections, but seem to be tailored to the situation at that church. Notice that here He is the resurrected Lord (v. 8) and that He promises resurrection to the overcomers (v. 11). Also notice that all of these letters are addressed, not just to the specific church, but also to "all the churches" (v. 11).

Life can be tough and seemingly unfair. God promises that it will be worth it all when we see Jesus.

Revelation 2:12-17

What is the writer saying?

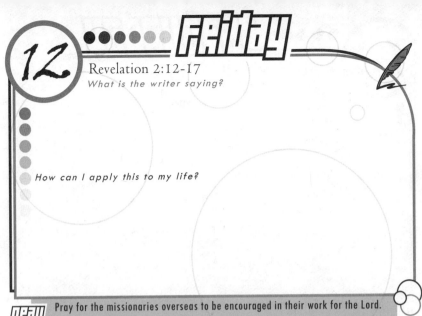

How can I apply this to my life?

PRAY Pray for the missionaries overseas to be encouraged in their work for the Lord.

Pergamos is also spelled Pergamum. It means "citadel." The name refers to an actual military stronghold on a hill towering 1000' above the city. It was a center for parchment and paper manufacturing and at one time had a large library with 200,000 books, which were eventually moved to the famous library in Alexandria, Egypt. The city was honored by the Roman government and given freedom in determining some of its affairs without first consulting Rome. This included "ius gladii," the Latin legal term for "the right of the sword" which referred to capital punishment. The believers were therefore under immediate threat of death at the whim of the local courts.

Notice that Christ is introduced as one who also possesses a mighty sword and that martyrdom is mentioned as a problem for the church. The city had several prominent religious expressions including an altar to Zeus, a temple to a serpent god (the god of healing who was also called "savior.") Pergamos was the first Asian city to have a temple for emperor worship (29 B.C. for Caesar Augustus). The man's name, Antipas means, "against all."

Balaam was that unusual prophet in Numbers 22-24, 31:16 who was hired by King Balak of the Moabites to curse the children of Israel, but every time he tried, God put a blessing in his mouth. He eventually encouraged Balak to seek Israel's destruction by "religious syncretism," namely, that if the Jewish men fell in love with the Moabite women they would then worship the gods of the Moabites and Jehovah would judge them. Here it is called the "teaching" of Balaam. In Jude 11 it mentions the "error" of Balaam (thinking that you can manipulate God) and in 2 Peter 2:15 we have the "way" of Balaam (religion for hire).

Those who are faithful will eat heavenly food (manna), have a transformed life (new name), and free access into heaven (white stone, often used in ancient times as a ticket).

How can I apply this to my life?

pray Indonesia — For missionaries to reach every inhabited island to share the Gospel.

Thyatira means "castle of Thya," in honor of a regional goddess. It was a "religious" town with each trade guild supported by a patron religion. Lydia, the "dyer of purple" (Acts 16), was from Thyatira. Scholars know the least about the church in this town, but this is the longest of the seven letters. Christ is presented as one who can see through phonies and is unmovable in judgment. The letter contains five compliments including even the "love" which Ephesus lacked! By ancient tradition, a woman founded the city. It was also the seat of a prophetess—established cult named "Sambatha." If Lydia also founded the church here, we can understand the influence of women in this church. Christ criticizes the error of a female church member. "Sufferest" (v. 20) is worse than the "hast" of 2:14. Since this condemnation was read publicly before the whole church, can you imagine the reaction in the church the Sunday it was read?

The word "tribulation" is used for persecution or judgment in general and also that special time of future judgment first presented in Daniel 9:27 (the seven-year tribulation period). Christ's warning of impending judgment will also find fulfillment in the lives of the apostate Christians who miss the Rapture and enter the tribulation period. We don't know what particular heretical sect this woman promoted, but it is similar to one version of the ancient Gnostic error that claimed, "In order to defeat Satan you have to experience evil deeply." Verse 27 contains the triumphant imagery of Psalm 2:9. This judgmental destruction and victorious ruling is further described in chapters 4-22. The "morning star" is the planet Venus, which is often visible at just before dawn. It is used of Satan in Isaiah 14:12-14 ("Lucifer" means "morning star") as the usurper and also of Jesus Christ who is the "true" morning star (Revelation 22:16).

Attack from within is more dangerous than persecution from without.

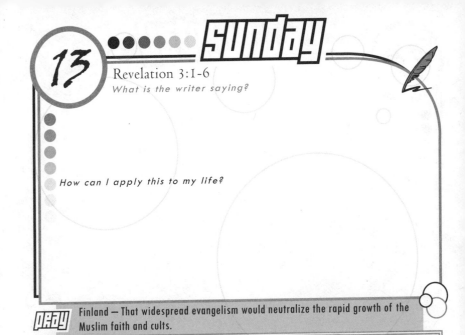

13

Revelation 3:1-6

What is the writer saying?

How can I apply this to my life?

pray Finland — That widespread evangelism would neutralize the rapid growth of the Muslim faith and cults.

Sardis derived its name from a gemstone that was a deep red color. The city also claimed to be the first to dye wool. These two physical facts plus the content of the letter has led some to refer to Sardis as the "stained church." Christ is presented as the one who "hath" the seven Spirits of God. This implies His authoritative possession of the Holy Spirit and the fact that as the Lord of the churches, He bestows the Holy Spirit on whomever He wills. The plurality of "Spirits" simply indicates that the Spirit is available for all seven churches (not seven different Holy Spirits). The seven "stars" would be the seven "angels" (either guardian angels behind the scenes or the human pastors) of the seven churches.

Archaeologists have uncovered coins with the inscription: "Sardis, the First Metropolis of Asia and of Lydia and of Hellenism." This would not have been the case in A.D. 95, so it speaks of a past glorious heritage. Christ says that they had a "name" (reputation), but in actuality they were "dead" (time had passed them by). The patron goddess of Sardis, Artemas, supposedly could raise the dead. Christ implies that they shouldn't assume Artemas would be able to help them in this deadly spiritual state. They were stained by the world and becoming indistinguishable from the world. They practiced "inoffensive Christianity."

Verse 3 warns the believers of the importance of vigilance. It is significant that even though Sardis was located on steep cliffs, twice in her history she was conquered in sneak attacks (by the Persians in 549 B.C. and by the Greeks in 214 B.C.). The word for "thief" ("kleptes" as in "kleptomaniac") refers to the furtive "cat burglar," not the armed robber who strikes in broad daylight. The letter concludes with more color analogies. Their garments were "defiled" ("dyed" by dirt) but for the over comer, garments "dyed" white were waiting in heaven.

Our society is consumed by fashion. What is the color of heaven? It is white, trimmed in white with white accessories!

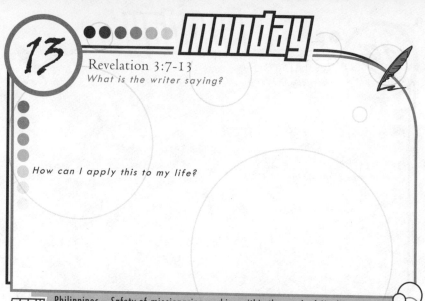

13

monday

Revelation 3:7-13

What is the writer saying?

How can I apply this to my life?

Philippines — Safety of missionaries working within the reach of Muslim extremists in Mindanao.

Philadelphia means "City of Brotherly Love." It was located at the end of a narrow valley and therefore was known as the "Gateway to the East." The city was founded specifically to spread the Greek culture eastward. In the sequence of the seven churches, it is a rose between two thorns (Sardis the dying church and Laodicea the useless church). The "open door" (v. 8) in general refers to ministry opportunities, but specifically has the messianic kingdom in mind. While their Jewish adversaries (v. 9) prided themselves as the object of God's messianic plan, it was these faithful New Testament saints who would receive the "key of David" (v. 7). The true Jew is the one who believes in Jesus of Nazareth. The Jewish Messiah loves the Gentiles rejected by the Jews of Philadelphia. Verse 10 is the strongest statement of the pretribulational timing of the Rapture of the church. Note that it is not only the judgments that the believers will escape but also specifically the time period during which the judgments occur. The exact same phrase ("keep from") occurs in John 17:15 and a similar phrase ("save from") occurs in John 12:27. In both cases only total exclusion from the situation would make sense. Therefore, total separation from the period of judgment (not just protection through the time period) seems to be the promise. That this promise extends beyond the church at Philadelphia to all churches is assured by the repeated final challenge, "He that hath an ear, let him hear what the Spirit saith unto the churches."

The region around Philadelphia was subject to earthquake activity. They had a devastating earthquake in A.D. 17. An interesting feature of architecture, the laws of physics and earthquakes is that while roofs and walls fall down, many times pillars do not (e.g., "Weebles wobble but they don't fall down.").

Life stEP

Believers will stay standing like pillars, will feel safe, and God will give them a threefold name, not "666."

Revelation 3:14-22

What is the writer saying?

How can I apply this to my life?

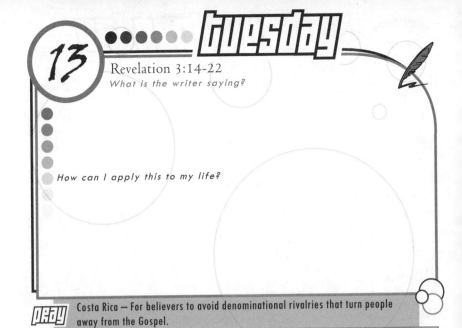

pray — Costa Rica — For believers to avoid denominational rivalries that turn people away from the Gospel.

Laodicea was named for a king's wife, Laodice, but the word also means "justice of the people." It was a wealthy city famous for many business enterprises. These included banking, black wool processing, medical schools, ear and eye medications, and hot spring resorts. Their wealth and self-sufficiency is noted in the fact that after an earthquake in A.D. 60, they rebuilt their city with no financial help from Rome. The city did not have safe drinking water. Drinking water was piped in from ten miles away, which meant they rarely enjoyed cold drinking. We know from Colossians 4:16 that this church would have received a copy of Ephesians and perhaps Colossians as well.

Christ is introduced as the "Amen" or "truth personified" as contrasted with Satan, "the father of lies" (John 8:44). He is also the "beginning" because he was the "Beginner." Hot water and cold water are both desirable for drinking (e.g., hot coffee or iced tea).

Room temperature beverages are undesirable or even nauseating. Despite their financial wealth, despite their famous black wool for clothing, despite their medicines and doctors; they were poor, unclothed, and sick. In place of their self-efforts for physical and spiritual wealth, God offers them His gold (genuine faith), His white garments (righteousness), and His eye salve (spiritual insight).

We often think of the "door" as the door to our life. Christ seeks entrance for fellowship with both unsaved and the saved. It also reminds us of the door to the messianic kingdom. Christ is ready to return to the planet and wants to have face-to-face fellowship with repentant believers. The "eating" would be the sharing of "the marriage supper of the Lamb" (Revelation 19:9). Overcomers then join the 12 apostles on the thrones of the kingdom (Luke 22:29).

In the world we see anarchy; in Christendom we see apostasy. Could it be that in the evangelical church we are in danger of apathy?

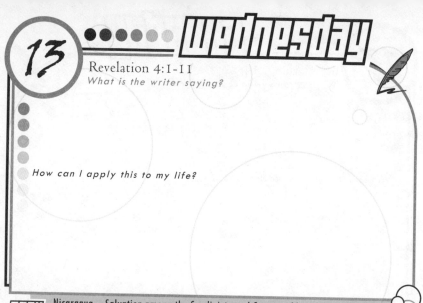
How can I apply this to my life?

PRAY — Nicaragua — Salvation among the Sandinista and Contra soldiers left disillusioned and angry from the war where they saw many atrocities meted out.

Chapters 4 and 5 form a unit that presents "throne room theology." In chapter 4 we are introduced to the "Creator God." In chapter 5 we view the "Redeemer God." "After this" means "after the messages to the seven churches" and perhaps also implies after the Church Age. John is also taken up to heaven for this information, as the church will be at the Rapture.

Notice that the first individual John sees in heaven is faceless and formless. Only His glory is described. He is God the Father, the Ancient of Days, the Universal Judge. Jasper is a clear gem like our diamond and perhaps speaks of God's holiness. Sardius (cf., the city "Sardis") is ruby-red, perhaps speaking of the righteousness supplied by Christ's blood. The green rainbow reminds us of God's mercy as shown to Noah, the first human to behold a rainbow. The 24 elders could parallel the 24 courses of priests in the temple service rotation or perhaps 12 representative Old Testament saints and 12 representative New Testament saints (as also appearing in the city of Jerusalem in Revelation 21). These elders wear the "victor's crown" (not a diadem or "kingly crown"). It indicates that they have run a race and have won. The reflecting pool magnified the light in the throne room and set God apart from creation by His purity. The word "beast" translates the word "zoa" which refers to a "living being" (and is also the root of the word "zoo"). These beasts are almost certainly the class of angel called Cherubim ("Watchers" of the holiness of God) or Seraphim ("burning ones"). The four faces also appear in the vision in Ezekiel 1. They represent the highest creature in their particular category of living creatures and also bear an uncanny resemblance to the theme of each of the four Gospels (e.g., "lion" for Christ the King in Matthew, etc.).

Life stEP

This splendid vision of God in heaven leads to an outburst of praise that we have turned into a praise chorus, "Thou Art Worthy."

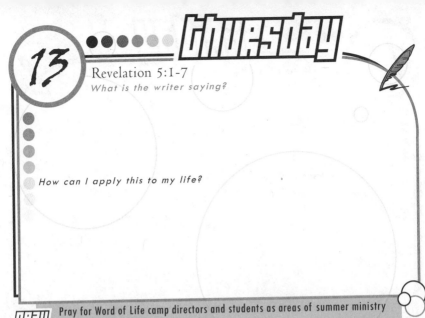

How can I apply this to my life?

The right hand in biblical times was a place of authority, privilege, and advantage. Both the Romans and the Jewish people used multiple-sealed scrolls for legal documents such as wills and title deeds. In Jeremiah 32:8 we see Jeremiah receiving such a title deed for land he had purchased. That there would be writing on the outside does not necessarily mean that there was abundant information. These title deeds would consist of two copies. Inside, protected by the legal seals, was the official copy, while a second copy was outside the seals for reference sake. The sealed copy could only be opened in a court of law. Archaeologists have recovered title deeds where someone had altered the boundaries in the outer copy!

Notice the dynamic nature of this scene with a "strong" angel and a "loud" voice. Twenty times in Revelation something is described as being "loud." "Worthy" means "of proper weight," referring to an intrinsic or earned quality. Initially, no one is found who can even look at the scroll, let alone open it. John is emotionally devastated by this problem. Some suggest that he was crying because he wanted to know the prophecies that the scroll contained. There are other times in Scripture when men are told that they cannot know something, and they don't respond by crying. It seems that the scroll signifies more than just information to John. His outburst is stemmed by the announcement that the Lion has prevailed to open the book. This statement is in the past tense, yet the scroll has not yet been opened. This illustrates that certain facts in Scripture are legally true before they are practically accomplished. When an entity steps forward to open the scroll, it is described as a lamb. In fact, not a strong adult ram, but rather a unique term used 29 times in Revelation that means "young lamb."

Life stEP

When is the lamb a lion and the lion a lamb? When we are viewing the person of Jesus Christ!

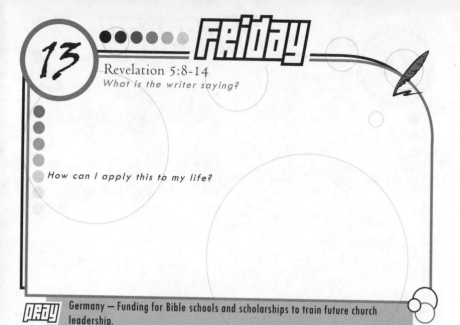

13 Friday

Revelation 5:8-14

What is the writer saying?

How can I apply this to my life?

PRAY Germany — Funding for Bible schools and scholarships to train future church leadership.

Notice that the 24 elders claimed that the Lamb had redeemed them, indicating that they were humans, not holy angels. Harps and gold are two of the standard items associated with heaven. The Greek word for "harp" is the same word from which we get "guitar." In biblical times this stringed instrument had 10-20 strings.

Of all the prayers that saints have prayed over the last 1900 years, which one has probably been repeated the most? Would it be, "Our Father which art in heaven, Hallowed be thy name. Thy kingdom come. Thy will be done in earth, as it is in heaven"? If so, then here we have a very specific and practical application of those prayers. These saints revel in their current citizenship status as kings and priests while noting that their actual reign is still in the future. Despite the fact that the Jews were said to be a "kingdom of priests" (Exodus 19:6) here people of all ethnic backgrounds are included in the assembly of the redeemed. All rational creatures in every nook and cranny of the universe join voices to praise both the Father and the Son. These include both the angelic creatures and redeemed humanity. As in chapter 4, this heavenly vision in chapter 5 gives us a popular praise chorus, "Worthy is the Lamb." In verse 6 the lamb was described as a slain lamb. Now in verse 14 it is described as a lamb that will never die again.

Theologically, some conclude that because New Testament saints are described by some of the phrases used of Old Testament saints (e.g., "kingdom of priests") this means that the church has replaced Israel in God's program. We would argue that such analogies are not mutually exclusive. Both Israel and the church can be a "kingdom of priests" without contradiction or the subservence of the one to the other.

God lives regardless of our existence, activities or thoughts; but He becomes alive to us in our praise. If you want to know God better, praise Him better.

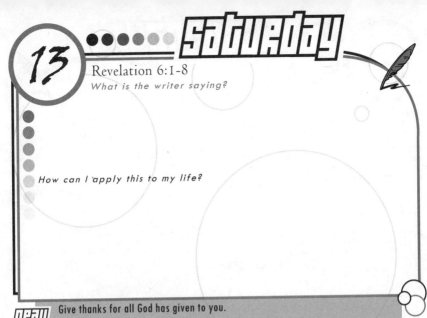

13

Revelation 6:1-8

What is the writer saying?

How can I apply this to my life?

---

pray   Give thanks for all God has given to you.

Revelation 6:1-8:1 describes the seven seal judgments. As each seal is opened on the scroll, John witnesses a prophetic event. The first four seal judgments are also known as the "four Horsemen of the Apocalypse." Notice that the four living creatures of chapter 4 call these horsemen forth. The thunderous voice of the first living beast implies judgment. The color "white" speaks of victory and perhaps counterfeit purity. While the horse and bow are both instruments of ancient warfare, perhaps the absence of arrows implies a political conquest (Daniel 7:8, 24). It says that the rider of the white horse "was given" his authority ("crown") indicating that these events are initiated from the throne of God and therefore, would be classified as God's wrath being poured out on the sinful earth as a judgment.

While no specific chronological markers are given here in chapter 6, both Daniel and Matthew associate war with the entire seven years of the tribulation period. Therefore, we could suggest that the opening of the seals begins shortly after the Rapture of the church and that the white horse represents the beginning of the Antichrist's rise to world dominance. The "red" horse speaks of the bloodshed of war. The "black" horse represents the famine that comes in the wake of war. The voice that describes the symbolism of the third horse is God's (from the midst of the four living creatures) indicating once again that this is God's judgment on sinful mankind. Wheat is more nutritious than barley. The prices mentioned indicate tenfold price inflation. Since olives and grapes grow wild, these items are not immediately affected. The famine is limited and the wealthy still have their food. The last horse is yellowish green (the word is "chlorine" in Greek). It represents death in general ("green around the gills"). "Hell" (actually "hades" representing the grave) is like the hearse, bringing up the rear.

If this happened tomorrow, 1.5 billion people would die. Are your friends safe?

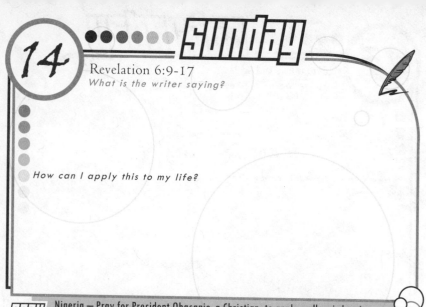

How can I apply this to my life?

The four horsemen seem to be analogous to the "four severe terrors" predicted in several Old Testament passages (Ezekiel 14:21). These are usually listed as sword, wild beast, famine, and plague. The fifth seal is not so much a judgment as it is a justification for judgment. Apparently enough time has transpired in the tribulation period for a significant number of people to have accepted Christ as their Savior and then be martyred for their faith. (The Greek word for "testimony" in verse 9 is the source of the English word "martyr" because so many of the early Christians lost their lives for their testimony). They address God with a special Greek word for Lord, the word "despotes" from which we get the English word "despot." It means "absolute master." The concept "earth dwellers" in the book of Revelation refers to unsaved mankind hostile to God. God encourages the martyrs with pure clothing and the promise that it will only be a short time until their murder is avenged (at least we could say "less than seven years").

The sixth seal involves catastrophic "cosmic signs." Matthew 24 describes earthquake activity prior to the midpoint of the tribulation period (which is marked by the establishment of the abomination of desolation in the temple). These unusual events in the physical world are calculated to make men think that the universe is coming apart at the seams. All men, great and small, are unnerved and apparently think that they can escape God's wrath by dying. In Scripture, God's end-time wrath ("day of the Lord" wrath) is said to come upon sinners "like a thief in the night" (1 Thessalonians 5:4). If that is the case, then the comments of these distraught humans form an announcement that the seal judgments are day of the Lord events, not that the seventh seal will be the start of the day of the Lord. "Who is able to stand?" may be a rhetorical question, but we will find an answer in chapter 7!

Life stEP

"It is a fearful thing to fall into the hands of the living God" (Hebrews 10:31).

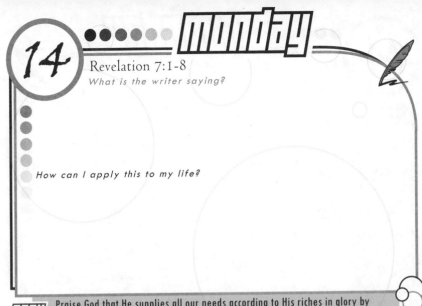

14 — monday

Revelation 7:1-8

What is the writer saying?

How can I apply this to my life?

The seventh and final seal is not opened until 8:1. In chapter 7, we take a break from the chronological sequence and step back to fill in details of some of the other things that God is doing during the first half of the tribulation period. In 7:1-8 we are introduced to the 144,000 sealed Jews who are protected from the divine judgments and apparently become the evangelists on the planet after the Rapture of the church. Ancient Jewish superstition claimed that winds blowing from the "corners" (east-northeast, etc.) of the compass were harmful. The direction of the rising sun (East, v. 2) is associated with the following positive concepts in Scripture: paradise; the direction that the Shekinah glory of God takes when returning to the temple; the Magi; and the messianic title, "Dayspring" (Luke 1:78). God is called the "living God" as contrasted with the "dead" gods of paganism.

The ancient world was familiar with tattoos and distinctive cuttings in the flesh for tribal, military, trade guild, or religious purposes. In Revelation 13 we will be introduced to the infamous "mark of the Beast," 666. Here, as in a parallel situation in Ezekiel 9, the individuals are marked on the forehead. In Ezekiel 9:4 the "mark" was actually the Hebrew letter "tav" or "t." At that time, the Hebrew letter even looked like a small cross!

In the Bible, there are many different arrangements of the "12 tribes of Israel." In addition to the original 12 sons of Jacob, we have the two sons of Joseph, Ephraim and Manasseh. Levi is left out in some lists since as priests they were given cities throughout the country and not territory. Joseph is left out in many lists to make room for his sons. In this list, Dan and Ephraim are missing. Perhaps Dan is missing because that tribe left the original tribal allotment in the south, moved to the extreme north, apostatized, and was absorbed into Syrian paganism. Perhaps Ephraim is missing because that tribe opposed Judah and David.

Life stEP God does dangerous things, but always with great care for those who are part of His master plan.

Revelation 7:9-17
What is the writer saying?

How can I apply this to my life?

pray France — Passionate outreach to the nearly 50,000,000 people who have no real link with a Bible-believing church.

"After this" could mean "the next thing I saw," but a tighter understanding would be "as a result of the sealing of the 144,000, many people came to know Christ as Savior." We are not introduced to the "two witnesses" until Revelation 11; however, it is clear that they are mighty preachers during the first half of the tribulation period. We could suggest the following chronology. At the Rapture, for the first time in human history, there will not be one saved individual left on the planet. To provide a renewed witness, God sends the two witnesses. They help lead the 144,000 to Christ. The two witnesses are killed by the antichrist at the middle of the Tribulation, but the 144,000 continue preaching to the end. It is their converts from seven years of missionary work that we see here in chapter 7.

Palm branches (called "lulav" in Jewish ceremonies) were standard joyous decorations for both Jewish and Roman celebrations (cf. the Triumphal Entry on Palm Sunday). The Roman emperor claimed the title "Savior" (v. 10). Here God is the rightful bearer of that title. Verse 12 repeats the seven attributes from Revelation 5:12 with just the slight change of "thanksgiving" instead of "riches."

Note that these saved individuals come from the entire earth; every ethnic group is represented. The number is also significant. The number is so great that no man could count it. In Revelation there are many numbers. The largest is the number 200,000,000 (v. 9:16). Therefore, we could conclude that even during the world's darkest hour, over 200,000,000 people will come to salvation by God's gracious intervention.

Life stEP "God is great and God is good," but mostly He is good. He didn't have to offer salvation during the time of well-deserved judgment, but He does. As a believer, you are convinced of His eternal graciousness. He also wants to show you grace right now, today, as you trust Him.

Revelation 8:1-13

What is the writer saying?

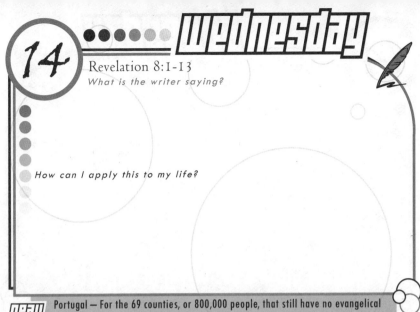

How can I apply this to my life?

PRAY   Portugal — For the 69 counties, or 800,000 people, that still have no evangelical congregation.

Chapter 8 begins with the opening of the seventh and final seal. All of heaven is shocked into adoring silence with the realization that the title deed to planet earth is now back in the hands of the rightful owner and the official copy is now open in the heavenly court with the breaking of the last seal. Satan, the usurper, is in the process of being defeated and expelled from his squatter claim. Adoring silence as a mode of worship is observed in other passages such as, "Be still and know that I am God" (Psalm 46:10). In biblical times, trumpets were used to get attention, call people together, and announce important events. Both metal and ram's horn trumpets (the "shofar") were known and used. It is not clear here what type is being used. Earlier we noted that "Thy kingdom come" is probably the most frequently uttered prayer. The altar of incense symbolizes the prayers of the saints going up to God. Here, the coals from that altar are also symbolic of the judgment to fall upon the rebellious earth.

The accompanying physical traumas heighten the judgmental aspect of these trumpets. Note that the seventh seal is not a specific judgment, but rather contains all seven of the judgments in this next series of judgments. The first four trumpet judgments fall on nature and indirectly attack man. The first trumpet judgment attacks green vegetation. The second trumpet judgment affects the salty sea. The third trumpet judgment attacks fresh water. Wormwood is "absinth," a bitter chemical used to kill intestinal parasites. Amazingly, it is also the meaning of the name Chernobyl, the city in the Ukraine with the tragic nuclear reactor malfunction. The fourth trumpet judgment affects the heavenly light. A similar phenomenon took place in one of the ten judgments upon the Egyptians and also the day Christ died.

"God is great and God is good." Here His greatness is on terrible display.

How can I apply this to my life?

At the end of chapter 8, John is told that there are three more trumpets to sound and that they will be the three (final) woes to fall upon mankind. Actually, this is a very accurate statement as the third woe, seventh trumpet, is in fact the final series of judgments, the vial (bowl) judgments. The devastation these judgments bring is cataclysmic. If you take one-fourth of a number (the fourth seal judgment) and then one-third of the remainder (the sixth trumpet judgment) the result is half of the original number. There are over six billion people on the planet today. This would represent a death toll of over three billion people! The "star" (v. 1) represents a spirit being. He has authority to open the bottomless pit. Smoke comes out, darkening the sun and also mimicking the darkening of the sun produced by a great swarm of locusts. These are not normal locusts but demonic locusts. Instead of eating vegetation, their "diet" is human flesh.

Their "sting" is like that of a scorpion. Some scorpions have deadly stings but these do not. The sting of a scorpion has been described as the equivalent of being stung by two wasps at the same time. Torment for God-haters is the stated mission for these horror-film creatures. That they would do so for five months is significant because that is the length of the lifespan of a normal locust. It is not clear why these tormented men cannot commit suicide. Perhaps it means that they are in so much pain they wish and think they should die from the stings but don't. Some have speculated that the fanciful description of these demonic beings was the best John could do in describing weapons of modern warfare. While God can use modern equipment to produce such torment, it would not be surprising if this were a literal description of the fearful appearance of these bizarre creatures. Both "Abaddon" and "Apollyon" mean the same thing, "Destroyer."

Life stEP

We have a choice. We can fear God now in reverential awe that leads to eternal salvation, or we can fear Him later in stark terror.

Revelation 9:13-21

What is the writer saying?

How can I apply this to my life?

The sixth trumpet or second woe is a precursor to Armageddon. The announcement comes from the altar of incense where the prayers of the martyred saints ascend to God. Since the four angels are bound, this would indicate that they are fallen angels (demons). The Euphrates River in the Bible is the border between Israel and the Gentile empires of Assyria, Babylon, and Persia. It runs for 1700 miles from the mountains of Turkey to the Persian Gulf. In Revelation 16:12-16 the River Euphrates is dried up to allow the kings of the East to come to the Valley of Armageddon in Israel.

Some have noted the parallelism between the two passages and have suggested that the 200,000,000 demons of chapter 9 indwell the armies of chapter 16 to induce them to come to Armageddon. Some commentators have imagined some sort of modern weapon with guns belching fire from the front and tail. We can just as easily imagine God using the traditional and modern representations of demons and extraterrestrial monsters to scare and punish sinful mankind. They are colorful. "Fire" would be golden, "jacinth" can be reddish-orange, blue, or purple, and "brimstone" (sulfur) is yellow. They kill with fire (burning), smoke (asphyxiation), and brimstone (chemical poisoning?). These creatures and their weapons kill one-third of the remaining people. Those who survive amazingly do not recognize God's hand in the matter and continue in their sinful ways. Demonic activity on earth peaks when the Messiah is about to establish the kingdom (in both His first and second comings). The Greek word translated "sorceries" is "pharmakeia," from the same root as "pharmaceuticals." The ancients used drugs to achieve an altered state of consciousness when worshiping. They would then become "in theos" ("enthused") or "indwelt by the gods."

You are possessed by what you value. Value Satan's things and he will claim you. Value God's characteristics and you will be His eternally.

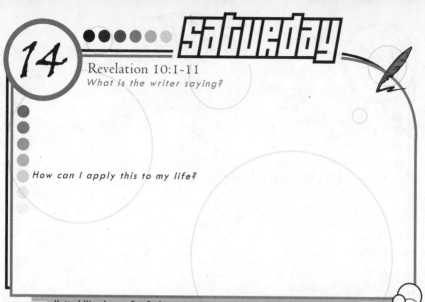

What is the writer saying?

How can I apply this to my life?

pray United Kingdom — For God to raise up a new generation of vibrant, doctrinally sound Bible teachers.

Saints feel inferior to and afflicted by the unsaved. However, God and His helpers are described in majestic language. Here the announcing angel is "mighty." He has the glory clouds of God (Daniel 7:13-14). The beauty of the rainbow adorns his head (since Noah's day, a symbol of God's mercy). His face is radiant like the sun. His feet are burnished by fire as were Christ's in Revelation 1:15. He is large enough to straddle the land and sea. His voice is powerful like the kingly lion. The little book (actually a scroll, since "books" as we know them were not invented yet) represents the judgments. Apparently we could have had another series of seven judgments, the "Thunder Judgments," but God wouldn't let John write that information down. This indicates that there is more to the story than we know and therefore, we have to trust God when certain elements don't

seem to make sense because we do not have all the data. Notice the emphasis on God as the Creator God. His puny creatures are in big trouble because they have offended their Creator.

Verse 7 indicates that once the bowl judgments begin, events will run rapidly to the conclusion. "Eat" (v. 10) means to "internalize" or "read" (Psalm 19:9). Ezekiel also had a similar experience (Ezekiel 3:1-4). The scroll was sweet to the taste because it was the very Word of God and His words are sweeter than the honeycomb (Psalm 19:10). However, since it contained judgments, it was bitter in John's stomach. Verse 11 indicates that while the bowl judgments lead quickly to the end, there are other details about the tribulation period that God wants John to include in his prophecy. These are covered in chapters 11-14.

Life **stEP**

"For we walk by faith and not by sight" (2 Corinthians 5:7). It would be great if God told us everything, but then we would not be practicing a "faith walk" if we already knew everything.

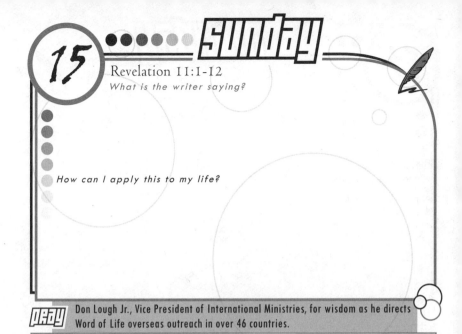

15 · SUNDAY

Revelation 11:1-12

What is the writer saying?

How can I apply this to my life?

PRAY Don Lough Jr., Vice President of International Ministries, for wisdom as he directs Word of Life overseas outreach in over 46 countries.

Some theologians argue that the Book of Revelation was written prior to the A.D. 70 destruction of the temple and that most of the prophecies herein were fulfilled in A.D. 70. They see no future Jewish Temple. However, in 2 Thessalonians 2:4, Paul envisions worship of the antichrist in the temple. Since this did not happen in A.D. 70, it must be a future event. "Measuring" implies ownership and authority. God lays claim to the temple even while predicting its desecration. It would seem that the "42 months" refers to the second half of the tribulation while the "1260 days" refers to the first half. For the first 3½ years of the tribulation, the two witnesses will preach in Jerusalem. This is the same length of time as Jesus' public ministry. They will be invincible until it is God's time for their martyrdom by the Antichrist as he dominates Jerusalem for the second half of the tribulation. Verse 4 uses the imagery of Zechariah 4:1-14. Elijah announced a drought on Israel and called fire down from heaven. He is also the predicted forerunner of Christ (Malachi 4:5). Moses is also mentioned in Malachi 4:4 along with "Mt. Horeb" (Mt. Sinai) which both men visited in their ministries. Both men also appeared with Christ on the Mount of Transfiguration. They are good candidates for the two witnesses. The "Beast" is defined as the antichrist in Revelation 13:1-18. The abyss defines his satanic origins and perhaps a resurrection from a mortal wound. The whole world will know of the two witnesses' death and will rejoice. Today satellite TV makes this possible. In earlier times, ambassadors in Jerusalem from every nation would have made this possible. They do not rise until the fourth day proving that indeed they were dead and that this is a supernatural resurrection.

Why does the world hate us so much? It is because their father, Satan, hates our Savior, Jesus Christ.

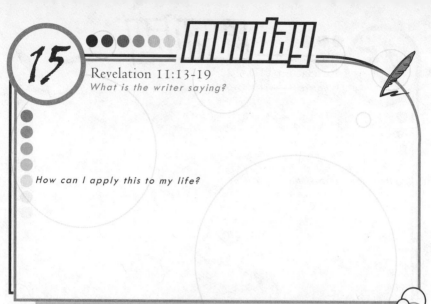

Revelation 11:13-19

What is the writer saying?

How can I apply this to my life?

PRAY Czech Republic — For increased growth and depth within Bible-believing churches.

An earthquake accompanies the resurrection of these martyrs, as was the case with the death of Christ and the resurrection of some Jerusalem believers (Matthew 27:50-54). The resurrection of the two witnesses, like all miracles in the Bible, is a sign of God's existence, power, and authority. Even unbelievers are moved to worship. Verse 15 beautifully describes the majesty of God and rings in our ears as the "Hallelujah Chorus" in George Frederick Handel's oratorio, "The Messiah." Some ancient manuscripts do not contain the future tense "art to come" in verse 17. While His future existence is certain, to leave out the explicit statement might be a purposeful literary devise implying that this great person "which art" and "wast" will certainly exist into eternity. As the impending doom of sinners and the sin-cursed earth is announced, John sees into the inner sanctum, the Holy of Holies in heaven, where the ark of the covenant is kept. In the earthly tabernacle and temple, only one man, the high priest, could enter the Holy of Holies and only on one day per year. Even then it took elaborate preparations and animal sacrifices to open the door to the presence of God. On the day that Christ died, that doorway curtain was ripped from top (heaven) to bottom indicating that man now has free access into God's presence through the death of Christ. Perhaps this is why so many priests believed (Acts 6:7). Here in Revelation 11:19, the Holy of Holies is open in judgment. The ark of the covenant ("testimony" and "testament" are equivalent to "covenant") contained in the Law of Moses. Mankind is about to be judged by the Law.

Life stEP

Gifted men can write amazing stories in moving detail, but the storyline and phrasing of these verses seem beyond mere mortal invention. Only a supreme being could create such an amazing description of the transition from the "age of God's absolute rule" on planet earth.

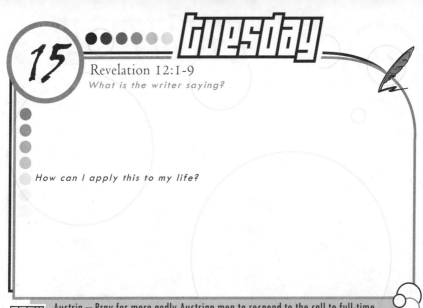

What is the writer saying?

How can I apply this to my life?

pray Austria — Pray for more godly Austrian men to respond to the call to full-time Christian service.

Chapter 12 adds more actors and activities to the tribulation story. The man-child is obviously Jesus so the woman would then represent the nation of Israel. This is affirmed by the 12 stars, which would represent the 12 tribes of Israel. In the Joseph story in Genesis, the sun and moon represented Joseph's father (Jacob) and mother (Rachel). The red dragon is obviously Satan (and so identified in v. 9). He appears as a serpent in Genesis. The color red may reflect Egyptian mythology that featured a fearsome red crocodile. The "stars" swept from heaven may refer to the angels that joined Satan's rebellion (v. 9). If so, then we would have the added bit of information that 33% of the angels followed Satan becoming "demons."

Revelation 12 is the first of several passages that speaks of Satan's end-time kingdom as composed of ten or seven countries/kings. Daniel 7:7-8 teaches that ten confederated kings will be dominated by Satan's antichrist who eliminates three

of them leaving seven kings over ten territories. In a parallel description in Revelation 13:1 there are ten horns, seven heads, and ten crowns instead of the seven crowns mentioned here in Revelation 12. Another important observation from this chapter is the freedom with which the prophecies jump around the timeline. For instance, from 5a to 5b we jump from Jesus' birth to His ascension (33 years). From 5b to 6 we jump over the entire Church Age (1970+ years) to the tribulation period. We can conclude that biblical prophecy does not have to be strictly chronological or inclusive. Verses 7-9 would seem to be a mid-tribulation event providing the reason why the second half is more intense than the first half of the tribulation. "Devil" means, "slander." "Satan" means "accuser." He is the original and master deceiver. Verse 6 describes what Israel does to escape the dragon, namely, hide in the wilderness for the last half of the tribulation.

God has a master plan and He is in control of even His enemies.

How can I apply this to my life?

PRAY Slovakia — God to mobilize broadcasters committed to producing programming in the Roma language.

Satan has a number of "falls" in Scripture. First, he fell from holiness when he rebelled against God. Next, he fell when the disciples were ministering during the time of Christ (Luke 10:18). He fell at the cross and Resurrection. Here he falls as he is cast out of heaven and limited to the earth for the duration of the tribulation period. He is a false high priest as he accuses the saints before the heavenly throne instead of interceding for them the way our Great High Priest does (Hebrews 4:14, Romans 11:2). Zechariah 13:8 indicates that 66% of all the Jews, at least of those living in Israel, will be killed by the Antichrist. According to Daniel 11:41, the countries of Edom and Moab will not be conquered by the Antichrist, making this wilderness region around the Dead Sea a safe place for the Jews. Notice another way to refer to half of the tribulation period: "time" (1) + "times" (2) + "half a time" (½) = 3½ years. The region around the Dead Sea is very rugged with many valleys and mountains.

Edom was noted for trusting in her mountain fortress (Obadiah 3). Edom (now in the country of Jordan) has whole cities carved out of the side of the mountains such as Petra, the Rose City. The area geographically has been called the "back door" of Israel, the place to flee to when danger comes in the "front door" (from the Mediterranean). Herod the Great had several mountain retreats throughout this region. The wilderness is also a dry place, unable to support many citizens, so it is a place to get away and be alone. Many churches had monasteries in the wilderness during the Middle Ages. The locals were also afraid of the demons they thought lived in the wilderness. To this day, every year several people are killed in flash floods as they are trapped in steep ravines when a sudden rain comes.

Life stEP

There are four women in Revelation. Two are evil (Jezebel and the Harlot) and two are good (the woman and the bride). Which two appeal to you?

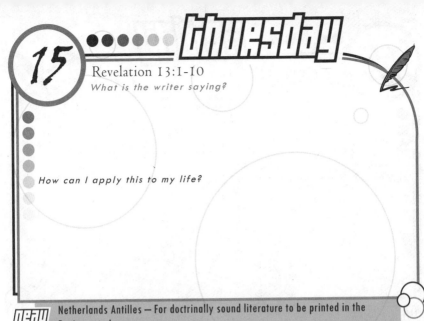

thursday

15

Revelation 13:1-10

What is the writer saying?

How can I apply this to my life?

pray Netherlands Antilles — For doctrinally sound literature to be printed in the Papiamento language.

The Greek word for "sea" is the same word translated "abyss" in Revelation 11:7 and 17:8. In context, "abyss" refers to the lower parts of hades from which satanic evil emerges. Here it clearly refers to watery depths, but elsewhere the watery sea is a symbol of the Gentile nations in sinful turmoil (Luke 21:25). The beast is a symbol of both the kingdom of the antichrist and the Antichrist himself. That the beast comes out of the sea indicates its Gentile (European) roots. The ten horns and crowns refer to the ten European (former Roman Empire) nations that the Antichrist controls.

"Blasphemy" refers to the Antichrist's claim of deity. Even in Roman times the emperors were worshiped as gods. The Emperor Domitian called himself "Dominus et Deus noster" ("Our Lord and God"). The description of the beast in verse 2 is similar to the description of the terrible fourth composite beast in Daniel 7:7. "Fatal" (v. 3)

is the same word describing the slain lamb in Revelation 5:6. It can refer to the death of the Antichrist or a crushing military defeat from which he miraculously recovers. This "resurrection" would be at the midpoint of the tribulation period as he then is dominant for the next 42 months (v. 5, cf. 11:2). "Who can wage war with him?" is a rhetorical question but it will receive an answer in chapter 14, tribulation saints can!

The book of life (v. 8) is patterned after the typical citizen's lists of the ancient cities. All citizens were listed until they died, then their names were erased. Honored citizens were even inscribed in gold lettering. Verse 9 contains a sentence repeated seven times in Revelation 2-3, but now has one phrase missing, "...what the Spirit saith unto the churches." This strongly implies that the church is no longer on the planet and that these saints should be identified as "Tribulation saints," not "church saints."

 Life **stEP**   Even in the world's darkest hour it is clear that God is still in control and that His people will be remembered and protected.

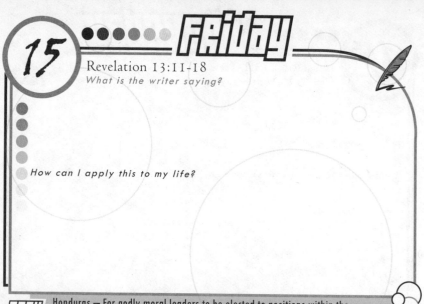

15

FRIDAY

Revelation 13:11-18

What is the writer saying?

How can I apply this to my life?

PRAY — Honduras — For godly moral leaders to be elected to positions within the government.

This section introduces a second beast, the "false prophet." His job is to promote the Antichrist. He comes from the "earth." Since "the land" in Scripture often refers to "the land of Israel," this description may indicate that the false prophet comes from Israel. We now have three main characters in Revelation 13. The dragon is Satan, "the father." The first beast is Antichrist, "the son." The false prophet, "the unholy spirit," completes Satan's counterfeit trinity. This "false prophet" also illustrates Satan's desire to imitate the messianic offices of prophet, priest, and king. The false prophet calls down fire from heaven like the two witnesses did in Revelation 11. Ezekiel 38 also predicts the use of fire to destroy an enemy of Israel during the tribulation period. Perhaps the false prophet is also claiming that the Antichrist defeated this enemy of Israel.

Believers are warned in Deuteronomy 13:1-3 to ignore miracles if they lead to the worship of other gods. The false prophet will oversee an image of the Antichrist which Matthew 24:15 and 2 Thessalonians 2:4 indicate will be placed in the temple in Jerusalem. Those who refuse to worship the image of the Antichrist by taking a distinguishing mark will not be able to buy food. They will also be liable for immediate execution.

The ancients used images to represent the power of a king, sometimes using tricks such as ventriloquism to manipulate the citizens. Even modern societies are fascinated with the image of a respected leader whether it is a painting, statue, or even the preserved body (cf. Lenin and Mao). Computer technology would certainly accomplish what is described here, but Satan could also use demons to control people.

Life stEP

The infamous "mark of the beast" will certainly mean something to the believers who are on the planet at that time. For us, the best we can say is that "seven" is the number of perfection. "777" would then represent the trinity. Satan's unholy trinity is less: "666."

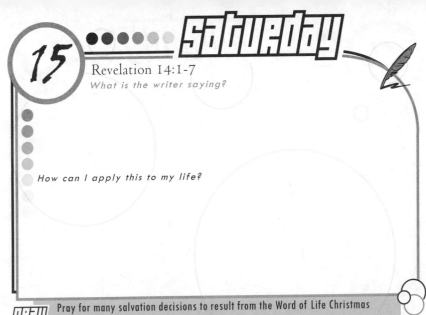

15

Revelation 14:1-7

What is the writer saying?

How can I apply this to my life?

PRAY Pray for many salvation decisions to result from the Word of Life Christmas presentation in Florida.

In answer to the question, Who is like unto the beast? Who is able to make war with him? (v. 13:4) Revelation 14 presents the 144,000. Instead of the mark of the beast (v. 13:16) they have God's name on their forehead. The lamb with them would be the "lamb as it had been slain" of Revelation 5:6. "Sion" refers to the temple mount specifically but Jerusalem in general. Powerful sounds emanate from heaven honoring their testimony. The four beasts (cherubim) and 24 elders (representative Old Testament and New Testament saints) of Revelation 4 are there worshiping. The 144,000 are called "virgins" (v. 4). This could be physically true, although since Hebrews 13:4 says that the marriage bed is "not defiled," this might be a reference to spiritual purity. They did not defile themselves by association with Jezebel (v. 2:20). They are "first fruits." This is a reference to the religious practice of giving some of the first grain to ripen to the Lord as thanks for the full harvest to follow. These 144,000 do not represent all the humans who are saved during the tribulation period, but rather the first group to be saved with many more to come. Deceit does not exist in their lives (as opposed to Satan). They are blameless (as opposed to the beast and false prophet).

The word "gospel" means "good news." There are several "gospels" in the Bible. For salvation effectiveness they all rely on the cross work of Jesus Christ. However, they emphasize different aspects of God's good news for humanity. The gospel of the kingdom in Matthew is "Repent: for the kingdom of heaven is at hand." The Gospel of the Church Age is the death, burial, and resurrection of Jesus Christ (1 Corinthians 15:3-5). Here, the emphasis of the gospel of the tribulation period is "Repent, you have offended the Creator God."

Life st**EP**

What a rude awakening when arrogant sinners are brought face to face with God their maker!

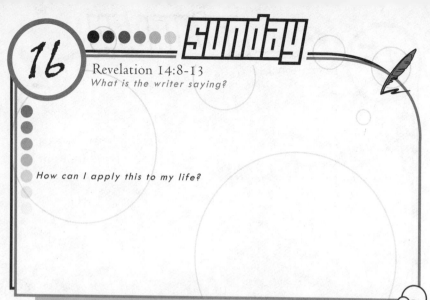

Revelation 14:8-13
What is the writer saying?

How can I apply this to my life?

PRAY Spain — Wisdom for pastors ministering in a society staggering under drug abuse, unemployment, and gambling addiction.

Chapter 14 is actually a review of the entire tribulation period. In verses 1-7 we are re-introduced to the 144,000 Jewish evangelists, the message they preach, and the worship their lives will produce in heaven. In verses 8-13, we are reminded of the predicted defeat of all of God's enemies and the ultimate vindication of all the saints. This is the first of six references to "Babylon" in Revelation. Genesis 10:10 is the first mention of Babylon (as "Babel") where we are told that the city was founded by Nimrod. In Jewish legends, Nimrod was the inventor of polytheism. The Greek historian Herodotus (c. 450 B.C.) also claimed that Babylon was the source of polytheism. The next mention of Babel is in Genesis 11. After the flood, Noah's family was commanded to spread out across the face of the earth. Instead, some descendants decided to try to maintain their unity by building a tower

on the flat plain of Babylon. Ever since Genesis 11, Babylon has been a symbol of man's government in rebellion against God. The early church referred to the Roman government as "Babylon" (1 Peter 5:13). Therefore, Babylon probably refers to the government of the Antichrist. In Revelation 17-18 this will have political, economic, and religious aspects as the Antichrist seeks to develop a unified world governmental system.

Ancient wine was cut 50-66% before being used as a daily beverage. The wrath of God against sinners will not be diluted (v. 10). There are some verses in the Bible that could be understood to teach that sinners are burnt up and go out of existence when they are cast into hell (theologically, this is called the "Annihilation Theory"). Here in 14:11 it is clear that not only is their status permanent, but their conscious punishment is also never ending.

God has the power to stop persecution. He clearly chooses not to for His own purposes, but notice His compassion and encouraging words for those who must endure a brief moment of affliction for His namesake.

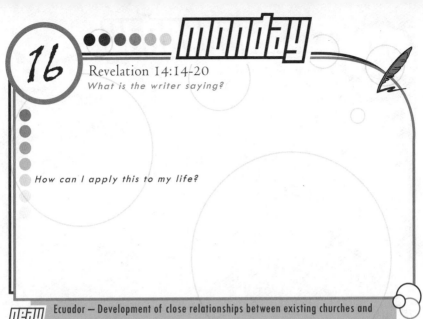

monday

16

Revelation 14:14-20

What is the writer saying?

How can I apply this to my life?

PRAY Ecuador — Development of close relationships between existing churches and new missionaries.

The tribulation review in chapter 14 concludes with the battle of Armageddon at the second coming of Jesus Christ. The "white cloud" and title "Son of Man" come from Daniel 7:13-14. "White" speaks of purity. "Clouds" are often associated with the glory of God. "Son of man" was Christ's favorite title for Himself. He used it twice as often as any other title (e.g., "Son of God"). "Son of" means "characterized by." This is demonstrated in the response the Jews had to Christ's claim to be the "Son of God" (i.e., "characterized by deity"). They hated Him for making that claim and called it blasphemous. "Son of Man" identifies Jesus with us; he is a man like we are.

God the Father in the heavenly temple sends an angel to tell Jesus to start the final harvest. "Ripe" (v. 15) is the word for "over-ripe" such as sun-dried "golden waves of grain." The "sickle" (v. 16)

would be the large instrument used for harvesting grain. The next "sickle" (v. 17) would be a smaller instrument, designed for cutting grape stems. "Fully ripe" (v. 18) means "peak condition" and for grapes would mean "full of juice." The juicy clusters of grapes represent sinful humanity with their life-preserving blood. In ancient times, grapes were thrown into large stone vats with a framework overhead from which straps hung. The unmarried men and women would remove their sandals, hike their robes, hang onto the straps, and crush the grapes as they joyously stamped to music. In this final judgment, the blood of Christ's enemies will flow the entire length of the land of Israel (about 200 miles). A horse's bridle stands about 4.5 feet from the ground. Assuming a literal river of blood about five feet wide, these dimensions would require about one billion people.

Life **stEP**   While God is a loving God, He also is a just God. While gruesome, the judgment of sinners is legally and eternally just for they deserve the punishment that they receive.

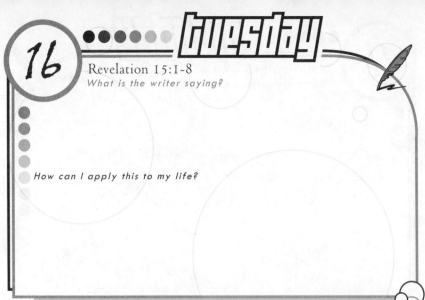

Revelation 15:1-8

What is the writer saying?

How can I apply this to my life?

Chapter 15 re-introduces the last series of judgments. In Revelation 10:6 and 7 we were told these judgments will come quickly, be intense, and climax the tribulation period. However, as a literary device, God keeps us in suspense through chapters 11, 12, 13, and 14. The sea of glass would magnify all the colors and lights in heaven. That "fire" is reflected from the sea of glass heightens the sense of impending doom and judgment. The martyrs sing the "song of Moses." Moses created two songs in his public ministry.

Exodus 15 praises God for the safe and miraculous exodus from Egypt. Deuteronomy 32 covers all of Israel's history up to Moses' day. Here they not only praise God for His attributes, but as fitting to the context, they specifically praise Him for His intent to judge their enemies. John sees the temple in heaven open. The inside is described as the "tabernacle." This word means "tent" or "dwelling place." It underscores the fact that in the tabernacle and later in the temple built by Solomon, God dwelt with His people. He was present in the Holy of Holies, residing above the ark of the covenant (testimony) between the two sculpted cherubim. The top of the ark was called the mercy seat because on the day of Atonement (Yom Kippur) the "covering" blood was sprinkled on the top and God was "satisfied" ("propitiated") that the just price for sin had been paid. Here we see mercy and punishment emanating from the same location. The seven angels are dressed like priests indicating that their job of judging was a holy, priestly job. One of the four beasts (cherubim) passes out the seven bowls of wrath. The temple is filled with smoke, as it had been with God's glory cloud when Solomon dedicated his temple in his day (1 Kings 8:10-11). The temple is then closed until the job is complete.

God's payday is coming some day. We might be frustrated now with the arrogance of sinful man, but God's longsuffering will come to an end.

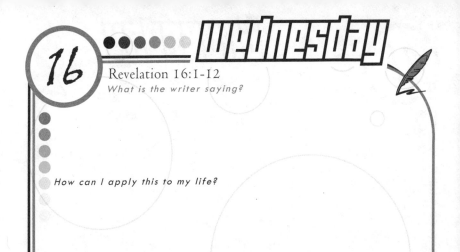

wednesday

16

Revelation 16:1-12

What is the writer saying?

How can I apply this to my life?

PRAY Germany — For youth ministries to develop creative and relevant means of sharing the Gospel.

The first four bowl judgments parallel the first four trumpet judgments, although they are more devastating. In the trumpet sequence, only one third of each category was damaged. In the bowl sequence there is total destruction in each category. The first bowl produces horrible skin eruptions on all the beast worshipers. The second bowl kills all life living in salt water by making the water coagulate like blood does. The third bowl kills all life living in fresh water by turning it into blood. The saints and angels in heaven find this particularly appropriate since the beast worshipers were so quick to shed the blood of God's saints. The fourth bowl intensifies the effects of the sun. This may just be increased heat or it could include the damage produced by unblocked ultraviolet light as well. Not only does ultraviolet light increase the incidence of skin cancer, but it also hastens cataract formation, inhibits crop growth, and damages plankton in the sea. Sinful humanity refuses to acknowledge God's hand in these events and repent. Perhaps they think these are natural disasters or the result of human (nuclear?) warfare. While perhaps not believing in God they still use His name in their curses!

The fifth bowl plunges the world into a tormented darkness. Perhaps the pain is psychological (fear and dread). Or maybe they stumble around hurting themselves even more. Or perhaps the darkness lets them sit still and concentrate on the pain of their existing wounds. The sixth bowl causes the great Euphrates River to dry up allowing troops from the east to easily march to Israel. For years now Turkey has had the power to shut off the flow of the Euphrates with a system of hydroelectric dams. This is also predicted in Isaiah 11:15.

One of the necessary features of "freewill" is that it is free to be totally irrational. Man's depravity produces the most illogical response, which leads to eternal loss.

thursday

16

Revelation 16:13-21

What is the writer saying?

How can I apply this to my life?

pray El Salvador — For godly leadership training; war, lack of finances, and lack of staff has crippled efforts.

Frogs are "unclean animals" (Leviticus 11:10). These demonic frogs perform "sign-miracles" to convince the kings of the earth to come to Israel. The phrase "I come as a thief" is never used in Scripture of the Rapture. It always is used of the judgments associated with the day of the Lord in general or the second coming specifically ("great day of God Almighty" and "Battle of Armageddon," vv. 14, 16). The word "thief" refers to a "cat burglar," not an armed robber (hence the popular phrase, "thief in the night"). Even after all these "signs of the times," the unsaved at the end of the tribulation period will still be caught off-guard by the appearance of Christ, "the thief." The surviving saints, however, will discern the times and welcome their Messiah. "Armageddon" comes from two words, "Har" ("mountain") and "Megiddo" ("place of troops"). Megiddo was the name of a strategic city that controlled the roadway through the Carmel mountain range into the huge Jezreel ("God Sows") Valley. It is in the shape of a triangle about 20 miles on a side. It also goes by the name "Plain of Esdraelon" (Greek form of "Jezreel"). It has always been a fertile valley. The earliest battle in human history with recorded details (on the walls of the Temple of Karnack in Thebes, Egypt) occurred there between the Canaanites and Thutmose III around 1450 B.C. During the time of the judges, Barak and Deborah fought the Canaanites there, who were led by Sisera, the man eventually killed by Jael as she drove a nail through his head while he slept. Gideon also defeated the Midianites in this valley. Unlike the seal judgments and the trumpet judgments, the seventh bowl judgment is a specific judgmental event. It caps all the judgments with the worst earthquake this old world has ever seen. In addition, 100-pound hailstones rain down on what remains of the earth.

The final conflict leads to eternal victory for the people of God and His Christ.

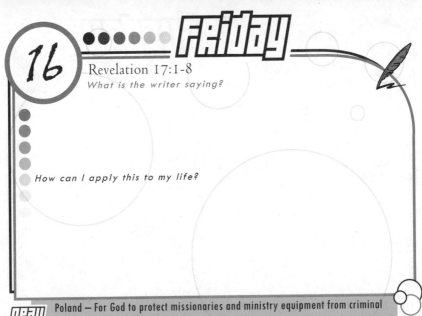

Revelation 17:1-8

What is the writer saying?

How can I apply this to my life?

pray Poland — For God to protect missionaries and ministry equipment from criminal activity.

In Revelation 13 the beast represents the Antichrist and his kingdom. Here a woman rides the beast, which is now described as a "scarlet" beast. Isaiah 1:18 likens the stain of sin to "scarlet" and "crimson." She is an immoral woman and has immoral connections with all the kings of the earth. She is symbolically named Babylon. In the Old Testament, God likened the pagan religions to strange lovers and accused Israel of spiritual adultery when she went after the other gods (Ezekiel 23:37). The woman is dressed like royalty. Purple traditionally has been the color of kings because the color was so expensive to produce. It took 10,000 murex shellfish to produce one ounce of the colorfast purple dye. "Mystery" probably refers to the deceitfulness and treachery of false teaching. She is "the great" because of the size of her organization, activities and the extent of her apostasy. 2 Thessalonians 2:3 indicates that the revelation of the Antichrist will be accompanied by "the falling away (apostasy)." She is the "mother" of harlots and abominations as the source and greatest offender. In addition to false teaching and immorality, she is guilty of murdering those who love the Lord. John is puzzled and the angel begins to explain the scene. He first describes the beast. Satan loves to counterfeit Christ's program in an attempt to replace it. Note the similarities between Revelation 17:8 (describing the antichrist) and Revelation 1:18 (describing Christ). Both have a "death," "burial," and "resurrection." In the tribulation period, the Antichrist will start to organize his kingdom in the first half (v. 8, "was"). He will then be killed or suffer a devastating political setback ("and is not"). He will descend into hades, be indwelt by Satan, and then "arise" to renew his goal of world domination ("and yet is").

Life stEP

"Good" people are not necessarily holy. Some of the greatest evils are done in the name of or hiding behind God.

Revelation 17:9-18

What is the writer saying?

How can I apply this to my life?

Revelation 17:3 says that the woman is sitting on the beast with seven heads. Verse 9 says she is sitting on seven mountains. Both "heads" and "mountains" are used symbolically of kings or governments elsewhere (cf. Isaiah 14:13; Ezekiel 35:2; Daniel 2:44-45, 7:6). They could be simultaneous and in fact the horns and crowns (12:3, 13:1) do seem to refer to contemporary associates of the Antichrist. They could also be sequential and that seems to be the case here. "Five are fallen" (v. 10) in Israel's history would be Egypt, Assyria, Babylon, Persia, and Greece. "One is" in A.D. 95 would be Rome. "The other is not yet come" would be the revival of Rome under the Antichrist. "He must continue a short space" refers to the first half of the tribulation before the Antichrist is "killed." Notice that there is a connection between the "seventh" and the "eighth." The Antichrist is also the "eighth" as the satanically indwelt "resurrected" wonder for the second half of the tribulation period.

The number ten is interesting. In Jewish thought, her enemies come in groups of ten (cf. Genesis 15:19-21; Psalm 83:6-8; Jeremiah 41:1). Revived Rome under the Antichrist will probably control the same territory as ancient Rome. Rome controlled all of Western Europe to the Rhine and Danube Rivers. She controlled northern Africa and the Middle East to Euphrates. The Mediterranean was the "Roman Lake." The Antichrist and his associates use the woman until they have no more need for her and then they discard her. If she represents a false religious system, then her destruction would take place at the middle of the Tribulation when the Antichrist enters the temple for the world to worship him.

Life stEP

There was a time when the Vatican was the most powerful city in Europe. For a short time, another religious center will have temporal power.

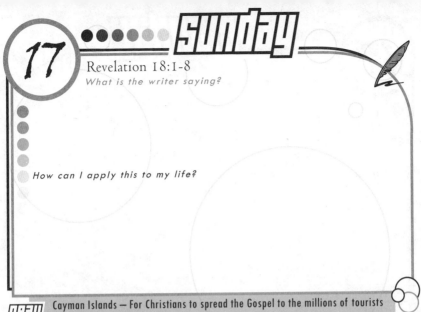

17

SUNDAY

Revelation 18:1-8

What is the writer saying?

How can I apply this to my life?

pray Cayman Islands — For Christians to spread the Gospel to the millions of tourists that pass through each year.

Chapter 17 seems to emphasize the religious aspect of "Babylon" as the Antichrist's ecumenical movement, the "One-World Church." Even so, 17:18 still maintains the political connection, as does 18:2 where "Babylon" is viewed as a place where things live. It would seem that chapter 18 emphasizes the political and economic influence of this "city." It is not unusual for a literal city to also represent a philosophy, way of life or, entire government. Therefore, we can't say whether the passage is referring to the ancient geographic location of the city of Babylon (somewhat restored in modern Iraq), or a religious center (The Vatican or Jerusalem), or a region (the European Union), or a commercial center (New York City), or the evil system in general. Just as God urged Lot to flee Sodom, believers are warned to vacate corrupt Babylon (v. 4). Babylon smugly says to herself that she will never be a widow or mourn, implying that her husband (the Antichrist?

Satan?) will always be a victorious soldier. It is fitting that on October 12, 539 B.C. the ancient city of Babylon fell "in one day" as Cyrus of the Persians diverted the river that ran under her walls and sent soldiers into the city by way of the riverbed. At the second coming of Christ, He will speak and the Antichrist and the false prophet will be thrown alive into Hell. The armies will be killed and in a brief period of time, "Babylon" will be punished with utter destruction. Nimrod ("he rebelled") founded Babylon. He is called a "mighty hunter before the Lord" (Genesis 10:9). The phrase can also mean "against the Lord." Legends claim he was the first idol worshiper and that after his death his wife, Semiramis, miraculously conceived and bore Tammuz, his reincarnation. She was the original "mother goddess." From Babylon spread this cultic idea, which was eventually absorbed into Roman Catholicism with the adoration of Mary and the Christ child.

 Life stEP

Satan's program changes shape over time but is still recognizable.

163

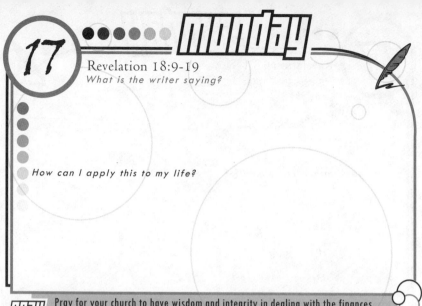

17

monday

Revelation 18:9-19

What is the writer saying?

How can I apply this to my life?

pray Pray for your church to have wisdom and integrity in dealing with the finances entrusted to it.

The destruction of the kingdom of the Antichrist and the city that represents his achievements is greatly lamented by those who benefited from her financially. The items listed are typical of any great port city in the first century. John spent time at Ephesus and certainly would have firsthand knowledge of these pleasant, desirable, and decadent luxuries. Since this is a vision and is designed to convey truth through "signs" or symbols, we do not need to imagine each detail happening only as it is described here. The fulfillment will be even more involved than the details provided in this selective report. For instance, it says that the kings of the earth stand a way off from her and lament her destruction. This does not necessitate that every king be present. That others would eventually hear the news or view it on television and

mourn would also be included. The implication is that the devastation is so great that whomever was present would react the way these kings and merchants react. This concept would also apply if "Babylon" were not just one city, but representative of the whole kingdom of the Antichrist. As the news gets out about the kingdom's destruction and the inability of the Antichrist to benefit the economies of the world, the whole world slips into depression and mourning. Notice that the destruction is sudden and completed in a short amount of time (v. 10). "Thyine wood" is a dark hardwood used by the ancients for fine furniture. Cinnamon is interesting because in the ancient world it was only grown and exported from Southeast Asia indicating the amazing trade network in John's day.

Life stEP

In addition to all the products, God curiously adds the "souls of men." Is this an elaboration on the horrors of slavery, or is it a frank admission that Babylon as the source of ancient polytheism and the seat of the Antichrist's false religion was a trafficker in the very souls of men?

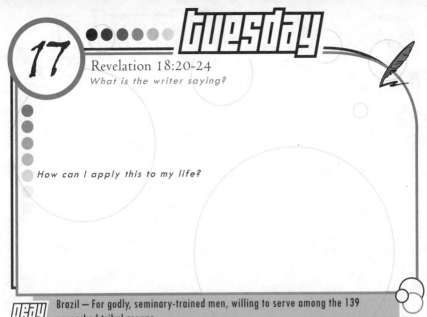

Revelation 18:20-24

What is the writer saying?

How can I apply this to my life?

pray Brazil — For godly, seminary-trained men, willing to serve among the 139 unreached tribal groups.

While sinners lament on earth, the halls of heaven ring with praise for the destruction of this icon of Satan's attempt to overthrow the kingdom of God. "Apostles" ("sent ones") only appear in the New Testament. "Prophets" appear in both. Satan has motivated the death of both in history, but in the context it seems to be referring to people living during the tribulation period. The two prophets certainly would be avenged by this destruction. Perhaps the 144,000 would be considered "apostles" in the sense that they were "sent" on their mission and supernaturally protected as they performed their ministry. We must be careful how we express this because the "office of apostle" is defined as someone who had seen the resurrected Lord (Acts 1:22) and performed miraculous signs (2 Corinthians 12:12). This office was limited to the early church as we are built on the foundation of the apostles and prophets (Ephesians 2:20).

A heavy stone thrown violently into the sea represents the violent overthrow of Babylon. In addition to earthquakes and volcanoes, modern man is concerned about devastating tsunamis (tidal waves). A wall of water from a sudden shock (landslide, earthquake, or asteroid strike) sends a swell of water outward. In open water the wave does not look like much, but great volumes of water moving at hundreds of miles per hour grow to high walls of water in the shallow coastal areas and violently strike the shore. John is told that joyful sounds will be silenced in that doomed city. Even everyday work sounds, like the grinding of grain, will cease. Babylon will be erased from the earth and from the memory of man. "Sorceries" refers to the magical (demonic) arts, but is the translation of the Greek word "pharmakeia," the root for the English word "pharmaceuticals." Mind-altering drugs are part of Satan's arsenal.

 Life stEP Satan was a murderer from the beginning. His world system continued that character flaw but now, hallelujah, she is no more.

Revelation 19:1-8

What is the writer saying?

How can I apply this to my life?

PRAY For Word of Life missionaries who will be separated from family and friends this Christmas season.

"Hallelujah" ("alleluia") is such a popular word of praise that it is hard to believe that it only occurs in one chapter in all the New Testament: Revelation 19. There are four hallelujahs: one for salvation (v. 1), one for judgment (v. 3), one for worship (v. 4), and a final one for the sovereignty of God in all these judgments (v. 6). In these verses we have the answer to the question asked by the souls of the martyrs under the altar in Revelation 6:10, "And they cried with a loud voice, saying, How long, O Lord, holy and true, dost thou not judge and avenge our blood on them that dwell on the earth?" The 24 elders and four beasts of chapter 4 are still part of the story, here worshiping God in the courts of heaven. We can't tell who the owner of the voice is. It could be one of the four beasts or an unnamed angel. "Our God" almost implies a human, which would be one of the 24 elders, but Revelation 7:12 has the four beasts using the phrase "our God" in worship. "Omnipotence" ("all powerfulness") requires demonstration, otherwise it can't be known by others. It is now an observable characteristic of human affairs. God is obviously on the throne and His will will be done on earth as it is in heaven. It is announced that the "marriage of the Lamb" is come. His bride is ready, not just willing but also spiritually qualified. She had been impure, but as a redeemed individual her past has been forgiven and forgotten. She is given white clothing to illustrate her purity. What does the fashion-conscious person wear in heaven? They wear white trimmed with white and with white accessories!

Life stEP

Nothing can match the beauty and excitement of a bride on her wedding day. What a day that will be when our Savior we will see and our Bridegroom He will be.

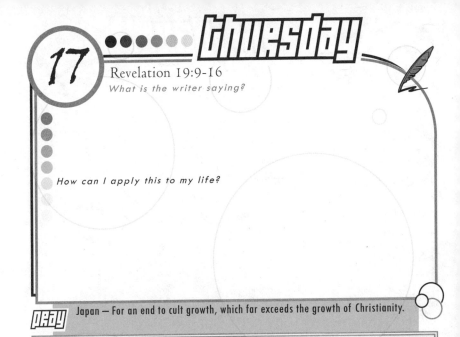

How can I apply this to my life?

The person talking is not identified beyond the statement that he is a fellow servant and not worthy of the worship due God. He is an angel. Angelic guides are a normal feature of Jewish prophetic literature (cf. Zechariah 1:19; 2:3; 4:1). The angel tells John that those called unto the "marriage supper of the Lamb" are blessed. This, in effect, is what the two witnesses and 144,000 will be doing for the entire seven years of the tribulation period. The "marriage of the Lamb" (v. 7) takes place at the Rapture of the church. In ancient Jewish weddings, for the first seven days after the wedding, the bride was kept in seclusion. At the end of that week, the groom would proudly bring her out of the bridal chamber and introduce her to the wedding guests. They would then enjoy another week of celebration with their guests.

At the second coming of Christ, the bride of Christ will return to the planet to reign with Him. Those who accept Christ as their Savior during the Tribulation will be "friends of the bridegroom," a designation that John the Baptist used of himself (John 3:29). They will enter the messianic kingdom and rejoice, as the marriage supper of the Lamb will be the first order of business when the 1000-year reign begins. The "spirit" of prophecy refers to its ultimate purpose. The ultimate purpose of the "revelation" of Jesus Christ is the unveiling of His glorious person for all to admire and worship. Revelation 19:11-16 describes this wonderful person as He returns to take possession of His rightful property as per the title deed of chapter 5, namely, planet earth. A secret name (v. 12) implies that even in the next mode of existence there will be mysteries to explore and learn. Christ returns to the planet like a Roman general in a triumphal parade of "spoils" before his adoring countrymen. He has His title on His thigh, where a Roman would wear his weapon, the sword.

Life stEP

What a day that will be when the rightful heir returns to His throne.

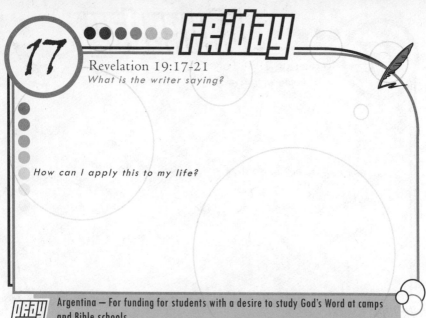

17

Friday

Revelation 19:17-21

What is the writer saying?

How can I apply this to my life?

PRAY Argentina — For funding for students with a desire to study God's Word at camps and Bible schools.

The imagery in Revelation is calculated to inspire awe. Here the angel has the sun as his backdrop implying the glory of God that cannot be directly viewed by mere mortals. Everything is done on a large scale. For the thirteenth time in the book, something is described as "loud." Another feature of inspired Scripture are the intricacies woven into the story line. In Revelation 19:9 we have an invitation to the marriage feast of the Lamb. Here in Revelation 19:17 there is an invitation to the marriage feast of the Antichrist! In this case, it is not humans but rather the carrion-eaters of the avian world that are invited. Humans are invited (16:14) but they are invited to be eaten, not eat. Every stratum of human society winds up on this gruesome banquet table. The Antichrist and false prophet escape becoming a meal only to find themselves cast alive into hell.

Revelation 19:14 pictures the armies of heaven following Christ back to the planet. This is a common Old Testament concept. "Jehovah Sabbaoth" means "Lord of Armies." "Sabbaoth" is sometimes translated "hosts" or "almighty" which obscures the point that the angels in heaven also perform a military function. Despite all this fire power, which would include both the holy angels and the Church Age saints, notice that only Christ does any fighting, and that by the spoken word. This episode is the conclusion to Satan's complicated maneuverings during the last half of the tribulation period. He has "resurrected" the Antichrist, empowering him to kill the two witnesses, to claim worship from the world, to reject the ecumenical church and to further his quest for world domination. Satan, knowing that Christ will attempt to return to the planet, wants all available fighters present. He entices the kings of the east to attack the Antichrist. As they prepare to fight each other at Armageddon, they see Christ return and join forces against Him.

All of Satan's efforts are thwarted with just the words of the Lamb.

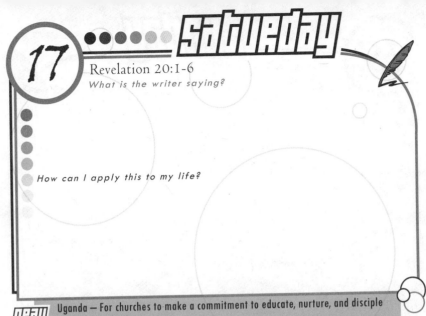

17

saturday

Revelation 20:1-6

What is the writer saying?

How can I apply this to my life?

pray Uganda — For churches to make a commitment to educate, nurture, and disciple their young people.

Satan, the mastermind, is treated with greater severity than the Antichrist. He is placed in the lowest part of hell. The chains and locked door picture maximum security. Revelation 20 is the first time in Scripture that the messianic reign is said to last for 1,000 years. All statements to this point have been open-ended. This number is repeated six times in the chapter, leading some commentators to conclude that it is to be taken as a literal, not symbolic figure. Good and godly men have argued otherwise. A popular conclusion is that the entire Church Age, at least since the A.D. 70 destruction of the temple in Jerusalem is this "1,000 year reign of Christ." They conclude that the binding of Satan is also figurative, implying a drastic restriction on his activities, but not total inability to function. This interpretation not only handles "1,000" figuratively, but

also many other statements in Scripture about the nature of the messianic reign. We then have the problem of limited men deciding that their multiple and subjective conclusions are better than a literal and objective conclusion, pointing to a specific future scenario. Since the number "1,000" is used elsewhere (Psalm 90:4) to describe the difference between man's time and God's time there is reason to believe that the number is not arbitrary but purposely chosen. God's original perfect lifespan was 1,000 years. Adam sinned and died in the "day" (less than 1,000 years) that he sinned. Now as Christ returns there is a restoration of edenic conditions including the lengthening of the human lifespan. This is reinforced by Isaiah's contention that a human struck dead by Christ for disobedience at 100 years of age has died tragically as a "child" (Isaiah 65:20).

Life stEP In Scripture there are only two options. Either we are saved and part of the "first resurrection" (Old Testament, New Testament, Tribulation and millennial saints) or we are unsaved and part of the "second death."

Revelation 20:7-15
What is the writer saying?

How can I apply this to my life?

Elsewhere in Scripture the messianic era is described as a period of blessedness for all mankind (Jew and Gentile) under the benevolent dictatorship of Jesus Christ. He will not tolerate any open rebellion. The Spirit will be poured out on all flesh, and holiness will be the hallmark of that time. Humans will enjoy freedom from disease and natural disasters. There will be no war or crime. Every human need will be met.

Despite these great conditions, there will be humans born during this long period of history who will outwardly conform, but never truly acknowledge the Lordship of Christ over their personal life. At the end of this initial phase of the messianic kingdom, Satan will be released for a brief period, enabling him one final opportunity to spark a rebellion. While seemingly unbelievable, the father of lies will once again succeed in deluding men with their inherited sin nature into joining his cause. The rebels are called "Gog and Magog." These were actual Gentile peoples first mentioned in Genesis 10 and later in Ezekiel 38. In Ezekiel 38, they are involved in an attack on Israel during the tribulation period. The occurrence of the same names does not automatically mean it is the same event. It is not unusual in secular or biblical literature to use one catastrophic human event as an illustration of another. For instance, we say that someone has "met his Waterloo" to refer to a humiliating defeat. This is based on Napoleon's defeat at Waterloo. Likewise, this post-millennial event is presented as similar to the mid-tribulation event of Ezekiel 38. They both involve treachery by Gentiles and conclude with God's enemies in flames. In preparation for "eternity" (by definition, no more babies being born to continue human history) John views the final judgments that result in sinners of all ages receiving their fair trial and assigned degrees of punishment in hell.

Life stEP

If you can't make fire fall from heaven and He can, obey Him.

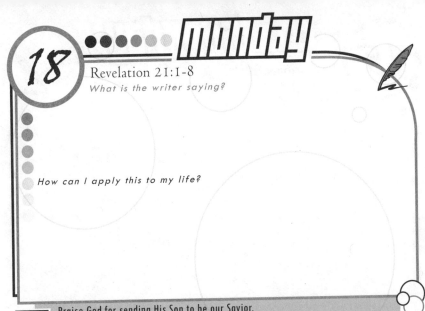

How can I apply this to my life?

pray Praise God for sending His Son to be our Savior.

Human history is complete. Sinners and saints have been evaluated, rewarded, and placed in their respective eternal homes. Several passages describe the renovation of the physical universe to purge it of all vestiges of sinful humanity (cf. 2 Peter 3:10-13). Why would God's heaven need purging? Job 1 pictures Satan and his demons coming to the halls of heaven, so even God's abode will be renovated. John views no sea in the new earth. The "sea" speaks of sinful nations in turmoil. It was also the "front door" by which evil Gentile armies entered Israel. Instead of the false religious system, the harlot of Revelation 17, we now have the New Jerusalem as a bride. Psalm 37:29 promises, "The righteous shall inherit the earth." For all eternity, "heaven" will be on earth. In the book of Hosea, God says that Israel will be "lo ammi" because of their rebellion. The phrase means, "not My people." Now (v. 3) redeemed humanity will be "ammi" ("My people"). The blessedness of heaven includes healed memories. Imagine the release a godly rape victim will experience when that horrible memory will no longer affect her. Some would argue that God has to wipe tears of regret from our eyes. Since this passage is 1007 years after the judgment seat of Christ, that would not be an appropriate conclusion. Even once safely entered into eternity, we are reminded that salvation is a free gift (v. 6). Being "fearful" (v. 8) does not seem like a gross sin worthy of eternal damnation. In context, it is referring to a lack of respect for God and the shame a sinner has in associating with Christ. This "fearful unbelief" condemns an individual to a Christ-less eternity. There are several words for after-life punishment. "Sheol" (Hebrew) and "Hades" (Greek) are the terms for the current place of punishment. Gehenna (Hebrew), hell, and the lake of fire refer to the eternal place of punishment.

Heaven will be greater and hell worse than we could ever imagine.

18 tuesday

Revelation 21:9-16

What is the writer saying?

How can I apply this to my life?

PRAY Guatemala — Reconciliation between the Mayan and Spanish-speaking believers divided by past war.

Earlier in Scripture, the church is called the bride of Christ. Here the eternal abode of the church (the New Jerusalem) is called the bride. It is a glorious sight. John chooses the prettiest gemstones of his day to describe the beauty that he sees. "Jasper" usually has some color (light green) but here it is clear like crystal (no impurities, the impurities impart the color). The city is well protected. It has a high wall, gates, and guardian angels. It is laid out in a square with three gates in each wall. On each gate is inscribed the name of one of the tribes of Israel. Each gate is made of a single pearl (v. 21). Must be amazing oysters to produce those pearls! The city has 12 foundations and on each is the name one of the 12 apostles. This very graphically indicates that while God has a separate program for Old Testament Israel and the New Testament church, both are treated equally as brothers and sisters in Christ for all eternity. The city is huge.

The conversion from reeds to miles would give 1500 miles per side. The tabernacle Holy of Holies, where the Shekinah glory of God dwelt, was a cube. Perhaps the three equal dimensions are designed to remind us of God's holiness and His presence with His people. However, the text does not require a cube. It could also be describing a pyramid (which has a square base, v. 16, and in the center rises to the same height as the length and width). Either way, this is a tremendously large object to reside on the planet. The distance of 1500 miles would be from Maine to Florida and the Atlantic to beyond the Mississippi. There are satellites that orbit the earth at an altitude of 90 miles, which makes the height of the city seem amazingly high. Physically, it would be impossible for the current earth to rotate with that lopsided weight, but of course this would be on the new earth designed for such a city.

Eye has not seen nor ear heard all that God has prepared for His saints.

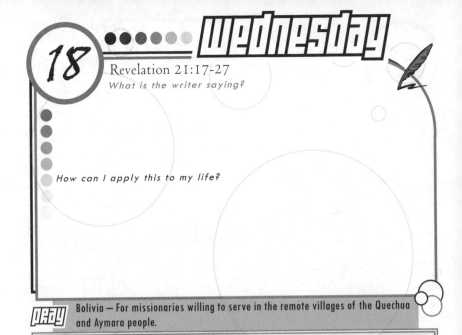

18

Revelation 21:17-27

What is the writer saying?

How can I apply this to my life?

Converting from cubits to feet, the wall would be 216 feet high. That is impressive until you imagine a building towering 1500 miles above it. Note the incidental information that angels (at least when they appear to men) are the same size as men. The wall is made of clear crystal. The city is made of gold, but it is also described as clear glass. Perhaps John is describing the purest, shiniest gold imaginable. It is from this chapter that the popular image of heaven emerges with pearly gates and streets of gold. John goes on to describe the 12 gemstones used for the foundation. The exact identities of these stones are debatable as the various types of gemstones had different names in various periods of human history. It is interesting to remember that the High Priest's breastplate also contained 12 gemstones representing the 12 tribes of Israel.

Several times in chapters 4 through 19 John saw the temple in heaven. In the new heaven, there is no need for a temple. First, everyone is saved so there is no need for the atonement represented by the temple. Second, Satan is no longer entering the courts of heaven so all of heaven itself can now be the temple without fear of any contamination.

In the new heaven there is no need for the sun or moon for God will provide the light from His person. "Gates" (v. 25) represent both access and safety. However, the city is so safe that they are never closed. The passage talks as if there are people other than the citizens of heaven living on the new earth and coming into the New Jerusalem. It is better to say that among the citizens of the New Jerusalem are kings and representatives of the various nations (Gentiles).

The Old Testament Hebrew society was agricultural, so the Old Testament pictures "heaven" as an agricultural paradise (cf. Zechariah 3:10). The New Testament Greek society honored city life, so it pictures heaven as a city. Actually, heaven will be on the new earth.

Revelation 22:1-7

What is the writer saying?

How can I apply this to my life?

pray Dominican Republic — For evangelicals to have the same freedom from legal restraints as Roman Catholics.

This sinful world is contaminated with a depressing amount of moral and ecological sewage. In heaven, the moral and ecological climate will be perfect, as pictured by the crystal-clear water flowing from the throne of God. One of the strong arguments for the intelligent design of the universe is the fine-tuning necessary to produce the narrow range of parameters in which biological life can exist. One of those important ingredients is water. A little closer or further away from the sun and our earth would not have water. A large percentage of our body mass is "just" water. We can survive for weeks without food, but only a few days without water. In our eternal home, life-giving water is in abundant supply. Apparently, our glorified bodies will process food. No mention here of beef steak, but 12 kinds of fruit sound refreshing. The tree reminds us of the Garden of Eden where man's moral problems began. One of the stated reasons for expelling fallen Adam and

Eve from the garden was to prevent them from eating of the tree of life and thereby sealing themselves in their fallen state for eternity. Now the saints have returned to Eden and can profitably eat of the tree of life. The leaves are for "healing." If heaven is perfect, why would there be a need for healing? "Healing" does not require a pre-existing sickness. It is a preventative or therapeutic health regimen.

God the Father and Jesus Christ the Lamb both have thrones and are a delight to the citizens of heaven. We will see God face to face. He will be our light. His name, instead of the mark of the beast, will be on our foreheads. The saints will reign. What will they reign over? That is one of the mysteries not revealed in Scripture. Verse 6 begins the conclusion to the whole book. The trustworthiness of the information is affirmed. Christ speaks stating that He will come "quickly" meaning that He can come at anytime, unannounced.

If these things are so, how then shall we live?

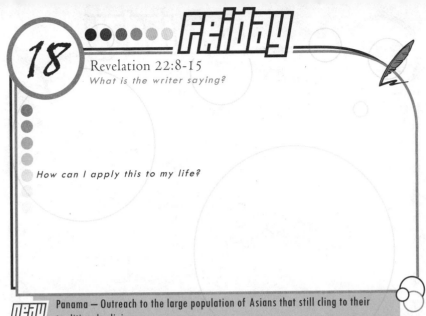

How can I apply this to my life?

John solemnly reaffirms he indeed observed and heard the prophecies that he wrote. For a second time he tries to show respect for the angel who has guided him through his vision. For a second time the angel reminds him that he is only a fellow servant and that worship should be reserved for God and God alone (cf. 19:10). The angel tells him not to keep the information private, but to share it with all believers. This is different from the command given to Daniel in Daniel 12:4, "But thou, O Daniel, shut up the words, and seal the book, even to the time of the end." The Tribulation information revealed in Daniel was not imminent since so many other things had to happen first. John's prophecy was and still is imminent in that nothing has ever had to happen first before the timeline predicted in Revelation could start. That is why the angel can say, "The time is at hand" and Christ can say, "And, behold, I come quickly." These phrases do not require that Christ come "soon," but rather that He can come at anytime, and when He comes, it will be abrupt, sudden and then all the events in the book will in succession quickly unfold. These statements of imminent divine intervention would also strengthen the warnings to the seven churches in chapters 2-3. The tribulation period might not start for 2,000 years, but Christ's chastisement upon the church at Laodicea might be fulfilled within a few years.

Verse 11 seems contradictory to God's normal challenge for sinners to repent. Perhaps it is phrased to warn that at any moment the world is liable to be swept into the final judgments and that if you want to be on the side of righteousness you need to be there today, tomorrow will be too late. Christ refers to Himself as "Alpha and Omega" (v. 13), a description that God the Father uses of Himself in Revelation 1:8.

Life stEP The company on the road to hell and outside the gates of heaven are not the sort of people that we would want to have as neighbors!

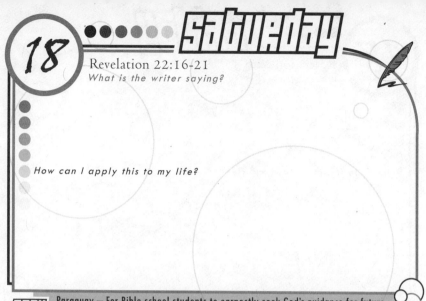

Revelation 22:16-21

What is the writer saying?

How can I apply this to my life?

pray Paraguay — For Bible school students to earnestly seek God's guidance for future areas of ministry.

It is interesting how the identity of the speaker to the reading audience changes without warning. John is writing it all down, so he is often the speaker (as in 22:8). Sometimes God the Father speaks (1:8). Sometimes Jesus speaks (vv. 16:15; 22:7, 12-13, 16, 18). The whole chain of Revelation starts with Jesus (v. 16), goes to an angel, then to John, next to the seven churches of Asia Minor, and finally, down through the centuries to us. In the Old Testament, "the branch" is a messianic title referring to the Messiah's connection with the "soil" of humanity in general and the family of David specifically (cf. Jeremiah 33:15). The "morning star" is the planet Venus because it is the brightest of the heavenly bodies after the moon and is often visible just before dawn. "Lucifer" is the Latin name for "morning star," applied to Satan in Isaiah 14:12 (in the sense that he has attempted to usurp the title). The Messiah is the "light" to the Gentiles (Isaiah 9:1-2). The "Spirit" (v. 17) is the Holy Spirit. The "bride" could be a personification of the New Jerusalem (as in 21:9), implying that the city calls out for more inhabitants. Or it could refer to believers (as in 19:7) and would be a timeless representation of one believer calling another of the elect to salvation. This is illustrated by the next phrase, "And let him that heareth say, Come." Verse 18 pronounces a curse on those who tamper with the material. Some commentators have tried to use this as proof that the Book of Revelation is the final book of inspired information in human history. However, the word "book" is the Greek word for "booklet" and therefore refers only to the Book of Revelation, not the whole Bible. In fact, an identical statement occurs in Deuteronomy 4:2 and 12:32. It obviously means that nothing should be taken away from or added to the information in that book. Only an unsaved person would do so, hence the warning of eternal damnation.

"Maranatha" (1 Corinthians 16:22) is Aramaic for "Our Lord Comes!"

1 and 2 Kings

For 120 years the Kingdom of Israel was united having three kings: Saul, David and Solomon. Saul was of the tribe of Benjamin and David and Solomon of the tribe of Judah. David's declining strength and final death is seen in the earlier chapters and the coronation of his son Solomon just prior to his death. A great part of the book deals with the reign of Solomon. After his death the sad division of the kingdom is recorded. Rehoboam ascended to the throne after Solomon and at the outset of his reign made a series of unwise and unpopular moves. In view of his folly, Jeroboam was successful in persuading the tribes to follow him. From this point on the kingdom is divided. There are two kings and later two capitals. Judah's capital remained at Jerusalem until the Babylonian captivity. Israel's capital (the ten tribes) was in Samaria until the Assyrian captivity.

The message of the book is: "Jehovah, sovereign ruler over Israel, blessed when obedient and punished when disobedient." The key phrase is "As David his Father." The key concepts are "glory" and "disruption."

The author of 1 Kings is unknown. Jewish tradition says the author was Jeremiah.

Of King Solomon, Scroggie says, "Solomon was a strange character, and he may be regarded in various ways; personally, officially and typically. Viewed personally, he was characterized by wisdom and wickedness; greatly gifted intellectually, he was very weak ethically. His mind and his morals were not on the same level. Viewed officially, his great work was two-fold: the material development of the Kingdom, and the erection of the temple. Viewed typically, it is not difficult to see an anticipation of Christ's Millennial Kingdom, when, after the extirpation of all His foes, there will be peace."

Solomon wrote 3,000 proverbs, 1005 Psalms, and three books: Proverbs, Ecclesiastes and the Song of Solomon. Both the books of Kings and Chronicles cover the same period of time. Just as the Gospels present different aspects of the ministry of our Lord, so the Kings and Chronicles give different viewpoints without contradiction. Kings gives the history of kings from the prophetic viewpoint whereas Chronicles gives the history of the kings from the priestly viewpoint.

 I and 2 kings

The Divisions of the book are:

I. The establishment of the
   kingdom   1,2
II. The glory of the kingdom
                              3-10
III. The disruption of the kingdom
                              9:12:24
IV. The decline of the kingdom
                              12:25-22

1 Kings 1:15-18, 29-37

What is the writer saying?

How can I apply this to my life?

PRAY Ukraine — For God to give youth a passion to live for Him and reach their land.

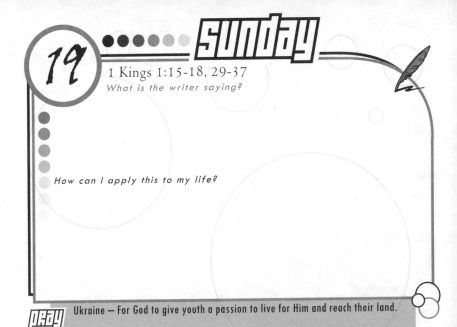

There was a serious problem. David is dying and one of his sons, Adonijah, makes a move to be accepted as king. Like his brother Absalom, he throws a great feast. It was obvious that Solomon was to be his successor; Nathan must have known it. As a prophet and aware of previous prophecies (Genesis 3:15; Genesis 49:10; Numbers 24:17; 2 Samuel 7:13) he was aware of the coming king. 1 Chronicles 22:9 show definitely that it was Solomon who was in line for the throne. God had told him so. And David had shared it with Bath-Sheba (v. 1:13). Why then was there so much confusion at this time? Could it be that David, loving his sons, did not want to openly share what he knew to be true? While a great man with some exceptions, he was the head of a dysfunctional family (See 1 Kings 1: 6).

Because of the emergency situation, Nathan urges Bath-Sheba to approach David and remind him of his promise. It was arranged that Nathan would break in on the conversation and agree (v. 23). At stake was not only the occupier of the throne, but their own lives. It was a custom to do away with contenders (Note: in the banquet of Adonijah, Bath-sheba and Nathan were not invited).

God's will was done! David declares that Solomon would reign (vv. 29-32). He was to ride on David's mule and be brought to the Gihon spring. Zadok the priest and Nathan would anoint him; the horn was to be blown with the shout "God save king Solomon". Note that three times we have reference to Solomon as king (vv. 34, 39, 51).

Life *stEP* Compromise always brings confusion. Take a stand, even if it must be with friends and family.

monday

19

I Kings 2:1-12

What is the writer saying?

How can I apply this to my life?

PRAY For many students to commit to full time service during Word of Life Bible Institute Missions Conferences.

This chapter gives the final charge of David to Solomon. You might want to number each charge to Solomon in the first three verses (There are six). Each of them is great advice for the believer today! It becomes very obvious how important obedience to the Word is. Keeping the charge, walking in the ways, keeping the statutes and commandments are emphasized. Note the similarity to God's charge to Joshua (Joshua 1:6-9). These, of course, are qualifications for real leadership.

When one reads Proverbs 4:3-9 we have Solomon's own account of his father's love for him and the spiritual help given him. While most of the sons of David lived questionable lives with questionable motives, Solomon seems to be an exception. We have already learned that they were not properly disciplined.

The importance of courage is emphasized and this courage had its source in the Lord. It is the only guarantee for success. It comes from obeying the Word. Be sure that you read 2 Samuel 7:12-13 and the Davidic covenant as a proper background for this passage in Kings.

Much unfinished business is attended to regarding Joab, Shimei and Barzillai. The first two were to be dealt with severely, whereas mercy was to be shown to Barzillai.

One can't help but think of the one who will occupy the throne of David in the millennium when the Lord will be merciful, but who will also judge in righteousness and truth. Vengeance will come from His hand and punishment for evildoers.

Life **stEP** Courage to take a stand on truth and principle comes from spending time in God's Word.

1 Kings 3:1-15

What is the writer saying?

How can I apply this to my life?

PRAY Peru – For churches as they seek to meet the needs of their congregations in which up to 70% of attendees are unemployed.

Solomon loved the Lord. That says it all. Those earlier years (in contrast to his later years) were years of obedience to the Lord's command and great respect for his own father David. Both sacrifice and prayer characterize this paragraph. What a delight to see Solomon and God at Gibeon where the Lord appeared to the king in a dream. The Lord asked Solomon what he wanted, promising him to give it. One wonders how Christians would respond to this question in view of such rampant materialism of the day. Here we have a review, a request and a divine response!

In the review you will note Solomon's words about the greatness of God and the respect he had for his father (v. 6) Note David walked (1) In truth, (2) In righteousness and (3) In uprightness. More importantly he walked with the Lord!

Now the request of Solomon was for wisdom. Great humility is seen when he said, in essence, "I don't have a clue as to how to be a king and I certainly don't know my way around; please give me wisdom" When one comes to the Lord with this spirit and attitude good things will result. Note the word "because" in verse 11. He had not asked for long life, riches of victory over enemies, but for wisdom. God honored Him and both gave him his request and those things for which he didn't ask.

Solomon is told to walk like his father and obey the Word. Blessing was assured.

Life stEP This whole paragraph illustrates the Lord's own words: "But seek ye first the kingdom of God, and his righteousness; and all these things shall be added unto you" (Matthew 6:33). Don't forget this principle as you serve Him today.

Wednesday 1 Kings 3:16-28

What is the writer saying?

How can I apply this to my life?

This paragraph illustrates the preceding one where the Lord promised to give Solomon wisdom and insight. Two harlots stood before the Lord with a grave problem. First let it be known that God loves all people, even those who had fallen. Rahab the harlot is a good example of this (Joshua 2:1). They were poor, having no servants to watch their children; they probably had no relatives who cared for them. In the night one woman accidentally killed her child lying on him in sleep (v. 20). As you read the passage you will note the problem. One child was dead, one alive; both claimed the living child and said the dead child belonged to the other woman. There were no witnesses to prove who was telling the truth. Solomon showed real insight and understanding of human nature and boldly suggested that the child be cut in half so each woman could have the child. While this seems cruel, it is obvious that he was going to determine by their reaction who the real mother was. The compassionate mother – the real mother – came to the forefront and insisted that the child should not be divided. Without a witness, Solomon determined who the real mother was and showed both boldness and insight.

We are reminded of one "greater than Solomon" that will someday rule as king and do so in righteousness. Gaebelein writes of Solomon: "In his wisdom he is a type of our Lord Jesus who is the wisdom of God. And the justice he administered in his Kingdom is typical of the righteous judgment of our Lord when he rules as King over the earth."

"He shall not judge after the sight of his eyes, neither reprove after the hearing of his ears: But with righteousness shall he judge the poor…" (Isaiah 11:1-4). Someday God will set all things straight on this planet and evil men will not succeed!

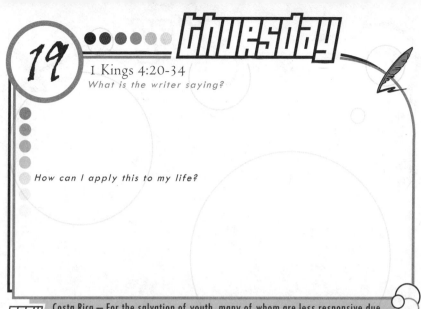

19 thursday

1 Kings 4:20-34

What is the writer saying?

How can I apply this to my life?

pray Costa Rica — For the salvation of youth, many of whom are less responsive due to addiction to drugs.

How great was Solomon's kingdom! Read these verses and you get some idea of his wealth and wisdom. When we read that Judah and Israel were many, "as the sand which is by the sea" (v. 20) we are reminded of the Abrahamic covenant where this language is used. The faithfulness of God is seen as he keeps, and will continue to keep his promises (Genesis 15:3-6; 18-21). Both the dimension of the land and the analogy to "sand" and "stars" are familiar words. This is but a foretaste of the ultimate millennium kingdom when Christ, of the seed of David, will reign. While often, when a new king came to the throne, there was opposition by others to test it; such was not the case here. There was peace "all the days of his life" (v. 21). When you read the provision listed in the next five verses remember that this is what it took for one day in his house. Converting the provision into our measurement there were 150 bushels of flour, 300 bushels of meal, etc. His dominion is listed (v. 24) and the defensive power is seen in terms of chariot horses. But most important, God gave Solomon wisdom, understanding and knowledge too vast to be measured. It exceeded the wise men of the East and Egypt. An examination of verses 32-33, gives the extent of his knowledge and wisdom, with kings coming to observe and listen to him.

Earlier we read that they (Judah and Israel) dwelt safely "every man under his vine and under his fig tree" (v. 25) language used by future prophets to describe the future Messianic kingdom (Micah 4:4; Zechariah 3:10).

It is regrettable that while Solomon had much knowledge he was more knowing than doing. While his head was full of knowledge and his lips articulated it to the amazement of all, his life was far from being holy. Let's be sure that our lip and life are both a credit to God's name.

1 Kings 6:1-14, 38

What is the writer saying?

How can I apply this to my life?

pray Local Church Ministries writing teams to develop lessons with biblical content, clarity, and creativity.

At last, the temple was being built. When you think of the temple, think of a permanent tabernacle. Everything said about the tabernacle, as a dwelling place of the Lord can be said of the temple. In the Bible, there would be several; first, the tabernacle referred to in Hebrews, then came Solomon's temple and later a more simple building built by the returned exiles. Then there was the ornate Herod's temple. But the greatest temple will be that erected in the millennium, when Christ reigns. Today there is a temple too; it is each Christian: "Know ye not that your body is the temple of the Holy Ghost?" (1 Corinthians 6:19) Again, it is the dwelling place of the Lord.

When considering the size of the temple think of it as being twice the size of the tabernacle. 1 Chronicles 28 tells us that David drew up the plans that "he had by the Spirit" (1 Chronicles 28:11-12). Specifically the temple was 90 feet long, 30 feet wide and 45 feet high with 2700 square feet. While it was not large, it was beautiful with white limestone, cedar and a gold exterior. It also had a front porch adding 15 more feet to its length.

Think of it: The temple was erected with precut and pre-fitted materials. Finally the temple was the "house" for the name of the Lord. But there was more than the beauty of the house involved here. It was important that Solomon obeyed the Word of the Lord. Ritual was not sufficient; rather obedience was demanded. We will see that this was not done and the glory of the temple became a place where there was no glory.

How important that our bodies (the temples of the Holy Spirit) bring glory to the Lord beyond mere ritual or external beauty.

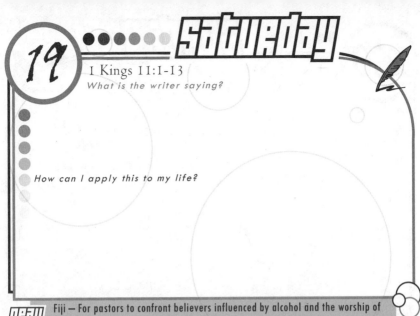

1 Kings 11:1-13

What is the writer saying?

How can I apply this to my life?

This is an amazing paragraph. After everything the Lord had done for Solomon, how could he have gone after strange gods? Note some of the blessings. He had appeared to Solomon twice (v. 9). He had directly received the commands of the Lord from the Lord (v. 11) He didn't need proof that God was there and ready to bless him; even the name that was given him: "Jedidiah" means "loved by the Lord." He was placed on the throne by the Lord and assured wisdom and success by Him. Again, how could this be? The answer isn't hard to find because it is repeated frequently today as well. First he tolerated such an attitude in his household and became accustomed to it and conformable with it. He participated in such idolatry with his wives. It was a gradual thing. While he didn't totally renounce the Lord he was not fully devoted to Him. This is the way Satan works, with the "thin end of the wedge" inserted, leading to further compromise. Well as one commentator said, he "was a great man, but he had feet of clay." He was spiritually unable to survive his disobedience to God's prohibition in Deuteronomy 17:16-17 on taking more than one wife" (Patterson and Austel in The Expositors's Bible Commentary). Warnings had been giving against intermarrying with Canaanites because of their degeneracy (Genesis 19; Leviticus 18). Doing so brought toleration and then opens involvement with their practices.

Instead of being an example of doing right, he was an example of disappointment. Being the king made it worse. Where there is greater position there is greater responsibility. Worshiping Ashtoreth (v. 5) involved fertility rites. He was the "perfect" example of the Ecumenical movement of his days showing no favoritism; treating all gods alike.

Life stEP

While it is difficult to believe that a man of God should sink to such depths, we need to "take heed lest we fall" (1 Corinthians 10:12).

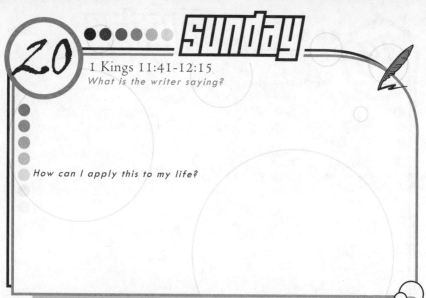
How can I apply this to my life?

Rehoboam, Solomon's son, was as weak as his father was wise. The people were obviously tired of Solomon's heavy taxes and the strenuous labor necessary for his personal projects. Idolatry was rampant in that Favorite gods and their corresponding priests represented foreign cultures. Solomon left the kingdom in a dreadful state.

The Request: 12:3-5. The people requested that the heavy yoke be lightened. Rehoboam consulted the old men and they assured him that if he would be a servant to the people and speak good words they would be his servants forever (v. 7). Then he took counsel of the young men. It is interesting that when you compare the relationships of Rehoboam to these two groups, he spoke to the old men using the word "I" (v. 6).

He asserts his authority. When speaking to the young men (v. 9), he said, "What counsel give ye that we may answer this people?" He identified with the younger men and prized their opinion.

The Kings Stupidity: It is not always wise to seek advice from our peers over that of those who are more experienced and wise. Rehoboam was weak as water. This is seen in his fleeing from the people. Enveloped by his peers and threatened by Israel, he made rash decisions.

God's Sovereignty: Verse 15 ought to be read and considered as similar to God's dealing with Pharaoh (See Exodus. 4:21). While Rehoboam was responsible for his own action, we see the sovereign plan of God. It is encouraging to know that God is still in complete control of events.

Life **stEP**   Let's be willing to learn from the mistakes of those who have failed. Remember what was written before is "for our learning." (Romans 15:4).

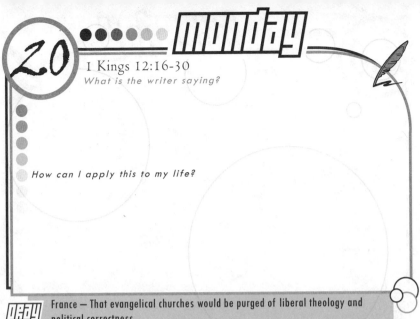

1 Kings 12:16-30

What is the writer saying?

How can I apply this to my life?

The ill-advised action by Rehoboam precipitated a revolt. The people insisted that Jeroboam be their king and Israel rebelled against the house of David. The division that is apparent from this time forward began here. Both Rehoboam and Jeroboam are seen sinning and making poor decisions. Rehoboam sent Adoram to quell the situation. This was idiotic in view of the fact that Adoram was over the tribute. He was not the solution to the situation, but part of the problem. His second mistake was his inclination to war against his own people. The prophet came to him and he reluctantly listened.

The right thing – the wrong way

Jeroboam's sin is obvious too. Remember he had been told that there would be a division in the kingdom. Rather than wait for the will of God to be implemented, he took matters into his own hands and depended on his own wisdom. His first sin was one of idolatry; the second was simply distrust in the Lord. He is seen doing the right thing in the wrong way. Not only did he change the symbols of religion to the calves (like those in Egypt) but also the centers of worship, the priesthood and the religious calendar. Everything was altered and changed as part of his master plan. He was foolish to devise this shameful plan in his own heart rather than listen to the prophet. The center of worship was changed to Bethel, which was 11 miles north of Jerusalem in Ephraim. It was on the main road that the pilgrims would use in going to Jerusalem.

According to the law, the Feast of Tabernacles was to be held in the seventh month (Leviticus 23:24). He changed the time of the feast to the eighth month. It was a man-made feast and a perversion of the will of God not unlike what has often taken place in Christendom.

Life stEP

We need to remember that God's Word is our only guide. Depending on our own wisdom can be fatal. Doing the right thing the right way is the only way.

1 Kings 13:1-10

What is the writer saying?

How can I apply this to my life?

pray Indonesia — For the Muslims to be exposed to the Gospel by the few missionaries remaining.

Again a man of God appeared on the scene; and crying against the altar, he made one of the most astounding prophecies in the Old Testament (v. 2) This passage was fulfilled 360 years later (See 2 Kings 23:15). The prophet also gave a sign, stating that the altar would be rent and ashes would be poured out. When Jeroboam heard of this thing, he put forth his hand from the altar and it was dried up. Entreating the prophet for help, his hand was restored. Wouldn't you think that when Jeroboam heard the message, attested by a miracle, that he would have given heed? He was more interested in his own will than in the revelation from God.

The Believer's Reaction

Apparently grateful for the healing he invited the prophet to his house and assured him of a reward. The answer was a definite no. He insisted that he wouldn't be identified with Jeroboam and that he must obey God rather than man. We read, "So he went another way" (v. 10).

The prophet was courageous in such a response. He was faithful to the trust the Lord had given him.

The prophet's response should challenge our hearts. How important it is to obey God's Word regardless of what might be offered to us. To do the right thing and not the expedient thing is to know the blessing of the Lord. We need to "go another way."

1 Kings 13:11-25

What is the writer saying?

How can I apply this to my life?

---

pray Nigeria – For Nigerian missionaries in West Africa to receive their financial support unhampered.

We now have an unfortunate turn of events. What Satan could not get the prophet to do for money and compromise with the king; he did get him to do as a result of a religious disguise. There was a prophet in Bethel who had been told what had happened. We know little about this prophet except that he was obviously out of fellowship with God. First, he was at Bethel. Thus he was at least giving tacit approval, if not outward and open approval, of the calf that had been erected there. He had already compromised his position, and now he was setting out to get the man of God to compromise his own. The godly prophet was asked to come home to eat bread, but this time it was with the prophet. When the man of God responded that he could not do so, the old prophet said, "I am a prophet also as thou art; and an angel spake unto me by the word of the LORD, saying, Bring him back with thee into thine house..." (v. 18) His response should have been: "though you or an angel from heaven speaks any other word unto me than that which God has spoken unto me, I will not hear it. God's word is absolute and true and I receive that word directly from Him. I must test your revelation and test the truthfulness of what you've said by what God had given to me." (We are reminded of Paul's words in Galatians 1:8).

Deceived – However, we note that the man of God went back with the prophet. How pitiful that what could not be accomplished through the royal invitation was accomplished through religious disguise.

Life stEP

We, too, should always be alert and aware that Satan has not changed his tactics. Should we be asked to change our position by one who is obviously sinful and at odds with our purposes, we should strongly and forthrightly decline.

I Kings 16:29-17:7

What is the writer saying?

How can I apply this to my life?

Without question one of the most outstanding men to appear on the world's scene was Elijah. Even the times in which he lived were similar to today. Idolatry, apostasy and indifference to the things of God all characterized the age. Ahab, king of the North, was perhaps the most wicked of all. His father arranged him to be married to Jezebel, an arrangement that was politically convenient. She was as wild as she was clever. The conditions were awful, but in the midst of such conditions God had a man – Elijah the Tishbite (v. 17:1). Suddenly, like a bolt out of heaven; Elijah appeared on the scene boldly proclaiming there would be no dew or rain. What boldness this man had in a day of compromise; what clarity of speech, when it would have been convenient to be fuzzy. He was from the rough and rugged mountains of Gilead.

The Preparation – We should remember that God does not grow His strongest plants in hothouses or in the sheltered nooks of the world. Elijah's ministry required lengthy preparation. When God takes a Moses and uses him, He often puts him in a desert for 40 years. He was a man of laboring prayer (James 5:17). And He was a man of like passion – he was not an angel, but a man. In our passage, we see him at Cherith, where the Lord had sent him. But, now the brook had dried up. How do you explain that? He was being tested. Carmel was to come where he challenged Ahab. But, before Carmel, comes the brook Cherith, waiting on the Lord, obediently responding to the Lord's command.

Life stEP

"Dry brooks" come to us in various ways; it could be a sickbed, bereavement or a time of seclusion. But if God is pleased to put us by drying brooks we should yield to His will. He knows what He is doing. After testing comes great opportunity.

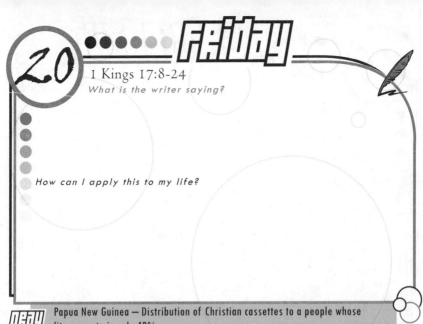

How can I apply this to my life?

pray Papua New Guinea — Distribution of Christian cassettes to a people whose literacy rate is only 43%.

From the brook Cherith, Elijah was transplanted to Zarephath (v. 17:9). Can't you see Elijah in the midst of a drought, daily measuring the water and seeing it decrease, yet believing that God had something "down the road" for him? Finally the word of the Lord appeared and he was told to go to Zarephath, which was the very area from which Jezebel came. Zarephath means a "smelting furnace." God often puts us through such crucibles in order to purify us and make us "meet for the master's use" (2 Timothy 2:21). But it looked like he was "out of the pot and into the fire" making matters worse. A widow appeared on the scene who was poorer than he was and a Gentile. God put him in a strange land with a woman of meager resources and uncertain background (v. 10). The story is a precious one. The man sent from God was able to replenish the meal (v. 14). When the widow's son died, he raised him from the dead (v. 23). Elijah, tried and tested, now was instrumental in helping others who were weak. The testing at Cherith prepared him. There are dividends in trust and faith. Someone has said, "The trials and difficulties are to faith what gymnastics are to muscles." "The barrels were filled," D.L. Moody said, "Trust in yourself, and you are doomed to disappointment; trust in your friends, and they will die and leave you; trust in money, and you may have it taken from you; trust in reputation, and some slanderous tongue may blast it; but trust in God, and you are never to be confounded in time or eternity."

Life stEP A minister was once asked how long it took him to prepare a sermon. He answered "a lifetime." The early years in the hard country of Gilead, the drying book of Cherith, the testing times at Zarephath: all are necessary for the blessing of the finished product.

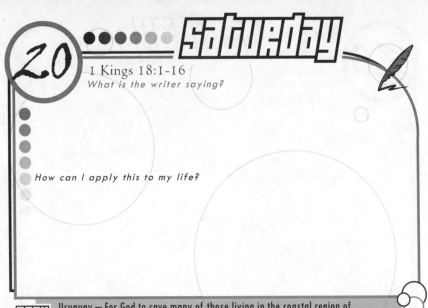

What is the writer saying?

How can I apply this to my life?

pray Uruguay — For God to save many of those living in the coastal region of Montevideo.

As we study the New Testament, we learn that there are three kinds of people in the world today: the natural man (who is unsaved) the carnal man (who is saved but not living like it) and the spiritual man (who is controlled by the Spirit and living the "normal" Christian life. In this chapter we have a picture of the three kinds of men. Ahab would be the natural man; unsaved and bent on doing harm to the Lord. Elijah is in step with the will of God (the spiritual man) and Obadiah is an example of a vacillating carnal Christian. As you read about him, notice that he is trying to please everybody, both Elijah and Ahab. He was neither "fish nor fowl nor good red herring." He was willing to be involved with the people of God as well as with those against God. How pitiful that he looked for grass for Ahab's horses while others were starving. Elijah was taking a stand "outside the camp" while Obadiah was holding onto the world, still seeking to serve God in some degree and yet in a place of carnal compromise. Characteristic of a carnal man, Obadiah was more concerned about his own skin than he was in being obedient to God and standing with Elijah. Also, he was self-deceived, stating that he wasn't "all that bad" having hid 100 of the Lord's prophets in a cave. He thought he could do more within the camp by mixing with the crowd and taking their part, than to stand with Elijah. Compromise will not work! This is so in marriage, in partnerships and in church membership.

Life stEP

We don't need "good mixers" but good "separators" Such lack of separation, such carnal compromise, is contrary to the Word of God (2 Corinthians 6:17). Be true to the Word of God; take a stand.

21 ● ● ● ● ● ● ● SUNDAY

1 Kings 18:17-29

What is the writer saying?

How can I apply this to my life?

PRAY Finland — For God's Word to ignite a passion in Finnish hearts to overcome apathy and nominalism.

Elijah was a man of dauntless courage. We see this in several ways.

With Ahab When Ahab and Elijah met, it was a most dramatic scene. Ahab's first words were, "Art thou he that troubleth Israel?" It was as though all the problems which existed were Elijah's fault. Rather than focus on the sin of the people, and indeed, on Ahab himself, the king "passed the buck" to the prophet. Elijah dealt with this forthrightly and made it clear that he was not the guilty party; rather, it was Ahab and his father's house.

With Israel Not only was Elijah courageous in dealing with Ahab, but also with His own people. Note his penetrating question "How long halt ye between two opinions?" The people were vacillating between two opinions. They were leaning to both sides. Every backslidden believer

today should listen to that question. We dare not play both ends from the middle (See Matthew 6:24).

In Preaching The priests of Baal are put to the test (vv. 26-29). Note the counterfeit nature of this religion. There were plenty of ritualistic actions as they dressed the bullock. There were empty prayers and self-flagellations, but it was counterfeit, exposed as such by Elijah.

The one lone prophet of God standing against the 450 priests is a precious picture of dauntless courage. Seen from a human standpoint, the odds were insurmountable; but from a divine standpoint, one with God is certainly a majority. The Baal bunch was about to be defeated. It was the courage of Elijah coupled with the almighty power of God that made the difference.

Are you willing to be courageous for God? Remember He never asks us to do anything without giving us the power and strength to perform it. Standing against the enemy, speaking out when necessary is a vital part of the believer's life.

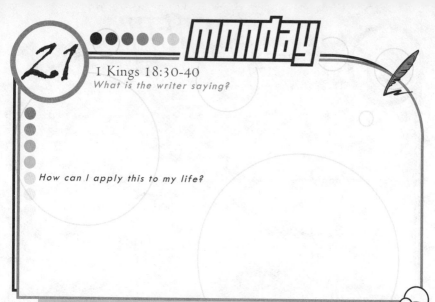

1 Kings 18:30-40
What is the writer saying?

How can I apply this to my life?

PRAY Nicaragua — God's guidance for pastors counseling the many devastated by death, poverty, and divorce.

Now that the "god's of Baal" failed, showing their true nature, Elijah comes to the forefront and we see a powerful act of God. What a day of victory! Note the instructions given and the reaction to them (vv. 31-39). Note also Elijah's prayer and how much his obedience to God meant to him. He prayed that they might know: (1) that God is the God of Israel; and (2) that he had obeyed God according to His Word. There is a precious application of this demonstration of God's power. If we are to know the power of God as Elijah did, there are several prerequisites that must be considered:

1. Our altars need to be repaired, rebuilt – the living sacrifice of our body is what the Lord requires (Romans 12:1-2).

2. We need to be rebuked for our past sins. Elijah chose 12 stones; the people were reminded of their folly and disunity. Their compromise and their contact with Ahab made them powerless. Much compromise with the world leaves us in that same state.

The conditions for power are repaired altars, rebuke for our past sins and implicit obedience to the Word of God in faith. Notice how step-by-step the 12 stones were arranged, the bullock was cut in pieces and the barrels of water were poured on the altar. Also, there was a refusal to recognize this act as impossible. After all, water poured on the altar and expecting fire defies human reasoning But they obeyed God and "Faith laughs at impossibilities And cries 'it shall be done'."

Life **stEP** To the person who asks, "Where is the Lord God of Elijah?" the simple answer is another question: "Where are all the Elijahs?" God's power is available to His obedient child today.

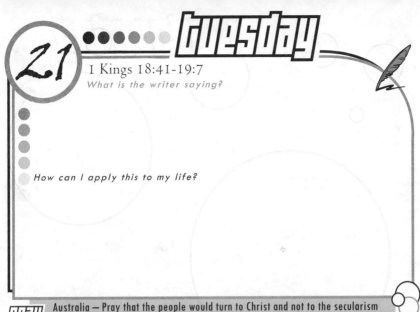

tuesday

1 Kings 18:41-19:7

What is the writer saying?

How can I apply this to my life?

pray Australia — Pray that the people would turn to Christ and not to the secularism that pervades society.

Elijah depressed and inconsistent. Each of us, at times has found ourselves sinking into the valley of despondency or wandered away from the center of God's will. This passage gives a good example of that. Note first that Ahab promptly told Jezebel what Elijah had done. That's how the world saw it. It was really what the Lord had done, not Elijah.

While a great man, Elijah, who had experienced one of his greatest days, is now seen inconsistent. He is seen despondent.

Fear of Man. Once we get our eyes off the Lord and begin to look at circumstances rather than the Lord Himself, we are liable to be despondent and depressed. The high point of victory and success at Mount Carmel was followed by fear and trepidation.

Feeling of Failure. A person feeling that they have failed often causes depression. We need to let God be the judge of that. Need of Rest and Refreshment. Elijah needed rest and refreshment. God intervened; He knows our needs.

In the New Testament we read "Elias was a man subject to like passions as we are" (James 5:17). Yes, he was human and vulnerable. He fled and jogged 150 miles to Beer-Sheba, left a servant there and traveled another day's journey into the wilderness. Depressed, exhausted and frustrated by Jezebel's threats, he sat under a juniper tree and prayed that God would take him. This is almost humorous. If he had just "slowed down" a bit he wouldn't have had to pray to be taken. Thank the Lord that He doesn't always answer our prayers the way we feel He should!

Life stEP Make sure that you get your eyes off of circumstances today and look to Him. The God, who brought us this far, will be there when we need Him most. As He cared for Elijah, he cares for you.

What is the writer saying?

How can I apply this to my life?

pray Pray for unity among the staff and the membership of your local church.

Elijah was told to stand on the mount to meet with the Lord. A wind came, and then an earthquake and then a fire, but God was not in these. Then came a still, small voice and it was God's. Then the directions were clear. Elijah was to return on the way to the wilderness of Damascus He was to anoint Hazael to be king over Syria, and Jehu to be king over Israel and Elisha to be his successor (vv. 15-16).

Divine Assurance God assured him of his place of service as well as God's control of the situation. God will have His way (v. 17). Also, contrary to Elijah's complaint that he was alone, God assured him that there were 7,000 in Israel who hadn't bowed their knees to Baal (v. 18). God has His men today to do His work; and while they are a minority, God will take that precious minority and use it to His glory.

How Elijah must have longed to be called again and used again. The appointment of Elisha emphasizes that God's work and plan are not thwarted. Jehu was the answer to Elijah's concern over the Israelite's apostasy and Elisha was the answer to Elijah's own failure. We need to remember that God isn't mocked; He is sovereign in Israel (v. 18). What seemed hopeless and helpless from man's viewpoint was not so from God's. God gives Elijah a second chance. The Lord still used him.

We should be careful to judge ourselves when we sin (1 Corinthians 11:31). We also need to stop feeling sorry for ourselves. Then, we need to let the Lord prune us with the holy knife of His Word in order that we can be most fruitful for Him.

21 thursday

1 King 21:1-16

What is the writer saying?

How can I apply this to my life?

pray Canada — For "fruit that remains" within the local churches where Bible institute ministry teams serve.

Covetousness is a sin (Hebrews 13:5-6). The Lord revealed the awful nature of covetousness by placing it along with other sins usually considered much worse (Mark 7:21-22). Ahab, consistent to his nature, was absorbed with himself. First we see him looking for grass for his mules; here he was looking for a vineyard for his house. He was an immature, pouting sinner with one objective: the satisfaction of his own fleshly desire.

The consistency of Naboth

First, he knew the Word of God understanding that his land was given to him as an inheritance from his father. To sell the land would violate Scripture (Numbers 36:7). Second, he obeyed the Word of God. He was willing to pay the price of obedience.

The cunning of Jezebel

In Revelation 2:20 Jezebel is called crafty and deceptive; one with evil plans. Ever since Ahab had won her hand, he was under her thumb! She controlled her husband, controlled the court and was as crafty as she was sinful. But the Lord will have the last Word.

Life stEP

Covetousness is a temptation for the believer. "Search me oh God and know my heart. Help me to be content and not covetous" should be our prayer.

I Kings 21:17-29

What is the writer saying?

How can I apply this to my life?

pray Aruba — Pray for an end to rivalry among churches, as it hinders the effectiveness of their witness.

Here we see the sowing and reaping principle. Ahab and Jezebel sinned against the Lord and were about to reap a harvest of barren regrets. With this background note the direction of the prophet Elijah. First, he is serving again! He waited and God gave him a new task.

Second, he was confident again. No vacillation is seen here. He was out of his despondency, out of the cave, and back into the will of God, taking a stand for God.

Third, we see him standing strong. By doing so he was surely a credit to the name of the Lord. He is used again to proclaim the righteousness and justice of God. His stand against sin is clear and forthright. And so should ours be.

Note that Ahab calls Elijah his enemy. The message from the prophet is clear and plain. That's the way it should always be. Neither Ahab nor Jezebel would escape. The reaction of Ahab caused the Lord to temporarily stay the execution (but not for Jezebel). But there is no indication that Ahab's character was changed by genuine repentance and faith. But, in spite of it all, the Lord is gracious and ever loving with boundless mercy. We are reminded of what Peter said: "the Lord is not slack concerning his promise, as some men count slackness; but is longsuffering to us-ward, not willing that any should perish, but that all should come to repentance" (2 Peter 3:9).

God is longsuffering. We cannot presume upon this quality as eventually His judgment falls, but as long as there is life there is hope. It is never too late to repent until you are dead.

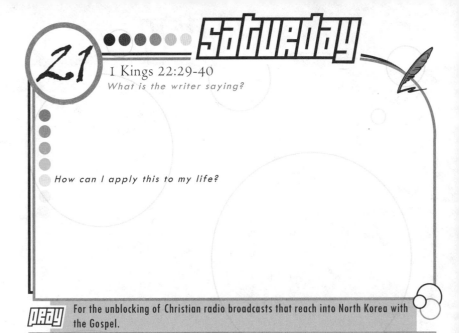

21 · SATURDAY

1 Kings 22:29-40

What is the writer saying?

How can I apply this to my life?

PRAY For the unblocking of Christian radio broadcasts that reach into North Korea with the Gospel.

When you read the verses preceding this paragraph you will note that there was an unholy alliance between the King of Judah and the King of Israel. The godly prophet Micaiah had prophesied defeat. Yet, the two kings went out to battle. Ahab did so disguised (v. 30). Jehoshaphat almost lost his life as he was mistaken for Ahab. He cried out to the Lord for help. In the 2 Chronicles account we have these words added. "But Jehoshaphat cried out, and the LORD helped him; and God moved them to depart from him (2 Chronicles 18:31).

Again, the Lord is in full control. Even the "random" arrow that smote Ahab was not "random" at all, but according to God's plan. Ahab insisted that his dying body be propped up in his chariot (v. 34). Earlier God predicted that Ahab would be slain. "Because thou hast let go out of thy hand a man whom I appointed to utter destruction, therefore thy life shall go for his life, and thy people for his people" (1 Kings 20:42). Again, "…Thus saith the LORD, 'In the place where dogs licked the blood of Naboth shall dogs lick thy blood, even thine'" (1 Kings 21:19). And again, "And the LORD said, 'Who shall persuade Ahab, that he may go up and fall at Ramoth-gilead?' (1 Kings 22:20)"

God is Sovereign So, while we see an unholy alliance, disobedience and compromise on the part of man and what seemed to be random events taking place as a result of a bad decision, we actually see the guiding hand of the sovereign Lord. One commentator has written, "That arrow was guided by a higher hand." How we thank God for the "higher hand" intervening and working in spite of man's inclination to disobey.

Life stEP Surely as we look at events around us we must understand that the Lord is not unaware of what is taking place. He is sovereign and His "higher hand" controls every situation. Someday His voice will be heard: "Come up hither" and we will be called home.

199

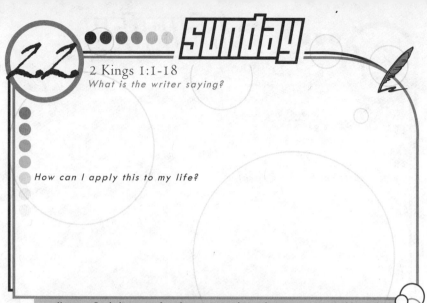

2 Kings 1:1-18
What is the writer saying?

How can I apply this to my life?

PRAY Kenya — For believers to forsake previous ethnic religious practices and be unified by biblical truth.

No longer do we see Elijah cowering beneath the threats of Jezebel, hiding in a cave of Moab or pining beneath the juniper tree. The man that we recognize as being forthright, a prophet of fire, is seen in his true character. King Ahaziah had a stroke and fell through the lattice of his upper chamber. He sent messengers to inquire of Baal-zebub whether he would recover from his illness. This was a direct violation of the law, "thou shalt have no other gods before me" (Exodus 20:3). Baal-zebub means "lord of flies." Apparently this god was worshiped in the form of a fly. The tradition of the rabbis tells us that this was so much a part of the Jewish religion in this time of awful idolatry that they carried a small image of a fly in their pockets and kissed it from time to time. Elijah declared the king would die. When the king heard of it, he sent messengers to Elijah in three successive groups of 50 soldiers. The first two times, Elijah called fire down from heaven consuming the 50 soldiers (v. 10, 12). The third time the commander of the 50 pled for their lives. Elijah finally went with the men (v. 15) and declared again that the king would die.

Grace from Heaven We are reminded of the request of James and John when they said, "Lord, wilt thou that we command fire to come down from heaven, and consume them, even as Elias did?" (Luke 9:54) Christ's answer was "Ye know not what manner of spirit ye are of. For the Son of man is not come to destroy men's lives, but to save them" (Luke 9:55, 56). This is the difference between law and grace.

Today God encourages men in grace to come to Him. He came not to condemn, but to save. But those who reject the grace that God offers will certainly be the objects of his wrath in fire (Romans 1:18; 2 Peter 2:9).

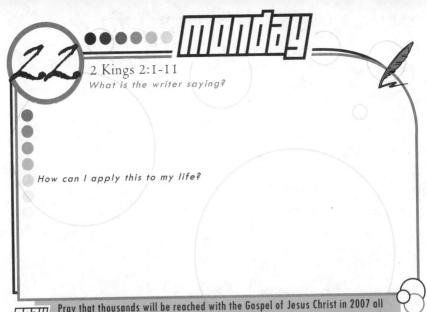

How can I apply this to my life?

PRAY Pray that thousands will be reached with the Gospel of Jesus Christ in 2007 all across the world.

We come to the final chapter in Elijah's life, his translation. Elijah was preparing to leave the world scene. He looks back confidently at Gilgal. He must have rehearsed the victories the Lord gave there (Joshua 4:19). He apparently wanted to be alone with his thoughts (v. 3-4). Then he pondered Israel's future in his absence. Notice Elijah's influence over young Elisha, as well as other sons of the prophets, along with his patience with them. His route is interesting: from Gilgal to Bethel, to Jericho, to Jordan and then home! He was called into the presence of God! Each of these places are filled with biblical history.

Elijah's departure is certainly a picture of the believer's rapture. How precious it must have been for this man to leave the earthly scene where he had learned so much about the Lord and to be ushered into His very presence. Indeed there were many high points in Elijah's life, but this is the highest. Faith is made sight; service on earth comes to an end in God's presence and the blessings that attend that presence have just begun.

There are two men in the Bible who did not see death. One is Enoch and the other is Elijah. It should be said, however, that the translation, which shall someday be ours is far greater than what we see here. Christ Himself will come. We shall meet Him in the air and enjoy the blessings of eternity with Him in incorruptible bodes (I Corinthians 15:1-58; I Thessalonians 4:13-18).

Life stEP

The next event on God's prophetic calendar will be the rapture. It is imminent. It is the "blessed hope" of the believer. We are "waiting for His Son from heaven." What a day that will be! Are you ready to meet Jesus?

2 Kings 2:12-22

What is the writer saying?

How can I apply this to my life?

PRAY Aruba — For outreach among those who have immigrated from Latin America, the Caribbean and, Asia.

As Elisha gazed into heaven, Elijah went up in a whirlwind, leaving his mantle behind. Elisha performed his first miracle using Elijah's mantle to part the waters and cross over on dry ground. When the sons of the prophets saw Elisha, they said, "The spirit of Elijah doth rest on Elisha" (v. 15). These sons of the prophets were seminary students, trained in the school of the prophets. They did not necessarily know Elisha as Elisha had long been Elijah's traveling companion. They had done well in their training in that there is no indication of any pride. They weren't so self-centered that they wouldn't recognize a leader who didn't come up from their own ranks. It would have been very natural for them to say, "Who is this leader, Elijah, so unlike our former president?

He is at best a farmer boy. Is he our leader?" This was not their spirit.

Elisha's second miracle is in this chapter. The water was bitter, and the men of the city called the condition to Elisha's attention. He cast salt into the springs of water making the poisonous, bitter water sweet. This pictures the Gospel. As it is preached, regeneration ensues. God can take the poisonous and barren and make it sweet and useful. We also have a picture here of what the Lord will do when He comes in power and glory at His second coming (Revelation 19). As He establishes His kingdom, He will make sweet all nature that is subject to the curse. His bringing in righteousness will put an end to a world, which is presently under the curse of the fall.

Life stEP

One gauge of spirituality is our willingness to follow a spiritual leader whom God has sent to us, even if he is different from us in many ways.

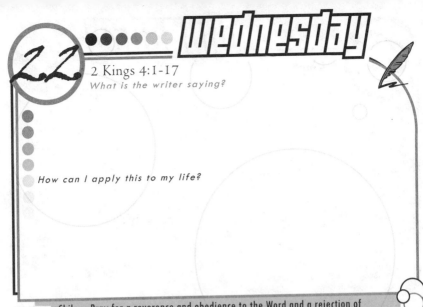

22 wednesday

2 Kings 4:1-17

What is the writer saying?

How can I apply this to my life?

pray Chile — Pray for a reverence and obedience to the Word and a rejection of sensational religiosity.

A series of miracles concerning little people are before us in chapter 4. Elisha was interested in widows and the needs of seminarians and the theological school of the day; "The Sons of the Prophets". The widow woman of verse 1 was the wife of a student; probably a young woman left with a series of bills after her husband's unexpected death. The creditor, in keeping with the law (Leviticus 25:39) was coming to take her two sons. Elisha didn't tell her to forget the debt, but rather showed her how it could be paid. This reminds us to also pay what we owe (Romans 13:8). He told her to get vessels and fill them. The vessels had to be filled. It was an act of faith on her part. The blessings of supply were not limited by the amount of oil but by the number of vessels she could find. So it is with us. God will supply our needs, but the degree of supply is often determined by the measure of our faith: in this case, the more vessels, the more oil. Then Elisha said, "Go, sell the oil, and pay thy debt, and live thou and thy children of the rest." (v. 7).

A Great Woman — The next miracle involved a woman of Shunem. This woman was a great woman. What does this mean? Probably that she had a great interest in the Lord's work. She recognized Elisha's greatness (v. 9) She and her husband build a "prophets chamber" (v. 10). Then we are told that Elisha announced that she was to have a child. The situation seemed hopeless (like many others in the Old Testament) but, God performed a miracle and the woman bore a son. Here we see that God was great and merciful. This is one of greatest miracles in the Old Testament.

Do we trust the Lord the way we should? Are we mighty in faith in both small and great things? Are you willing to trust the Lord for something special today? How many vessels will you submit?

2 Kings 4:18-37

What is the writer saying?

How can I apply this to my life?

PRAY New Zealand — For the emergence of a new generation of godly Maori leaders to evangelize their culturally alienated people.

This is a touching story. It is quite similar to an earlier event when Elijah was used of the Lord to raise a widow's son to life (1 Kings 17). In both cases a child was involved and the miracle was done in the prophet's chamber. More detail is given to this event. A son has died, probably of sunstroke as he had been working in the field (v. 18). He was on his mother's knees till noon and then he died. Remember this is the same son that had been given to her in a miracle (v. 17). Now, it looked like the Lord was taking away what he had given. Later the woman reminded Elisha of this very thing (v. 28). But note that while she didn't understand why this was all happening, there was still faith on her part. Rather than prepare the child for a funeral in final arrangements, she sent for the prophet. He is referred to as "The man of God."

She also knew where to find Elisha, at Mount Carmel. Elisha meanwhile recognized her when she came, but did not know why she was coming. God had not revealed it to him. He was limited in knowledge and indeed apart from the Lord, limited in power.

What a wonderful example of prayer on the part of Elisha. He shut the door and prayed unto the Lord. This continued (vv. 34-35) and after stretching himself on the child, the child sneezed seven times and opened his eyes. Such detail is interesting and even exciting. What joy must have been in that room! Prayer was made, God's power was manifested and the child came alive. There are so many indications that the woman was a woman of faith (vv. 8-10, 21, 22, 24, 25, 27, 30, 37). Her faith was rewarded.

Life stEP

There are many troubles in life; unexpected circumstances beyond our understanding. Blessings are followed by puzzling events. But we must remember "all things work together for good" (Romans 8:28). He is in control today. Trust Him.

Friday

22

2 Kings 4:38-44

What is the writer saying?

How can I apply this to my life?

PRAY Hungary — Effective outreach and godly teachers in public schools where Christianity is welcome.

Have you noticed the difference between Elijah and Elisha? While both performed similar miracles and spoke with authority, they were quite different. Elijah was bold, fearless and a forthright individualist. Elisha was on the other hand industrious, loyal and mixed well with people. God uses all types of people. In this chapter we have one of the "smaller miracles" which characterizes Elisha's ministry. It was not a Mount Carmel experience calling fire down. Rather it is the healing of poisonous pottage. There was "death in the pot" so they could not eat. Meal was cast into the pot and it was changed; "healed." In Leviticus the meal is a type of the Lord. It could be considered the same here. The meal was cast into the death scene and healing resulted. Out of death comes life.

Certainly we were once dead in sins (Ephesians 2:1). We were "alienated from the life of God." (Ephesians 4:18) "But she that liveth in pleasure is dead while she liveth" (I Timothy 5:6). We were alive physically but dead spiritually. But, having trusted Christ as Savior, out of death came life. "This is the record, that God hath given to us eternal life, and this life is in his Son. He that hath the Son hath life; and he that hath not the Son of God hath not life" (I John 5:11-12). How important to understand that as the meal was cast into the pot, life ensued.

In Matthew 13 we read a parable of a woman who took leaven and hid it in three measures of meal." While interpretations vary, the meal there could refer to Christ and the attempt to put leaven in the meal can be seen as an attack on the person of Christ (Matthew 13:33). (Leaven is always used in a bad sense). But here, life deals with death. So it is with us in salvation.

Life stEP

The Lord is the life giver for all who will trust Him. Share Him with someone today and pray that they might have life in Him.

2 Kings 5:1-16

What is the writer saying?

How can I apply this to my life?

PRAY Bulgaria — For godly, biblically trained missionaries to get past the prohibitive visa process.

In the paragraph before us is a description of what God can do for the sinner who puts his trust in Him. Naaman was captain of the Syrian host with great power and high moral character, but he was a leper! What a picture of an unsaved man. Power, prestige and human acquisition could be his, but he was a sinner. Naaman's wife had a servant who was a constant witness and told her about Elisha. How we thank the Lord for the "Naamans" in today's world who witness and speak of the Lord. Naaman was on the wrong track. The king of Syria, trying to help the captain, sent a letter to Israel's king. (He went to the wrong person.) Naaman took ten talents of silver and 6,000 pieces of gold (he had the wrong means). So it is in salvation. Man seeks salvation in a religion or in a church and seeks to find help through works.

When Elisha heard of the problem, he urged Naaman to come to him and he instructed him to "Go and wash in Jordan seven times" (v. 10). It was, like salvation, simple and uncomplicated. Christ came "into the world to save sinners" (1 Timothy 1:15). We could call it "Seven Ducks in a Muddy River." Naaman's reaction was one of pride, there were bodies of water "better than" Jordan" like Abana and Pharpar. So today, the Gospel is foolishness to the world (1 Corinthians 1:23). But when he did what was requested he was healed; the seeker was saved. It took seven dippings. Five times did not heal him five sevenths. It was instantaneous. If you haven't yet trusted Christ remember that salvation cannot be yours by doing, giving or reasoning. It has been finished at Calvary. Cleansing comes through faith in His blood.

Life stEP Praise God for the uncomplicated cleansing that is ours through the work of Christ. We are redeemed by His blood. (1 Peter 1:18) Never let that truth become stale. "Jesus paid it all, all to Him I owe."

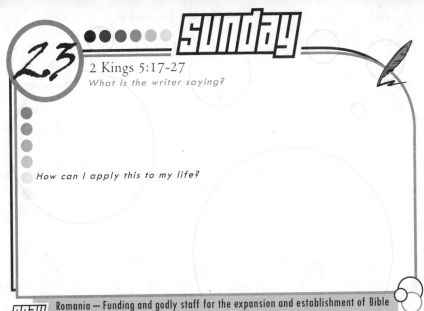

2 Kings 5:17-27

What is the writer saying?

How can I apply this to my life?

PRAY Romania — Funding and godly staff for the expansion and establishment of Bible schools and seminaries.

You would think that the servant of Elisha would be a godly man. After all, he had a good example. But we must remember that even Christ had a Judas who betrayed him. When Naaman offered to give something to Elisha out of gratitude for what he had done, he refused it. Much like Abraham (Genesis 14:23), he did not want to be beholden to a man. But after Naaman left to go back, Gehazi ran after him to "take him up on his offer" for Gehazi's own benefit. He covered it up by lying and claiming it for one of the sons of the prophets. He was covetous and greedy and lied to get the benefit. Certainly, "For the love of money is the root of all evil" (I Timothy 6:10). What's worse, it never satisfies (Ecclesiastes 5:10). Covetousness blinded his eyes and hardened his heart. How does a person become covetous? It starts in the heart. Then, it engrosses the heart. As believers we need to ask the Lord to help us get our eyes off of material possessions. Think of it, this man was so near the prophet of God, but was so far from God. He had become accustomed to the arena of holiness. Paul writes: "Let your conversation be without covetousness; and be content with such things as ye have: for he hath said, I will never leave thee, nor forsake thee" (Hebrews 13:5). If we really get into His presence we will not covet the world's presents. Covetousness is to be put to death (along with fornication and uncleanness). The Bible calls it idolatry (Colossians 3:5). The result of Gehazi's sin is that he "went out from his presence a leper as white as snow" (v. 27).

Life stEP When you practice His presence and understand His heart (who became poor that we might be rich 2 Corinthians 8:9), the things of the earth so inviting to most humans will become "strangely dim."

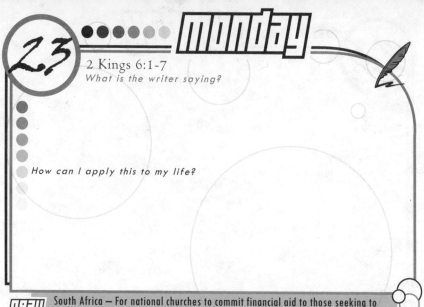

2 Kings 6:1-7

What is the writer saying?

How can I apply this to my life?

What could be less significant than the loss of an axe head? Apparently the theological seminary had expanded numerically and more buildings were needed. The students could help, but they wanted the seminary president to join in the building. Elisha welcomed the opportunity (v. 3). In the process of building they were cutting a beam and an axe head fell into the water. This was a borrowed axe head. Seminary students didn't have a great deal for themselves and even the tools they used were borrowed. When Elisha found where the axe head had fallen, he cut down a stick and cast it in the water "and the iron did swim" (v. 6). The greatest miracle of all is to be lifted out of the muck and mire of this world and to be empowered to live for God. The seminarians showed diligence and zeal by trying to help in this situation. When the axe head was lost, they also had the sense to stop swinging the handle. After all, like many today, they could have thought that just "going through the motions" was enough. But, as in the Christian life, when you've lost your cutting edge you have lost your ability to "change the scenery." Yes, if a believer wants to determine whether or not he (or she) has "lost their cutting edge" just ask: "Has there been a change of scenery? Am I making difference? Or are we in the "same-old-same old?"

What was needed was a miracle. That's exactly what happened. The stick was thrown into the water and the iron came up. Now what? Elisha said take it up. Yes, and then what? Well, secure the axe head, get it on the handle, and get back to work.

Life stEP

The principle of "divine-human cooperation" is seen here. It is the might of God and the efforts of man. Without Him we can do nothing, but in His power and might we can get to work again and be successful.

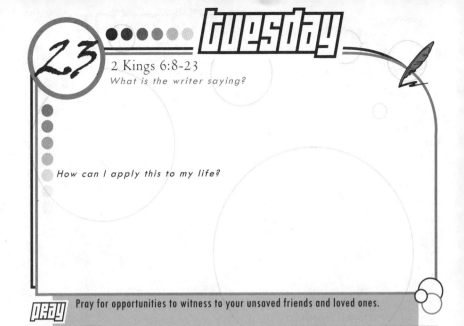

2 Kings 6:8-23

What is the writer saying?

How can I apply this to my life?

PRAY Pray for opportunities to witness to your unsaved friends and loved ones.

The king of Syria made war plans against Israel. Elisha was able to pass on to the king of Israel what had transpired in the secret war room of the enemy (actually, his bedchamber v. 12). When the king asked who had given the secrets of his battle plans, he was told it was Elisha. Horses and chariots were sent by night and surrounded the city. This caused no little consternation and fear on the part of Elisha's servant. Picture yourself, surrounded by a great host of Syrians with seemingly no help from the inside. But Elisha's response is in verse 16. By faith he was counting on God's invisible armies to intervene for them. The prayer he prayed is the prayer of a pastor's heart. "LORD, I pray thee, open his eyes that he may see." The servant's eyes were opened and "behold, the mountain was full of horses and chariots of fire round about Elisha" (v. 17). We should remember

that today angels are ministering spirits (Psalm 104:4). Yes, today there is an unseen, invisible host of angels, delegated by God to take charge over us in all our ways (Psalm 91:11; 34:7; Isaiah 63:9). God has His ways of protecting us, ways unknown and unseen to us; but they are very real and very able. Let us believe that in the invisible war about us, "greater is he that is in you, than he that is in the world" (1 John. 4:4). God's armies and resources are great indeed. When the forces came to Dothan, Elisha prayed that they would be smitten with blindness; then he led them into Samaria. This must have been one of the strangest processions in history. Elisha the prophet, led hundreds of men to Samaria. Imagine their surprise when they opened their eyes and found themselves there. Israel's king wanted to capitalize on the situation, but Elisha showed mercy.

Remember to trust the Lord today knowing that he watches over you and has a host of helpers to guide and guard. The Lord is with us; don't forget that.

23 wednesday

2 Kings 6: 24-33

What is the writer saying?

How can I apply this to my life?

pray Jamaica — Leadership within the government and churches to be untainted by corruption or compromise.

Ben-hadad, king of Syria, besieged Samaria. This resulted in great famine. The head of a donkey was sold for 80 pieces of silver, and dove's dung was used for fuel. Everything was financially beyond the people's reach. One might ask why God allowed His people to suffer such an awful condition at the enemies' hand. The answer is simple. The people had apostatized; they worshiped false gods and disobeyed the Lord. What happened was what God predicted would happen when they turned against Him (Leviticus 26:29; Deuteronomy 28:53). God is not mocked and what happened here was to happen again at the hands of Nebuchadnezzar (Lamentations 4:10). The blame was put on Elisha (v. 31); what a picture we have here of what happened to our Lord. After the Lord's gracious ministry, He was still hated and opposed. Forgotten were the mighty miracles of the Lord and the many ways he had shown compassion. As it was in the days of Elisha and in the days of the Lord, so it will be with us. The world is no friend of grace and often believers are treated with contempt while trying to show their Christian love.

True Experience? — Note that when the king of Israel saw the awful results of the famine he rent his clothes and had sackcloth on his body. But the repentance was only outward as he blames the whole thing on God's prophet. Also, it is quite obvious that he is angry with the Lord (v. 33) The language "Why should I wait for the Lord any longer" seems to mean why should I wait for the Lord to do any thing, or why even pray. Such is the extent of his turning away from the Lord.

Be careful that you walk with the Lord "in the light of his word" and then "trust and obey" Be careful that you aren't angry with the Lord when the fault is in your own heart.

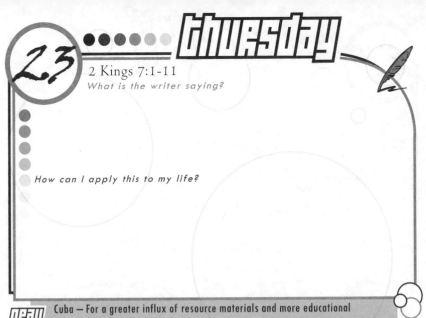

2 Kings 7:1-11

What is the writer saying?

How can I apply this to my life?

PRAY Cuba — For a greater influx of resource materials and more educational opportunities for pastors.

Before us is the story of four lepers. Rather than die in the city, they decided to ask the Syrians for food. They had nothing to lose; they figured that either way they were goners. When they came to the Syrians' camp, however, they found the Syrians had left; but all the tents, horses, asses, food, drink and silver were left behind. Verse 6 makes it clear that the Lord had divinely intervened. The Syrians heard the noise of chariots and thought the king of Israel had joined hands with another power and both were on their way to attack. So the camp had been abandoned, and all the goods in it had been left behind. Be sure to read the response of the lepers in verse 9. They spread word of God's deliverance around. Here again we have a beautiful application in the Gospel. Those of us who know Christ as Savior must remember that our day is also a day of good tidings. What a pity if we hold our peace. The lepers had found they were without money and without price. The answer to their awful condition had been offered. What a tremendous picture of God's grace. Do you agree that the Lord has been gracious to you in allowing you to hear the message of salvation? Should we not want to share it with others? Rather than be silent and quietly thankful for what he has done each of us should have a heart's desire to broadcast it "Holding forth the Word of Life" to a lost and dying world. Well does Gaebelein write: "It was a day of good tidings? Such is the still lasting day of salvation, the day of grace. The lepers who had their fill first and had tasted God's great salvation could not hold their peace."

Life stEP

As your move out into the day-to-day world ask the Lord to help you meet someone with whom you can share the good news of the Gospel.

2 Kings 7:12-20

What is the writer saying?

How can I apply this to my life?

PRAY Dominican Republic — For God to send workers to the 4,000 villages that have no Gospel witness.

There is good news and bad news. The good news is that the Lord has provided the bread of life for any who hunger (John 6:35). The bad and unfortunate news is that not all will receive it. Remember in chapter seven Elisha predicted that a great supply of food would be available. Remember the four lepers entered into the enemy's camp and found that it was true. It was good tidings and it was told to the king's household (v. 9), but there was suspicion and distrust. The king thought that the Syrians were up to no good and that actually there was a plan to trap them. Thinking this was so, a plan was arranged for some horsemen to check it out. So two chariots were sent "after the host of the Syrians." On the way they found garments and vessels the Syrians had cast away in their haste (Remember, the Lord was in this for they were "spooked" by the noise they heard (v. 6). So God had intervened. Elisha had predicted that they would find food, yet there is suspicion and unbelief. When it was discovered that the Syrians had fled indeed and word got out, the hungry people surged into the area to get the food. The king's official appointed to maintain order was overrun and killed. So while some in belief enjoyed the booty, another in disbelief didn't. The lesson is simple. We can rely on God's promises. He is good to His Word. The prophet had spoken the mind of God and it was believed by some and rejected by others. Again, the good news was that God had showed His hand. The sad news was one of beholding it with their eyes, but not eating of it (v. 19).

Can we just believe the Lord? Do we need to get it confirmed by external sources? Can we say God said it, I believe it and that settles it?

saturday

23

2 Kings 9:1-10, 30-37

What is the writer saying?

How can I apply this to my life?

PRAY Ukraine — For believers willing to translate biblical resource material into the Ukrainian language.

In this chapter, Jehu is anointed as king over Israel. God instructed Elisha to gird his loins, take a flask of oil and go to Ramoth-gilead and find Jehu, take him into the inner chamber and anoint him to be king. This was done as commanded. We also read that he was not to "hang around" but do the work and get out and get going (v. 3). Sometimes when the work of God is done we need to get out of the way and not take away from what God has done. The second important thing here is that the king was to be God's instrument to smite the house of Ahab and avenge the blood of his servants of the Lord (v. 7). God's patience had run its course. He was about to make the house of Ahab a "zero." Also, the dogs would eat Jezebel in Jezreel and there would be no one to bury her. So, the message was plain, anoint the king and instruct the king. When we come to the second portion of our devotion we

see this carried out (vv. 30-37). Jezebel was waiting for Jehu (v. 30). She taunted him seeking to humiliate him. Jehu is called "Zimri" which was synonymous with "traitor." At the command of the king she was thrown down and killed. The king left her there, but later decided that they should go back and at least give her a decent burial since she was a king's daughter. It was too late. As predicted by Elijah (1 Kings 21:23) dogs had eaten her flesh. So this evil woman was slain as God had ordained. That had been prophesied 15 years earlier, now it had come to pass. We are reminded in the book of Revelation that all "Jezebels" will be judged (Revelation 2:20). In the Old Testament, a prophecy was given and fulfilled; in the New Testament, a prophecy was given and will be fulfilled. We can expect the Lord to have the last word.

Here we see the sowing/reaping principle. God is longsuffering and patient. His silence today does not mean that He is unaware of the world's conditions. His payday is coming someday.

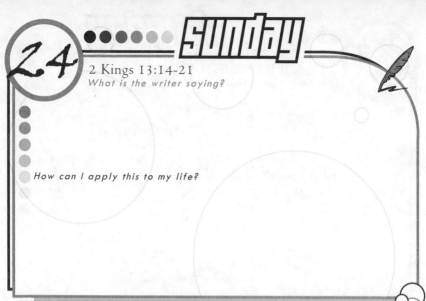

2 Kings 13:14-21

What is the writer saying?

How can I apply this to my life?

This paragraph deals with King Joash. He reigned from 798-782 B.C. His name means "Jehovah gifted." Under this king, Israel began to recover. Perhaps this man is known best for the bedside scene when Elisha died. Elisha was now an old man. Like Nebuchadnezzar when he was old, little attention was paid to him in the last few years of his ministry. Elisha, at his deathbed, told the king to take the bow and shoot the arrow. He said, "The arrow of the LORD'S deliverance, and the arrow of the deliverance from Syria: for thou shalt smite the Syrians in Aphek, till thou have consumed them" (v. 17). Joash obeyed; but rather than smite upon the ground five or six times, as Elisha had commanded, he smote three times and stopped. This was a definite lack of faith on the part of the king. According to his faith, he won but three victories (2 Kings 13:25).

There is one last miracle given in conjunction with Elisha. Sometime after Elisha died a funeral procession was taking place and a looting party attacked them (v. 21). Members of the procession quickly buried the dead body in an available tomb, which happened to be where Elisha was buried. The dead man revived. What was the significance of this? Could it be that the sign was given assuring the king that as the man had been restored, Israel could be too if they would turn from their sin and turn again to God. God was the God of the living. Certainly God would in a future day be gracious to Israel. We know that God is not through with Israel. Someday He will use the Tribulation (the time of Jacob's trouble) to bring Israel to their knees and they will recognize the Messiah and be saved.

Life stEP Do we still revere and respect older servants of God? Elisha had been forgotten and neglected. Thank the Lord for faithful servants of the Lord.

24 monday

2 Kings 17:6-23

What is the writer saying?

How can I apply this to my life?

PRAY Brazil — For godly government officials who will put an end to corruption and discrimination.

This chapter records one of the great turning points in the history of Israel. It records her captivity and the reason for it. The plain fact is "Israel had sinned against the Lord their God" (v. 7). If you list the sins in this paragraph you will find 18 (vv. 6-17). Every kind of idolatry was practiced, beginning with the calves of Jeroboam to the Asherah pole and even human sacrifice was practiced. Add to this divination and sorcery and you have a picture of a corrupt nation. God's wrath is evident. Note the word "therefore" in verse 18. They sinned (v. 7) therefore (v. 18) we should note that while there were some good kings in Judah there were no good kings in Israel. They were all corrupt, some more than others. Out of the 19 kings which reigned, seven were murdered, one died on the battlefield, another fell out of a window and another was struck down by God's judgment. Finally one committed suicide. This chapter traces Israel from their redemption out of Egypt until their demise (v. 7) Words to note here are they "did secretly those things that were not right" (v. 9). God had plainly spoken to them about the need for holy living. The prohibitions were plain (Exodus 20:2-6; Leviticus 18:4, 5, 26; 20:22-23; Deuteronomy 5:6-10). If you take time to look these verses up you will find a clear contrast as to what God said and how they responded.

Is God all through with them? Did they have a chance and were abandoned by God forever? Is the church the new Israel? The answer to all of these is a definite "No!" Read Romans 11 for the explanation.

Today there is "blindness in part" but it is only till the "fullness of the Gentiles be come in." The "fullness" speaks of the completion of the church and the rapture (Romans 11:25). Then the Lord will restore Israel.

Life stEP

You can count on God's promises, whether it is to Israel, to the church or to individual believers. We can "stand on the promises" of God even though man fails and stumbles.

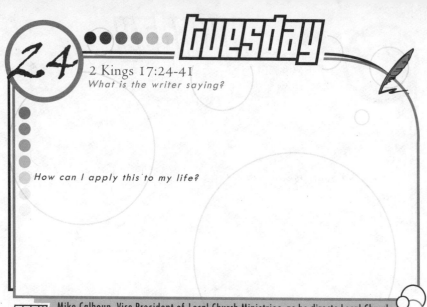

How can I apply this to my life?

PRAY Mike Calhoun, Vice President of Local Church Ministries, as he directs Local Church Ministries and missionaries.

Remember when the Lord met the Samaritan woman in John Chapter 4, and how there was an obvious division between the Samaritans and the Jews? This chapter gives us the necessary background to understand that condition. The king of Assyria, now in control, decided that he would repopulate Samaria with non-Jews and he brought them from other areas (v. 24) While Israel had sinned and was being punished by God, the Lord was still offended and wanted a witness to Him to remain. He allowed lions to threaten the people. "The lions were a reminder of the broken covenant and of God's claim on the land (Leviticus 18:24-30)." (Expositor's Bible Commentary) So, the king, respecting Jehovah as another god (remember they were polytheists) brought back a priest to represent Jehovah and calm down the situation. But the priest was probably an idol worshiper himself who worshiped the golden calf. So we have an exchange: people taken out of the land and people and their gods brought in. This was an Old Testament ecumenical movement. Indeed, it is characteristic of the modern pluralism that prevails in our own day: everybody's right, nobody is wrong, all religions are good and we all have the same god. This was an offense to God who made it clear that there were to be no other gods (Exodus 20:3). This syncretism was not acceptable to God, nor is it acceptable today.

In early church history, Rome had no problem accepting Christianity as another religion alongside of the others. This is also the case in many foreign lands today. But, the fact of the matter is, Christ is the way (not a way) the truth and the life (John 14:6). "Neither is there salvation in any other" (Acts 4:12).

Life stEP Do not be fooled with this "everybody's right" philosophy. While we will be considered narrow we must say that there is only one Savior, Jesus Christ.

2 Kings 19:5-20

What is the writer saying?

How can I apply this to my life?

pray Bolivia — For the Holy Spirit to bring about maturity in the lives of those studying for the ministry.

We must commend Hezekiah for going to the prophet. We read Isaiah's answer in Isaiah 19:7. God's ways are always best, and He controls all things. He is always concerned for His own. The King of Syria heard of Ethiopia and their advances. Realizing that the condition was worse than ever, he again sought to threaten Hezekiah and press him into submission (vv 8-13). His final argument was that all the gods of other kingdoms had failed, and his would too (vv. 19:12-13).

We now come to Hezekiah's prayer (vv. 14-19). This is a choice passage because Hezekiah received the enemy's message and spread it before the Lord (vv. 14). We need to spread our burdens and problems before God and leave them there. Rather than resort to the "intelligence department" of his own kingdom and then seek to outmaneuver the enemy, he took his burden to God and sought God's mind in prayer. God answered through Isaiah, and one of the greatest defeats in history took place. Hezekiah's prayer reminded God of His uniqueness (v. 15). There is none like Him. The enemy had been defeated because there "were no gods" to help the enemy. This would glorify God. We also learn from Jehovah's words that He is the omniscient (v. 27) omnipotent (v. 35) God.

Clearly we see from this passage the interest the Lord had in individuals. He is a prayer-hearing and a prayer-answering God.

As you come to the Lord today, are you willing to bare your heart and spread before Him your needs, even the most seemingly insignificant needs? "He who sees the sparrow fall, will hear your call."

2 Kings 19:35-20:11
What is the writer saying?

How can I apply this to my life?

PRAY Argentina — For godly, trained, Argentine leaders to become missionaries to lesser-reached, Spanish-speaking countries.

One of the greatest battles recorded in Scripture is found here. One hundred, eighty-five thousand people were defeated in one night, and Sennacherib's evil power was brought to an end. It has been pointed out that prophetically this pictures the ultimate end of the Assyrians who will enter the land of Israel during the Great Tribulation and like Sennacherib, be defeated.

Next we have Hezekiah's illness. God's advice was "set your house in order." Then the king prayed for an extension of life. God not only hears our prayers, but also sees our tears (v. 20:5). In answer to his prayer, 15 years were added to his life. The prophet Isaiah had figs placed on the boil as a token of God's power and might. God did the seemingly impossible, making the shadow retreat, which implies that the rotation of the earth had been reversed, but He could

have accomplished the miracle in some other way, such as bending the shadow. But...Hezekiah

At this point it would be helpful to read the parallel account of this event in 2 Chronicles. Here we read an added dimension not mentioned in 1 and 2 Kings. Something took place during those 15 additional years. "But Hezekiah rendered not again according to the benefit done unto him; for his heart was lifted up: therefore there was wrath upon him, upon Judah and Jerusalem. Notwithstanding, Hezekiah humbled himself for the pride of his heart, both he and the inhabitants of Jerusalem, so that the wrath of the LORD came not upon them in the days of Hezekiah" (2 Chronicles 32:25-26). The Word of God shows the blemishes as well as the beauty of the king. He had a relapse, but thankfully recovered from it.

Life stEP

While God gave the king more years, as he requested; all those years were not spent serving God correctly. Let us be on guard for tendencies to fall back spiritually. Let us use every bit of time given to us by the Lord to glorify Him.

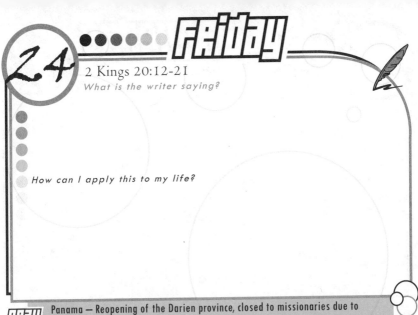

24 Friday

2 Kings 20:12-21

What is the writer saying?

How can I apply this to my life?

PRAY Panama — Reopening of the Darien province, closed to missionaries due to kidnapping and violence.

Hezekiah's life ended with an unfortunate exposure of his treasures to Babylon. If Satan can't get us to concede to the enemy, often he works in our hearts in the area of pride. Perhaps Hezekiah wanted to convince the Babylonians that he wasn't a second or third-rate king. Babylon had sent letters to Hezekiah to congratulate him on his healing. Also the Babylonians were inquisitive about astrology, change in the heavens and perhaps the sun's turning backwards. This prompted their coming. In any event, he showed them "his precious things", and it was said that "…there was nothing in his house, nor in all his dominion, that Hezekiah shewed them not" (v. 13). He didn't point to God's greatness or power of the Lord. God promptly rebuked him for this; and he was told that the day would come when the nation would be carried into Babylon, and nothing would be left. Not only do we need to have the short view of consequences, but the long view of repercussions from our disobedience. Much can be learned from Hezekiah's life about conditions of revival. The way verses 17 and 18 were fulfilled is well known to us.

High Points The chapter ends with references noting some of the high points and achievements in the king's life. The water conduit is mentioned. It deals with the waters of the Gihon spring directed inside of Jerusalem's walls via a tunnel leading to the pool of Siloam. It was a tunnel of 1,777 feet, making the waters available in case of a siege.

Life stEP

One of the greatest dangers in the Christian life is the "booby trap" of pride. It is so insidious and is a part of the world system (I John 2:15-16). Ask the Lord to help you in this matter so prevalent in Christendom today.

**24** •••••• **saturday**

2 Kings 22:3-10; 23:1-3

What is the writer saying?

How can I apply this to my life?

pray Uganda — Compassionate evangelistic outreach among the estimated 3,000,000 people living with AIDS.

As you read this passage it would be helpful to also read 2 Chronicles 34:8-18 and 1 Chronicles 34:29-31 for the full story. Because Josiah was concerned that the house not only be purged, but also repaired, Josiah sent Shaphan and Maaseiah along with Joah to repair the house of the Lord. The people's faithfulness in their work is noted (2 Chronicles 34:12). Hilkiah the priest, found a book of the law of the Lord given by Moses. This was some 73 years since Hezekiah's reign. Wickedness had prevailed since that time. Apparently under the reigns of Manasseh and Amon, it was against the law to read the Bible and to quote Scripture. Now, in this time of reconstruction and reformation, the long-ignored book of the law had been discovered. Hilkiah, the priest, delivered it to Shaphan the scribe, who in turn carried the book to the king. What a pity that it had been so long neglected! This is true in our lives. When we neglect the Word, we can expect the same kind of results.

The law was read to the people and the Passover was kept. We read "there was no passover like to that kept in Israel from the days of Samuel the prophet" (2 Chronicles 35:18) Thirty years of happiness, peace and prosperity were the portion of God's people. Looking at Josiah's life in retrospect, we praise the Lord for his stand and love for the Lord. But one wonders just how sincere the people were in their attitude toward his reform. Listen to a contemporary of Josiah: "For my people have committed two evils; they have forsaken me the fountain of living waters, and hewed them out cisterns, broken cisterns, that can hold no water" (Jeremiah 2:13).

Life stEP

We must look beyond the surface, the superficial pretense, and seek God with all our hearts. Not reformation but regeneration is important. Not a new leaf, but a new life; a real relationship with God that comes from the heart (Matthew 12:34).

The fourth Gospel was penned by the beloved Apostle John around A.D. 90. Early tradition holds that he wrote his Gospel from the city of Ephesus. One might wonder why God commissioned four biographies of His Son's earthly life, but certainly each account gives us a new appreciation and perspective of our Savior. Matthew writes to Jews, presenting Jesus of Nazareth as their prophesied Messiah.

He quotes many Old Testament passages in the process. As such, Matthew presents Jesus as the Lion of the Tribe of Judah, taking his genealogy back to Father Abraham. Mark writes to a Gentile Roman audience that knows so little about the Jews that he has to inform them that the Jordan is a river. The Romans care little for Jewish customs but know a lot about slavery, servanthood and obedience. As such, Mark presents Jesus as the perfect servant.

No one cares about the background of a servant so Mark provides no genealogy. Jesus is pictured as a busy man, "immediately" springing into action as He bustles around doing the will of His Father in heaven. Luke writes for a Greek audience. They admired both the human intellect (Plato, etc.) and body (the Olympics). As such, Luke presents Jesus as the greatest man who has ever lived. He takes Jesus' genealogy all the way back to Adam. Finally, John presents Jesus of Nazareth in His full-blown deity. Since God always existed, there is no need for a genealogy of Jesus in John. In comparison with the other Gospels, John bears the following distinctives: 27 personal interviews and the mention of six Jewish holidays. Jesus Christ is presented as greater than the law, temple, shekinah and holidays. John records seven great "I AM" claims.

- The Bread of Life (6:48)
- The Light of the World (8:12)
- The Door (10:7)
- The Good Shepherd (10:11)
- The Resurrection and Life (11:25)
- The Way, the Truth and the Life (14:6)
- The True Vine (15:1)

The purpose for the fourth Gospel is clearly stated by John in 20:31" But these are written, that ye might believe that Jesus is the Christ, the Son of God; and that believing ye might have life through his name." The miracles recorded in the book are signs of Jesus' deity that should lead people to believe unto eternal life. In fact, "sign" is the only word that John uses to describe a "miracle." In this book John presents seven signs, each highlighting an aspect of the salvation that only Jesus Christ could provide.

Sign	=	Salvation

1. Water into wine = The outpouring of God's grace
2. Cleansing the temple = The future perfect sacrifice
3. Nobleman's son = The necessity of faith
4. Lame man = The sovereignty of God
5. Feeding of the 5000 = The sufficiency of Christ's sacrifice
6. Blind man = The cleansing of forgiveness
7. Raising of Lazarus = The resurrection unto eternal life

Belief is the response that John seeks. The word "believe" occurs 98 times as compared to only eight times in Matthew, 13 times in Mark and nine times in Luke.

The following outline is provided by Dr. Merrill Tenney, whose commentary on John is highly recommended. It is based on the reaction of the Jewish authorities to the person of Jesus Christ.

1. Consideration	1-4
2. Controversy	5-6
3. Conflict	7-11
4. Crisis	12
5. Conference	13-17
6. Consummation	18-20
7. Commission	21

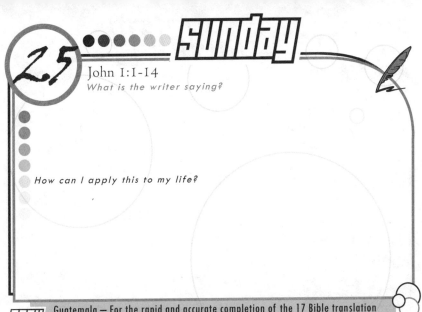

sunday

25

John 1:1-14

What is the writer saying?

How can I apply this to my life?

 PRAY Guatemala — For the rapid and accurate completion of the 17 Bible translation projects in progress.

John starts his account of the person of Christ in a style reminiscent of the book of Genesis, "in the beginning." Here, beginning does not imply a time when God did not exist, but rather just the opposite. John is saying that at the origin of human history, God was already there.

The terms Word (Greek, "Logos"), life (Greek, "Zoa") and Light (Greek, "Phos") here applied to Jesus Christ, speak of His being the revelation of God to mankind (see John 14:8-9), and the source of eternal life to those who believe.

Verse three plainly states that Jesus Christ is the Creator. What a blessing to read the account in Genesis 1 knowing it is an infallible account of the creative work of the Son of God. In verse five, we see the Light was met with opposition-darkness. The darkness is said to not comprehend the Light. The idea is not that the darkness did not understand the Light, but rather that it could not overpower it.

This section also introduces us to one sent to testify about the Light, John the Baptist. John is the prophesied forerunner (Isaiah 40:3; Malachi 3:1, 4:5-6). Those who should have been the best prepared to receive the Light, the Jews ("His own," v.11), rejected Him. To those who received the true Light, He gave the power (right) to be called children of God. Verse 13 states that this new birth came about by the will of God and not by any agency of man.

Life **stEP** Jesus Christ became flesh and blood that He might take upon Himself the sins of mankind. God became one of us so that He could be our substitutionary sacrifice... What sacrifice are you willing to make in return?

monday

25

John 1:15-28

What is the writer saying?

How can I apply this to my life?

In this section, John again turns his attention to John the Baptist. Here we see two aspects of John's life – his ministry and his message.

John the Baptist's ministry had created no small stir, evident in the fact that the Pharisees sent a delegation to investigate who he was and what he was doing (vv. 19, 24). John gave clear testimony to the nature of his ministry in verses 20-23. He told his investigators clearly he was not the Messiah, neither did he claim to be Elijah (Malachi 4:5), or the prophet (Deuteronomy 18:15). John simply referred to himself as "the voice" (see Isaiah 40:3).

Not only do we learn of John's ministry, but more importantly his message. John's ministry was to prepare the nation of Israel to receive Jesus. He proclaimed His eternality. He came after. Jesus was born after John and began his ministry after John, yet He was before, a clear declaration of Christ's pre-existence. He was from eternity past. John also describes the nature of Christ's ministry. His ministry is full of two Old Testament character qualities – grace (loving kindness) and truth. He provides "one gracious gift after another" (v. 16). Moses gave the law, not without grace and truth, but Christ would usher in a new dispensation that would fully unveil the grace of God in truth. Jesus Christ is the One who declares or explains the Father to us. The Greek root form of the word being translated declared is the source of our word exegete (to explain or unfold divine mysteries). Jesus explained the truth of the Father to man (v. 18).

Life stEP The ministry and message of John the Baptist points us clearly to Jesus Christ as the promised Messiah of Israel. John teaches us that Jesus is the eternal Son of God and the ultimate demonstration of the grace of God. Have you received God's gracious gift of salvation?

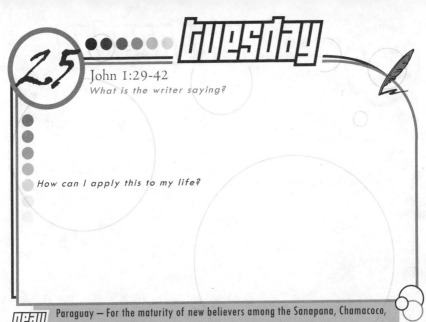

John 1:29-42

What is the writer saying?

How can I apply this to my life?

pray Paraguay — For the maturity of new believers among the Sanapana, Chamacoco, and the Guarani Indians.

It is clear from his calling Jesus the Lamb of God, that John knew Jesus was the promised Messiah (Isaiah 53:5-11). In the Jewish sacrificial system, an unblemished lamb was sacrificed during the celebration of Passover for each household. The blood of the sacrifice was a covering for sin, but could never take their sin away (Hebrews 10:4). John recognized that Jesus was the Promised One who would become the substitutionary sacrifice that would take away the sins of those who placed their faith in Him. Jesus' sacrifice was sufficient to atone for all of mankind (1 John 2:2).

The Jews were looking for their Messiah, but they were looking for one who would come and deliver them from their national political problems. What a tragedy that most were not alert to the time of their visitation (Luke 19:44)!

John gives us insight into how he knew Jesus. It had been revealed to him by God that the One upon whom the Holy Spirit descended and remained was the Christ.

The first four chapters of John describe a period of consideration when seven different people or groups of people consider the claims of Christ. First, John the Baptist recognizes Him as the sacrificial lamb. The second consideration involved the calling of His first disciples, Andrew and John, with Andrew later bringing his brother Peter as the third. Andrew is most prominently seen introducing others to Jesus (see John 6:8-9; 12:22). Andrew tells Peter they have found the Messiah, and John adds a translation note that Messiah means Christ. When Jesus meets Peter He gives him the name Cephas, which is Aramaic for rock.

Life stEP

Meeting Jesus is life changing. John and Andrew were never the same. John the Baptist pointed them to the Lamb of God, and they followed. Whom are you pointing to Christ? Whom are you following?

John 1:43-51
What is the writer saying?

How can I apply this to my life?

PRAY Taiwan — For godly Bible teachers and evangelists who know their cultures and how to relate Scripture to the root issues that hinder growth.

In John 1:43-51 Jesus adds Philip and Nathanael. Philip is from Bethsaida, as are Andrew and Peter. Bethsaida will later be one of the cities Jesus pronounces a woe upon (Matthew 11:21) for their lack of repentance, even in the face of some of Christ's greatest miracles.

Philip, like Andrew, found someone else to introduce to Christ, Nathanael. Nathanael, however, is not impressed with the news that Jesus is from Nazareth. Nazareth was small, had poor soil with no well, and housed a Roman garrison. This became the basis for the later accusation of Jesus' illegitimate birth.

The fig tree (v. 48) was a place of meditation and study. Guile is supplanter, the name for Jacob in Genesis 28. Perhaps Nathanael was meditating on that passage and Christ's knowledge of his thoughts convinced him of Jesus' Messiahship and thus his declaration Son of God, King of Israel. Jesus is amazed that Nathanael so quickly turns from skepticism to belief. Greater evidences lay ahead for Nathanael as He would soon see Christ do the first of many miracles that demonstrated His deity. The reference to angels ascending and descending is another connection to Jacob (Jacob's Ladder).

Son of Man was a favorite title the Lord used of Himself. This is the first of 11 times the title occurs in the book of John and carries the idea of Christ's union with mankind through the incarnation. At His birth, He became fully man so that He might be able to offer Himself a sacrifice for mankind. Jesus willingly laid aside the glories of heaven to become the ultimate servant and all-sufficient sacrifice (Mark 10:45).

Life stEP

When introduced to Christ, people react in different ways. Some, like Philip, are immediately sold-out. Others, like Nathanael, are skeptical and cautious. What a great example we see in Andrew and Philip, men who did not need the spotlight but quietly brought others to Christ.

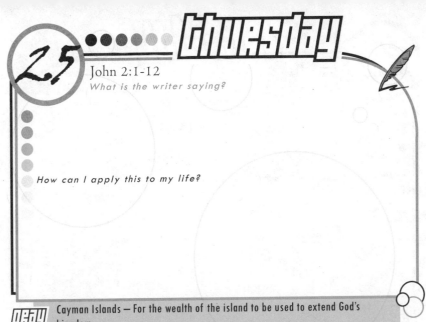

John 2:1-12

What is the writer saying?

How can I apply this to my life?

pray Cayman Islands — For the wealth of the island to be used to extend God's kingdom.

The wedding at Cana of Galilee provided the third opportunity for considering the person of Christ. We are told that the wedding was on the third day, which would be Tuesday. This seems strange to us, but actually, this was a popular day for Jewish weddings. Perhaps the reason Mary felt compelled to do something about the wine shortage was because so many extra people had gone to the wedding with her (Jesus and His disciples). This also points to the fact that Jesus was not seeking notoriety, for the occasion of His first sign was a small, family type of gathering. Christ's response to Mary's request was not impolite. Woman was a proper title similar to saying lady. Jesus protests that His hour (to reveal Himself as Messiah) had not yet come. The six large pots held water for washing hands. If only the guests knew where the wine came from! His creative act, bypassing both the growth stage of the grape and the proper aging of the wine, underscores God's ability to create with the appearance of age just as He did when He created Adam and Eve. Jesus came to bring the new wine of God's grace in a measure that exceeded man's need just as surely as the six large pots of wine surpassed the need of this small wedding party. This is the first sign of seven signs that John records. Remember, John's goal is to bring the reader to a place of belief in the deity of Jesus Christ. Surely, His power over natural processes was very convincing to those who knew and understood what had taken place.

So far we have seen Jesus as the Word, God, Creator, Light, only begotten Son, Lamb of God, Son of God, Messiah, King of Israel and Son of Man. Which title best speaks to you in your relationship with the One who even concerns Himself with trivial happiness and avoiding social blunders at a wedding?

John 2:13-25

What is the writer saying?

How can I apply this to my life?

pray Columbia — For an end to violence and widespread corruption within the government.

During the Passover, many of the scattered Jewish nation made a pilgrimage to Jerusalem to take part in the celebration and remembrance of God's grace, mercy, and deliverance from their bondage in Egypt. Because many had traveled in from distant lands, merchants had developed a thriving business providing the animals for sacrifice and the necessary currency exchange so those traveling would be able to pay their temple tax. Jesus charged these merchants with making God's house a place of merchandise. The word being translated for merchandise is the word from which we derive our word emporium. Jesus' zeal was for purity in the house of God! (See Psalm 69:9.) Jesus demonstrated the power to overturn the hypocritical spiritual state that was so prevalent and restore purity in the worship of the Almighty God. The Jews questioned His authority to challenge this accepted compromise. They demanded a sign as a sort of credential. The sign He offered went right over their heads as He spoke of His bodily resurrection. Here, as in other places in this book, John gives us a glimpse of the effect these events had on the disciples. His disciples, remembering this event later, were strengthened in their faith (John 12:16).

During these days in Jerusalem Jesus obviously did other signs (v. 23) that were causing people to believe He was a great man, believing in His name. That their belief was surface curiosity, and not saving faith in Him as the Christ, is evident from the statements in John 2:24-25. Jesus knew their hearts, and knew the quality of their belief and was not willing to believe in them.

God is not interested in the show of religion, but in purity of heart. He demands this not only from those who would worship, but especially from those who take part in the leading.

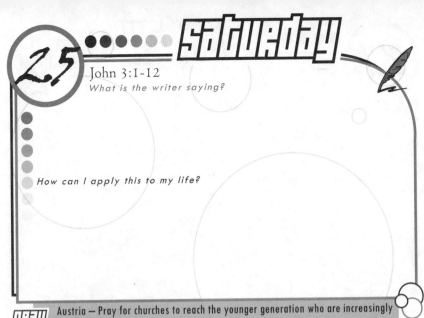
John 3:1-12

What is the writer saying?

How can I apply this to my life?

Christ's fourth encounter in chapter two was no low-key event. On His first trip to Jerusalem, He marches into the temple and runs out the moneychangers, instantly gaining the attention of the rulers of the Jews. The temple was to be a place of worship, not merchandise. In chapter three, we meet one of these rulers as Jesus has His fifth encounter with a ruler named Nicodemus. Nicodemus was a Jew and he came to Christ with intellectual needs. In the religious circles Nicodemus traveled in, he was a recognized authority (v. 10), yet he was spiritually blind. He was a Pharisee, a teacher (3:10), and part of the Sanhedrin. Jesus introduced Nicodemus to his need for rebirth. He initially understood this to be a physical rebirth, which would be impossible. Jesus helped him to understand that He spoke of a second birth into spiritual life (v. 6).

Jesus uses the wind (v. 8) to illustrate the ministry of God's Spirit to Nicodemus. Just like the wind, God's Spirit moves according to His sovereign will and His effect is unmistakable upon the hearts of mankind.

Nicodemus is only mentioned in the Gospel of John and only three times. In the three passages, it seems that John focuses on the progression of his spiritual life. Nicodemus appears first in chapter three, but leaves with no apparent change. Then in John 7:50 we find him defending Jesus against charges made by the Sanhedrin. Last, we find him at the Crucifixion (John 19:38-39), with Joseph boldly and publicly standing as a disciple of Christ.

Life STEP

Many who are brilliant and highly intellectual have a hard time grasping the simple truths of God's Word. Have you been born twice? To be alive is to have experienced physical birth. To be born again is to receive eternal life through placing your faith in Jesus Christ. You must be born again!

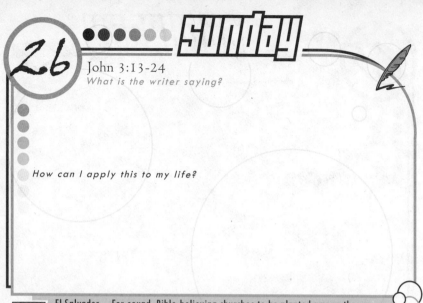

How can I apply this to my life?

PRAY El Salvador — For sound, Bible-believing churches to be planted among the Amerindian people.

Nicodemus was not a novice. However, when Jesus taught using a simple earthly comparison between physical birth and spiritual birth, this great teacher could not grasp the simple truth. How would he ever understand heavenly things, which no one had seen (3:12-13)?

Jesus was trying to relate to Nicodemus in terms he could grasp. He uses the account from Numbers 21, which tells of a time in the history of Israel when they complained against Moses and God sent serpents among the people. Many were dying and God instructed Moses to make a bronze likeness of a serpent and raise it on a pole. Those who were bitten were to look upon the serpent and they would not die. This required them to believe and look in faith. In the same way, at the cross, Jesus Christ would be raised up, and those who place their faith in God's substitutionary sacrifice would be saved. Nicodemus eventually appeared to understand (John 19:39).

Verse 16 shows the breadth (world); length (gave); depth (not perish) and height (everlasting life) of God's love. Christ has paid the price for the sin of all men of all time- past, present, and future (1 John 2:2). That means that the only issue left is whether men will believe and receive what has already been provided for them. This means that men go to hell, not because of their sins (plural), but because of the sin (singular) of unbelief. Once in hell, they then pay for their own sins (plural) having rejected Christ's gift of eternal life.

Again, John picks up the theme of light and darkness. Jesus came to bring light to those in darkness. Those who desire to know God are attracted to the light. Those whose deeds are evil reject the light and flee from it, not wanting to be exposed by it.

Are you attracted to the things of God or do you avoid them? Those who are of the light love the light and want to be near it.

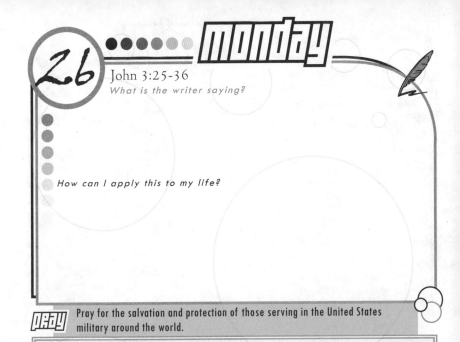

John 3:25-36

What is the writer saying?

How can I apply this to my life?

Pray for the salvation and protection of those serving in the United States military around the world.

Jesus was from above, heaven, and as such, His ministry was superior to that of John the Baptist. John was among the greatest of men, but did not compare to the Son of God. Jesus came with a message from heaven, but many were not receiving the message. Those who did receive Him had gone on record to the fact that God is true. However, those who rejected Christ were rejecting God and calling Him a liar, for they rejected His messenger and therefore His message. (See Luke 20:9-18.) Believers in Jesus Christ have the Holy Spirit living within them (1 John 4:13; Ephesians 1:13-14). At salvation, we have all of the Holy Spirit there is to receive. Verse 34 does not teach that Jesus had the full measure of the Holy Spirit, while we only get small allotments; but rather, this is in contrast to the Old Testament prophet who was only temporarily empowered by the Holy Spirit for a specific task. Jesus had the Holy Spirit permanently, as do those who place their faith in Him.

Verse 36 ends chapter three with a clear statement of what it means to be saved. The one who is saved is one who believes and by faith receives His Son, who alone gives everlasting life. In the same way, those in Numbers 21 had to believe Moses and look upon the serpent to escape death. The one who does not obey reveals a heart of unbelief, and will not see everlasting life, but will remain under God's wrath. God's abiding wrath is not a new condition, but rather a continuation of the condition they were already in due to their unbelief.

Life stEP

The Holy Spirit is not given to believers in installments. The question is not how much of the Holy Spirit do you have, but how much of you does the Holy Spirit have? Obedience is not a requirement of salvation, but rather a demonstration of it.

John 4:1-15

What is the writer saying?

How can I apply this to my life?

pray Ecuador – Praise for effective Christian radio ministry that encourages believers and spreads the Gospel.

The woman at the well, a Samaritan woman with deep spiritual needs, will prove to be everything that Nicodemus was not! The rulers, in this case the conservative Pharisees, were concerned about Jesus' growing success and, unlike John the Baptist, they were not happy. Unwilling to escalate the confrontation at this time, Jesus leaves the area of their concentration (Judea) and heads for safer, neutral ground in Galilee. Galilee was safer because ever since 930 B.C. non-religious Jews, and then even Gentiles starting in 722 B.C., had inhabited the area. In verse 4 must is a moral necessity, not physical, as they could have done what religious Jews did when traveling north. They could have bypassed the Samaritan area by crossing the Jordan River, traveling up the east bank. The sixth hour was high noon, normally too hot for the work of carrying water, but apparently this woman avoided the other women of the city out of shame for her lifestyle. Jesus does the unexpected and asks the woman for a drink. Note that John finds it necessary to explain that socially Jews would normally not stoop to speak to a Samaritan, much less a woman. Jesus crosses both boundaries to reach this woman. Jesus uses a known item, water, to introduce this woman to the unknown, spiritual life. The gift of God that He offers is salvation. Those who have been born again become life-giving streams to those with whom they share the good news of the Gospel.

Life stEP

To catch fish you have to go where the fish are! Christ takes the road less traveled and is busy doing His Father's business. Jesus used things people knew and understood to unfold spiritual truth.

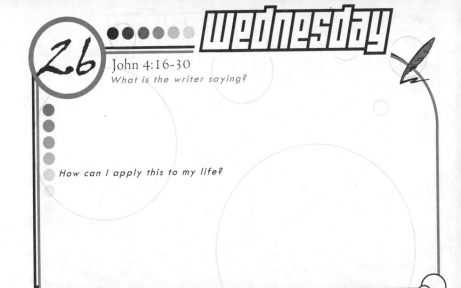

John 4:16-30

What is the writer saying?

How can I apply this to my life?

PRAY — Mexico — Believers to realize their responsibility to contribute to the support of ministers of the Gospel.

Up until this point, the Samaritan woman has been proud and argumentative. Jesus responds to her graciously, obviously impressing her since Jewish people of the day disdained the Samaritans as half-breeds and theological competitors. Racially, they were the product of the Assyrian foreign policy of population transfer to quell rebellion. The Israelites were moved out and Gentiles brought in.

Verse 18 indicates that marriage is more than sexual relations. Christ's request to return with her husband would cause her to walk a mile in the noonday sun. Embarrassed and confused, the woman resorts to the tactic of changing the subject and launches into a theological discussion. She tries to bog the conversation down by introducing a point of contention between Jews and Samaritans – where they should worship. Worship comes from worthship, recognizing and appreciating the worth of God. The central issue was not where one was when worshipping God, but rather the heart with which they approached God. God desires a pure and true heart from those who would worship Him (Psalm 24:4). Jesus intercepts her and brings her back to the central issue, a vital heart relationship with the Creator.

The disciples return, oblivious to the ministry that has been taking place, and are amazed that Jesus has crossed this cultural line. The Samaritan woman leaves her water pot and rushes to the city to tell her fellow-citizens, "Come and see, could this be the Messiah?"

Life stEP

Jesus was more concerned for the spiritual needs of this woman than what people would think about Him talking to her. Are you allowing culture to decide whom you will tell about Christ? The woman's first response was to try to avoid conviction with a debate. Are you seeking truth or holding to tradition?

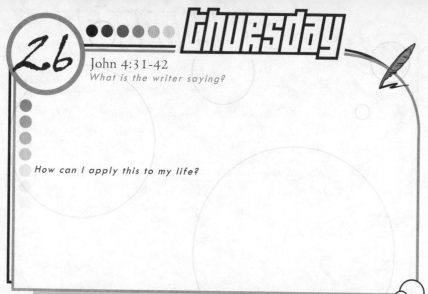

26 thursday

John 4:31-42

What is the writer saying?

How can I apply this to my life?

pray Honduras — For righteous men to be appointed as judges to halt corruption and institutional violence.

Upon returning, the disciples try to get Jesus to eat. He refers to the spiritual food He was already enjoying and confuses them in the shift from the physical to the spiritual realm. As the Samaritans were making their way down the road from the village to the well, Christ explained to His disciples that the harvest was not four months away, but that the fields were white unto harvest. Heads of grain would look white, but Jesus is probably referring to the white robes of the Samaritans coming toward Him! At a time like this, food should be the last thing on their minds. During the harvest, the reapers often are focused on the task of getting in the harvest to the neglect of meals. This is the case here. This is no time for eating; it is time to bring in the crop. Jesus also shares an important ministry principle. Not everyone gets to do the harvesting. Some plant, some water, some cultivate, and others often bring in the harvest. In the case of the disciples, they now had an opportunity to reap that which others had sown.

The final verses of this event (vv. 39-42) show us that the Samaritans first believed because of the woman's testimony. However, to the people of this culture, the testimony of a woman was inadequate. They would have to hear and see for themselves! Jesus did not share this condescending attitude toward women as was evident from His dealings with her.

Are you willing to set aside your comfort for the sake of the ministry God gives you to accomplish? Are you looking to the needs of others or are you too preoccupied with your own needs to see others? What part are you playing in the harvest of God?

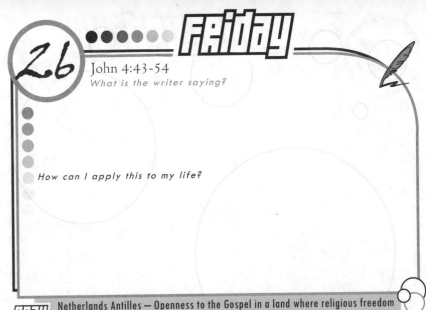

26 Friday

John 4:43-54

What is the writer saying?

How can I apply this to my life?

pray Netherlands Antilles — Openness to the Gospel in a land where religious freedom has yielded little fruit.

Unlike the argumentative initial response of the Samaritan woman, in this section we see the humble plea of a father for his child. This sign was again to demonstrate who Jesus was in order that the people might believe and be saved. Cana, where Jesus met this nobleman, was over 20 miles from Capernaum where the boy lay sick. Jesus, being God, is omniscient, and therefore just as capable of healing this child at a distance as if standing at his bedside. Jesus' first response to the nobleman seems rather harsh but is probably intended for the broader audience who may have heard. The Jews were always seeking a sign and were often reluctant to receive Christ at face value. The nobleman was more than likely a Jew, possibly an important member of Herod's court. The nobleman did not appeal to his position, nor did he defend himself in light of Jesus' charge, but rather in earnest faith again appealed to Him to save his dying son. The man asked Jesus to come to Capernaum, but Jesus sent him away with the simple statement, "Your son lives." The nobleman did not question, but returned the 20 miles home. When he learned of the hour of his son's healing, the nobleman believed, and in turn led his family to belief in Jesus.

Life stEP

Are you willing to take God at His word? How often have we seen God deliver only to then question it or explain it away? The miracles of Jesus demonstrated who He was, so that men might believe, not to draw attention or attract a crowd.

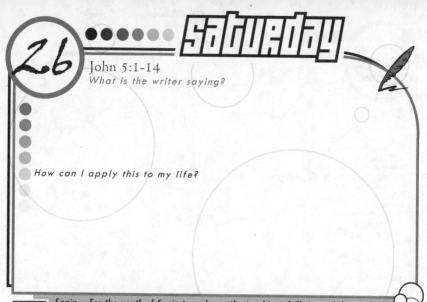

John 5:1-14

What is the writer saying?

How can I apply this to my life?

Spain — For the youth of Spain to embrace the teaching of Christ and the relevancy of God's Word.

Unlike the nobleman in the previous section who sought Jesus out to heal his sick son, this man who had been sick for 38 years was not even aware it was Jesus who healed him! The description of the angel stirring the water and subsequent healing of the first to enter the water (vv. 3b-4) is not found in the earliest manuscripts prior to A.D. 400. The fact that this may have been only a local legend adds to the sadness of the situation. How many today cling to false hope built upon the traditions of men rather than the Word of God? This type of healing is unique in Scripture. Jesus has compassion on this individual knowing the number of years he has suffered. His direction to the man is simple, "Take up thy bed, and walk." The Jews give the man a hard time about carrying his pallet, seeing this as a violation of the Sabbath rest. This once again is an example of man's tradition being exalted to the same level as God's Word. Jesus obviously did not stay around to be mobbed by the others at the pool. By sovereign choice, He had shown grace to this man who did not even know whom He was. Later Jesus found him in the temple and warned him. His condition may have been the result of his sin. A similar situation is found in Matthew 9:2, where a man's sins are forgiven resulting in his healing.

Life stEP

In the world many cling to false hope and false religion based upon myth and superstitions. We who know the truth are to be a light in the darkness for those who are lost. Many of life's great tragedies are directly traceable to lifestyle choices!

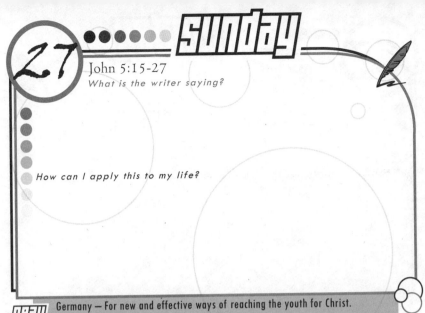

27 — sunday

John 5:15-27

What is the writer saying?

How can I apply this to my life?

PRAY — Germany — For new and effective ways of reaching the youth for Christ.

The first four chapters of John were characterized by consideration, but we now move to a new section of John, chapters 5-7: The Period of Controversy. The controversy begins as Jesus heals a man, who had been lame for 38 years on the Sabbath. He meets the man at the Pool of Bethesda (beth is "house" and hesed is "loving kindness," one of the Old Testament words for "grace"). Verse 16 demonstrates the Pharisees' irritation over Sabbath desecration. Verse 18 voices another complaint, that He claimed equality with God, by calling Him "His own Father" (Greek idiom as in idiosyncrasy). Jesus will say, My Father or Your Father, but not Our Father in His discussions with the Pharisees! In today's passage, Christ builds on His claims to a special relationship with God, which the Pharisees correctly interpret as claims of equality with God. Throughout this passage, Jesus declares His commitment to doing the Father's will. He had come to fulfill all that the Father had given Him to do. His statement in verse 17 and following made it clear that this was only the beginning, and He would continue His work as the Father directed. Verse 24 makes it clear that one cannot have a valid faith in God the Father apart from a faith in the Son of God.

Life stEP — Many today live their Christian lives under a cloud of do's and don'ts. The Pharisees missed Jesus because He did not fit their mold. God wants us to follow Him from the heart not by a system of man-made religious regulation. The key is a relationship, not regulation.

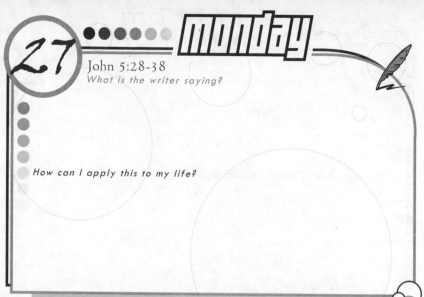

monday

27

John 5:28-38

What is the writer saying?

How can I apply this to my life?

PRAY — Czech Republic — For God to raise up believers who can influence public policy in their society.

Jesus concludes His response to the challenge that came from the Jews by stating that the resurrection and subsequent judgment will verify His authority. Some day all those who have died will hear His voice and arise (see Daniel 12:2). Two distinct outcomes await those who will arise. The open arms of their Savior will greet some, while others will meet their final Judge (Revelation 20:11-15). Good and evil in verse 29 are not conditions of salvation, but the evident fruit of their lives.

The Pharisees argue that a man cannot be his own character witness. Jesus in 5:31 picks up this thought and states that if He alone bore witness of Himself, His witness would not be true. True here, in the sense of admission into a legal defense. Therefore, in verses 30-47, Christ brings five testifiers to the witness stand: 1) 5:30-31 – Himself. The point here is not that He never bore witness of Himself. He did, but that He was not alone in His witness. 2) 5:32-35 – John the Baptist, whose life and ministry prepared the way for the coming of Christ. 3) 5:36 – His works. When John the Baptist doubted in prison, Jesus let His works speak for Him to assure John that He truly was the Messiah (Matthew 11:2-6). 4) 5:37-38 – His Father (three times: baptism, transfiguration, and after the triumphal entry), 5) 5:39-48 – Scripture.

Life **stEP**

The unbelieving heart is often oblivious to the evidence that is clearly seen by those who are open to hear God's voice. Hard hearts are often only softened by a consistent loving demonstration of the life of God lived out by those who truly know Him.

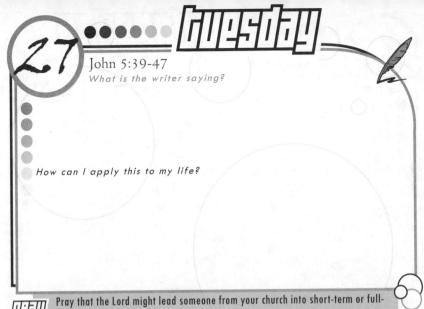

27 tuesday

John 5:39-47

What is the writer saying?

How can I apply this to my life?

PRAY Pray that the Lord might lead someone from your church into short-term or full-time missions work.

The religious leaders of the day thought themselves to be experts in the Scripture. They equated their strict observance of the Law given by Moses with their salvation. Yet, Jesus turned this against them when He stated that Moses wrote of Him (v. 46). If they would not believe Moses whom they held in the highest esteem, how could they believe Him whom they despised? Even in the face of overwhelming evidence, the unbelieving heart often is not softened, but grows even harder. Jesus did not fit the mold they had cast for their Messiah and as a result, they were unwilling to hear Him, much less humbly confess their need before Him. Their pecking order was well established, yet He needed none of their recognition (v. 41). Their glory did not come from God, but rather was self-imposed as they compared themselves to one another.

Moses was the human author of the first five books of the Old Testament: Genesis, Exodus, Leviticus, Numbers, and Deuteronomy. One does not need to look far to find Moses' prophetic words relating to Jesus. Genesis 3:15 points directly to the cross work of Jesus Christ where He dealt Satan the defeating blow that sealed his doom. This is only the beginning of many such prophecies in Moses' writings.

Life stEP Self-righteousness is the worst sort of blindness to plague mankind. The writings of Moses should have brought the Jews to a place where they were humbly seeking a Savior. Yet they twisted his words and missed his highest thoughts. How do you view yourself in the light of God's Word?

John 6:1-14

What is the writer saying?

How can I apply this to my life?

PRAY United Kingdom — For many teens to be saved through Christian camping and outreach events.

The feeding of the multitude was the fourth sign done by Jesus. Each sign was a demonstration of who He was, God the Son. John chose each one carefully to underscore an aspect of saving faith. John gives a tremendous picture of God's abundant supply for man's greatest need. Here bread was broken to meet man's physical need. In only a few verses Jesus will show that He is the true bread come down from heaven and that His sacrifice is more than sufficient to meet the needs of all humanity (1 John 2:2). In this Gospel we learn of some interesting details the other synoptic Gospels do not give: the nearness of the Passover feast, the testing of Philip (v. 5), and the type of bread used (barley was a coarse, cheap bread). Once again, Andrew is seen bringing someone to Jesus. Some would like to cheapen this event by saying that each person only received a small fragment, a token taste. However, verses 11 and 12 quickly dispel that notion. Each man ate all he wanted, and the fragments that were gathered amounted to 12 baskets full. Interestingly, Jesus' insistence that "nothing be lost" (v. 12) was nearly identical to His words in John 3:16; 6:39; 10:28; and 18:9 where He states that none of those who trusted Him for salvation would be lost

Life stEP

Just as Jesus was not limited by physical circumstances, in the same way His sacrifice is sufficient to meet every spiritual hunger of mankind. Because He is God, His sacrifice is infinite and His gift of salvation is secure. Have you partaken of the Bread of Life?

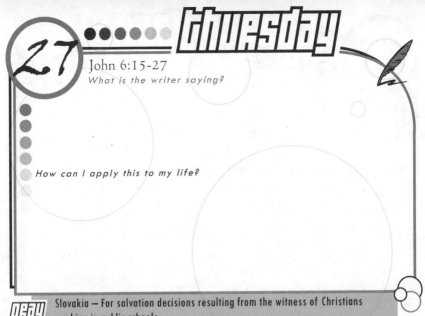

John 6:15-27

What is the writer saying?

How can I apply this to my life?

pray Slovakia — For salvation decisions resulting from the witness of Christians working in public schools.

The response offered by those who had been miraculously fed was not what Jesus intended, He wanted them to see Him as their Messiah, but they wanted to make Him their king. His rebuke (v. 26) exposes their wrong motives. The miracles were proof of His true deity, yet the people were only thinking of the physical. Jesus instructs them to labor for the meat that remains (Consider the water that satisfies in John 4:14). The food is Christ Himself.

As He often did, Jesus came apart from the crowd to be alone on the mountain. The place was on the western bank of the Sea of Galilee near the city of Bethsaida (Luke 9:10). Jesus had sent the disciples on ahead and had possibly agreed to meet them near Bethsaida (Mark 6:45) on their way to Capernaum. He had remained to see the crowd off and then had gone up into the mountain to pray (Mark 6:46). The disciples had not expected to see Jesus coming to them walking on the sea. This fifth sign demonstrated His power over creation and the ability to transcend the physical limitations that bind mankind. "With God all things are possible" (Mark 10:27). The crowds, upon discovering Jesus' departure, quickly follow to Capernaum. Jesus confronts them, exposing their motive in seeking only a free meal. Sealed in verse 27 is similar to our idea of something that is certified. The Father placed His certification upon the ministry of His Son.

Life **stEP** Many today seek after the miraculous and the spectacular. God's desire for man has not changed. It's that we might look to the Son and seeing, believe. What is your motivation in following God?

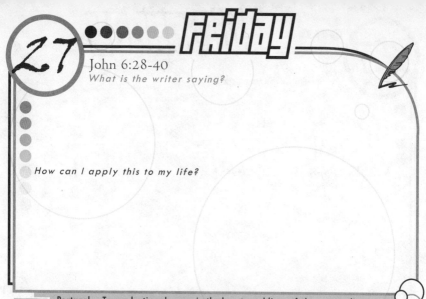

John 6:28-40

What is the writer saying?

How can I apply this to my life?

PRAY Portugal — To see lasting changes in the hearts and lives of those attending Christian camps.

John 6:35 is the first of the seven great "I Am" statements in John. Most of these statements have a predicate nominative (in this case, bread). Nevertheless, all reflect the naked "I Am" of Exodus 3, the covenantal name of Jehovah (Yahweh), by which God wished to make Himself known to His chosen people. Based on the Hebrew verb to be, it conveys both His eternality (past, present, and future or the eternal present) and His self-sufficiency. The backdrop to "I am the bread of life" is the miracle of the feeding of the 5,000 (John 6:1-21). When confronted with the need for food to feed the fainting masses, Philip (the accountant) calculates that it would take 66% of a man's annual salary to feed the crowd. Andrew (the visionary) finds a boy's lunch and talks him out of it! This is the only miracle recorded in all four Gospels. Only John mentions that the people of Galilee were ready to force Jesus to be their king. The people are rather brazen in their request for more food and further signs of Christ's Messiahship. The implication of verse 31 is "Feed 2.5 million people for 40 years like Moses did and then we'll consider your claims!" Jesus quickly corrects them stating that it was God who supplied the bread in the wilderness, and now the true bread from heaven was come down to them.

Life stEP

"Whose god is their belly (Philippians 3:19)." It is not a pretty picture when human existence is reduced to "gimme, gimme." Let us not overlook true spiritual food in our lust for physical things.

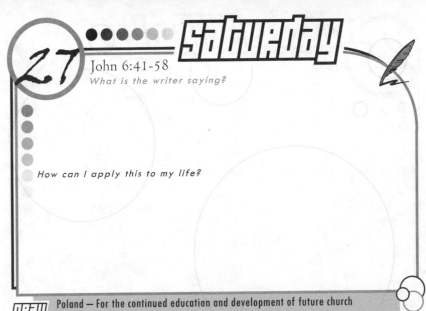

John 6:41-58

What is the writer saying?

How can I apply this to my life?

pray Poland — For the continued education and development of future church leadership.

Jesus has an extended conversation with the people of Galilee. They want Him to throw off the yoke of Rome and meet their physical needs. However, it is clear that they are not interested in His spiritual program. Verse 44 makes it abundantly clear that apart from the working of God, no one would come to Christ. Jesus states that the bread, which He was offering, was different from the manna, which their fathers had eaten in the wilderness (v. 49). Those who ate that bread were dead. He was offering Himself as the true Bread of Life, which brings eternal life. Elsewhere, Christ told His disciples that He spoke in parables to discourage the unbelievers (Matthew 13:13). In this passage, He uses a similar tactic, making His teaching sufficiently difficult to weed out the marginal disciples. They don't follow the analogy of eating His body (appropriating His sacrificial death) for (spiritual) nourishment. In light of the emphasis on salvation by believing and the many analogies that Christ uses in John, it is clear that He is not referring to taking Communion as the basis of salvation, and eating the body and blood of Christ. The entire passage speaks of a spiritual consuming and internalization of Him, the logos of God, via belief.

Life **stEP** Those who have partaken of the Bread of Heaven will never hunger again. It is only through the broken fellowship of unconfessed sin that the pangs of spiritual want return. Is your soul satisfied today?

28

SUNDAY

John 6:59-71

What is the writer saying?

How can I apply this to my life?

PRAY Papa New Guinea — For the leaders of this land to seek righteousness and guidance of God in the affairs of their nation.

Apart from the work of the Holy Spirit, genuine belief would not be possible (v. 63). The statement that Jesus knew from the beginning uses the same Greek word as found in John 1:1 where we read that the Word was with God in the beginning. This is a clear statement of His foreknowledge, an attribute applicable only to God. As He stated earlier (John 6:37), He again declares the need for God's intervention to bring man to saving faith. Left alone no one would come to the light. Verse 66 makes it clear that even being a follower does not guarantee that a person is a true believer. As some drift away, Jesus challenges the disciples. Spokesman Peter eloquently professes their trust in Him. He uses a perfect tense of the verb (a present condition based on a previous act) saying, "We have been and are currently believing that You are the Holy One of God" (v. 69). It is interesting that elsewhere a demon makes the same identification (Mark 1:24) and that Jesus responds by saying, "Yes, but one of you has sold out to Satan." Again, John switches roles from that of the narrator of the story to interpreter, as he explains to the reader that Jesus' words in verse 70 are directed toward Judas. Judas, although chosen to be one of the 12, was simply going through the motions of belief, but did not posses genuine faith.

Life stEP

Profession and possession are not the same. True faith is not a matter of mere words. A living faith will be active and visible in the fruit of the life. Those who only profess faith will not endure over the long haul (1 John 2:19).

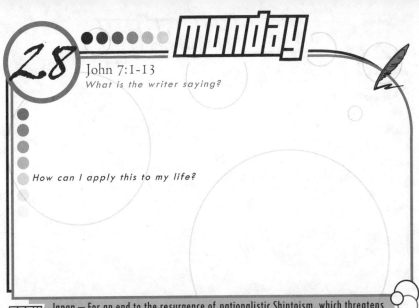

How can I apply this to my life?

pray Japan — For an end to the resurgence of nationalistic Shintoism, which threatens religious freedom.

During this time in Jesus' ministry, it was getting dangerous for Him to travel openly in Judah for the Jews sought His life. However, during the Feast of Booths (Tabernacles), He again teaches in the temple in Jerusalem. The Feast of Booths was a time when the Jews were reminded of God's provision during their wandering in the wilderness. They were to make booths and stay in them for seven of the eight total days of the feast (see Leviticus 23:42). Each day offerings of the fruit of the harvest were being made. The eighth day all were to gather for corporate worship and offering.

Some think that to have been alive when Christ walked among men would have been a great advantage to believing. In the last chapter, John has shown that many of Jesus' followers did not believe in Him (6:66) and that even one of the 12 was not a true disciple. Now here, in this passage, we learn that His own brothers were not believing in Him (v. 5). Their tone appears to be taunting (vv. 3-4). Jesus is not prepared at the time to go up to Jerusalem, but chooses to wait and depart sometime after His brothers have already gone up. The climate in Jerusalem is volatile (vv. 11-13), but He begins to openly teach in the temple in spite of the danger.

Life stEP

The deceitfulness of the human heart can blind even those of great opportunity to observe the work of God. Be careful never to get so accustomed to seeing God work that you treat His grace and mercy as a common thing.

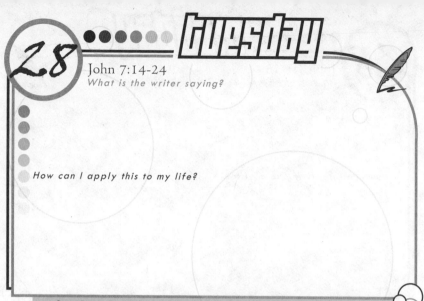

John 7:14-24

What is the writer saying?

How can I apply this to my life?

pray Costa Rica — For godly young people to embrace their role in reaching their generation for Christ.

When Jesus began to teach, the people marveled. They could not understand how one who had no formal training could teach with such power. Yet, the wisdom of the teaching of Christ was from above. The things He taught were from above, from the Father.

The requirement of God for man is to believe, to take God at His word by faith. Verse 17 is such an appeal, "Take me at my word and see the truth of what I am teaching." Too often men look to one another instead of looking to God for truth.

The one deed (work), referred to in verse 21, is a reference to the healing of the lame man at the pool near the Sheep Gate (John 5:1-15). Because this healing had taken place on the Sabbath, the Jews had labeled Him a sinner, violating the Law. Jesus picks up on their discontent and reveals the hypocrisy of it. If it was not a violation of the Law of Moses to circumcise on the Sabbath, how could making the man whole be a violation? Judging by appearance (v. 24) was looking only at the letter of the Law and not the Spirit behind it. The Jews had reduced their worship of God to a legal code that must be followed to the letter. God was looking for heart obedience based in a relationship with Him.

Life stEP

What is the basis of your faith? Ritual or relationship? Those who heard the Son of God speak were often too stuck in their ritualistic mindset to hear what He was really saying.

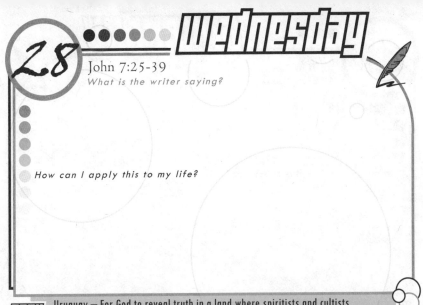

28

John 7:25-39

What is the writer saying?

How can I apply this to my life?

pray   Uruguay — For God to reveal truth in a land where spiritists and cultists outnumber true believers.

Many of those who had made the pilgrimage to Jerusalem were obviously not familiar with Jesus, but were able to connect Him to the whispering they had heard among the crowds. The Jews held a common conception that the Messiah would burst on the scene seemingly out of nowhere, but with Jesus, they knew where He came from. Jesus responded that while they may have known Him and where He came from, they do not know the Father who had sent Him. Many who heard His words were convinced that He was their Messiah and believed, yet the Jewish leaders only increased in the hardness of their hearts and their rejection. As Jesus began speaking of the time of His return to the Father in heaven, His words went right over their heads.

Tabernacles is the harvest home festival, much like our Thanksgiving. In honor of the 40 years of protection in the wilderness, families would take their joyful meals outdoors in gaily-decorated shelters. Everyday the High Priest would lead a procession from the Pool of Siloam with water in a gold pitcher to pour out at the temple. With this as a backdrop, Jesus stands on the eighth day and calls out to the spiritually thirsty crowds (v. 37).

Against this backdrop, Jesus proclaimed that He was the source of true satisfaction and that those who find this satisfaction would become a source of refreshment to all. John (v. 39) interprets His comments as pertaining to the Holy Spirit, whom those who believe would receive upon their salvation.

Life **stEP**

Those who responded in faith to the ministry of the Savior found eternal life. There is a great difference between hearing God's Word and receiving it.

John 7:40-53

What is the writer saying?

How can I apply this to my life?

The opening verses of this section show the range of opinions about Jesus that swirled around the Jerusalem streets. Some said He was the Prophet (see Deuteronomy 18:15-18), while others (v. 42) said He was the Christ (Messiah), and yet others were sure that He could not be the Messiah, because He was to come from Bethlehem and they thought that Jesus was from Galilee. Their statements show both their lack of knowledge concerning Jesus and their impulsiveness, for in verse 44 they are ready to seize Him. Their inability to lay hold on Him shows that everything was moving forward on God's timetable, not man's.

In typical Pharisaical fashion, they upbraided the people for being taken in by Jesus' words. Their statement says little about their knowledge, but much about the hardness of their hearts. The claim that none of the Pharisees were believing in Jesus (v. 48) begins to lose its weight as Nicodemus speaks. The first time John introduced Nicodemus was in chapter 3. There, he came in the darkness to interview Jesus having seen the miracles He did. Now, he defends Jesus' right to a fair hearing. The response of the Pharisees (v. 52) "Art thou also of Galilee?" was an insult and an erroneous one at that, seeing that the prophet Jonah was from Galilee (see 2 Kings 14:25).

Our words always reveal the attitudes of our hearts. James said it best when he asked if the same fountain could bring forth both fresh and bitter water. What are your words telling about the condition of your heart?

28 Friday

John 8:1-11

What is the writer saying?

How can I apply this to my life?

Finland — For believers to abandon church hopping and become committed church members.

The episode in chapter 8 is designed to entrap Jesus and discredit him. The scene begins on the Mount of Olives where He is already ministering to a constant stream of people (v. 2: "were coming" indicates constantly). The Pharisees show up with a woman taken in the very act of adultery. (Where was the man?) The tense of the verb say (v. 4) indicates that they were repeatedly saying. Their statement about the Mosaic Law was accurate although God in His grace did not always insist on capital punishment, such as in the case of King David. They were hoping to either accuse Him of contradicting Moses or of contradicting Roman law, which did not allow the Jews to inflict capital punishment. It seems that Jesus was embarrassed by the crassness of their treatment of the woman (v. 6). He brilliantly avoids the trap by putting it back on them to fulfill the Law, if they are worthy.

Christ succeeded in turning another challenge back on His interrogators when questioned about the tribute money ("Render therefore unto Caesar the things which are Caesar's; and unto God the things that are God's." Matthew 22:21). In neither case did He really answer their question, but rather He exposed their ulterior motives for asking the question. Out of gratitude for His gracious treatment, the woman awaited His direction. It is established that not one of the men stayed to pursue the matter. Jesus does not condone the woman's sin, but releases her with the admonition to cease her life of immorality.

Life stEP

We are to hate the sin, but love the sinner. Jesus associated with the dregs of society. They were the ones who needed the doctor. He did not water down His demands, however. Sinners were forgiven, but expected to repent and forsake their sin.

28 — SATURDAY

John 8:12-24

What is the writer saying?

How can I apply this to my life?

pray Peru — For the Quechua and Aymara people to reject superstition and accept Christ as their Savior.

Jesus is still in Jerusalem at the Feast of Tabernacles. John again picks up the theme of light and darkness. This is the second of the seven great "I am" statements of Jesus that John records. The priests in the temple would light the Court of Women for dancing and singing, making large lamps and using worn out priestly linen garments as wicks. In the light of these festive hanging bonfires, Jesus made the analogy to His spiritual illumination. The Shekinah Glory had lighted the way of redemption for the children of Israel from Egyptian bondage and through the 40 years of wilderness wanderings. That same light is now available for daily guidance in righteousness. Soon, at the Feast of Pentecost, it would descend from heaven and enter individual believers in the form of the indwelling Holy Spirit. Jesus' testimony was valid because He knew the answers to the big questions of life: Who Am I? Where did I come from? Where am I going? The Pharisees could not answer those questions. Christ's second witness of validity (satisfying the demands of the Law for two witnesses in a court of law) was the testimony of His own Father, who not only empowered Him for His miraculous works but also spoke from heaven on three different occasions stating His approval of His Son (baptism, transfiguration, and after the triumphal entry).

Life stEP

It is stunning to see the hardness of the human heart. The Pharisees were intelligent men. Though they argued vehemently with the Lord, they must have felt the power of His words. They never denied the reality of His miracles. Yet in the face of such obvious power, they persisted in their opposition.

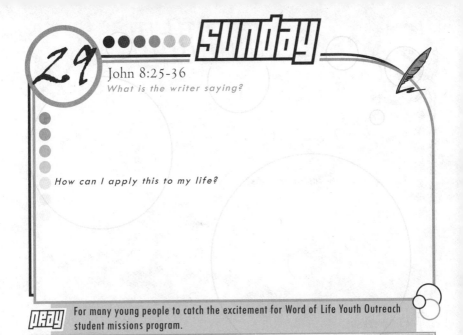

John 8:25-36

What is the writer saying?

How can I apply this to my life?

PRAY For many young people to catch the excitement for Word of Life Youth Outreach student missions program.

This is the second time that Jesus mentioned that He was going away and that where He was going they could not go (because they weren't righteous and wouldn't be welcomed into heaven). The first time they wondered if He was planning to leave the country to live among the Jews in the area outside of Palestine (John 7:35). Now they wonder if He is planning to commit suicide (John 8:22). In 8:24, Jesus literally says, "If ye believe not that I Am he, ye shall die in your sins." This again is an allusion to the name Jehovah in Exodus 3 (although they and many translators assumed He meant, I am he). Jesus is exasperated with their insolence, and rightly so, since He clearly claimed to be the Messiah sent from heaven with the signs to verify the claim. Lifted up normally means glorified, but here, as in chapter 3, it refers to His crucifixion. Christ predicts His own death and specifies death by crucifixion so that when it happens, the people can remember His prediction and know that He was telling the truth.

True believers will automatically demonstrate their genuineness by their continuation in the faith. It is the unsaved pretenders who do not have the inner energy to persevere. Verse 32 mentions three highly prized commodities: knowledge, truth, and freedom. His Jewish audience bristles in their pride of being Abraham's Seed. Their claim of never being enslaved is strange in light of 400 years in Egypt and their current domination by Rome (v. 33)!

The prophecies in the Old Testament about the coming of Messiah and the teachings of Jesus seem so clear to us living after the fact. How many teachings of our duties during the Church Age will seem equally clear after the return of Christ? We need to be diligent students of the Word so we are not embarrassed.

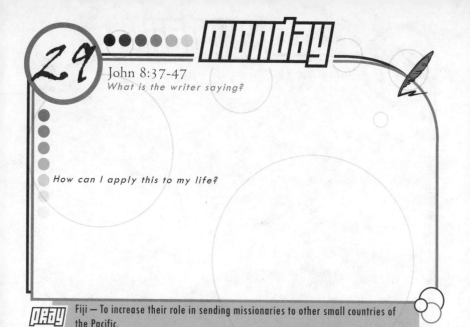

29 monday

John 8:37-47

What is the writer saying?

How can I apply this to my life?

PRAY Fiji — To increase their role in sending missionaries to other small countries of the Pacific.

The discussion gets heated as Jesus points out that their father is really Satan as demonstrated by their murderous intent (vv. 38, 44). When they attempt to claim Abraham as their father, Jesus exhorts them to act like it! Verse 41 comes out of the blue and might be a jab at the rumors surrounding Christ's virgin conception and birth (cf. 48). In 6:66 we noted that even discipleship does not guarantee that a person is a true believer. We see this as some drift away from Christ. In today's passage, Jesus shows that true discipleship depends on having the right Father. Jesus refers to your father three times (vv. 38, 41, and 44). The Jews claimed to be the sons of Abraham in verse 39, but Jesus shows this to be false. They were of Abraham's physical seed. This is true. However, Abraham is not their spiritual father. The Jews also claimed to be sons of God in verse 41. Again, Jesus shows this to be false by showing that if you love the parent, you will not hate the son which they were doing. Last, Jesus says they are sons of the devil (v. 44), the father of lies, for they were knowingly doing his works as is seen in verses 38, 41, and 44.

Jesus substantiates His claim to be speaking the truth on the premise that no one could charge Him with sin. His enemies often debated whether Jesus was a sinner. (John 9:24; 18:38; 19:4, 6). Christ answers His own question of why the Jews would not believe Him. They have rejected Him because of their relationship to the devil. Indeed, they were not of God!

Life stEP

There are many who claim to be disciples of Christ, but this does not mean that they are! The only way for a person to be a true disciple is to first have the right lineage. To whom do you trace your lineage? If it is to anyone but God the Father, then you are not a disciple of Christ.

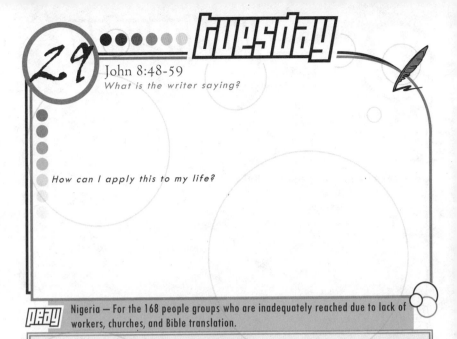

John 8:48-59

What is the writer saying?

How can I apply this to my life?

PRAY Nigeria — For the 168 people groups who are inadequately reached due to lack of workers, churches, and Bible translation.

To call Jesus a Samaritan was the equivalent of calling Him a religious fraud. The Jews begin hurling all kinds of abuse at Him, even to the point of saying He was demon possessed! In verse 55, Jesus says that these Sons of Abraham had not come to know the heavenly Father (this word for know means to come to know by experience) while He knew the Father (a different word for know which means to know inherently). Jesus' words in verse 51 do not miss their target, as the Jews clearly understand the implication of shall never see death. They fume over the fact that these statements would clearly make Him superior to Abraham and the prophets! "Who do you think you are?" would be how we would say it today (v. 53). We can almost feel the indignation coming from the crowd! Jesus understands their frame of mind, but makes it clear He is not attempting to exalt (glorify) Himself, but simply carry out the will of His Father.

Your father Abraham (v. 56) is stated in the ancestral sense. What he rejoiced to see was the promise of future salvation through his seed. How much Abraham understood is not known. The Jews again are stuck in the present because they do not recognize the deity and therefore, the eternality of Christ. That Jesus would have first-hand knowledge of Abraham is beyond their comprehension. The discussion comes to an explosive climax with Christ's clearest "I Am" (Jehovah) claim in verse 58!

Life stEP

How do you respond when those who do not agree, challenge the basis of your claim to have a relationship to God? We can imagine in this event in Christ's life that His accusers were livid, while He remained calm and confident (see Philippians 1:28).

253

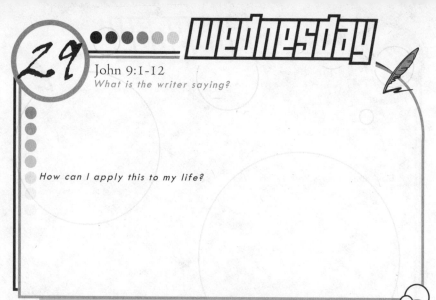

John 9:1-12

What is the writer saying?

How can I apply this to my life?

pray France — For believers to be evangelizing to the 150,000 known French Muslims.

John 9 is the fascinating story of the healing on the Sabbath of the man born blind (the second Sabbath healing in John that infuriated the religious establishment). This is the only recorded miracle of one defective from birth. A number of Christ's miracles involved the healing of the blind in fulfillment of Messianic passages such as Isaiah 35:5. The event begins with a philosophical discussion among the disciples as to why the man was born blind. In verse 34, the Pharisees will voice one popular opinion. As far back as the book of Job, we find that those who suffered were considered to be under God's judgment for their sins. Christ however, states that it was for this very moment that he had been born blind, that the Father might be glorified. Christ makes clay, anoints the man's eyes, and tells him to wash in the pool of Siloam (sent). The clay encouraged the man to display faith.

Throughout his Gospel, John has highlighted specific miracles (signs) to show that Jesus is God and to bring his readers to the point of believing in Him. Jesus had previously stated before the crowd in the temple that He is the light of the world (cf. John 8:12; 9:5). Now He clearly illustrates this truth by bringing one born in both physical and spiritual darkness into the light. Just as this man had to wash the clay from his eyes, so our sins must be washed in the blood of Christ.

We are all born blind. It is to the glory of God that some sense the clay of God's Word and respond in faith receiving their spiritual sight and a new way of life!

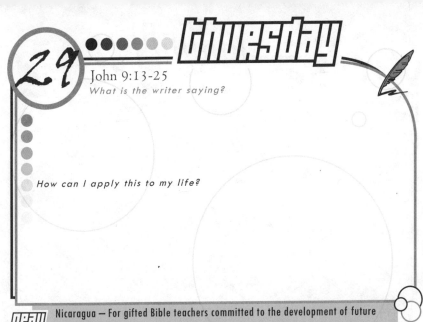

29

John 9:13-25

What is the writer saying?

How can I apply this to my life?

pray Nicaragua — For gifted Bible teachers committed to the development of future church leadership.

This portion of John's Gospel shows the tragedy of following man's tradition rather that walking with God. Clearly there were no sustained doubts from anyone present that a miracle had occurred, but it was against the Pharisaic Code to knead clay on the Sabbath (vv. 13-15) and therefore, they labeled Jesus a sinner (v. 16). Previously, when Jesus had healed the lame man at the Pool of Bethesda, the Jews had taken issue with the man because he had taken up his bed and walked, just as Jesus had told him (5:10). The religious Jews were so blind that they could look right past a great miracle and only see a technical violation of their tradition. Here in this passage the very same thing is again taking place.

The exchange between the Pharisees and the blind man is amazing! The blind man's opinion of the identity of Jesus goes from the man (v. 11) to prophet (v. 17) to Lord, I believe (v. 38)! The response of the man's parents is sad. How could they not be overjoyed at the healing of their son? Yet their fear of the Jews caused them to shrink back from a great opportunity to embrace Jesus as the Christ. This is a great illustration of the truth taught in Proverbs 29:25, "The fear of man bringeth a snare."

The Jews greatest deterrent to seeing Jesus as the Christ was their spiritual blindness and zeal for their traditions. What best describes your spiritual walk? Religion or relationship?

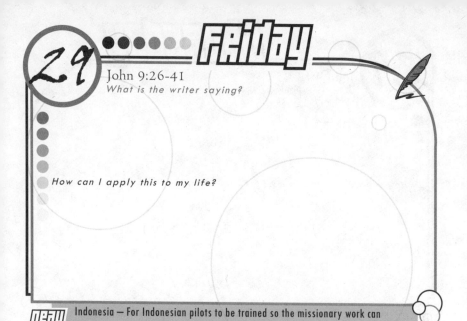

John 9:26-41

What is the writer saying?

How can I apply this to my life?

PRAY Indonesia — For Indonesian pilots to be trained so the missionary work can continue.

This passage shows a profound truth. Often the simple must instruct those who claim to be learned. The blind man holds to a simple faith, "I once was blind now I see." He knows that God's power had been demonstrated through his infirmity and cannot but believe in the One who made him whole. The Jews call Jesus a sinner because they placed their Sabbath regulations above the spirit of the Law. When one was born blind, the common belief was that the family was being judged for their sin. The disciples certainly thought this way (John 9:2). When the man refused to call Jesus a sinner (John 9:24), they turned on him and claimed he had been in sin since his birth (v. 34). Cast him out means they kicked him out of the synagogue, the local assembly of the Jews, similar to our churches.

Jesus, hearing the man was cast out of the synagogue, finds him and affirms His deity to him. How gracious of the Son of God, to care so much for this man that He sought him out. Obviously, the Pharisees are still hovering about this man (v. 40) and feel the weight of Jesus' statement about the blind receiving sight and the seeing being blind. Because they were not willing to admit their sin (blindness) and need for healing (salvation), they would remain in their blind state!

Life stEP

What great darkness surrounds those who are religious, yet apart from Christ? Only by coming to the Savior will they ever truly see the Light of Life.

John 10:1-13

What is the writer saying?

How can I apply this to my life?

pray Philippines — For missionaries to the 13,000,000 plus living in Manila to affect every level of society.

This section is a continuation of the exchange that took place between Jesus and the Pharisees at the end of chapter 9. Here He makes the third and fourth of the seven "I am" statements in the Gospel of John (vv. 7, 11).

Christ is the door to the sheepfold. A shepherd literally was the door as he lay down in the doorway of the stone enclosure sometimes topped with brambles for barbed wire that protected the sheep during the night. The enclosure had only one entrance. Anyone getting to the sheep had to come through the shepherd first. Today many would like us to believe that there are many roads that lead to God. The message of the cross is very exclusive. There is one door

(v. 7), one way (John 14:6), one God and mediator (1 Timothy 2:5).

The Pharisees were spiritual thieves, robbers, or at best, hirelings (vv. 8, 12). Perhaps Jesus had in mind the words of the prophet Zechariah as He made these statements (Zechariah 11:4-9, 17). Christ is the Good Shepherd because He gives His life for the sheep (v. 11, Psalm 22). For us, that is His past ministry. He is the Great Shepherd because He presently guides the sheep all the way to glory (Hebrews 13:20; Psalm 23). He is also the Chief Shepherd of the sheep and in the future will return to reward all the under shepherds or pastors (1 Peter 5:4 cf. Psalm 24).

Life stEP Christ is the only door into the security of the sheepfold. There is no other way of salvation than through the sacrifice of Jesus Christ. One of our great comforts as believers is the knowledge that the Great Shepherd has placed us into the fold.

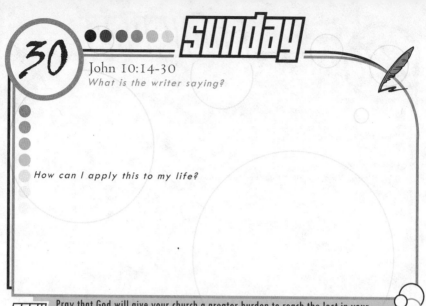

sunday

John 10:14-30

What is the writer saying?

How can I apply this to my life?

pray Pray that God will give your church a greater burden to reach the lost in your community.

The Good Shepherd has a special relationship to His sheep. This is seen by the nature of the relationship. The shepherd is not a hired hand but rather the owner of the sheep (my sheep); and the relationship is reciprocal (know and known). The Father loves the Son because of His willing obedience. Other sheep (10:16) refers to Gentiles who would believe and be joined with the Jewish believers (this fold) into one body (see Ephesians 2:13-16). Verses 17 and 18 teach clearly that Jesus was in total sovereign control throughout the events leading to His crucifixion. No one took His life from Him but rather, He willingly offered Himself as our substitutionary sacrifice. A worthy shepherd would sacrifice himself to save his sheep and Jesus proved He was our Good Shepherd at Calvary.

John indicates (v. 22) that this confrontation takes place during the time of the Feast of Dedication, which took place in the winter. This feast is present day Hanukkah and was a celebration of the rededication of the temple by Judas Maccabeus in 165 B.C. after its desecration in 168 B.C. by Antiochus Epiphanes.

Even though it had been weeks since Jesus' last confrontation with the Jews much hostility toward Him remained. The Jewish leadership continues in their unbelief, which shows they were not a part of God's fold (v. 26). This section concludes with a powerful declaration of the security of our salvation (vv. 27-30).

Believers are in a spiritual war zone. The battle has already been decided, yet it still rages. To bring men to Himself, Jesus endured much suffering and abuse. How willing are you to stand for Him?

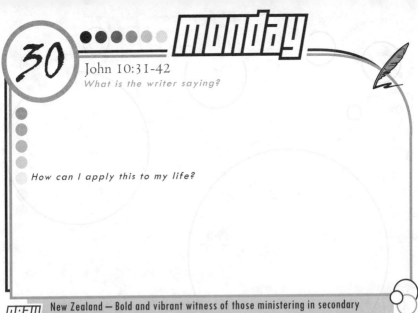

What is the writer saying?

How can I apply this to my life?

New Zealand — Bold and vibrant witness of those ministering in secondary schools and universities.

If anyone ever doubted whether Jesus claimed to be God, He put the question to rest as He plainly says, "I and my Father are one!" (v. 30). The Jews understood perfectly that by making such a statement Jesus claimed to be God. In response, they lashed out stating that His claim was blasphemy! Yet Jesus used the Scripture to silence their complaint. In the passage He quoted (Psalm 82:6), the psalmist used the common Hebrew word for God, Elohim, to identify key men who spoke for God. How much more should the incarnate Son Himself be free to speak of His oneness in nature with the Father!

Once again, Jesus was willing to let His works speak for Him (vv. 37-38). If

they could not believe His words, they only needed to examine His works to see that He did all that the Prophets had said that Messiah would do when He came (cf. Isaiah 35:4-6).

As so many times before, the Jews wanted to grab Him, but He eluded their grasp. Each time we are reminded that Jesus was in complete control of every situation (v. 39).

Withdrawing to the Jordan, His ministry now comes full circle to where it all began (John 1:28 ff.). Though most of the religious leadership had rejected Him, yet many sought Him and believed upon Him there.

Life stEP

The security of our salvation stems from the trustworthy nature of the one who provided it. He endured the painful sacrifice required to purchase our redemption and has an active involvement in keeping those who have believed unto salvation.

30 tuesday

John 11:1-15

What is the writer saying?

How can I apply this to my life?

PRAY Cuba — For mission boards to be sensitive to God's leading as they anticipate coming political change.

Chapter 11 contains the last and greatest of Jesus' sign miracles prior to His own resurrection. Bethany (house of dates) was a small village on the backside of the Mount of Olives about two miles from Jerusalem.

Lazarus (Whom God aids!) is not as well known as his two sisters, Mary and Martha. On hearing the news of his friend's sickness, Christ explains that this episode is predestined to glorify the Son. He means not just in the miracle, but also in the aftermath for this miracle was to cause the final confrontation leading to His crucifixion. Verse 9 poetically relates that as long as you are walking in the center of God's will, no harm can befall you. Verse 14 is also a miracle because

He knew what took place over 20 miles away. Verse 6 tells us He waited two days and verse 17 tells us that Lazarus had been dead four days. (The Jews believed that the soul did not leave for heaven until three days had passed.) Christ purposely waits until the fourth day to increase the drama and impact of this His crowning sign miracle before His death.

Throughout his Gospel, John has highlighted many of miracles done by Jesus, but draws particular attention to seven that he identifies as signs, each underscoring some aspect of what it means to believe. This final sign points to the newness of life that awaits those who have trusted Christ as Savior.

Christ taught the masses but focused on individuals. He poured His life into individuals who then turned the world upside down when He was gone.

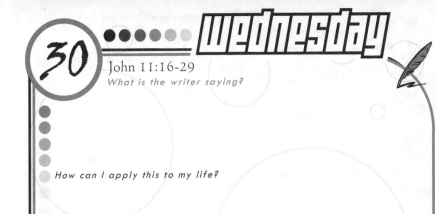

John 11:16-29

What is the writer saying?

How can I apply this to my life?

PRAY South Africa — Boldness for pastors in a society that no longer holds to moral absolutes, and where the media has pushed legalized abortion, pornography, prostitution, and gambling.

Didymus means twin (as does Thomas), perhaps the twin brother of Matthew because they are frequently mentioned together. Thomas gives us a glimpse into what is going through the minds of the disciples. They were greatly concerned about the mounting hostility against Jesus.

The contrast in the personalities of Mary and Martha makes an interesting study (John 12 and Luke 10). Luke 10 is the famous Martha/Mary Syndrome where Martha is busy preparing a meal for the Lord and rebukes Him for allowing Mary to sit and listen to Him while she did all the work. Martha is told that Mary has chosen the better part, sitting at the feet of Jesus! Here in John, Martha is active, running out to meet Jesus while Mary passively mourns in the house. Martha aggressively announces her hurt in losing my brother (Greek emphasis), whereas Mary tenderly mourns my brother (v. 33). Martha is vocal and Mary is tearful. Christ and Martha have a rational discussion about the resurrection, whereas Mary just falls at Christ's feet and worships. That Martha called Jesus the Teacher (Master) is interesting because the Pharisees would not teach women, but Jesus did (v. 28). The friends, who have come to comfort, are staying close to Mary, while Martha must have appeared to be holding her own.

 Life stEP

God always deals with us as individuals. Martha needed instruction, while Mary needed to be comforted. Ask God to help you meet people where they are. What a blessing it is to know that those who believe in Jesus will live even if they die!

How can I apply this to my life?

pray Aruba – Praise God for the growth in the evangelical witness and that the growth will only increase.

Jesus' response in verse 33 is a display of anger at Satan for the heartache he has brought to mankind. Groaned is used of the snorting of a warhorse. Death, to Christ, was not an impassable barrier, but a call to battle! The wept of verse 35 was a quiet, dignified weeping.

This passage is filled with emotion. Martha goes to fetch Mary having had a few moments with Christ outside the village. She calls her sister unobtrusively. The Jews, who had stayed with Mary consoling her and had not followed Martha when she went out to meet Jesus, followed Mary as she rises to go. They thought she was going to the tomb to weep, and they wished to share in this activity.

Mary's words were almost identical to Martha's and as such were a firm conviction that Christ's power could have saved Lazarus from death. No one was expecting a resurrection! But then, Jesus exceeds all that we ask or think, doesn't He?

At the tomb, Christ orders the stone removed and reminds Martha of His previous statement to her. He offers a thanksgiving prayer before the miracle. Lazarus, upon hearing the voice of the Omnipotent, responds and comes forth! Christ had to specify "Lazarus, come forth," lest the whole cemetery empty out!

Life stEP

Many Christians are like Lazarus as he comes out of the tomb… alive in Christ, but still bound by the grave clothes of the world. They cannot work for their hands are bound, nor witness because their mouths are bound. Christ wants us to be free! Oh, that we would proclaim Christ's words to those dead in sins, "Whosoever will may come!"

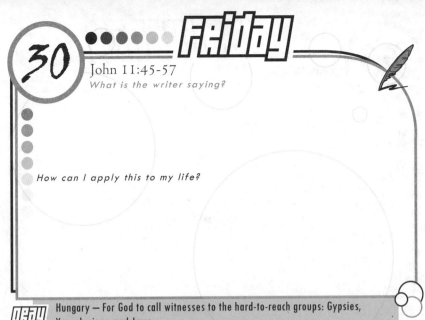

Friday

30

John 11:45-57

What is the writer saying?

How can I apply this to my life?

PRAY Hungary — For God to call witnesses to the hard-to-reach groups: Gypsies, Yugoslavians, and Jews.

When Jesus gives the command to loose Lazarus, it would appear that the miracle is finished. There is more though! In verse 45, we see that because of Jesus' prayer, many believed! Sadly though, some merely went to report the incident, their hearts hardened to the truth. The religious authorities were not happy campers! The place they were afraid of losing was the temple. Caiaphas offers what he believes is the expedient thing to do, sacrifice one man for the good of the whole nation. Caiaphas, being the High Priest, is speaking prophetically (v. 51), yet he himself does not have God's will in mind but rather the removal of a nuisance for the good of the whole. Earlier, Jesus had told them they were of the devil and would do his works ("a murderer from the beginning," John 8:44). Here we see them plotting that very thing. Verse 52 speaks of the scope of Christ's sacrifice, sufficient not only for the nation of Israel but for the Gentile also. This day marked the beginning of the Jews' open plans to kill Jesus. Verse 55 is an amazing backdrop. The Passover was at hand! Jesus was soon to be the ultimate Passover lamb. The blood He would shed would be a once-for-all sacrifice that would serve not as a covering for sin but as the satisfaction of God's righteous demands (1 John 2:2) and the basis of cleansing from their sin, to those who believe (Hebrews 10:10-14).

Life **stEP**

The substitutionary sacrifice of Jesus Christ at the Cross is the basis for our forgiveness. This forgiveness is made available to every man yet is only known by those who believe and place their faith in Christ. What a tragedy to know of God's grace and yet not receive it.

263

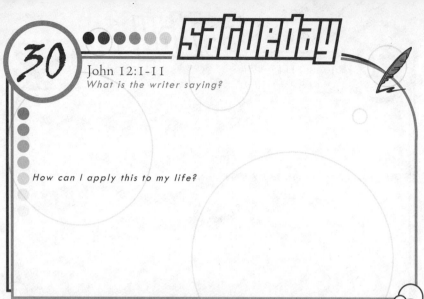

John 12:1-11

What is the writer saying?

How can I apply this to my life?

PRAY Jamaica — For Christian workers to have greater access to and interest in biblical resource materials.

We are now six days before the crucifixion. It has been no more than three months since Lazarus was raised (from the Hanukkah of John 10 to Passover is about 100 days). Martha is still active, and Mary is worshiping! This was apparently a special meal as the Greek text says that they reclined at the table. Only the wealthy regularly ate this way. The poor would only do so at special meals like Passover. In the reclining position, it was easy for Mary to reach the Lord's feet. Normally a servant would wash the feet. It was also unusual for a woman to let her hair down in public. These acts of humility are impressive.

The value of the perfume is overwhelming. Three hundred pence (denarii) represents about a year's wages for a common laborer. The spikenard (nard) was expensive because the closest that it was grown and processed was northern India.

The mean-spiritedness of Judas is shocking. It is hard to imagine whom he thought he was to interfere. The Lord graciously protects Mary and turns Judas' complaint back on him. If he was so interested in the poor, he could make that his personal ministry for the rest of his life! John interjects the commentary that Judas was insincere, although no one suspected him at the time. In verse 10, we see that sinful intent is multiplying. The religious leaders started with plans to kill one man for the sake of the nation. They have now added a second. Having crossed the line, they now can rationalize almost anything to preserve their place.

Martha, Lazarus, and Mary are wonderful examples of service, fellowship, and worship. All are necessary, but worship is the starting point.

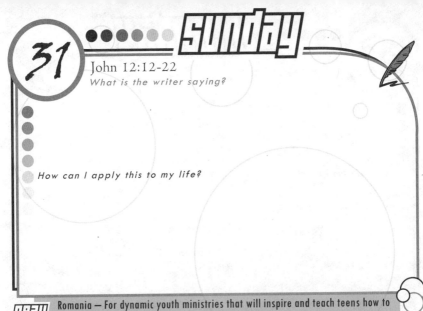

John 12:12-22

What is the writer saying?

How can I apply this to my life?

PRAY Romania — For dynamic youth ministries that will inspire and teach teens how to live for Christ.

This section, often referred to as the Triumphal Entry, is common to all four Gospels. Here, many in the crowd of people coming to Jerusalem to celebrate the Passover began to continually call out (the verb is in an imperfect tense) to Jesus as He enters the city.

The palm branch, a symbol of happiness, is used to this day in the Feast of Tabernacles celebration. Hosanna is a transliteration of the Hebrew or Aramaic meaning, please save. Both this phrase and he who comes are found in Psalm 118:25-26. The crowd obviously has these messianic ideas in mind as they greet Jesus. His entry, riding on a donkey's colt, is a direct fulfillment of Zechariah 9:9.

Unlike the pomp and circumstance usually associated with the coming of a king, Jesus' entrance is humble. Nonetheless, the Pharisees are greatly agitated and are stirring one another up as a result of their perceived ineffectiveness at squashing His popularity with the people.

John editorializes the event (v. 16), showing the disciples lack of understanding about what was happening as the events unfold. Later, after the Lord's Resurrection, they were able to put the events together. Throughout the book it is clear that John is writing both to a Jewish and Gentile audience. The mention of the Greeks (vv. 20-22) is important in that Jesus' death was for the sins of all of mankind, not just the Jews.

Life stEP

The fulfillment of Scripture is a common theme among the Gospels. God's Word will not fail. The things written concerning Jesus will all be completely fulfilled. Are you ready for His promised return?

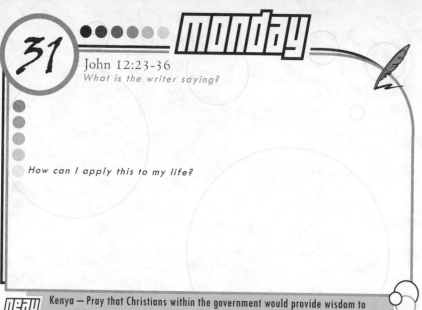

John 12:23-36
What is the writer saying?

How can I apply this to my life?

PRAY Kenya — Pray that Christians within the government would provide wisdom to avert political collapse.

The Greeks (previous section) were God-fearers, Gentiles who were impressed with Judaism but didn't want to be circumcised. Possibly, they came to Philip since he had a Greek name (Lover of Horses) and was from a Greek area. It is touching to see the way Philip goes to Andrew for advice. You will notice that no more mention is made of this request, but Jesus uses it as an opportunity to predict His imminent death, (the hour) towards which the entire story has been moving. It is significant that Gentiles trigger this announcement because through His death we are elevated to equality with Jews in the family of God! Verse 24 applies the law of the harvest to the spiritual realm. Verse 25 is a paradox. Those who wish to save their life, living for their own selfish ends, will destroy (present tense) that to which they desperately cling. Those who hate their lives (by comparison), gain (future tense) that which is true life indeed.

The Father thunders His approval from heaven (v. 28). Lifted up (v. 32) normally means exalted. The cross is a triumph, not a defeat! It was here that the serpent received its head wound (Genesis 3) and the prince of this world system was cast out (v. 31)! John returns to familiar themes of light versus darkness and that which leads to belief. Jesus' warning is to respond (in faith) to the light at hand, lest the opportunity for belief is snatched away due to their procrastination (vv. 35-36). See also (Matthew 13:4, 19).

Life **stEP**

We fear death because it makes no sense to us that out of death and decay can come another life. Nature encourages us, whether it be the dead grain of wheat or the stunning metamorphosis of the lowly caterpillar into a mass of jellied protein and then the stunning butterfly!

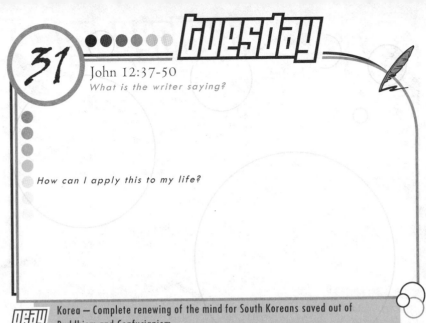

31 ●●●●●● tuesday

John 12:37-50

What is the writer saying?

How can I apply this to my life?

pray Korea — Complete renewing of the mind for South Koreans saved out of Buddhism and Confucianism.

Verse 36 announces Christ's withdrawal from the public. In chapters 13-17, He limits His ministry just to the disciples. Verse 37 announces the reason for going private. Verse 38 quotes Isaiah 53:1, and verse 40 is part of Isaiah's call to the ministry (Isaiah 6:10). In Isaiah's day (700 B.C.) he was told that he would have a ministry of hardening and so did Jesus. Those who reject the deity of Christ did so with the claim that in Scripture Jesus is not referred to by the name Jehovah (the Greek Kurios for Lord can also mean sir). John 12:41 is the one place in Scripture where there is a direct connection between Jesus and the name Jehovah. In Isaiah 6:1, it is Jehovah high and lifted up that Isaiah views, but John tells us that the prophet was beholding the glory of Jesus!

Like Nicodemus, some of the Jewish religious leaders were coming to faith in Christ (v. 42). However, they kept this to themselves fearing the reproach of their peers. Though they are generally the exception, not all of the priests would remain hostile to the Gospel (see Acts 6:7). John, looking back upon this event, notes that it was the fear of men that motivated their silence. They sought the approval of men more than the approval of God.

Those who reject Jesus Christ will only have themselves to blame ultimately. Jesus makes it clear that those who hear and reject the Gospel will be judged by the very Word of God from which they have turned away (vv. 47-50).

Life stEP His contemporaries missed the predictions of Messiah's death (Psalm 16, 22; Isaiah 53). We are tempted to give them the benefit of the doubt, but Christ expected them to know these hard passages.

John 13:1-11

What is the writer saying?

How can I apply this to my life?

PRAY Word of Life Inn leadership and staff, as they minister and equip their guests to better serve the Lord.

Chapters 13-17 contain seven lectures designed to prepare the disciples to carry on Christ's work in His absence. Seven times in these chapters He says, These things have I spoken unto you. In four of these, we are given the purpose for His teachings:
1) For their joy (15:11)
2) For their confidence (16:1)
3) For their memory (16:4)
4) And for their peace (16:33)

Chapter 13 contains the account of the Last Supper. Verse 1 states that Christ loved His disciples to the uttermost (fullness of His love). He leaves them with an example of humility to follow. Prior to chapter 12 Jesus had four times stated that His hour had not yet come. Now however it had come. Hour is a reference to the whole series of events leading up to and including His death, burial, and resurrection.

In the exchange between Peter and Jesus (vv. 6-11) much more than dirty feet are being discussed. Peter's initial refusal quickly becomes an overreaction as he requests a complete cleansing. The reply of Jesus (v. 10) is a reference to salvation. He that is washed, (saved) needs only to wash his feet (confession of daily sins for unbroken fellowship). The statement that they are not all clean, is a reference to the unbelief of Judas.

Life **stEP**

Peter always tries to control the situation. In his befuddlement, (probably because he was seated where the assigned foot washer would sit) he first rejects the washing then requests a whole bath. Consistent with 1 John 1:9, Christ strikes the balance. Believers are bathed in the blood of Christ for salvation and kept in fellowship by the confession of daily sin.

31

John 13:12-20

What is the writer saying?

How can I apply this to my life?

pray Chile — Outreach among the middle and upper classes who have proven resistant to the Gospel.

Jesus has just washed the disciples' feet. This was a task performed by the servant of a household. In the absence of any subordinate, no one was jumping to be the one to carry out this task. Jesus takes on the role of servant to the group and performs this menial task.

Returning to His place at the table, He now explains the importance of this act to His disciples. His pre-eminence among them was never an issue (v. 13). The terms they addressed Him by were terms of respect and honor. If their teacher, the Lord, was not too good to serve them by washing their feet, they too were not too good to serve one another. The example (v. 25) He left them was not of washing feet but rather of service. Blessing (v. 17) is found not in the knowledge of what pleases God, but in doing those things that please Him. Verse 18 is a fulfillment of verse 19. Jesus was going to tell His disciples plainly of His betrayal before it occurred, so when it happened, their faith would not be shaken but rather strengthened. The cross was not a mistake but part of God's plan. The betrayal was a necessary element on the road to Calvary.

Verse number 20 shows the connection between the Lord and His servants. Those who minister unto the servants of God are ministering to the Lord. A great example of this is found in the Olivet Discourse (Matthew 25:34-40). The heartbeat of God is that of service. If our Lord was not too good to wash the feet of His disciples, then who are we to consider ourselves above any aspect of ministry unto our brethren?

Service is not glamorous, but it is Christ-like. Jesus was not pretending to be a servant, but using this opportunity to demonstrate vividly that to humble one's self to serve others was not above Him, and should not be too much to ask of us!

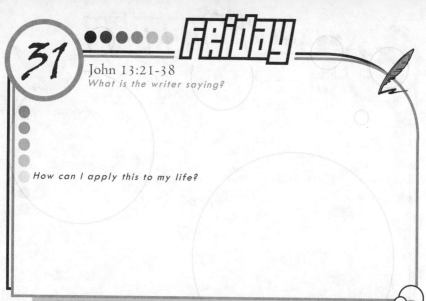

John 13:21-38

What is the writer saying?

How can I apply this to my life?

In the next section (13:31-14:31), Christ tells His disciples, "Brace yourselves, I'm leaving!" He affectionately calls them little children and certainly they would behave so in the next 72 hours!

Peter persuades John (the disciple whom Jesus loved, v. 23) to ask Jesus who His betrayer would be. Jesus plainly identifies Judas, however many of the disciples are still oblivious to his treachery (v. 29).

Peter ignores the Lord's challenge to love the brethren and goes back to His statement in verse 33, "Whither I go, ye cannot come." When Christ said that to the religious authorities (7:34; 8:21), He implied never (since they refused to repent and believe). In verse 36, He softens the statement for the disciples indicating that their separation would be temporary, not permanent. Peter gets the drift and protests his intent to lay down his life as well. Christ calls his bluff and states the reality that at the crisis time no one will stand with Him. He will go through the valley of the shadow of death alone. Peter's denial is recorded in all four Gospels.

In this first private discussion after Judas' departure, Christ is asked four questions by the puzzled and increasingly alarmed disciples. Peter: Where are you going? (v. 36) Answer: Somewhere you can't.

Thomas: How can we get there? (14:5) Answer: Through Me!

Philip: Can we take a peek? (14:8) Answer: Look at Me!

Judas: Why the change in the program? (14:22) Answer: Belief required.

Life **stEP** Despite being truly repentant of their sins and desirous of obeying God and His Christ, the disciples had the same disease that afflicted the Pharisees. They wanted physical manifestations of the kingdom of God in this world. Where have you set your affections?

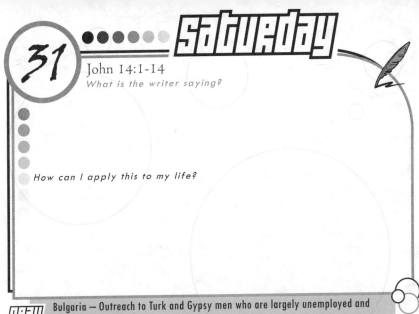

SATURDAY

John 14:1-14

What is the writer saying?

How can I apply this to my life?

PRAY Bulgaria — Outreach to Turk and Gypsy men who are largely unemployed and enslaved by alcohol.

Christ does not want His disciples to be in turmoil. Belief is the key. Mansions is from the Greek root meno, meaning to abide. It is not referring to palatial country estates but rather, dwelling places (rooms in a father's house for the children). The only other time this word occurs in scripture is in 14:23 where it refers to our heart as Christ's home!

Christ promises to return for the disciples. Theologically, this is a unique proposition since up to this point in their understanding of the Bible, the coming of Christ was for the sake of establishing a kingdom on the earth, not taking saints back to heaven. As such, verse 3 becomes a major witness for the Pretribulational Rapture of the church! Believers will spend the seven years of the tribulation period in seclusion with the Bridegroom in the heavenly bridal chambers before returning to help establish Christ's Kingdom in the same arena where He was originally rejected.

Verse 6 contains the sixth of Christ's great "I am" statements. Jesus, being one with the Father, was of the same essence as the Father. To know Him was equal to knowing the Father. Those who know Jesus know the way home.

In response to Philip's request (v. 8), Christ offers His own life as an open book about the Father. The astounding statement that the disciples would do greater works should be understood as works greater in scope. Christ was localized and could only minister to so many people per day. However, when He leaves and sends the Holy Spirit, the Holy Spirit will work through all believers.

Life stEP

What work could be greater than seeing the dead raised? Today we have the privilege of seeing lives changed through the power of the Gospel. To know Christ is to pass from spiritual death to spiritual life.

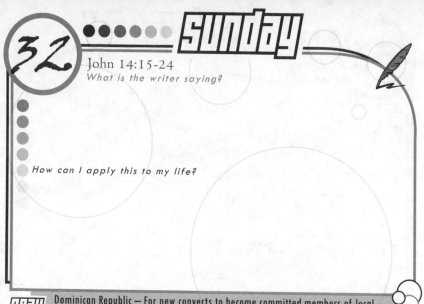

John 14:15-24

What is the writer saying?

How can I apply this to my life?

pray Dominican Republic — For new converts to become committed members of local churches.

Christ will ask the Father to send another Comforter. There are two words for another in Greek. Heteros is "another of a different kind" such as the false gospel that was no gospel at all in Galatians 1 or our word heterosexual. The other, which is used here, is allos, which means "another of the same kind." Both Jesus and the Holy Spirit are comforters.

In 1 John 2:1, the term being translated comforter, is used of Christ and translated advocate. When we slip into sin, Jesus Christ is our advocate with the Father. The Greek term is paraklete, a compound word composed of para (alongside; parallel) + kaleo (to call): one called alongside to help in time of need. It was used as a legal term- aid, counsel, or intercessor. Even our English word comfort helps us appreciate the Holy Spirit's ministry.

It too is a compound word, com (with) and fort (strength). He doesn't just comfort us when we get hurt but strengthens us before we go out into battle!

Verses 15 and 24 are like the bookends of this section. The life of the true believer is characterized by obedience to the commandments of God. Jesus had set the ultimate example of love and obedience and now expects His followers will walk according to that pattern. The one who says he loves God and yet lives a life of habitual disobedience to the Word of God is deceiving himself but not God (1 John 2:4). This being said, maturity does not happen instantaneously when one is saved. We must leave room for the immature Christian to grow into maturity and obedience as their knowledge of God increases.

The function of the Spirit is to make the reality of God convincing to all men in the same way that Jesus did to His disciples. How are people being impacted by your life and testimony?

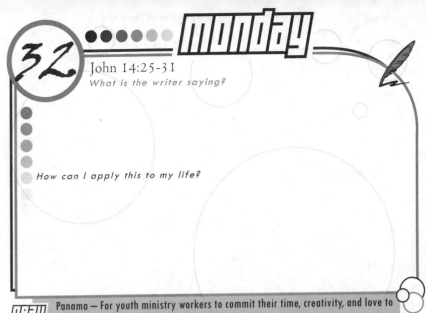

32

monday

John 14:25-31

What is the writer saying?

How can I apply this to my life?

pray Panama — For youth ministry workers to commit their time, creativity, and love to Christ's use.

One of the ministries of the Holy Spirit was temporary and limited to the disciples. This resulted in the book we hold in our hands almost 2,000 years later, the Bible. He would cause the disciples to remember all that Christ said, even though they didn't understand much of it at the time it was spoken.

He emphatically states that, "My (kind of) peace I give unto you (not the world's peace) (v. 27)." Christ wants the disciples to be happy for His imminent reunion with the Father. He also implies that He has to go away for this special gift of the Holy Spirit to come. It is clear that the ministry of the Holy Spirit is different after the cross than before. The event that makes the difference is the cross work of Christ. The actual payment for the sin of mankind gave the Spirit of God greater influence in the lives of men than what was normally experienced by the Old Testament saints. This could be one of the reasons why we see so many of the Old Testament saints falling into gross sin (cf. David and Solomon) while most heroes of the New Testament stayed faithful to the Lord.

Christ knew that the disciples were in a state of shock, but He informs them of these things now so when they happen, the disciples will have further proof that He was right and indeed is the Messiah.

The prince of this world (v. 30) is a reference to Satan, whom soon would throw everything he had at the Son of God. In unwavering obedience and submission to the will of the heavenly Father, Jesus Christ walked full face into the adversary's fury.

Life stEP

It is sometimes tempting to say, "God is not doing anything special in my life. I want to see some power!" But in the sweep of human history, the impact the Bible has had on culture is a demonstration of incredible power!

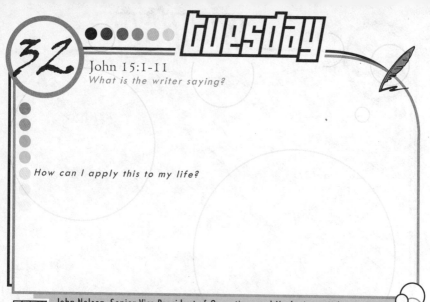
How can I apply this to my life?

pray John Nelson, Senior Vice President of Operations and Marketing, wisdom in meeting organizational challenges.

Chapter 15 is lecture number two, a lecture on relationships. At the end of chapter 14, Christ said to the disciples, let us go (from the site of the Last Supper). As they make their way out of the city to the Garden of Gethsemane (Olive Oil Press), He uses an agricultural analogy to describe the relationship of the believer to Himself (vv. 1-11). The grapevine was a powerful symbol in Israel, like our bald eagle.

The progression given (v. 2) is that of increasing fruitfulness. The vinedresser works with the branches of the vine to maximize their fruit bearing. Jesus told His disciples that they were already clean or pruned because of the word He had spoken to them. They were ready to bear fruit, but the key for them would be their abiding in Him, the vine (v. 4). On their own they could produce nothing (v. 5) but in Him they would bear much fruit.

The branches that are burned (v. 6) can picture the following things: 1) unproductive Christians who are taken home prematurely because of their disobedience 2) branches containing dead wood that is cut away during the pruning process. Here the branch is only the dead wood that is thrown into the fire, and not the whole person. 3) Those, like Judas, who professed to be followers of Jesus Christ but did not continue in faith, demonstrating that they were not genuine (1 John 2:19). Verse 7 is not a blank check but rather a promise that as His disciples walked in obedience they could rely on Christ to meet their needs. The relationship that Christ was unfolding for His disciples was based upon love (v. 9) and obedience (v. 10) just as His relationship with His Father. Their walk of love and obedience would result in glory to the Father and fullness of joy for them.

Life stEP

Notice the progression of what Christ expects from His vines (vv. 15:2, 5): fruit; more fruit; and much fruit! How do you measure up?

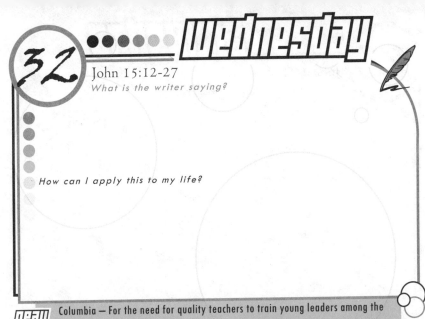

John 15:12-27

What is the writer saying?

How can I apply this to my life?

PRAY Columbia — For the need for quality teachers to train young leaders among the 20 theological schools.

Christ's second lecture to His disciples involves relationships. First, He discusses their relationship to Him as the vine and the branches (vv. 1-11). Second is their relationship to each other in brotherly love (vv. 13-17). Finally, He discusses their relationship to the world (vv. 18-27).

In the new set of circumstances, no longer will believers be the servants of God or just the children of God but rather adult sons in God's family (the theological definition of the New Testament word adoption). This gives us great authority, privilege, and responsibility. It is significant that the Church Age began on Pentecost, the anniversary of the giving of the Law. The great transition from the Age of Law to the Age of Grace begins on the same anniversary in the calendar. On that day, the disciples went from being children under the tutelage of the Law

(Galatians 4) to adult sons! In their day, students chose the rabbi they wanted to study under. Christ says that He reversed the process, choosing them (v. 16). He chose them to be fruit bearers. The authority they have in prayer is to fulfill that commission.

Jesus gives them fair warning that the world is not going to treat them kindly. There is a chain of guilt by association. The world hates the Father; therefore, it also hates the One sent from the Father (the Son). Since it hates the Son, it also hates those associated with the Son. It also resents that the Son has chosen them out from the world (v. 19). Verse 26 returns to the coming of the Comforter who will energize the disciples in their relationship to the world (as that of light, witness, and testifier). He is called the Spirit of Truth. Notice that His job is to magnify Christ, not Himself.

Life stEP We are free…free to choose to show our gratitude to our Savior by working for Him and His glory! Christ wants us to bear fruit, fruit that remains and thus glorify the Father.

John 16:1-11

What is the writer saying?

How can I apply this to my life?

The fourth relationship that Christ discusses is that of believers to the Holy Spirit. The parents of the blind man in chapter 9 were afraid of being excommunicated from the synagogue. In chapter 12 we find out that some of the Pharisees did believe in Jesus, but they were afraid to lose their position of prominence in society. Being put out of the synagogue was a serious event for a Jewish person. The Pharisees controlled the synagogue system (whereas the Sadducees controlled the temple). Birth certificates, marriage certificates, bills of divorcement, and burial rights were all controlled by the synagogue. All of Jewish life and society centered on the synagogue. Jesus warns them of their own excommunication so they are not caught off guard when it happens. By warning them ahead of time, He wants to keep them from despair, which can lead to apostasy.

The Apostle Paul is a good example of verse 2. Christ says it will be profitable to them for Him to leave (v. 7). This is the same word used by Caiaphas when he said that it was expedient for one man to die to save their position!! The Old Testament does not say much about the Holy Spirit's ministry of conviction. Now we are informed of three areas of conviction in verse 8 which are explained in verses 9-11: sin (of unbelief, v. 9); righteousness (now that my example is no longer in front of their eyes, v. 10) and judgment" (since it is coming soon, v. 11).

Here are the special relationships and ministries of the Holy Spirit: Spirit and World- Convict (v. 8); Spirit and Disciples- Guide (v. 13); Spirit and Christ- Glorify (v. 14).

Life stEP The fear of man is a snare. Let us not be concerned about our appearance in man's eyes, but rather, let us serve Christ in obedience. Satan is a defeated foe! He still roars and is dangerous in his death throes, but we can claim the victory in the power of the Spirit.

John 16:12-22

What is the writer saying?

How can I apply this to my life?

Having spoken of the Holy Spirit's convicting ministry, the Son of God now turns to His teaching ministry. By His use of the Old Testament Scriptures, quoted in various places in the Gospels and Acts, Jesus put God's stamp of authority on those writings. Beginning in John 14:26, Jesus pre-authenticates the whole of the New Testament writings. "Bring all things to your remembrance" (John 14:26) speaks of the Gospels. "Guide you into all truth" (v. 13) would occur as the Epistles were penned under divine inspiration. These letters would give the early church the direction and instruction it so desperately needed. "Shew you things to come" (v. 13) was the promise of the blessing of the completed canon, as the book of Revelation would foretell the final chapter of human history and the glorious future of those who enter into God's rest.

Today, we have the Scripture in totality. There is no need for new revelation. However, the Spirit of God still guides believers in understanding God's revealed Word found only in the Bible. "He shall glorify me" (v. 14); the ministry of the Holy Spirit is never to bring attention (glory) to Himself but to bring glory to Christ.

We saw in verse 16 how puzzled the disciples were since they had not comprehended the death, burial, and resurrection of Christ. Within 24 hours, He would be gone, but within another 48 hours He would be with them again in His resurrected body! He does not spell it out to them, but further illustrates the significance of their mood swings over the next 72 hours. They will be plummeted into the depths of despair. Their despair will be bitter as they hear the religious authorities mocking and rejoicing at His demise. Verse 22 speaks of the fullness and permanence of their joy at the other end of these events.

Life stEP

Anything said to be of the Spirit should match exactly the pattern laid in Scripture. One should ask, "Who is being glorified and what is the purpose?"

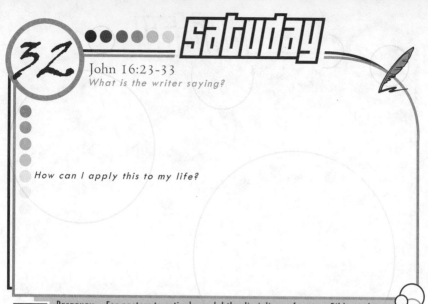

John 16:23-33

What is the writer saying?

How can I apply this to my life?

PRAY Paraguay — For pastors to actively model the disciplines of prayer, Bible study, and witnessing.

The phrase, *in that day* (v. 23), is a reference to the time after Jesus' resurrection. Up to this point, prayers were not offered in the name of Jesus. Christ explains the pattern of prayer that is followed during the Church Age. We are to make our requests to the Father in the name (authority) of the Son. This does not mean that it is out of the question to pray to Jesus or the Holy Spirit but that the normal pattern is to pray to the Father in the authority of the Son and empowered by the Spirit. The direct access to the Father that Jesus reveals to them would be a tremendous source of encouragement. The disciples say, "Yes, now we understand." One would think they would have been filled with questions. They clearly overstate their grasp of that which Jesus is saying to them as seen by His reply.

Jesus is clearly skeptical (v. 31) knowing that in a few hours the sheep would scatter (Zechariah 13:7). Even with that depressing acknowledgment, Christ leaves an example for us to follow in our lonely times as He rightly observes that the Father will be with Him. (This sets the stage for the horror of the three-hour period when even this was not true as He bore the sin of the entire world on His back and was temporarily abandoned by His own Father.)

Jesus states the reason that He has spoken these things to them, that they might have peace in the midst of the turmoil that was to come upon them. Overcome in verse 33 is the same as conquerors in "we are more than conquerors" (Romans 8:37). Three different Greek prepositions describe Christ's relationship to the Father in this section: verse 27, "out from" (para indicates authority or commission); verse 28, "out of" (ek, source); verse 30, "from" (apo, separation from the Father).

Life **stEP**

It is hard to think that anything could be better than having Jesus living with you in the flesh. In the plan of God, the indwelling Holy Spirit and His written Word gives us a richer relationship with the Godhead!

John 17:1-13

What is the writer saying?

How can I apply this to my life?

pray Argentina — For church leaders to know the Word, live in the Spirit, and disciple others to replace them.

John 17 is the real Lord's Prayer; His High-Priestly Prayer of Intercession. (Matthew 6 is better called The Disciples' Prayer). The structure of John 17 is very interesting. The bull's eye is eternal life with the following three sections, forming three concentric circles each section broader in scope than the former.

1) Verses 1-5 have two commands: glorify thy Son (that is, His authority as the Son to give eternal life due to His work on earth) and glorify thou me (that is, return my person to its pre-incarnate glory with the Father).

2) Verses 6-19 have two more commands: Keep them (that is, protect my disciples from evil) and sanctify them (that is, set them apart for the continuation of my work on earth).

3) Verses 20-26 contain two requests: I ask (v. 20) is a request for unity among all believers and I desire (v. 24) is a request to unite all believers with their Savior in glory.

Eternal Life (v. 13) is defined, not as endless existence (although it is that!) but as a living contact with God. Know is the present tense which means that even in heaven the contact and growth is ongoing throughout all eternity! (Know means more than just imparted knowledge.) The life now enjoyed by the disciples is revealed in this prayer as enlightenment (v. 8) and preservation (except Judas whose betrayal was predicted, Psalm 41:9, vv. 11-12).

Eternal life is not luxurious idleness, but purposeful labor for the Creator, both now and for eternity!

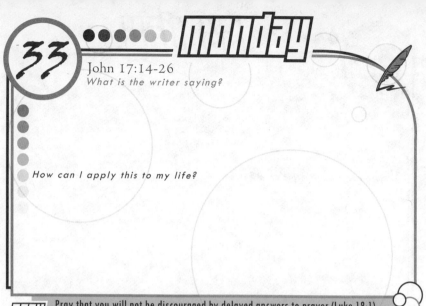

John 17:14-26

What is the writer saying?

How can I apply this to my life?

PRAY Pray that you will not be discouraged by delayed answers to prayer (Luke 18:1).

Continuing from yesterday, the life (v. 3) now enjoyed by the disciples is revealed in this prayer as joy (v. 13), sanctification (to set apart for God's use, v. 19), employment (v. 18, "So send I you!"); and is revealed in the prayer as unity of common belief, worship, service (v. 23), and fellowship (v. 24) now and for eternity!

The disciples are not of the world, as demonstrated back in verse 8 by the fact that they: 1) accepted His words, 2) recognized that Jesus came from the Father and 3) believed Him. That sets the disciples apart from the Pharisees. In verse 17, note the close association between sanctification and revealed truth. Verse 18 likens our mission to Christ's. We take up where He left off. Christ says that He set Himself apart that the disciples might also be set apart. Of course, His sanctification was

His self-sacrifice on the cross (v. 19)! With these 11 disciples there begins a long chain that reaches down the corridors of time to the 21st century, which has resulted in our salvation! There is much work to be done, but Christ looks forward to that grand day when labor is over and we can all meet in the Father's house. Jesus is anxious to introduce us to His Father! His Father is a very prominent theme in John, occurring over 120 times. Holy Father only occurs once in the Bible in 17:11.

The unity of the disciples was important for the evangelistic outreach of the early church. Verse 23 says that their unity will be a signal to the world that Jesus was the Messiah. The united testimony of the transformed disciples was the validation to the world that the Father truly sent the Son.

Life stEP

What can a watching world conclude by the relationship of believers in your town? Are you a promoter of unity or are you weakening the local Christian witness by sowing discord?

John 18:1-14

What is the writer saying?

How can I apply this to my life?

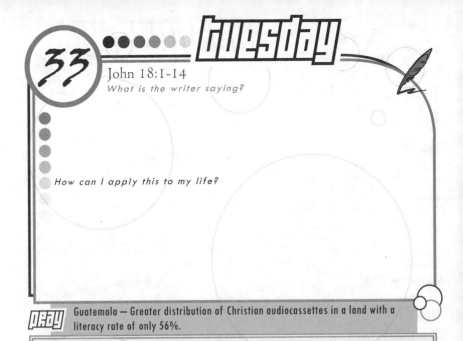

PRAY Guatemala — Greater distribution of Christian audiocassettes in a land with a literacy rate of only 56%.

We now enter the fifth major outline section of John, the Period of Consummation (chapters 18-20). They are just arriving at the Garden of Gethsemane. Apparently, chapters 15-17 were spoken en route or they stopped at another private location for these lectures. The other Gospel accounts speak of Jesus praying in the garden, although here in John He has already prayed an extensive prayer. It could be that the prayer of John 17 was spoken in the hearing of the disciples for their benefit; whereas the other Gospels mention the private agonizing that He did in the garden with only a few of the details known by the disciples (because they were asleep!).

The Kidron was a steep valley between Jerusalem (The Temple Mount) and the Mount of Olives. A stream runs through it all the way down to the Dead Sea 17 miles to the east. Today it provides a strip of green lushness in an otherwise bleak wilderness.

The band (cohort) of men that Judas brought would number 300-600 soldiers. Christ responds with the name of Jehovah, "I Am (he)." This display of raw power is a reminder that Jesus did not have His life taken from Him but that He laid it down willingly. The prediction that verse 9 fulfills was only minutes old, having been prayed in 17:12! Peter tries to take charge of the situation, however he does not realize that what is happening is a part of God's plan. Jesus stops him from any further embarrassment and announces His intentions to go with the men. He is taken to Annas, the real power behind the current High Priest Caiaphas (who had been deposed by the Romans earlier for political reasons).

Only the hardness of the human heart, blindness of sin and trickery of Satan could have produced this type of foolishness! How faithful are you to study God's Word that you might know truth from error?

33 wednesday

John 18:15-27

What is the writer saying?

How can I apply this to my life?

---

pray Angola – For medical missionaries laboring in a nation where landmines outnumber people and famine is widespread.

The other disciple was John. He doesn't mention his name out of humility but is the best candidate. John apparently came from a wealthy family who could move in such circles. Only 2 of the 12 have stayed with Jesus; 9 have scattered already.

The dignity of Jesus is in stark contrast to the seething anger of these men. The High Priest's questions were directed in two areas- His disciples and His teaching. The religious leaders have often been concerned about the number of people who were following Him (compare 12:19). Not only is His first response logically accurate, but His rebuke to the one who struck Him is also eminently reasonable. It further includes a legal term, bear witness which contains an implied request for a fair trial. As Isaiah 53 predicts that the suffering servant will be the victim

of a judicial murder. Annas then sends Jesus bound to Caiaphas. Although each of the Gospels mentions progressions in the arrest and examination of Jesus, John's Gospel is the only one to tell us that this initial examination occurred before Annas. The office of High Priest was for life and although he had been deposed, Annas still wielded much influence among the Jewish leadership. Interwoven with Jesus' questioning is the drama of Peter's denials in the courtyard. Comparing the other Gospels, some have complained that there is a discrepancy on the identity of his questioners. We need to realize that selective reporting is not the equivalent of error or deception. Many people around the fire could have questioned Peter. Each author reports the questioner that caught his attention in the retelling of the events of that fateful night.

 Life stEP

When the heat was on, most of the disciples scattered. How will you fare if persecution comes to you? Jesus remained calm under the pressure of examination. His strength is available to us as we stand for Him!

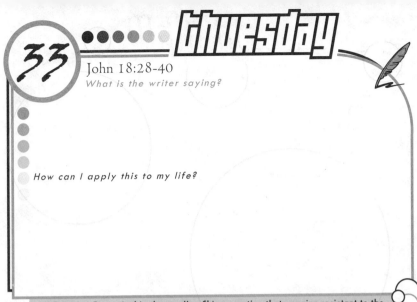

John 18:28-40

What is the writer saying?

How can I apply this to my life?

pray Taiwan – For revival in the one Han Chinese nation that remains resistant to the Gospel.

The Praetorium (v. 28) is a reference to the governor's official residence (see Acts 23:35). In order to remain ceremonially clean the Jews would not enter into a Gentile home. John notes that they did not want to be defiled that they might observe the Passover. How strange, in light of the fact that they were in the process of carrying out a murder!

As Pilate examines Jesus, we see another example to avoid. Pilate was not convinced that Jesus had committed any crime worthy of death. His decision was politically motivated and devoid of justice. The Passover was at hand, and Jesus, like the Passover lamb, was the innocent being offered for the guilty. Both Jew and Gentile had a part in His death. The Jews needed the participation of the Romans since the Jews were not allowed to execute anyone (v. 31). This seems strange in light of the fact that they had often taken up stones to stone Him! John interjects that their situation served to fulfill what had been prophesied concerning His death (v. 32).

As Pilate again interviews Jesus, he tries to verify the accusations the Jews apparently made that He is a political rival (v. 19:12). Jesus tells Pilate clearly that He is a king but that His kingdom is not of this world. It is amazing that Pilate does not probe this profound answer, but simply concludes that He is indeed claiming to be a king.

Much has been written concerning what is meant by Pilate's question, "What is truth?" However, what he does next seems to indicate that it was a pessimistic dismissal of Jesus' words. Pilate appears to neither believe in Him nor find Him to be a threat and looks for a basis for setting Jesus free.

Life stEP

Let us be quick to desire justice and not what is expedient.

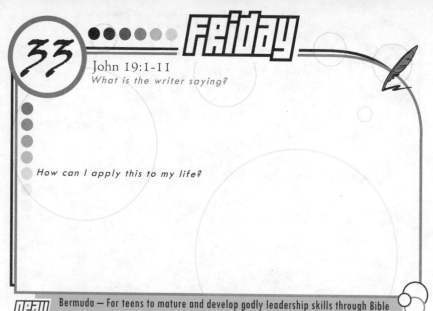

33 ● ● ● ● ● ● ● FRIDAY

John 19:1-11

What is the writer saying?

How can I apply this to my life?

PRAY Bermuda — For teens to mature and develop godly leadership skills through Bible clubs.

Pilate was the Roman governor of Judea from A.D. 26-36. He had a history of stormy relationships with the Jews that displeased his Roman superiors. He was anxious to avoid having another bad report sent back to Rome.

The crucifixion of Christ is variously dated from A.D. 29 to 33. In any case, Pilate would have already been in Judea for a number of years and would have several years thereafter to consider the error of condemning an innocent man. Despite his care here, Rome eventually recalls him for misadministration in another matter. Pilate was not willing to execute an innocent man and flogged Jesus to satisfy inherent blood-lust and perhaps arouse pity to let Jesus go. He also allowed his soldiers to take out their frustrations on the Jews by mocking

their king. The Romans played a game called the game of the kings to while away time. The climax involved mocking an innocent bystander, which might be the cultural background to their mockery of Jesus.

The original charge brought against Jesus before Pilate was that of treason (18:33) since the Sanhedrin thought that would be easier than explaining the real charge of blasphemy, which now slips out in their anger (v. 7) further confusing the issue. Jesus maintains a dignified silence (v. 9) fulfilling Isaiah 53:7. Jesus minimizes Pilate's role in His execution, placing the burden on the theocratic representative of the chosen people, Caiaphas (v. 11). Pilate skillfully baits his enemies into professing a heresy of their own: "We have no king but Caesar" (v. 15).

Life stEP

Pilate was in over his head, both in Judea and in this trial. You may lose (in this life) if you live according to your principles, but you will always lose if you don't.

33 saturday

John 19:12-22

What is the writer saying?

How can I apply this to my life?

PRAY Easter — Praise Him for giving us a living hope through the resurrection of Jesus Christ (1 Peter 1:13).

The point of Roman crucifixion was two-fold. First was the agony of the event, designed to discourage rebellion. The other was the total humiliation, from the cruelty of carrying your own instrument of death (like digging your own grave), to the shame of public nakedness, to the prying eyes and scorn of those who pass by reading the published charges. Paul, in Colossians 2:14 wrote that it was really our charges that were nailed there.

Jesus' death was the substitutionary sacrifice for the penalty of man's sin. His death is sufficient for every man but is only made effective to those who place their faith in Him. Pilate further insulted the Jewish authorities by having The King of the Jews placarded between two common thieves! Golgotha (skull) has been identified as a rocky outcropping just north of the current (Turkish) walls of Jerusalem, called Gordon's Calvary. It is a nice visualization of what the site might have looked like, but probably the real site was at The Church of the Holy Sepulcher, which is inside the Turkish walls today but was just outside to the northwest in Christ's day.

John does not detail the horrors of the crucifixion. Victims have been discovered by archaeologists with the spikes going through the heel bones as though the feet had been nailed to the side of the cross. Death came through a combination of blood loss, shock, and suffocation.

Life **stEP** We are physical beings. It is natural to concentrate on the physical horrors of crucifixion. Don't forget the spiritual ramifications of the humiliation, selfless love, sin bearing, and the spiritual death that were also involved.

How can I apply this to my life?

Psalm 22:18 and 69:21 are being fulfilled. You would have to stay up many nights inventing fulfillments of such passages in a fictitious story. God's sovereignty is evident, even down to the number of soldiers (four) present at His crucifixion (v. 24) and their casting lots for His tunic.

Also present are His mother, her sister (while the passage could be read to understand her name was Mary also, this would seem highly unlikely), two other devoted women, and John. While John does not record Jesus' prayer for His executioners (Luke 23:34) or His pardon of the repentant thief (Luke 23:43), he does record His words to His mother and the disciple He loved. His concern for His mother is touching. Woman was not a disrespectful way to address one's mother in that culture (John 2:4). "Behold thy son" was instructive to Mary as He commends her to the care of John, whom He loved. The care of a widow was the responsibility of the oldest son. Jesus entrusts his mother to the care of John, rather than His unbelieving brothers (v. 7:5).

Notice that He controlled His life to the very end and at the proper time He dismissed His spirit from His body (see John 10:18) after the victorious statement, "It (the provision for the salvation of mankind) is finished!"

Life stEP Jesus' love and concern for others was evident to the end. Even on the cross, His thoughts were for the needs of those with Him. Lord, help us to see with your eyes!

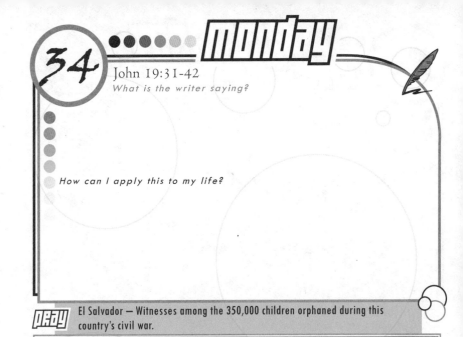

John 19:31-42

What is the writer saying?

How can I apply this to my life?

Despite suggestions for a Wednesday or Thursday crucifixion, Friday still is probable. All the biblical data can be explained to fit with a Friday crucifixion and it has the respectability of tradition behind it. (Lest we be too skeptical of tradition, let's remember that we also worship on Sunday for the same reason. Sunday worship can be illustrated, but not commanded from Scripture!)

This particular Sabbath was a high day because it occurred during Passover (either the first full day of Passover or the first day of the seven-day Feast of Unleavened Bread). It is possible that Christ celebrated the Passover with his disciples Thursday night according to one religious calendar (Essene) and then was crucified the very afternoon that Jewish fathers were butchering their lambs for the Passover meal Friday night according to the other calendar (Pharisaic).

John injects strong emotion in verses 35-37, identifying himself as an eyewitness (the disciple of verse 26) of the proof of Christ's death (water is the plasma that separates from the red blood cells once the heart stops) and His fulfillment of yet more specific Old Testament prophecies (Exodus 12:46; Zechariah 12:10). Two influential men procure the body, allowing it to suffer no more indignities. Nicodemus supplies a large amount of spices, such as would be used in a royal burial (2 Chronicles 16:14).

Life stEP

Not many mighty, not many noble are called into the family of God. Queen Victoria once praised the Lord for the letter "m" as it saved her from not any!

tuesday

John 20:1-10

What is the writer saying?

How can I apply this to my life?

PRAY   Japan — God to reveal Himself in this land where only 10% believe in the existence of a personal God.

Another argument for a Friday crucifixion is that the women were coming on Sunday to further adorn the body for burial, something that should be done as soon as possible, in this case, the Sabbath day intervening.

It is interesting that John records Mary Magdalene as the first eyewitness of the empty tomb (although she doesn't realize that Christ is alive until v. 16). She was a devoted follower of Jesus ever since He cast seven demons out of her (Luke 8). Actually, if John was making this story up he would have chosen a more respectable first witness since in that day women were not allowed to testify in a court of law.

John was younger and faster than Peter but not as bold, and it was Peter who entered the tomb first to inspect the proof of Jesus' resurrection, the empty tomb, and the abandoned grave clothes. That point in human history is the launch pad of the church, the event that turned cowards into dynamic, fearless testifiers of the risen Lord!

The ironic tragedy of the life of Christ which is resolved in the resurrection is this: "Although virtuous, He suffered all possible indignities; majestic, He died in disgrace; powerful, He expired in weakness. He claimed to possess the water of Life but died thirsty; to be The Light of the World, but died in darkness; to be The Good Shepherd, but died in the fangs of wolves; to be the Truth, but was executed as an imposter; to be Life itself, but He died quicker than the average crucifixion victim. The greatest example of righteousness the world had ever seen became a helpless victim of evil!" (Merrill Tenney, John, p. 52.)

The resurrection of Jesus Christ was a powerful demonstration of victory won over sin and death. Those who know Christ as Savior will experience this newness of life.

John 20:11-18

What is the writer saying?

How can I apply this to my life?

John explained in verse 9 that no one expected Christ to rise immediately from the dead. It wasn't until after the resurrection that they began to understand it from Scripture (such as Psalm 16:10, "Thou wilt not suffer thine holy one to see corruption.").

Mary missed Peter and John on the way back to the tomb and didn't receive any encouragement from their new-found conviction. She was sobbing broken heartedly (literally, wailing as in 11:33) when she decides to look inside. She sees the angels and talks with them, but nothing is registering. She must have thought it perfectly natural for two men to be sitting in a tomb! As she turns, she notices another man and launches into a fresh attempt to locate the body of her Lord. The inability of Mary and others (like the two disciples on the road to Emmaus) to recognize the Lord at first argues strongly against the theory that the resurrection is a myth of wishful thinking. Finally, through the blur of her tears, noting the urgency in the familiar voice, she finally realizes that she is talking to her Lord! Two natural acts followed: first, use of the familiar name, Master (Rabboni, My Teacher, normally used in prayer to God Himself) and then a grip that hinted she would never let go. Jesus did not want Mary to cling to Him because she needed to make the transition from reliance on Him to reliance on the Holy Spirit.

Life
stEP

Those forgiven much, love much. Jesus of Nazareth meant the world to Mary Magdalene, physically, spiritually, and emotionally. The day He died; her lights went out. Now, after 48 hours of weeping, her nightmare is over! What an explosion of joy.

John 20:19-31
What is the writer saying?

How can I apply this to my life?

pray For the Bible Institute Students as they go overseas to share the gospel with Missions Reality.

The word of Christ's resurrection must have spread like wildfire through both the ranks of the disciples and the Sanhedrin. Matthew records the attempts of the religious authorities to silence the rumor of the resurrection with hush money. John does not tell us how many people were gathered with the disciples. They were afraid of the Jewish authorities, but imagine how they must have been dissecting every little detail that Mary, Peter, and John could provide. Suddenly without a door opening, Christ is standing there in their midst! (Item #1: Glorified bodies can pass through solids!) He could have said a million different things but He settles on a routine "Hello" (shalom aleichim). The routine greeting of peace also allayed their fears, both of the sudden appearance and concern about the cowardly behavior less than 72 hours earlier. His next comment concerned their commission which requires empowerment (v. 22) symbolized by His breath (creative power) and actualized at Pentecost.

Since only God can forgive sin, verse 23 is talking about the results of the disciples' preaching ministry. Some will respond, be saved and as a result, have their sins forgiven by God. Thomas (the Twin) was not there and will forever be known as Doubting Thomas by his comments. Before we are too hard on poor old Thomas, let's remember that the very proof that he requested had already been provided for those who were there that night (v. 20). Those who believe having not seen the resurrected Lord (like us) are commended for their belief (v. 29). Thomas' testimony is the fitting conclusion to John's thesis, and John says so in verses 30 and 31.

We would like Jesus to be physically here, but the power of the Word and the internal confirmation of the Spirit are sufficient for us today.

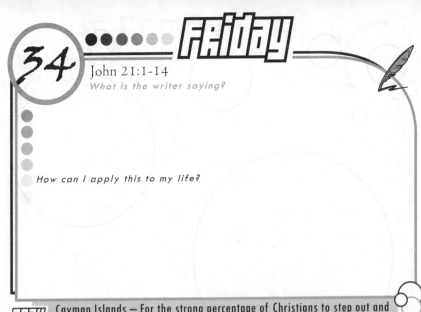

34 Friday

John 21:1-14

What is the writer saying?

How can I apply this to my life?

pray Cayman Islands — For the strong percentage of Christians to step out and share the Gospel.

John 21 is the final section of our outline: the commission. Having established the believability of the life and message of Jesus Christ, John now tells us how this message was spread throughout the world.

Seven of the eleven disciples gather together in their home territory of Galilee. That Christ would appear to them on their familiar home ground negated any lingering sense they might have had that perhaps what they experienced in Jerusalem was a product of their confusion and fear in a hostile environment. Once again, Christ appears unto people who should have recognized Him, but they do not. His question implies that He knows they didn't catch any fish. Now that it was daylight, the fish would be able to see and avoid the nets. They nevertheless obey the voice of the stranger on the shore with startling results. Christ had called them to the ministry with a similar miracle three years earlier (Luke 5).

Propriety (not necessarily modesty) called for Peter to be properly dressed to greet his Lord, despite the fact that it would be harder to swim thus attired. The Lord had already procured some fish (small sardines) which are cooking on the breakfast fire, a considerate gesture for men who had worked all night. We can only imagine the rush of memories, as Christ broke the bread and fish and fed them once again from His own hands. It left an indelible mark on Peter as he refers to it in Acts 10. This meal is a not-so-subtle reminder that He can provide for all of their needs. Just as a miraculous draught of fish initially convinced them to leave all and follow Him (Luke 5), they are to do so once again.

Life stEP

Hard work is therapeutic. It is proper to be busy as long as we are sensitive to the Lord's direction in our life when higher business calls.

How can I apply this to my life?

PRAY — Brazil — Pray for the more than 8,000,000 people practicing Spiritism to be delivered by salvation.

Peter had publicly denied the Lord three times after protesting greater love than the rest. Now, Christ gives Peter three chances to publicly affirm his chastened love for the Lord in front of the other disciples. Peter is not confident enough to tell the Lord that he agapes Him (self-sacrificing love, love given with no thought of a return) but phileo is strong enough (brotherly love as in Philadelphia). Christ probes the deepest in the third question by using phileo saying, "Okay, you can't say 'agape,' but do you really 'phileo' me?"

Both lambs and sheep are mentioned, representing all kinds of believers in different stages of development. The master shepherd mentions two aspects of shepherding: feeding the flock and caring for all their needs. Christ predicts Peter's death by martyrdom.

The last command to Peter was "Follow me." He still is a little slow on the uptake and turns around to see what everyone else is doing. He spies John, still nameless but identifiable by the descriptive phrases John uses. Peter blurts out, "What about John?" Jesus, no doubt with exasperation in His voice, says, "Mind your own business, and do what I told you to do! Follow me!" A rumor developed from Jesus' actual words, a rumor that John wanted to quell. However, he probably wasn't very convincing since, by the time this is written, all the others had met martyrs' deaths, and he was still going strong! He nevertheless asserts that his life is an eyewitness account of the greatest story ever told. His years of service, communion, and reflection have made him quite the wordsmith as well. He closes his Gospel with a precious tribute to the grandeur of the greatest man who has ever lived!

God is so gracious. Not only does He forgive our sins, He also uses us in His work giving us reward for what He plans, energizes, and executes through our lives!

In Bible usage, the word proverb denotes a terse saying of practical wisdom and often conveys moral direction. Ancient proverbs were designed principally for oral transmission. They were structured in couplets to impact the hearer and to be easy to remember. A frequent device was the contrasting couplet, "A fool uttereth all his mind: but a wise man keepeth it in till afterwards" (Proverbs 29:11). "Commit thy works unto the LORD, and thy thoughts shall be established" (Proverbs 16:3) is an example of a completive couplet; where as "Better is a little with righteousness than great revenues without right" (Proverbs 16:8) is a comparative couplet.

The Book of Proverbs includes not only proverbs, but also other types of literature, such as parables, poems, and oracles. Proverbs 1:1, 10:1, and 25:1 tell us that King Solomon authored Proverbs with the exception of the last two chapters where Agur and Lemuel are named as authors. According to 1 Kings 4:32, Solomon spoke 3000 proverbs.

1 Kings 4:31 says he was wiser than all men. That statement, of course, was no longer true when Christ became a man, for in Him are hidden all the treasures of wisdom and knowledge (Colossians 2:3). The story of how Solomon acquired such wisdom is found in 1 Kings 3:5-13.

Some of the virtues commended in Proverbs are the pursuit of wisdom, respect for parents, liberality, marital fidelity, honesty, humility, and piety. Vices condemned include lust, drunkenness, lying, cheating, laziness, strife, greed, pride, folly, gluttony, and vengeance.

The principle theme of the book is wisdom. The words wise and wisdom occur more than 100 times in the text.

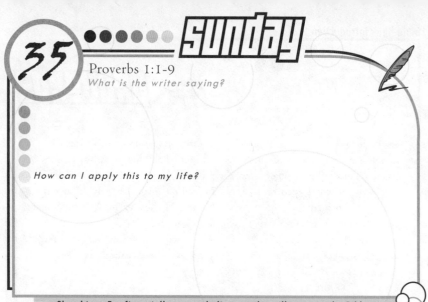

35

SUNDAY

Proverbs 1:1-9

What is the writer saying?

How can I apply this to my life?

The chapters of Proverbs in the Quiet Time schedule this year were written by Solomon. Some of the later chapters of the book were written by associates of Solomon. We must understand right up front that a proverb is a general truth from the Lord about life. The purpose of the book is stated in verses 2-3. The word wisdom implies the application of knowledge. Knowledge is the accumulation of facts that helps us form conclusions in our mind. Wisdom is taking the principles that knowledge learns and applying them to our lives. This is a key in living a Christian life. We are to study the Scripture and then apply it to our lives in the way of wisdom. The Quiet Time is set up just in that order. When wisdom is taught, the person who is unlearned will learn. And the person who is already learned will increase in the understanding (vv. 4-5). This tells us right up front that we can never know too much, for the more we learn, the more we have a capability to live a life of wisdom. In verse 7 we see that all true knowledge starts with the fear of the Lord. Fearing God is having a reverential trust in Him. A fool does not trust in the Lord and therefore can never become wise. We are told in verse 8 that knowledge comes from our parents, we are to listen to them carefully and obey them willingly. This is the way of wisdom. If we live like this, it will be an obvious sign to those around us that we are living in a wise way.

Life stEP

One of the signs of the end times is that children will not be obedient to their parents. Do you see this in the world today? It is vital for you to commit to the Lord right to lead your children effectively as a parent, or submit as a child. This is God's ordained vehicle for direction in our lives and we should take it seriously.

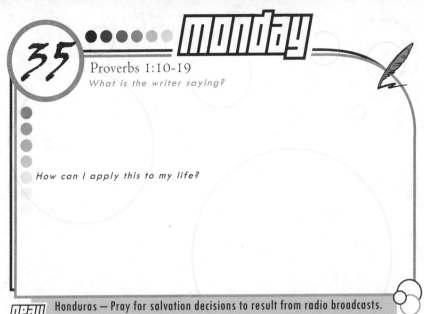

35 monday

Proverbs 1:10-19

What is the writer saying?

How can I apply this to my life?

Honduras — Pray for salvation decisions to result from radio broadcasts.

We live in a world where sinners dwell. One thing you will notice about those who sin is that they seldom want to sin alone. Sinners are constantly seeking to entice others to join in with them in their sinful ways. In verse 10, Solomon instructs us to stand firm when sinners entice us. In vv. 11-14, we see the way that sinners will entice. They will try to lure us in with promises of victory and spoil. One of the realities of sin is that it does bring pleasure. If it was a sin to stick needles in our eyes, we would all be safe! But we must remember that the pleasure of sin is only for a short period of time, then we will reap what we sow. Sinners never tell you that! The son of a famous evangelist told me of a time he was with his dad in the subway station in New York City as a youngster. On a billboard over the station was a large picture of a good looking man with a pretty blonde on each bulging bicep. He was holding a bottle of beer in his hand. It was an advertisement. Under the billboard there was a drunk sleeping off his stupor. The evangelist said (pointing at the billboard) "This is what the world tells you" and then pointing at the drunk, "and this is what the world gives you." That is a valuable lesson to remember. As Paul said, "We will reap what we sow" (Galatians 6:7). Solomon tells us here not to even hang out with them (v. 15). This means that we are not to go where they go and do what they do. We should ask them to come with us and to learn from the Word. If they stay on the path they are presently walking, it will be devastating.

Commit today to stay out of situations that will tempt you to compromise your full allegiance to Jesus. Seek to influence your unsaved friends instead of being influenced by them. Invite them to church this week and pray that the Lord will do a work in their lives.

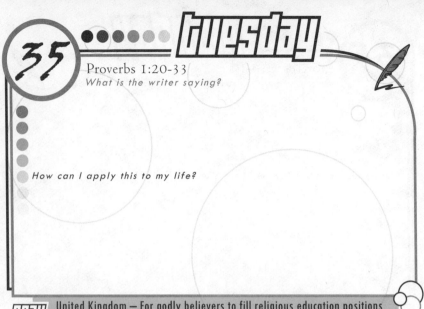

Proverbs 1:20-33
What is the writer saying?

How can I apply this to my life?

pray United Kingdom — For godly believers to fill religious education positions within the school system.

In today's passage we see wisdom standing in the market place crying out to anyone who will listen. This is a very picturesque way to teach us that the wisdom of God is available to anyone who is willing to open his heart and listen. Notice that in verse 22 the question is how long people will keep walking in their foolish ways. One of the most frustrating things is trying to show people the utter hopelessness of their godless life-style. Notice that fools hate knowledge according to this passage. Why do they hate knowledge? It is because they don't know the fear of the Lord. In John 3, Jesus points out that men love darkness more than they love light because of their evil desires. There is a call to repent in verse 23, and if they do, the spirit of wisdom will come on them. Most people do not have wisdom because they continue to entertain their sinful habits. If they continue in their hard-hearted rejection of wisdom, it may get to the point where it will be too late for them to turn. Notice in verses 28-32 Solomon says that there will be a time when they are reaping the results of their evil life that they will finally want wisdom and it will be too late. When is this point where people no longer can turn? We do not know. What we do know is that we are to encourage people to come to Christ while there is still time. According to Romans 1:19-26, people can get to the point where after continual rejection of the light that the Lord has given them, God will turn them over to their own lusts. Once that happens, they will reap the results and there will be great sorrow. In verse 33 the opposite is true, if we listen to wisdom, we will have a blessed life.

Have you been listening to the words of wisdom? Have you been applying the truth of the Word to your life? Now is the time to make sure that you are seeking to live God's way.

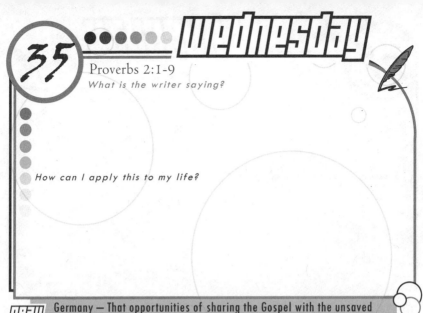

35

wednesday

Proverbs 2:1-9

What is the writer saying?

How can I apply this to my life?

pray Germany — That opportunities of sharing the Gospel with the unsaved will not be lost.

What would you do if you were told that there was $1,000,000 worth of gold buried in your back yard? Surely you would get busy digging to find it so you could take advantage of those riches!! The wisdom of the Lord is much more precious than all of the riches that the world has to offer. If we would be willing to dig hard for riches of the world, how much more should we be willing to dig for the biblical truth that will bless our life and the lives of others? In verses 4-5 Solomon tells us that we will understand when we are willing to seek with all of our heart. The word seek here carries the concept of a continual and dogged search. This is the kind of seeking that parents do when a child is abducted. They don't just casually look; they search with all of their hearts. That is the type of heart attitude the Lord is calling for in this passage. He has the wisdom stored up for us (v. 7); all we have to do is go to Him for it! When we walk in wisdom we can be assured that the Lord will protect us. That means if we are walking in wisdom, we can be sure that we are in the will of God, which is the safest place to be. Notice that as we walk in wisdom, applying God's truth to our lives, it is then we will understand what true justice is all about (vv. 8-9). Many times in our lives, we want to understand everything before we are willing to walk in obedience to the Lord. The opposite is seen here, in that we walk in obedience to the Lord, and then we will start to understand how He is working in our lives. That is the walk of faith that the Lord calls us to.

 Life stEP

Are you searching the Scriptures will all of your heart during your quiet times? Ask God to open your heart and give you a deep hunger for Him. Step out in obedience to what you know he desires of you and trust Him to give you understanding.

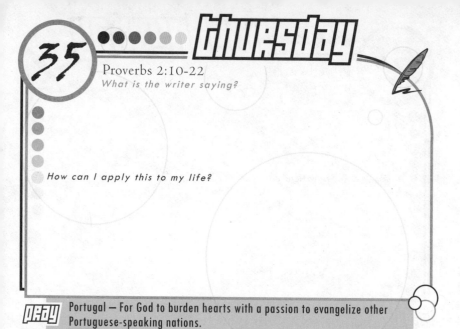

Proverbs 2:10-22

What is the writer saying?

How can I apply this to my life?

pray Portugal — For God to burden hearts with a passion to evangelize other Portuguese-speaking nations.

What is the result of having wisdom in your life? How can you tell if someone is a wise person? In verse 11, we see that the person who is walking in wisdom shows it by having discretion. Discretion knows the difference not only between right and wrong, but also between good, better, and best. In Colossians 1:9-10 Paul commands us to approve the excellent things in life. There is a difference between the good and the excellent, and those with wisdom will know what that difference is! We see in our passage that this discretion will deliver us from evil people (vv. 12-13). Wisdom can see the outcome of an action. If you are wise, you realize that there is a result to every action in life. We make the wisest decisions in our lives when we make our decisions based on long-term results of our actions as opposed to immediate gratification. The unwise make decisions to bring immediate gratification, and the result is long-term ruin (vv. 18-22). The illustration he uses here is that of falling for someone who is seducing you sexually. Would there be some immediate gratification from that? Most likely there would be, but notice the long-term effect in the passage. The wicked will be cut off by the Lord.

Life stEP

What is tempting you? Write it down, and then after you write it down, list the results of giving in to that temptation. After you do that, whenever you are tempted in that area, make sure you think of the results of that action and it will help you stand against that temptation. The second thing to do is to make sure you stay away from any opportunity that would open you up to that kind of temptation. We are told to flee youthful lusts. Last, ask the Lord for His strength in standing firm in your convictions. He will give you the strength and the grace to overcome the temptation (see 1 Corinthians 10:13).

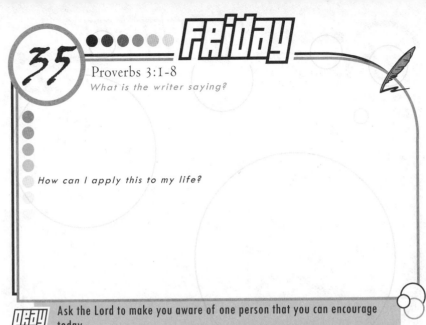

Proverbs 3:1-8

What is the writer saying?

How can I apply this to my life?

PRAY Ask the Lord to make you aware of one person that you can encourage today.

Don't forget to clean your room. Don't forget to take out the trash. Don't forget to do your homework. Sound familiar? One thing that is true of us all is that we have a tendency to forget! Over and over in the Word of God we are implored to remember certain things and not to forget the Lord. In verse 1, Solomon tells us not to forget the law of God. He instructs us to keep the commands of God from the heart. What does it mean to keep them in our hearts? It means that we don't just outwardly keep the commands, but we keep them on the inside too. In the Sermon on the Mount, Jesus shows us that God is looking not only at our actions, but also at the intent of our heart (Matthew 5:21). If we do that, we will have peace in our lives. How can we live a life that is continually directed by the Lord both in our actions and in our attitudes? The answer to that profound question is found in verses 5-6. The first thing we have to do is trust in the Lord. The word trust means to totally rely on, to lean on with all of our being. The second thing we do is refuse to trust in our own understanding. Every person has a propensity to rationalize away behavior that is not according to God's will, and we are to refuse to give in to that. The third step is to acknowledge the Lord in all of our ways, that is, to put His desires above ours in all of our plans. If we do that, we can be sure that the Lord will direct our paths. The Hebrew phrase can be translated, "He will make your path straight." The key to trusting like that is humility, not being wise in our own eyes (v. 7).

Life stEP

What is the will of God for my life? That question is on the heart of every Christian. The answer is in our passage today. Make a commitment to memorize Proverbs 3:5-6, and then ask the Lord to remind you of this truth every day of your life, and you will find that your decisions will be blessed!

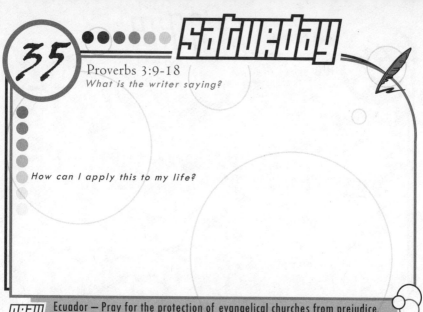

35

Proverbs 3:9-18

What is the writer saying?

How can I apply this to my life?

In our passage today there are three major principles given on making godly decisions. If we are trusting in the Lord with all of our heart (vv. 5-6) there will be results in every area of our lives. Solomon first picks out how walking in God's wisdom affects our riches. God wants us to honor Him with the possessions that He has entrusted to us. We, first of all, must remember that all we have in reality belongs to the Lord, and we are temporary stewards over it. Part of our stewardship is to honor the Lord with the first fruits. This means that the first one that we are to honor with our finances is the Lord. Many people will get their paycheck, pay all the bills, get what they want, and then give some to the Lord of what is left over. The Lord wants us to give to Him FIRST, and then to take care of the rest of our responsibilities. If we do that, we can be sure that the Lord will bless us. We are also to be good stewards of God's discipline. The Lord loves us enough to discipline us when we are wrong. Good stewardship of that discipline means that we will respond in humility and repentance. The third principle he covers in our passage today is our attitude toward wisdom. We take care of that which we treasure. If we treasure wisdom, we will be good stewards of that wisdom (vv. 13-18). Notice at the end of verse 18 we are told that the person who holds fast to wisdom will be truly happy. True happiness is an internal joy knowing that God is in control and all His plans are good.

Are you honoring God with your finances? "Are you kidding, I don't have much money," you might be thinking. The issue is to honor God with what you have, not wait until you have much more. Make it a habit now to give a portion of what you get to the work of the Lord. God will honor you for being faithful in this important area.

36

sunday

Proverbs 3:19-26

What is the writer saying?

How can I apply this to my life?

pray Czech Republic — For Czech citizens to turn to Christ to fill the void left by years of Communism.

How rich is the wisdom of God! There is much discussion going on concerning the origins of the earth. Some tell us that many years ago there were some random atoms in space that started to reproduce. After many years of reproduction, they formed into a hard core and continued to grow. After growing for billions of years, the enormous core blew up, spewing millions of spheroids all over the universe. Some of them got very hot and became stars, and some of them got cold, started rotating around the hot ones, and thus were called planets. On one of these small, cold spheroids (we will call it earth) there was water and land. In the water were some atoms that kept reproducing, and after millions of years started to swim. After swimming for years, they decided to get out of the water and try to walk. That took many years, but finally they could stand upright. They started thinking deep thoughts....and here we are! Now just off hand, that does not sound wise. We are told in verse 19 that it is by wisdom that God created the earth and all that is in it. To believe what the Bible says about creation, one must believe that there was one big miracle, and the rest makes total sense. God not only created the world, but he created it with great wisdom and care. The Creator has the right to rule over his creation, and that is one of the reasons why people believe evolution. If they believe that, then they don't have to be accountable to the Creator. As opposed to evolutionists, our trust is in the Lord (v. 26), and we are willing to submit to His words of wisdom.

Life stEP

It would be good for you to understand creation from a biblical perspective so that you can defend it in a world that for the most part rejects the biblical account. Believing that the Lord created us, we also must be willing to totally submit to Him.

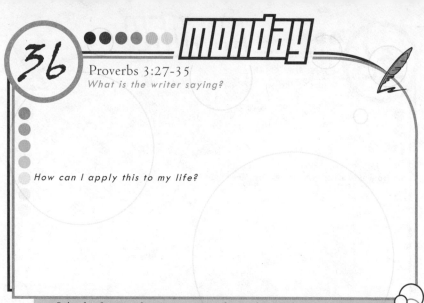

How can I apply this to my life?

pray Poland — Summer Camp ministries safety, salvation decisions, and sanctification commitments.

In the passage before us today, Solomon shares with us five principles concerning interpersonal relationships. Each one of the principles starts with the same phrase – "do not." The first one argues that we should make sure that we do good to others when we have the opportunity to do so. Many times in our lives, we have great intentions and forget to act. That leads to the second principle, which is give to someone when you have the ability to do so and don't put it off (v. 28). We all have a tendency to put off helping people instead of doing it now. The third principle in verse 29 tells us how important it is to treat our neighbors with grace. If we do, they will help protect us. The fourth principle is that we are not to get into an argument just for argument's sake (v. 30). There is a time to stand for righteousness and for the cause of Christ, but we are not to be argumentative. In verse 31 the fifth principle is that we are not to envy those who oppose us, even if they prosper. It is easy to envy people who have more than we do, and seem to have it better than us, at the same time knowing that they do not know the Lord. Asaph struggled with this in Psalm 73. We are to leave them to the Lord. The fifth principle is one with which many struggle. We wonder why the Lord would allow someone who does not serve Him to prosper in any way. One way to think of it is this: this is the best it will ever get for an unbeliever, and this is the worst it will ever be for a believer! If God shows some general grace on the pagan out of love, we shouldn't be upset should we? Humility is the key (v. 34).

It is interesting to see that wisdom applies to all of our relationships. This is the way that the world notices the difference that Jesus makes in our lives. Remember that people are watching you!

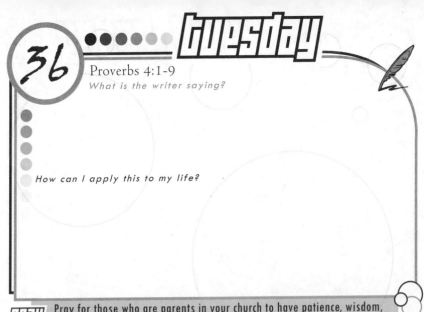

How can I apply this to my life?

There was an old television show called "Father Knows Best," and in this passage we see that this father does indeed know best, and we should listen to his instruction (v. 1). We are told to "pay attention" to what we are being taught for the instruction is good. The word used here in the Hebrew means morally excellent. We know that all of the instruction given to us in the Bible is excellent. Solomon talks about what he learned from his father when he was a child. We know that Solomon's dad was King David. David was described by the Lord as "a man after my own heart." He taught Solomon to carefully guard the teaching he received and keep it in his heart. One of the reasons that there is a strong emphasis in the Word of Life material on memorizing the Word of God is found in this passage. We are to hide God's Word in our hearts. Many people have been taught that the key to life is to "live and learn." Although that sounds reasonable, it is not a biblical concept. The biblical principle is that we are to learn and then live. Too many times we make bad mistakes and hopefully learn from them. How much better it is to learn how to live in wisdom and stay away from even making the mistakes! That is what David taught Solomon to do. When Solomon could ask for anything from the Lord, he asked for wisdom. It is most likely because of the way he was taught when he was young. The sad reality is that Solomon knew what his father was saying, yet later in his own life, he did not live by these principles.

The Bible tells us that we are to live biblically by applying wisdom to our lives. Ask the Lord to give you a heart that desires to know wisdom and never to depart from it. Remember that knowing what is wise is great, but we must live according to wisdom to please the Lord.

36

Proverbs 4:10-19
What is the writer saying?

How can I apply this to my life?

pray Mexico — For the full implementation of religious freedom at the national and local levels.

Solomon moves from telling us what his father taught him to teaching us as sons (v. 1). Notice that he tells his son that he leads him in "right paths." A "right path" is an unrestricted path, which is simpler to walk in. It is not always easier to live according to wisdom, but it is simpler. For instance, if you do not lie, you never have to remember the stories you tell, all you have to know is the truth. If you live according to wisdom, your life will stay simple. Sin only confounds and confuses. When you walk in wisdom, the Lord will bless you (v. 12) and keep you from falling. With that principle in mind, we are told that we need to hold on to wisdom with all of our might. We hold on tightly to that which we hold dear, so the point is that we are to hold wisdom to be important to us. After giving the positive, we are told what we are to stay away from. We are to stay away from those who do evil, for they will not be satisfied until they get others involved (vv. 15-16). This reminds us of the words of the Apostle Paul when he tells us that bad company corrupts good morals. It is a true principle that health does not spread, but sickness does. Sin is like a sickness of the soul and it spreads if it is not cut out of our lives. It is naïve to think that we can spend time continually around sinful activities and not be affected.

Life stEP

What people are influencing you to do evil? Are you finding yourself giving in to their influence? God has called on us to influence those around us and not to be influenced by them. Ask God to give you the internal strength to say no to ungodly influences when you know that you should. There are two kinds of people, thermostats and thermometers. Thermometers record the temperature and thermostats set the temperature. Let's commit to being spiritual thermostats!

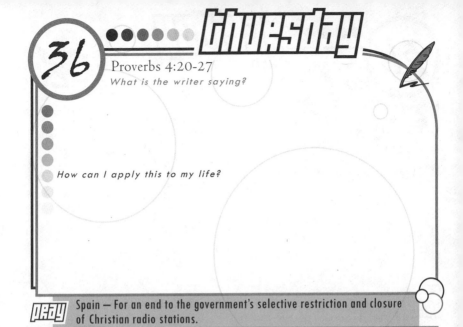

Proverbs 4:20-27

What is the writer saying?

How can I apply this to my life?

Did you ever see a scene where a person is dying and he is trying to say something? Everyone bends down toward his lips and listens carefully to see if they can pick up what he is saying. That is the word picture in verse 20. We are to incline our ears to the way of wisdom and listen carefully to what it teaches. The Word of God brings perspective and life to all of those who learn it (vv. 21-22). The emphasis in this passage is on what we let into our hearts. In verse 23, we are told that we are to guard our hearts. Men in the service are careful to guard the perimeter of their camp to make sure that only appropriate people get into camp. The concept is that we are to set up a garrison around our hearts to make sure only appropriate things get in. The reason is that what we put in our hearts will determine what

eventually comes out of our lives. In verse 24 we see that what we say comes from our hearts, so we are to watch what we put inside (v. 25). We are to look only at things that are righteous and build us up and to stay away from that which will tear us down. Have you ever heard someone say "I know there is bad language in that movie, but it doesn't bother me, after all that kind of language is used in the world all of the time"? That might sound good, but it is foolish on a number of levels. First, everything we listen to does affect us according to this passage. Second, there is a difference between hearing bad language when it is spoken in the world, and CHOOSING to listen to it when we have a choice. When you knowingly watch a movie with bad language, you are choosing to listen to it. Does that please God?

Is there some music that you listen to that does not reflect the wisdom of God? How about something you choose to watch? Are you willing to commit to God to guard your heart? Do it today!

Proverbs 5:1-14
What is the writer saying?

How can I apply this to my life?

PRAY Kenya — For the believers to live an exemplarily life and speak out against what is wrong.

There is no doubt that we live in a sex-mad world. Is this something new? No, of course not. People have always been drawn by their lusts to immorality. The difference today is that we have mass media and the internet, which brings the immoral images right into our lives in an instant. This makes these principles even timelier today. In verses 3-4, we are told that on the outside everything looks great and alluring, but the result of the activity is personal destruction. Sexual sin will eat away at your life unlike any other sin. Paul writes in 1 Corinthians 6:13-20 that there is something incredibly condemning about sexual sin. A Christian needs to realize that their body is the temple of God, and that our bodies belong to Him for His use only. In verse 8 we are told not even to go near the house of an immoral woman. Applying this today, we should stay as far away from compromising situations as we can. This would apply to what we see on the internet and what we view on the screen. Satan knows where we are weak and will seek to bring us down. Our defense is found in this passage. If we listen and apply these principles, we will have victory. Moreover, if we don't listen and obey, verses 13-14 tell us that we are on the verge of spiritual ruin.

Are you willingly looking at visuals that will make you lust? Job wrote that he would not stare at a virgin. What makes this interesting is that in Job's day the only thing you could see was a girl's eyes and feet (and those would be dusty!). Everything else would be covered up. How much more do we need to be on our guard today? Women need to be careful not to dress in such a way to draw a man's lust. The Bible says that we are to dress modestly, not to bring attention to our bodies. How are you doing in this area? Are you staying pure in heart?

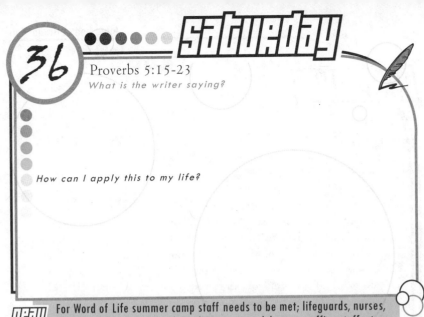
Proverbs 5:15-23

What is the writer saying?

How can I apply this to my life?

pray For Word of Life summer camp staff needs to be met; lifeguards, nurses, wait staff, housekeeping, boat drivers, groundskeepers, office staff, etc.

God is the one who created the sexual desires. Within the confines of marriage, sexual desire is a wonderful thing. Everything that God creates for good, Satan will seek to use for evil. Drugs are a wonderful and useful thing for those who are sick. Satan takes those same drugs and gets people totally hooked on them. God has created men with the ability to be creative with technology. Satan takes that same technology to promote his evil world system. This passage shows us that sexual activity is to be within the confines of a one woman and one man marriage relationship. In verses 15-20, we are told that when a couple comes together in a marriage relationship, they are to stay committed to that relationship for the rest of their lives. One of the greatest gifts that you can give your future spouse is a pure and holy life physically. Violating God's principles will carry implications in all of your future relationships, so it is vital to stay pure now. Current surveys tell us that the average age that a young person loses their virginity is between 13 and 14. As Christians, we are not to be average, we are to be exemplary, and show the world what Christ is all about. The last part of our passage today is an encouragement to remain pure. In verses 21-23 we are reminded that the Lord is omniscient (He knows all). Every time we sin, it is as if we marched right into the throne room of God and did it in His face, for all of our ways are before Him.

Life stEP You might have been burdened as you read the passage today because you have already violated God's purity principles. What can you do now? The great news is that God will forgive your sin and make you clean if you come to Him. The vital thing is from now on, ask God to keep you pure for the glory of God.

Hebrews

The theme of Hebrews is Jesus Christ in His present office as our Great High Priest. The purpose of the book is three-fold:

1. To present needed detailed information about our great priest,
2. To exhort believers to consider and act upon the information presented.
3. To warn of the consequences incurred by failure to heed the exhortations.

The exhortations and warnings are progressive after the general ones in Hebrews 2:1-4. Those in chapters 3 and 4 are focused toward believers who have no inclination to progress spiritually after being saved. In chapters 5 and 6 the emphasis is on those who have taken steps toward fruitfulness but have become stagnant. In chapter 10 mature believers in danger of sinning away future rewards are exhorted and warned. In chapters 12 and 13 there are many exhortations and few warnings directed at fruitful believers who have a great desire to continue in spiritual growth.

Since the heavenly author didn't lead the human author to reveal his name, we will call him simply the writer. Some respected students of Hebrews consider it to be in the form of a written sermon or other type of treatise. We will follow tradition in calling it a letter. The textual evidence indicates the original recipients of the letter are first century Jewish believers who possessed a good knowledge of the Old Testament. There is also ample textual evidence that the Holy Spirit had in view the entire body of believers from the original readers until the coming of Christ in power. If anyone needs confirmation that the exhortations and warnings of Hebrews are directed specifically to believers, we offer these sources: 1. The introduction to A Faith that Endures by J. Dwight Pentecost – Discovery House Publishers, 2. The first chapter of Studies in Hebrews by M. R. DeHaan – Kregel Publications 3, and Introductory Notes to Hebrews by Warren W. Wiersbe – Calvary Book Room.

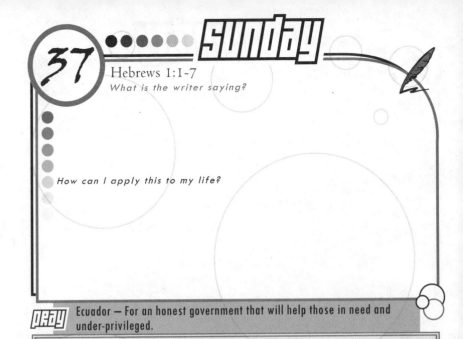

Hebrews 1:1-7

What is the writer saying?

How can I apply this to my life?

pray Ecuador — For an honest government that will help those in need and under-privileged.

Verses 1-3 present our Great High Priest, Jesus Christ, in essence (who He is) and in manifestation, (what He did, is doing, and will do). In essence, He is "the brightness of his [the Father's] glory, and the express image of his person." In His pre-incarnate ministry, He made the worlds, manifesting Himself as Creator. In His past earthly ministry, He filled the office of Prophet and then purged our sins as Savior. In manifestation of His present priestly office, He sat down on the right hand of the Majesty on high. In the future, He will manifest Himself as heir of all things.

The angels of God are wondrous beings with amazing attributes. They are wise (2 Samuel 14:20) and exceedingly strong (Psalm 103:20; 2 Thessalonians 1:7; 2 Peter 2:11). However, they have not been appointed heir of all things and are not seated on the right hand of the Majesty on high as is our Great High Priest.

In verses 5-7, the writer quotes from four Old Testament passages to prove by Scripture that our Great High Priest is superior to angels and worshipped by them. He has been given — a more excellent name — the name Jesus means Savior. The word angel means messenger. If anyone trusts an angel to save his soul, he will be doomed to the lake of fire. If anyone trusts an angel to mediate for him with God that one will never get through to God. Only the name of Jesus, God's Son and our Great High Priest can perform those services (Acts 4:12; 1 Timothy 2:5).

Today, millions are trusting angels to perform services and ministry not taught in the Bible. Our responsibility is to point out to others the only One who can both save and mediate, the Lord Jesus Christ.

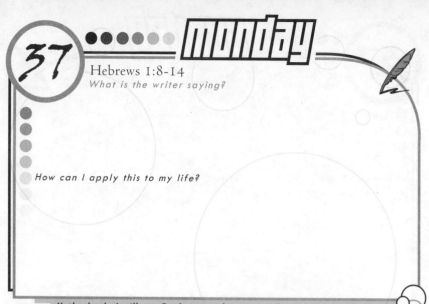

monday

Hebrews 1:8-14

What is the writer saying?

How can I apply this to my life?

PRAY Netherlands Antilles — For hearts to be open as the missionaries and pastors share the good news with them.

Verses 8 and 9 are quoted from Psalm 45:6-7. That Psalm is one of several designated as royal Psalms because they describe the Messiah as the King in His earthly kingdom. Reading the text carefully beginning with Hebrews 1:5, you'll detect that God the Father is addressing the Son as God. One purpose of chapter 1 is to make certain that you regard your Great High Priest as very God.

Verses 10-12 quote Psalm 102:25-27. The purpose is to expand upon the phrase in verse 2, "by whom also he made the worlds." Your Savior, now your High Priest, was pre-eminently the Creator. This truth is affirmed in John 1:1-14 and in Colossians 1:15-19. Perhaps we can understand the triune God in creation by considering how a magnificent edifice comes into reality. The Father is represented by the architect; He planned it all. The Son executed the plans of the Father, as did the contractor of the building. The Holy Spirit is represented by the various artisans who actually put the building together. Thinking in terms of your own salvation, the Father planned it in eternity past, the Son executed it at Calvary, and the Holy Spirit brought it to you at your conversion. The Son is Creator and Savior pre-eminently!

Verse 13 quotes from Psalm 110:1 to emphasize that angels do not possess the capability of mediating between you and God. Their proper ministry is pointed out in verse 14.

Life stEP Hebrews 1:14 indicates that God, foreknowing that we would be among His elect, appointed angelic protectors for each of us before we were born. To understand more about guardian angels, study Psalm 34:7; Psalm 91:10-12; Matthew 18:10; and Luke 16:22.

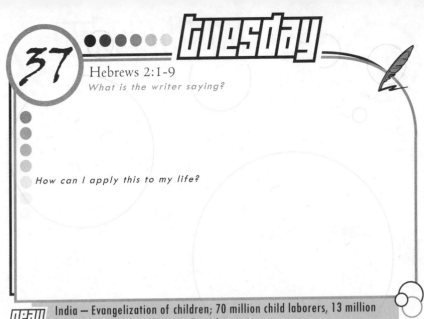

Hebrews 2:1-9

What is the writer saying?

How can I apply this to my life?

pray India — Evangelization of children; 70 million child laborers, 13 million homeless, and two million orphaned.

Verse 1 presents the first exhortation and first warning of the book of Hebrews. There is a danger of drifting away by neglecting the salvation we possess. In the Old Testament, when God's people failed to heed God's Word, there were dire consequences. That word was received by Moses through angels (Deuteronomy 33:2; Acts 7:53; Galatians 3:19). Now we have received God's Word through His Son, our Lord Jesus Christ, and His Holy Spirit empowered disciples. The book of Hebrews tells how our salvation can be neglected, the consequences of such neglect and God's provision to "hold fast the confidence and the rejoicing of the hope firm unto the end" (Hebrews 3:6).

The subject of verses 5-9 is the dominion which God gave to Adam. Adam forfeited to the angelic being, Satan. Verses 6-8 quote from Psalm 8:4-6 to confirm that dominion is intended for man and not angels. Writing about 1,000 years before Hebrews was written; the psalmist observed that man had not regained dominion. He still hasn't, but he will!

Dominion for man is in the process of being regained by the Man, Jesus Christ (Isaiah 32:1-2). "Now shall the prince of this world (Satan) be cast out" (John 12:31). When? "The God of peace shall bruise Satan under your feet shortly" (Romans 16:20). Our Great High Priest in heaven has a body on earth that He is using to regain dominion for man.

Life stEP The word neglect connotes lack of proper regard for the magnitude of the gift bestowed and received (2 Corinthians 9:15). Not to properly regard God's matchless provision of the Great High Priest described in chapter 1 is to neglect the salvation that caused Him to taste death for every man.

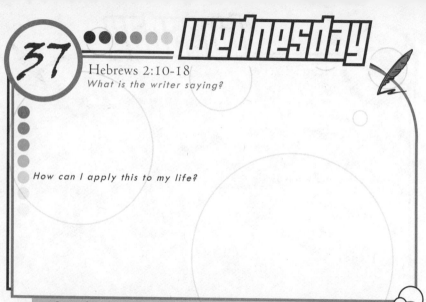

Hebrews 2:10-18

What is the writer saying?

How can I apply this to my life?

Only through the suffering of death as a member of the human race was Jesus enabled to become a perfect Savior. In no other way could the Creator (v. 10) call many His brethren. In verses 12 and 13, the writer quotes from two Old Testament portions to prove that all of these truths were foretold hundreds of years before Jesus became a man.

Angels do not die. Therefore, Jesus did not die for them. Jesus needed to be a descendant of Abraham (Matthew 1:1) because God made a covenant promising that dominion would come through him (Galatians 3:16). It has been the purpose of chapter 2 to show why Christ had to be a human being in order to provide salvation and regain dominion for man. We have already seen in chapter 1 the need for Him to be God in order to be our Great High Priest. In verses 17 and 18, we see that Jesus needed to be man in order to be our Great High Priest.

In Job 9:32-33, the ancient patriarch cried out in his need for a human mediator who could plead his case before an infinite God. He repeated his plea in Job 16:21. He needed someone who was on his level as well as God's. In Isaiah 59:16, sinful Israel needed a human intercessor; however, there was none available. First, they needed a redeemer (59:20). In Isaiah 53, the LORD had promised one who would be both Savior and Intercessor (53:12). We have the same need as did Job and Israel.

As our Great High Priest, the man Jesus is our intercessor (Romans 8:34), our mediator (1 Timothy 2:5) and our advocate (1 John 2:1). The main purpose of the book of Hebrews is to furnish us with the information we need to avail ourselves of His services.

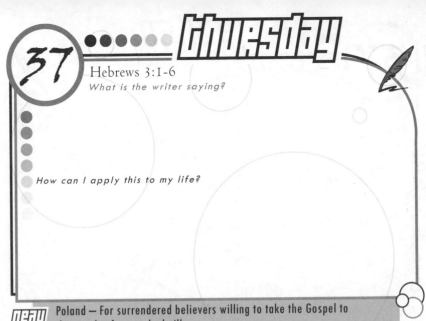

37

Hebrews 3:1-6

What is the writer saying?

How can I apply this to my life?

pray Poland — For surrendered believers willing to take the Gospel to thousands of unreached villages.

The original text was not divided into chapters and verses. Those were added for reference purposes. The word wherefore (therefore) ties 3:1-6 with the preceding verses. The holy brethren of 3:1 are the brethren of 2:11. They are members of God's family through the new birth (John 3:3; I Peter 1:23). The word apostle means sent one. In His earthly ministry, Jesus was the sent one (John 3:17; 6:57; 17:3). In His present ministry as High Priest, He is the seated one (Hebrews 1:3; Colossians 3:1).

Beginning with verse 2, we have a comparison between faithful Moses, a servant in God's house (Numbers 12:7) and faithful Jesus Christ, a builder over His own house. House can mean the building in which the family lives or the family that lives in the building. The context tells whether house or household is meant.

The family of God and the household of Christ are not precisely the same. In the story of the prodigal son (Luke 15:11-32), a member of the father's family disdained the privileges and responsibilities of the father's household and departed to a far country. Upon his repentance and return, the errant member of the family was again received into the household.

The purpose of the household of Christ on earth is to be a holy temple for a habitation of God (Ephesians 2:19-22) and to offer up spiritual sacrifices acceptable to God (I Peter 2:5).

Life stEP

A member of the family of God cannot be unborn out of that family. The evidence that I am an active, acceptable member of the household of Christ is confidence and the rejoicing of the hope. Membership in His household carries with it both privileges and responsibilities.

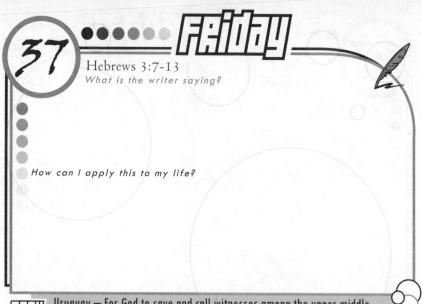

37 **Friday**

Hebrews 3:7-13

What is the writer saying?

How can I apply this to my life?

Verses 7-11 are a quotation from Psalm 95 in which the psalmist is warning his generation about a generation of their ancestors who missed the blessing of the LORD because they erred in their hearts. Verses 12 and 13 apply the same warning to us.

Speaking to Moses out of the burning bush (Exodus 3:8), God said, "I am come down to deliver them out of the hand of the Egyptians…" "unto a good land and large flowing with milk and honey…" That adult generation of Israel was freed from slavery, but never entered the Promised Land.

Forty years later Moses told the second generation that the land had houses full of all good things (Deuteronomy 6:11). The wells were already dug. The vineyards and olive trees were planted

and producing. Moses explained that God's purpose for bringing the nation out of Egypt was to give their fathers a land of abundance (Deuteronomy 6:23). Moses called that land "the rest and …the inheritance which the LORD your God giveth you" (Deuteronomy 12:9). A number of times in Joshua the conquered land is called Israel's place of rest.

"Then believed they his words; they sang his praise" (Psalm 106:12). "They believed not his word" (Psalm 106:24). The unbelief of Hebrews 3:12 is the unbelief of one who has been delivered from the slavery of sin but who does not go on into a productive Christian life. The brethren are warned to take heed and exhort one another daily (Hebrews 10:25).

We received a new heart when we were saved. God did not remove our sin nature and our wills at conversion. We must will to keep our new hearts clean "with the washing of water by the word" (Ephesians 5:26) and by confessing our sins (1 John 1:9).

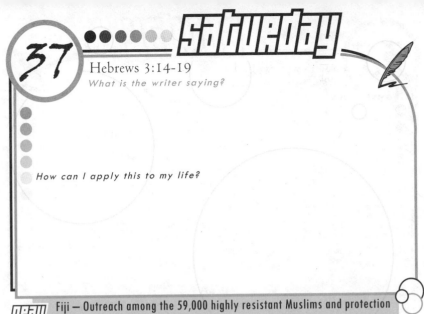

37

SATURDAY

Hebrews 3:14-19

What is the writer saying?

How can I apply this to my life?

"Christ in you, the hope of glory" (Colossians 1:27). As we appropriate the hope within us, our confidence is steadfast. When we are saved by faith, but fail to walk in that faith (Colossians 2:6), we are neglecting our salvation and wandering in the wilderness. We are exhorted to hear his voice. We hear the Lord's voice as we hear, read, study, and meditate upon God's Word. Our hearts are hardened as we fail to yield our bodies as instruments of righteousness unto God (Romans 6:13; 12:1).

Psalm 106 recounts the history of Israel from their deliverance from Egypt to their exile to Babylonia, about 850 years. The belief of Psalm 106:12 is recorded in Exodus 14:31 and was followed by the song of Exodus 15:1-19. The record of the unbelief of verse 24 is in Numbers 14:1-4. By faith, the people applied the blood of the Passover lamb and passed through the Red Sea, escaping the power of Pharaoh. Two years later; however, they refused to trust God to deliver the Promised Land into their hands.

My rest in Hebrews 3:11 and his rest in 3:18 refer to the abundant life God wanted to provide for His people in the Promised Land (Joshua 1:13; 21:43-45). Notice that those who sinned in Moses' day were the ones who were denied a part in God's rest. Joshua and Caleb believed God and later entered in because they wholly followed the LORD (Numbers 32:10-13).

Life **stEP**

If we fail to hear the exhortations and heed the warnings, we will suffer loss. We will spend our Christian lives following our own agendas, while our Great High Priest desires to work in us and through us that which is pleasing in His sight (Hebrews 13:21).

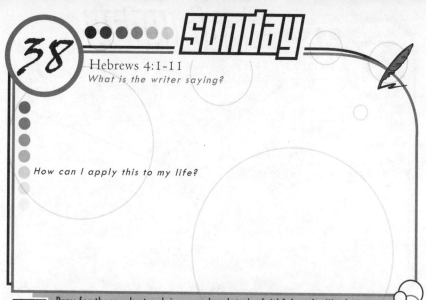

Hebrews 4:1-11

What is the writer saying?

How can I apply this to my life?

PRAY Pray for those who teach in your church to be faithful to the Word.

The Lord intended three stages of rest for the nation of Israel: 1. The redemption rest from slavery in Egypt (Exodus 6:5-7). 2. The possession rest in the Promised Land (Deuteronomy 12:9,10; Joshua 21:43-45). 3. The kingdom rest when Messiah reigns on earth (Isaiah 11:10; 32:18). These three rests typify three stages of rest God intends for every believer. 1. The rest salvation provides as a gift at conversion (Matthew 11:28). 2. The rest of soul satisfaction attained by being a productive part of His present earthly program (Matthew 11:29). 3. The eternal rest received when the labors and trials of this life are over and we are with Christ (Daniel 12:13).

The warning of Hebrews 4 is that saved people today can miss the second stage of their rest as did Israel. It is God's desire that we enter into the same type of rest He experienced (Genesis 2:2) at the completion of creation. Many Christians come short of the deep sense of satisfaction experienced from being just where God would have us be in this life.

The unbelief of Hebrew 3:12, 18-19 and 4:6, 11 is the failure to trust God for victories over the walled cities and giants of the Promised Land. It is failure to walk by faith after we have been redeemed by faith. Walking by faith produces that which "remaineth therefore a rest to the people of God" (v. 9). The exhortation of verse 11 is to exercise diligence so that we do not miss that which God intends for us through being yoked with Christ in doing His work on earth.

Life stEP

The key to finding such rest is learning more about Him. We were given a rest from the burden of sin when He saved us (Matthew 11:28).

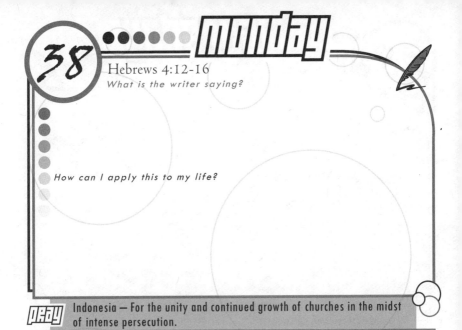

38 **monday**

Hebrews 4:12-16

What is the writer saying?

How can I apply this to my life?

pray Indonesia — For the unity and continued growth of churches in the midst of intense persecution.

From 4:12 to 6:8 the writer gives instruction, exhortations and warnings to believers who manifest a desire to heed the exhortations and warnings of 3:12 to 4:11. They will need: 1. A real desire to know Christ well enough to be an effective part of His present program on earth. 2. Sufficient attention to God's Word. 3. An understanding of the high priestly ministry of our Lord. The Word of God is capable of discerning our hearts and spotlighting hidden errors of thought and deed. It even has the power to produce the faith needed to believe all it says (Romans 10:17). When the Word points out our errors to us, even the sin of incomplete trust, we need the services of our Great High Priest. He knows and understands our spiritual infirmities. As we grow under His tender care, our love for Him increases until we have a compelling desire to spend enough time with Him to understand His person and His ways (Philippians 3:10). All of this is outside of the scope of the wilderness Christian who has his own agenda for this life. Attempting to run his own life he suffers loss of rest in this life and loss of eternal rewards. "There is a place of quiet rest, Near to the heart of God. A place where sin cannot molest, Near to the heart of God. There is a place of comfort sweet, Near to the heart of God. A place where we our Savior meet, Near to the heart of God. There is a place of full release, Near to the heart of God. A place where all is joy and peace, Near to the heart of God."

Life stEP

"Let us therefore come boldly unto the throne of grace, that we may obtain mercy, and find grace to help in time of need" (v. 16).

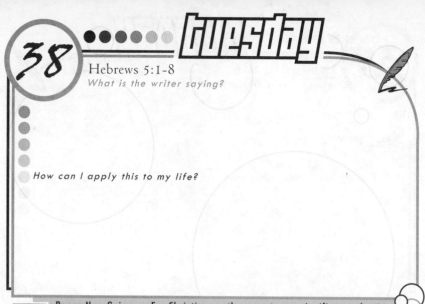

Hebrews 5:1-8

What is the writer saying?

How can I apply this to my life?

pray Papua New Guinea — For Christian youth camps to see significant salvation and consecration decisions.

Through Moses, God gave His people a system of procedures whereby a Holy God could dwell among a sinful people (Exodus 25:8). The key person in that relationship was Aaron, the high priest. A high priest is a man ordained of God who speaks to God for men, whereas a prophet is ordained to speak to men for God. Because he also was a sinner, Aaron first offered sacrifices for himself (Leviticus 9:7). Then he offered gifts and sacrifices for sins of ignorance and sins committed because one was out of the way due to the enticement of the flesh or the devil. There were no sacrifices for presumptuous sins (Numbers 15:27-31). This subject will be developed in chapter 10, after chapters 7-10 explain why our High Priest, Jesus Christ, is far superior to the Aaronic priesthood.

Verses 5 and 6 quote from Psalms 2 and 110 to let us know that God planned beforehand a high priest who is a sinless son instead of a sinful servant, and that His priesthood is forever. Verse 7 refers to the experience of our Lord in the Garden of Gethsemane. Jesus prayed to be rescued from death, not to escape death (Psalm 22:21; Acts 2:24). He knew that He was born to die. His resurrection proves that His prayer was answered. The word fear indicates Jesus shrank in horror at the prospect of being laden with our sins. Jesus learned by experience what it was like to suffer obedience unto death in order to be a perfect Savior and a perfect High Priest. He was always the obedient one (John 8:29).

If you have a desire to be effectively involved in that which the risen Christ is doing in and through His people today, you should be greatly interested in the Great High Priest.

How can I apply this to my life?

PRAY France — Outreach among the growing Muslim population. Islam is now the second religion of France.

At this point, the writer wants to explain what it means for Christ to be "an high priest after the order of Melchisedec" (v. 10). However, many are not spiritually mature enough to comprehend deep spiritual truths. He makes four accusations: 1. You're dull of hearing; 2. You must be taught again the basic principles; 3. Spiritually, you're like babies who must be fed milk when you ought to be adults able to digest meat; 4. You're unskillful in the words of God relating to righteousness. As a result, you're living according to your own standard of righteousness instead of God's standard. If you want to understand deep spiritual truths, you must first let the Word of God change your thinking about good and evil.

People of our day who are in the same category could have some of the following histories or practices: 1. They have had a genuine conversion experience. 2. They surrendered their lives to Christ at a campfire service. 3. They went forward at a dedication service. 4. They attend regularly at a Bible-preaching church and take part in church activities. 5. They have a daily Bible reading regimen. 6. In some manner, they have indicated a desire to live for Jesus. At the same time, some of the following may be true: They have a bad temper or other trait they excuse instead of calling it sin. About conduct, they say "I don't see anything wrong with it; or "Show me in the Bible where it says I can't do it"; or "So and so are good Christians and they do it." The problem may be resistance to the work of the Word rather than lack of the Word.

Bad moral thoughts, questionable pastimes, defensive attitudes, or devotion to vocation or avocation can interfere with absorption of the Word. Pride of accomplishment and critical remarks about others characterize those who are not exercised to discern both good and evil.

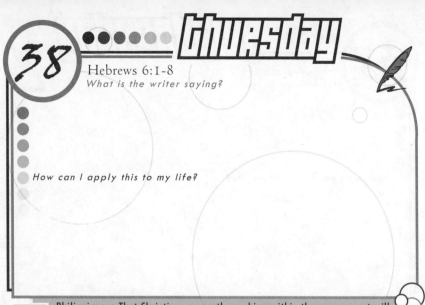

Hebrews 6:1-8

What is the writer saying?

How can I apply this to my life?

PRAY — Philippines — That Christians currently working within the government will use their influence wisely.

The resurrection and bodily ascension of Jesus to sit at the right hand of God is an example of foundational truth. That He is seated there to be a priest forever after the order of Melchisedec is deeper truth. Those described in 5:11-14 are exhorted to go on to deeper knowledge and spiritual maturity. But who are these who are not permitted to go on?

We are assured that the words of verses 4 and 5 describe born again people because of their usage elsewhere. The word enlightened is found in Ephesians 1:18 and is translated illuminated in Hebrews 10:32. The word tasted is used in Hebrews 2:9 and 1 Peter 2:3. It is translated eaten in Acts 10:10 to say what Peter would do when he was very hungry. The word partakers is in Hebrews 3:1, 14 and 12:8, 10 and several other places in regards to saved people.

Verse 6 is interpreted by 7 and 8. God is represented as a farmer. He has fields that produce, but others given the same loving care grow only thorns and briers. As a good farmer, he will burn up the product of the bad fields and leave them fallow. It is the product, not the field that is destroyed by fire. A similar truth is taught in 1 Corinthians 3:13-15.

The believers warned in chapters 3 and 4 were pre-figured by the Israelites who were delivered from slavery but denied the privileges of the Promised Land. These being warned here are pre-figured by the Israelites of Isaiah 5:1-7. They had position, preparation, protection, and privilege but no product for the Provider. They were in the land but denied a part in God's program.

Life stEP

Persistent rejection of the Spirit's call to repentance makes us unusable to God. We will be castaways, disallowed in the race (1 Corinthians 9:27) while awaiting the judgment seat of Christ (2 Corinthians 5:10).

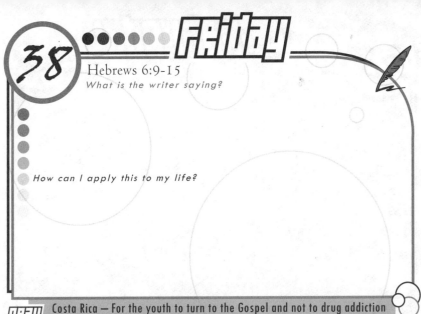

Hebrews 6:9-15

What is the writer saying?

How can I apply this to my life?

In verses 9 and 10, the writer assures his readers that they are not being classified with the unproductive Christians of verses 4-8. There has been continuous evidence of dedication to the Lord's work. The exhortation is to continue diligently through faith and patience. The warning is against slothfulness, which leads to rejection for service.

It was pointed out earlier that Hebrews is a book of instructions, exhortations, and warnings concerning the utilization of the services of our divinely appointed Great High Priest. After warning disinterested Christians in chapters 3 and 4 and unproductive Christians in chapters 5 and 6, the writer now proceeds to instruct dedicated Christians. There is little exhortation or warning until chapter 10.

In Genesis 12:1, we read that the Lord commanded Abraham to leave his own country and go unto a land I will show thee. He went by faith not knowing where he went. In verses 2 and 3, God made him a seven-fold promise. When Abraham reached the land of Canaan, God expanded the promise (Genesis 13:14-16). Later (Genesis 15:9-17), the Lord confirmed the promise by making an unconditional covenant with a blood sacrifice. In 17:6-8, the covenant was extended to Abraham's heirs. The covenant was restated in Genesis 22:17 as quoted in Hebrews 6:14.

After 25 years of waiting, at age 100, Abraham obtained the promise through the miraculous birth of Isaac.

Life stEP

The lesson for us is that waiting requires endurance, faith, and patience. Impatience, which is a lack of faith, may cause us to take matters into our own hands, as did Abraham with Hagar. Then God must wait to fulfill His promises while we learn to be patient.

How can I apply this to my life?

pray China — Wisdom and boldness to bypass restrictions against teaching creation and the Lord's return.

Verses 16-18 let us know that God had us in mind when He made promises to Abraham and then confirmed them with an oath (Genesis 22:16-18). Galatians 3:6-29 explains how we become heirs of Abraham. (Verses 7, 9, 16, and 29 are particularly pertinent). God wants us to have a strong consolation with a hope both sure and stedfast from a God who cannot lie (Titus 1:2). Our High Priest, Jesus our Lord, is already at our eternal destination. We are anchored to Him by a cable that is unbreakable! How could we be more secure?

The hope of Scriptures is not the concept that we express in everyday conversation. We hope it will rain tomorrow with no assurance that the hope will be realized. We hope our fortunes will improve or that some desire will be fulfilled. In the Bible, hope is the present appropriation of a future joyous certainty (Titus 2:13). In heaven, there is no need for hope. Fulfillment will be complete. There is no hope in hell. Hope is for present assurance!

Melchisedec is identified in Genesis 14:18 as king of Salem (Jerusalem) and the priest of the most high God. The pagan king of Sodom was coming to offer great riches to Abraham. Melchisedec intervened and as a result, Abraham vowed not to receive anything except from the hand of God. As priest, Melchisedec ministered to Abraham beyond the capabilities of an Aaronic priest. He kept Abraham from error; whereas Aaron could offer sacrifice only after the wrong was committed.

The Bible describes hope as — restful, strengthening, happy, glad, rejoicing, abounding, righteous, glorious, crowning, consoling, good, steadfast, better, living, indwelling and purifying.

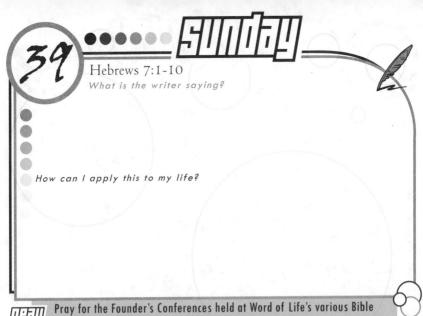

39 SUNDAY

Hebrews 7:1-10

What is the writer saying?

How can I apply this to my life?

pray Pray for the Founder's Conferences held at Word of Life's various Bible Institutes.

Melchisedec was "Without father, without mother, without descent (genealogy), having neither beginning of days, nor end of life; ...abideth a priest continually (perpetually)" (v. 3). Some expositors believe he was a pre-incarnate appearing of Christ (theophany). Verse 8 indicates that Melchisedec never died, as did Aaronic priests. Two objections to that interpretation are (1) Jesus had a mother; (2) it is said he is like the Son of God and therefore, could not be the Son of God. Jesus had no mother when Melchisedec appeared to Abraham and Revelation 1:13 says Christ was like the Son of Man, and He was the Son of Man. Would the writer be so emphatic about the greatness of Melchisedec above Abraham if he were less than deity?

Abraham gave to God's priest a tenth (tithe) of the wealth gained from the defeat of the enemy to acknowledge that it all belonged to God. It was God who gave the victory! God tested Abraham by requiring him to forfeit all and keep none! The Sabbath rest, animal sacrifice, circumcision, and tithing were procedures instituted by God before the law and later incorporated into the law. All four were fulfilled in Christ (Romans 10:4). The tithe required by law was for the sustenance of the tribe of Levi, which had no other means of income. Our instructions for supporting God's work are spread throughout the Epistles with detailed instructions in 2 Corinthians chapters 8 and 9.

Life stEP

"...but first gave their own selves to the Lord—" (2 Corinthians 8:5). When we willingly give ourselves to the Lord, we give Him all that we have. We then become His stewards of the material wealth that comes into our hands. It is His great pleasure to direct us in the distribution of that wealth as we learn of His work throughout the world.

monday

39

Hebrews 7:11-17

What is the writer saying?

How can I apply this to my life?

pray Nigeria — Protection for those working among the Fulani people and other Muslim groups.

Why did there need to be a change of priesthood? Because the Aaronic (Levitical) priesthood had imperfections. It was not possible for there to be a perfect priesthood until death was conquered through the resurrection of Christ following His offering of the perfect sacrifice on the cross of Calvary. The Law of Moses could not function without the Aaronic priesthood nor could that priesthood operate apart from the Law. The Law required that the high priest descend from the Levite family of Aaron. However, the Lord's decree in Psalm 110 required a priest forever after the order of Melchizedek who would be a descendant of David of the tribe of Judah. That would not be possible under the Law. Therefore, the law, along with its' priesthood, must be annulled to make way for a priesthood as decreed by the LORD in Psalm 110. The incarnation, death, and resurrection of Jesus Christ opened the way for a superior priesthood. We now have a great high priest after the power of an endless life. That power derives from the fact that our high priest is impervious to death or any other destructive power. Because He is a man, He understands our human needs. Because he is God, He has the capacity to know and meet our needs.

God's plans never included a permanent Aaronic priesthood. That was established to offer a temporary approach to God until those events transpired which would permit a far better priesthood.

Life stEP

What a pity that the majority of God's people have no real concept of God's gracious provision of such a Great High Priest. This is because they have not had their senses exercised by the Word of God. Their concerns are for the temporal rather than the eternal! Therefore, their spiritual food is still milk when they should be feasting on meat.

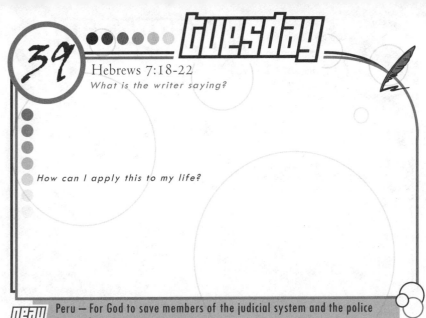

What is the writer saying?

How can I apply this to my life?

The word surety in verse 22 is translated guarantee in most modern versions. It is a very special type of guarantee. The word is found only here in the Greek New Testament, but the Hebrew equivalent is used at least eight times in the Old Testament. Consider such verses as Proverbs 6:1 and 11:15 for an understanding of the word. Webster's dictionary defines a surety as "one who assumes the obligation of default or failure in duty of another." Suppose a merchant needs funds in order to stock his store for Christmas sales. The bank will say, "We have the money to lend, but we aren't confident that you will sell enough goods to repay the loan." He must find a surety whom the bank knows can and will make up his shortage if he fails. The bank will enter into an agreement with him, but the one who is the surety must sign also. Jesus has signed with His blood as my surety. He makes up the difference between God's requirement and my performance. My record with God consequently is perfect! In his distress, Job cried out to God for a surety (Job 17:3). The psalmist expressed his need for one (Psalm 119:122). God's requirement is perfection (Matthew 5:48). That is His standard. Because He is perfect, He cannot lower His standard to accommodate my insufficiency. However, in His mercy He has provided Someone as my surety who meets His standard completely. An Old Testament high priest could not do that. "By so much was Jesus made a surety of a better testament" (v. 22).

Life stEP

Many Christians live from day to day with a sense of inadequacy, guilt or frustration. Our God wants us to walk joyfully. When our desire is to meet His standard of perfection, our great high priest continuously makes up our lack (Matthew 11:29-30).

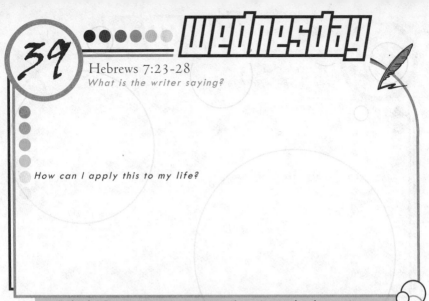

How can I apply this to my life?

In Hebrews chapter 7, the writer impresses his readers with the superiority of Christ's priesthood over that which was available under the Law of Moses. The theme is continued in verses 23 and 24 by pointing out that the old priesthood changed every time a high priest died, whereas the new priesthood will never change. Therefore, through His ministry of intercession, our Great High Priest is able to bring our salvation to its ultimate conclusion (v. 25).

Verse 26 presents the character and exalted station of our Great High Priest. He is holy and therefore can bring us to a state of holiness. He is harmless, that is, He has no motive except for our ultimate good. During His life on earth, He proved His eternal sinlessness and is already positioned in the place where we will attain sinlessness with Him. There is no position in heaven or on earth more exalted than His.

Verse 27 introduces a subject that will be stressed in the next several chapters. In His death on the cross, He offered up one all-sufficient sacrifice for sin. Under the system established before that sacrifice, it was necessary for the high priests to offer sacrifices every day as long as they were in the priesthood. Those daily sacrifices were of no avail until the high priest first offered sacrifices for his own sins. These were called consecration offerings. Our Great High Priest is consecrated for evermore by an oath of one who cannot lie (Hebrews 6:17-18). Such a one is available continuously and perpetually in the glory for our benefit.

Two questions face us. What will we do with this wondrous provision from God? What will be the nature of our loss if we neglect so great salvation? Chapter 10 will answer the second question and chapters 11-13 will be of value in answering the first.

Hebrews 8:1-6

What is the writer saying?

How can I apply this to my life?

After the LORD gave Moses the law (Exodus 20-23), He called Moses back to the mountain (Exodus 24). There He gave Moses specific details for the construction of a sanctuary called the tabernacle in the wilderness (Exodus 25-27). The structure was about 45 feet long, 15 feet wide and 15 feet high and was divided into two rooms separated by a heavy veil. The building was in an enclosed courtyard surrounded by a linen curtain. The only entrance was a gate at the east end. Just inside the gate was a large brazen altar. Between the altar and the building was a brazen laver. For a complete description of the court, the building and the furnishings see Exodus 35-38. In Hebrews 8:2-5, we learn that the tabernacle was an example or shadow of something in heaven called the true tabernacle. Four times it was made clear to Moses that the earthly tabernacle and all of its furnishings were to be made according to a specific pattern (Exodus 25:9, 40, etc.). Aaron and his sons went through an elaborate procedure of consecration and a system of worship was set up. God told Moses that the tabernacle, the priesthood and the procedures were for a purpose; "And I may dwell among the children of Israel, and will be their God" (Exodus 29:45).Our High Priest has now offered a better sacrifice and now mediates a better covenant established upon better promises made possible by the Resurrection of Christ.

Life stEP

The Old Testament system was never meant by God to be a permanent way for a holy God to dwell among sinful man. Let us yield our lives to the indwelling Holy Spirit through whom our Great High Priest administers His program in the world today. We have been made near to God by the blood of Christ (Ephesians 2:13).

Hebrews 8:7-13

What is the writer saying?

How can I apply this to my life?

Verses 8-12 are quoted from Jeremiah 31:31-34. Second Corinthians chapter 3 adequately explains how believers of this age are brought into the new covenant and also affirms that Israel will in the future enjoy the benefits of this covenant which was promised to the house of Israel and the house of Judah. (See also Jeremiah 32:37-40 and 50:4-5.)

We got our terms Old Testament and New Testament from the covenant God made with Israel at Sinai (Exodus 19:5-8) and the one prophesied by Jeremiah and quoted in Hebrews 8. The words testament and covenant are the same in the Greek New Testament. For a complete understanding of the old covenant read Leviticus 26:3-33. God said, "if ye walk… keep … and do" then "I will give … plenty (vv. 4-5) …peace (v. 6) … power (vv. 7-8) … presence (vv. 9-12)." Notice in Hebrews 8:10-12 there is no "if ye will." Rather, there is a five fold unconditional "I will." Jesus Christ has already performed our part to perfection!

There are two aspects of that which Christ has done for me in meeting God's requirements. For instance in suretyship (v. 7:22), all of my need has already been put to my account. As far as my eternal salvation is concerned, my need was total. There is nothing I could have done towards that debt and there is nothing I can ever do; Jesus paid it all. His righteousness has been put to my account and that settles it! As a practical matter, I am an effective servant as I appropriate the realization of His suretyship while I am serving.

Life stEP

I must constantly remember that I do not serve the Lord in order to gain His favor. I gained God's favor completely by receiving His gift of eternal life which is in His Son (I John 5:11). Now as I yield my will to the indwelling Spirit, He gives me a deep desire to join Him in His work.

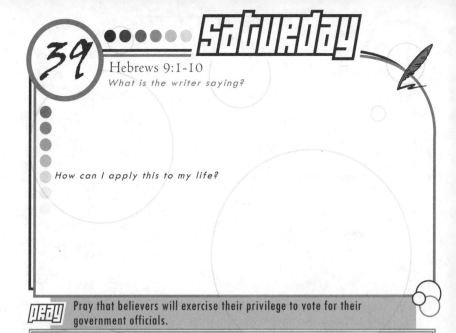

Hebrews 9:1-10

What is the writer saying?

How can I apply this to my life?

Every item and procedure concerning the tabernacle typifies some facet of the person or ministry of Christ. The two items of furniture in the courtyard typify that which Christ our Savior provided for our salvation and our sanctification. The items named in verse 2 are located in the first part of the sanctuary itself. They pre-figure that which Christ our Great High Priest is currently providing for our illumination and sustenance as we are in the place of service. The items of verses 4 and 5 have to do with our approach into His presence for communion and worship. Under the old covenant only a priest could enter the place of service and only the high priest could enter into the presence of the LORD and that but once a year on the day of atonement (Leviticus 16).

The purpose of this section of Hebrews is to impress us with the tremendous advantage we have in Christ over the old system which could not make him that did the service perfect, as pertaining to the conscience. Our consciences tell us what is right or wrong according to our own standard of righteousness. The Apostle Paul murdered Christians in good conscience before he yielded to the lordship of Christ and received a new standard of righteousness.

Life **stEP**

Let your conscience be your guide is bad advice though often given. Our consciences can cause us to feel guilty after we violate them. They can also warn of consequences. However, the conscience has no power over temptation and desire. It is the Holy Spirit's application of the Word of God that empowers to withstand temptation (I Corinthians 10:13).

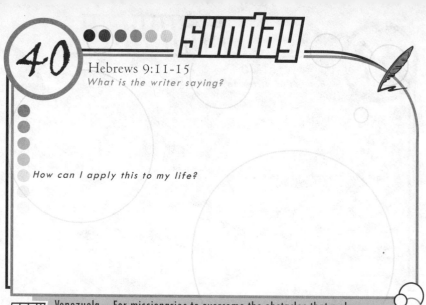

Hebrews 9:11-15

What is the writer saying?

How can I apply this to my life?

PRAY Venezuela — For missionaries to overcome the obstacles that make obtaining a visa a difficult process.

"For this he did once, when he offered up himself" (Hebrews 7:27). "By his own blood he entered in once into the holy place" (9:12). "Now once … hath he appeared to put away sin by the sacrifice of himself" (9:26). "Christ was once offered to bear the sins of many" (9:28). "We are sanctified through the offering of the body of Jesus Christ once for all" (Hebrews 10:10). "He had offered one sacrifice for sins for ever" (Hebrews 10:12). "For by one offering he hath perfected for ever them that are sanctified" (Hebrews 10:14). Every year under the old covenant, the high priest sacrificed literally thousands of animals to cover the sins of the people. That covenant was in force for about 14 centuries! The Holy Spirit, through the Word, wants to impress us with the fact that the one sacrifice of God's dear Son accomplished infinitely more than all of those sacrifices.

Even saved people can have weak consciences that can be defiled (1 Corinthians 8:7). Defiled consciences bring about impure minds and all kinds of evil (Titus 1:15). The conscience can be seared causing some to depart from the faith into false doctrines (1 Timothy 4:1-3). What then is the answer? Our consciences need to be purged by the blood of Christ. (Hebrews 9:14; 10:22, 1 John 1:7). When we are saved, the Holy Spirit comes into our beings to guide us (John 16:13; Romans 8:14). He uses the Word of God to inform us and empower us to live by God's standard of righteousness to the extent that we are exercised by the Word to discern good and evil (Hebrews 4:12, 5:14).

Life stEP

We have obtained eternal redemption by His own blood (v. 12) through the ministry of the eternal Spirit (v. 14). Now we glory in the promise of an eternal inheritance (v. 15).

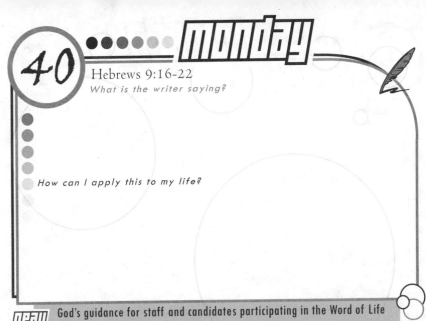

monday

40

Hebrews 9:16-22

What is the writer saying?

How can I apply this to my life?

pray God's guidance for staff and candidates participating in the Word of Life Missionary in Training program.

A covenant (testament) is a contract whereby a testator agrees to bestow benefits upon a recipient. Both the old and the new covenants required performance on the part of both parties to the contract. The great advantage of the new covenant is that my performance requirements have already been met by Jesus Christ! As in a will, death must precede the receipt of benefits. The measure of the value of sacrificial blood is a major point of contrast between the two covenants. What then is the value of the blood of Christ? Years ago, expositor C.H. Mackintosh observed, "The loftiest estimate which the human mind can form of the blood must fall infinitely short of its divine preciousness."

All of the following was wrought for me "by his own blood" (Hebrews 9:12): propitiation (Romans 3:25), justification (Romans 5:9), communion (1 Corinthians 10:16), eternal redemption (Hebrews 9:12), a purged conscience (Hebrews 9:14), access to God (Hebrews 10:19), sanctification (Hebrews 13:12), perfection (Hebrews 13:12), forgiveness of sins (Ephesians 1:7), peace with God (Colossians 1:20), reconciliation to God (Colossians 1:20) and continuous cleansing (1 John 1:7). Besides all of this, His own are "purchased with His own blood" (Acts 20:28), "made near (to God) by the blood of Christ" (Ephesians 2:13), and overcome by the blood of the Lamb" (Revelation 12:11).

The word blood is found 12 times in Hebrews 9. "Without the shedding of blood there is no remission" (v. 22).

Life **stEP** Some of our most cherished hymns extol the merits of the blood of Jesus Christ. In God honoring churches, you'll hear There is Power in the Blood and Are You Washed in the Blood sung with gusto. Among liberal groups these bloody hymns are disdained and have been removed from their hymnals.

Hebrews 9:23-28
What is the writer saying?

How can I apply this to my life?

pray Romania — Outreach to thousands of street children and orphans who possess Europe's highest HIV rates.

"...Now to appear in the presence of God for us" (v. 24) "... hath he appeared to put away sin by the sacrifice of himself" (v. 26) "... shall he appear the second time without sin unto salvation" (v. 28). These three appearings of our Lord represent the ministry of Christ in the three tenses of our salvation. In His past earthly ministry He saved us from the penalty of sin by that which He did for us. In His present high priestly ministry He is saving us from the power of sin by that which He does in us. In His future ministry He will save us from the very presence of sin through that which He will do with us.

It is historically true that of the billions of people who have lived on earth, all but Enoch, Elijah, and those still living on earth have met their appointments with physical death. The witness of God's Word is, except for the Divine intervention of the rapture of believers at the coming of Christ, that all that are now alive will meet that appointment. Some judgment for sins precedes death, but the ultimate judgment will surely come. No one will escape (Romans 2:3-6).

Now here is a happy thought for all who are in Christ Jesus (Romans 8:1). God considers you to have died with Christ and already to have been raised from the dead with Him! Your sins were judged on the cross. You have already kept your appointment with death and judgment. You are now alive on the resurrection side of death and judgment. If you do not live to see the rapture, the grave is but a doorway to His presence!

Do you want to know where in the Bible to read about being alive now on the resurrection side of death and judgment? See these passages: Romans 6:3-11; Colossians 2:12-13; 3:1-4. Then go and live in "the power of His resurrection" (Philippians 3:10).

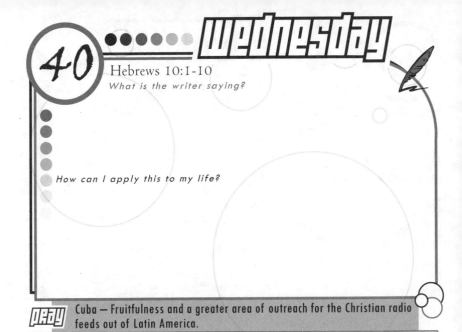

Hebrews 10:1-10

What is the writer saying?

How can I apply this to my life?

pray Cuba — Fruitfulness and a greater area of outreach for the Christian radio feeds out of Latin America.

The purpose of Hebrews 10:1-18 is to contrast the inadequacy of the Old Testament sacrifices with the sufficiency of the sacrifice of Christ. Those sacrifices were only a shadow of the good things that would be accomplished by Christ. They must be offered continuously year by year. His sacrifice was once for all. Those sacrifices could not purge the conscience because they could not take away sins. They could only cover sins until the perfect sacrifice was provided. God had no pleasure or satisfaction in the sacrifice of bulls and goats. Our sanctification through the willing sacrifice of Jesus Christ fulfilled His purpose of having a people for His holy name.

In order to demonstrate the complete willingness of the Son to offer His body as a sacrifice, the writer spotlights a prophecy from Psalm 40:6-8. The Holy Spirit, as author, reflects what has occurred between the time of the original prophecy and the writing of Hebrews. "Mine ears hast thou opened" of Psalm 40:6 becomes "a body hast thou prepared me" in Hebrews 10:5. Isaiah 50:4-7 applies to our Lord, an Old Testament way of indicating complete submission on the part of a servant (Exodus 21:5, 6). Notice the essentials in that procedure. There was a decision made willingly. The decision arose from a love relationship. There was a public demonstration of the commitment. The servant bore forever the marks of the commitment! What a beautiful picture of our Lord's willingness to be "obedient unto death, even the death of the cross" (Philippians 2:8).

Shouldn't such devotion by Christ to the will of the Father cause us anew to "consider the Apostle and high priest of our profession, Christ Jesus" (Hebrews 3:1)? The word consider means to bring about an earnest application of the mind.

Hebrews 10:11-18

What is the writer saying?

How can I apply this to my life?

PRAY Hungary — For churches to mature in their giving and support of nationals involved in Christian work.

Verses 11 and 12 contrast the sacrificial offerings of the Aaronic priests who stood daily ministering with the offering of our great high priest. He offered one sacrifice for sins forever and then sat down. In the tabernacle and later in the temple, there was no provision for the ministering priests to be seated, signifying that their work of offering sacrifices was never completed. It was unfinished work because it could never take away sins. On the other hand, our Lord completed His one sufficient offering for sins and is now seated at the right hand of God waiting for the fulfillment of until I make thine enemies thy footstool. That phrase is from Psalm 110:1 and is quoted six times in the New Testament.

Verses 16 and 17 repeat the essence of the new covenant as prophesied in Jeremiah 31:31-34 and quoted in Hebrews 8:10-12. There are three main points: 1. the laws of the Lord will be written in the hearts and minds of His people; 2. the sins and iniquities of His people will be erased from God's memory; 3. there will be no more sacrificial offerings because forgiveness will be complete.

What does God do with the sins that He forgives and forgets? He removes them "as far as the east is from the west" (Psalm 103:12). He makes them "as white as snow" (Isaiah 1:18). He casts them behind His back (Isaiah 38:17). He blots them out for His name's sake (Isaiah 43:25). He will "cast all their sins into the depths of the sea" (Micah 7:19).

Life stEP Why do so many of God's people carry a load of guilt? No doubt, there are several reasons: unconfessed sins (1 John. 1:9); failure to walk in the light (1 John. 1:7); willful ignorance of God's provision (Hebrews 5:11-14) and satanic accusation (Revelation 12:10).

Hebrews 10:19-25

What is the writer saying?

How can I apply this to my life?

PRAY Praise the Lord for His sovereignty over details of your life.

Under the old covenant, a veil barred the ministering priests from approaching the semblance of the presence of God (the Shekinah between the cherubim). Now, because of the value and the provision of the blood sacrifice of the body of Jesus, as described in verses 10-14, we may enter confidently into the very presence of God! He miraculously dramatized this by the renting of the veil in the temple at the death of Christ (Matthew 27:51).

In Hebrews 2:3, we were warned not to neglect so great salvation. This neglect could come from a failure to trust God to vanquish the enemy and to lead us into a place of restful service (Hebrews 3-4; Matthew 11:29). Neglect could arise from failure to become fruitful after evidencing a will to serve in the Lord's harvest field (Hebrews 5-6; John 15:2; I Corinthians 3:15).

In chapters 7 through 10, we have received information necessary in order to appreciate the provision of our Great High Priest. Now we need the additional exhortations of verses 22-25. A true heart in full assurance of faith comes by the daily "washing of water by the word" (Ephesians 5:26). Steadfastness of profession comes through proclaiming the Gospel message regularly. Love and good works are manifested through regularly meeting with fellow believers, especially within the God ordained structure of a Bible believing local church.

Let us put the three let us exhortations of verses 22-25 into Word of Life language: 1. Let us read from our Word of Life Quiet Time Diaries every day. 2. Let us be a missionary everyday by telling the world that Jesus is the way. 3. Let us be fruitful members of a local Bible believing church. How often should we attend church? "...so much the more as you see the day (of our Lord's return) approaching."

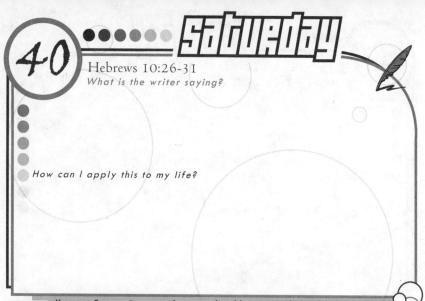

Hebrews 10:26-31
What is the writer saying?

How can I apply this to my life?

pray Korea — For seminary graduates to humbly commit themselves to less prominent, rural pastorates.

For those Christians who neglect so great salvation by failing to heed verses 19-25, there is the dire warning of verses 26-31. When a fully knowledgeable child of God persists in willful sin, the indwelling Holy Spirit will patiently convict and chasten. If that does not result in "sorrow to repentance" (2 Corinthians 7:9), then "the Lord shall judge His people" (Hebrews 10:30; 1 Corinthians 11:30-32).

Those who put their hand to the plow and look back (Luke 9:62) will be cut off as fruit-bearers (John 15:1-6). They will be cut off of the olive tree (Romans 11:22). Their works will be burned; they will suffer loss and be saved yet as by fire (1 Corinthians 3:15). They will be of no use as God's temple for showing forth God's glory on earth (1 Corinthians 3:17; 6:19, 20). They will be delivered unto Satan for the destruction of the flesh, that the spirit may be saved in the day of the Lord Jesus (1 Corinthians 5:5; 1 Timothy 1:20). They remove themselves from the benefit of intercessory prayer (1 John 5:16). They have had their candlesticks removed (Revelation 2:5). Notice in verse 27 that it is Satan and his agents who are devoured by God's fiery indignation against sin.

Under the Old Covenant, there was no sacrifice for presumptuous (willful) sins although there were extensive provisions for sins of ignorance, omission and defilement. (See Leviticus 4 and 5 and Numbers 15 for a complete explanation). Understand that verse 26 is not speaking of the magnitude or repulsiveness of a sin, but of the attitude of the sinning one towards God's provision for restoration.

Life stEP

Despite the difficulty in fully understanding a passage such as this, two things are clear in Scripture: 1. Salvation is by faith and faith alone and 2. God will chastise His sinning child.

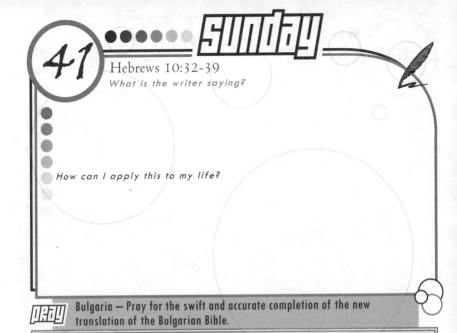

Hebrews 10:32-39

What is the writer saying?

How can I apply this to my life?

PRAY Bulgaria — Pray for the swift and accurate completion of the new translation of the Bulgarian Bible.

In verses 32-34, the author assures his readers that he is not classifying them with the willful sinners of verses 26-31. There he warns that it is possible even for mature believers to neglect their salvation.

It is our Lord's good pleasure to be a rewarder. Our reaction to adversities furnishes the basis for Him to reward (2 Corinthians 4:17). When we confidently persevere, He derives eternal pleasure through rewarding us out of all proportion to the service performed (Mark 9:41). By neglecting so great salvation we cast away that which has great eternal value to our Lord and to ourselves (1 Corinthians 9:24-27).

When our Lord comes, some will have an abundant entrance into His presence (2 Peter 1:11). Others will be "ashamed before him at his coming" (1 John 2:28).

Habakkuk is quoted in verses 37 and 38. Habakkuk 2:3 prophesies of an event. Hebrews 10:37 focuses on the person of the event by changing it to He. "But the just shall live by his faith" is from Habakkuk 2:4 and is also quoted in Romans 1:17 and Galatians 3:11.

When a saved person draws back (v. 38), the Lord is robbed of the pleasure of rewarding a faithful servant. Examples are Alexander (1 Timothy 1:20; 2 Timothy 4:14), Demas (Philemon 24; 2 Timothy 4:10), and Diotrephes (3 John 9). When an unsaved person draws back (v. 39) from receiving salvation, the Creator is robbed of eternal fellowship with His creature. Examples are Judas Iscariot, Simon the Sorcerer (Acts 8:20-23), Felix (Acts 24:25), and Agrippa (Acts 26:28).

Life stEP

The reason for the exhortations of Hebrews 3-6 is that the opportunity of earning rewards can be lost. The Bible also teaches that rewards earned can afterwards be lost (Revelation 3:11). Therefore, we need the exhortations of Hebrews 10:19-25 and the warnings of 10:26-31.

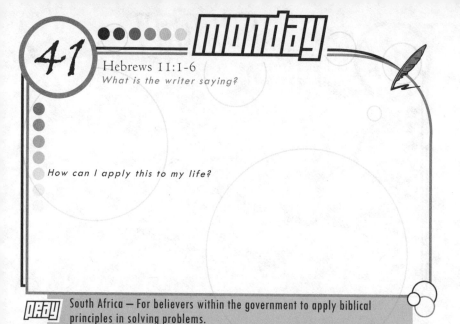

Hebrews 11:1-6
What is the writer saying?

How can I apply this to my life?

Scriptural hope is a cup of blessing filled with future good things promised by a God who cannot lie. Faith is the handle by which we lay hold of that cup. God measures out faith to us (Romans 12:3) as we rely upon what He says (Romans 10:17). Faith has such substance that it permits us to see the invisible. God's order is believe and you will see (John 11:40). Like Thomas we insist upon seeing before believing, whereby we miss the blessing (John 20:29).

By combining the story in Genesis 4:1-8 with the five times Abel is mentioned in the New Testament, we discover the following: Abel was a shepherd. He offered an acceptable sacrifice to God. He was declared righteous by God. He was despised by his brother because of envy. He was slain by his own kinsman although guiltless. He was faithful unto death. Though he died, he yet speaks. He was the promised seed. Another seed was appointed in his stead. He died without physical progeny. All of these statements are also true concerning Jesus Christ. Abel typifies the Christ that died.

On the other hand, Enoch typifies the Christ that lives. Enoch pleased God by a walk of faith on earth, and then God took him. Death had no hold upon him (Acts 2:24). God took Enoch to Himself by translation before He brought judgment upon the earth by flood. Thereby, he is also a picture of all God's saints who will be raptured out from earth before the judgment of the Tribulation.

Jesus Christ is the seeker of the lost (Luke 19:10). After we have been sought for and found by Him, we are told to seek Him. By consulting a concordance, we can find many promises for those who seek the Lord.

Hebrews 11:7-12

What is the writer saying?

How can I apply this to my life?

Abel manifested his faith in his worship. Enoch exhibited his faith by his walk. Noah demonstrated his faith through his work. Good works must arise from a proper walk which derives from a right spiritual relationship with God. Neither Noah nor his family gained eternal salvation by building the ark. They "became heir(s) of the righteousness which is by faith" (v. 7). "But Noah found grace in the eyes of the LORD" (Genesis 6:8) because he believed God. God chose (Genesis 6:8) and called (Genesis 7:1) Noah and his household. They responded to the call (Genesis 7:7) and God shut them in (Genesis 7:16). When the wind and the waves roared, they could have fallen while inside the ark, but they could never fall out of the ark. They were safe from God's judgment because they were sealed by God's grace. (See the New Testament parallel in Ephesians 1:4-14.)

"By faith Abraham ... went out" (v. 8). After Abraham "went out," he "went forth into the land" (Genesis 12:4-5). Some of us launch out for the Lord but never really go forth into the place of restful service. When Abraham was tested, he "went down into Egypt" (Genesis 12:10). When we are tested, we also are prone to go back into Egypt after being saved out of bondage. Although Abraham found riches in Egypt, he never built an altar there because he was out of the place of fellowship. So he "went up out of Egypt" (Genesis 13:1) and then "went on" (Genesis 13:3) "unto the place of the altar..." (Genesis 13:4).

"He looked for a city ..." (v. 10). Man's poor attempt at immortality is to build a city and name it for himself or his progeny (Genesis 4:17; 11:4).

The servant of God needs wisdom from the Holy Spirit in discerning the difference between faith and presumption.

Hebrews 11:13-19
What is the writer saying?

How can I apply this to my life?

pray New Zealand — For those helping immigrants with language training to be bold in sharing the Gospel.

Abraham didn't know where God was leading him (vv. 8-10). He didn't know how God would fulfill His promises (vv. 11-12). He didn't know when he would receive the promises (vv. 13-16). He didn't know why God would ask him to sacrifice Isaac (vv. 17-19). In order that we may have the opportunity to walk by faith; God often doesn't let us know where, how, when, or why. Faith extends our sight beyond the limit of our vision, in order to permit us to see afar off (v. 13). Only faith lets us see a better, heavenly country before we get there! Only by faith may we in this life see the city God has prepared for us (vv. 14-16).

Verses 17-19 give us the solution to the enigma of the story in Genesis 22:1-14. God had given to Abraham the promise.

"In Isaac shall thy seed be called" (Genesis 21:12; Hebrews 11:18). God had promised Abraham that only through Isaac would his descendants be as many as the stars of the sky and the sand of the seashore. Then God told him to travel for three days and offer up Isaac as a sacrifice! How could that possibly permit God to fulfill His promises? How could Abraham slay his beloved son of promise? "I and the lad will go yonder and worship, and come again to you" (Genesis 22:5). When Abraham said this to his servants, he had already counted his son dead three days earlier. He was now ascending the mountain to witness his son's resurrection; not his death! What a beautiful figure of why God the Father was able to permit the sacrifice of His beloved Son!

Life stEP

"For we walk by faith, not by sight" (2 Corinthians 5:7). When we desire signs, fleeces, miracles and other such manifestations, we hinder our own progress in walking by faith. "Without faith it is impossible to please him" (Hebrews 11:6).

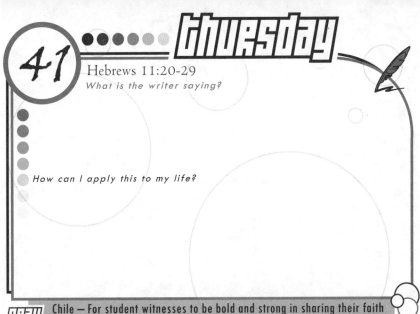

41

Hebrews 11:20-29

What is the writer saying?

How can I apply this to my life?

PRAY Chile — For student witnesses to be bold and strong in sharing their faith at their universities.

The Genesis account tells of many failings on the part of Isaac and Jacob. However, Hebrews 11 is not concerned with failings, but with faith that triumphs over failings. To the end of their lives their actions proved that they trusted the promises of God. The last recorded words of Joseph (Genesis 50:24-25) prove his faith even in dying.

The acts of Moses' parents prove that love conquers fear. Their faith in God made His infinite resources available to them. Refused, chosen, esteemed, respected, forsaken, endured, kept, passed through; faith brought all of these character resources to Moses! By faith, he willed, like Christ, to suffer reproach rather than to covet his exalted position. By faith, he saw that which was invisible.

The Feast of Passover and rules for its annual observance are recorded in Exodus 12. Deliverance from the destroyer required manifestation of faith by the application of blood. When the children of Israel saw the 600 chariots of Pharaoh pursuing them (Exodus 14:7-9), they murmured against Moses and wanted to return to the slavery of Egypt. Moses said to them, "Fear ye not, stand still, and see the salvation of the LORD ... the LORD shall fight for you ..." (Exodus 14:13, 14). In effect, Moses was saying, "faith is the victory." All they had to do was to sing a song of victory (Exodus 15:1-21)!

If the omniscient God had foreknown that Moses would choose Egypt rather than affliction with the people of God, He would have chosen someone else to bring deliverance to Israel. Moses would have drowned with Pharaoh and his army. That illustrates for us how short is the time available to enjoy the pleasures offered by the world in comparison with eternity!

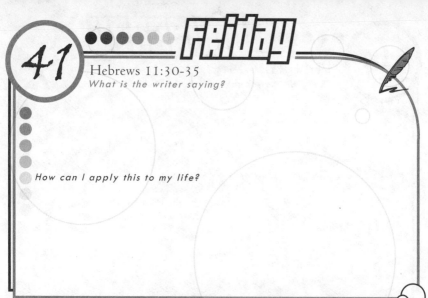

Hebrews 11:30-35

What is the writer saying?

How can I apply this to my life?

PRAY Pray for Word of Life summer camp counselors, supervisors, and teen staff to serve Christ wholeheartedly.

The conquest of Jericho described in Joshua 6:1-16, depended entirely upon believing and acting upon instructions from God which made no logical sense. Rahab aided that conquest because she believed, "…The LORD your God, he is God in heaven above, and in earth beneath" (Joshua 2:8-11). She proved her faith by her deeds (James 2:25) and therefore, perished not with them that believed not.

Two generations after the conquest of the Promised Land under Joshua, Israel forsook the Lord God and served the idols of the land. For several centuries, their history consisted of recurring cycles of rebellion, retribution, repentance, and restoration. God raised up a succession of leaders called Judges. He empowered them to miraculously deliver Israel from its oppressors when Israel repented. The four most prominent of the 12 Judges are named in verse 32 along with David, the foremost of Israel's kings, and Samuel, the first prophet (Acts 3:24) The exploits of verses 33 and 34 were far beyond the capabilities of the humans involved. They were supernaturally accomplished in response to faith on the part of those chosen by God to perform His purposes. In the Old Testament, there are two accounts of women who received their dead raised to life again (1 Kings 17:17-24; 2 Kings 4:32-37). In each case, the one raised from the dead was an only son, pointing to the resurrection of God's only begotten Son.

Life stEP "And greater works than these shall he do" (John 14:12). When Jesus went to the Father, He sent the indwelling, enabling Holy Spirit that each one of us might daily be involved in His most miraculous work; the transforming of hell-bound sinners into heaven-bound saints!

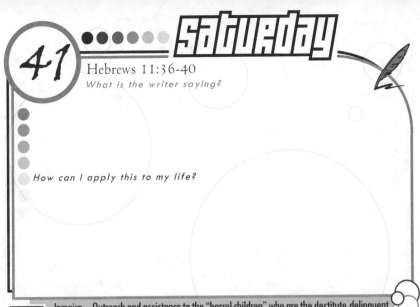

Hebrews 11:36-40

What is the writer saying?

How can I apply this to my life?

PRAY Jamaica — Outreach and assistance to the "barrel children" who are the destitute, delinquent underclass, whose parents have emigrated elsewhere and occasionally send them support.

The Apostle Paul was one who suffered all of the experiences of verse 36 (2 Corinthians 11:23-27). Zechariah (2 Chronicles 24:20-21), Stephen (Acts 7:57-60), and Paul (Acts 14:19-20) were among God's spokesmen who were stoned for their preaching.

God's people of every age, from the Old Testament prophets even until today, have suffered the atrocities described in verses 37 and 38. Why does God permit such persecution upon His loved ones? One reason is to demonstrate to the world the power of faith. Another reason is so the persecuted "might obtain a better resurrection" (v. 35). All of these afflictions produce something for the sufferer. That something is eternal and glorious (2 Corinthians 4:17). It is more precious than gold and will result in praise, honor and glory at the appearing of Jesus Christ (1 Peter 1:6-7).

Abraham "looked for a city" (11:10). We conclude from 11:13 and 11:39 that he has not yet seen that city. He, along with the other faithful ones of chapter 11, is waiting for our arrival (v. 40). They must be very desirous that we are "Looking for and hastening unto the coming of the day of God" (2 Peter 3:12). One day someone will lead a soul to Christ and the assembly of called out ones will be complete. The Lord has called us to be His instruments in His work of taking out a people for His name from among the nations (Acts 15:14). In His power, let us finish the task!

Life stEP As we review in our minds all of the individuals named in Hebrews 11, we ought to ask why God listed them for us. He had us in mind when He permitted them to be subjected to their trials. According to 1 Corinthians 10:11, He moved upon the writer to present this record in writing for our admonition. Let us be admonished!

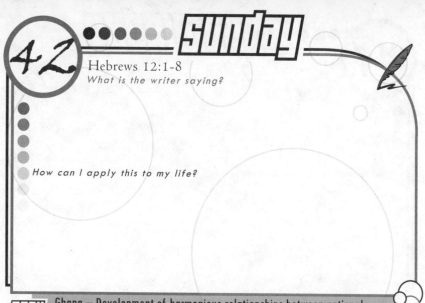

Hebrews 12:1-8

What is the writer saying?

How can I apply this to my life?

pray Ghana — Development of harmonious relationships between national pastors and missionaries.

Chapter 1 of Hebrews presented the deity of our Great High Priest. After warning against neglecting our salvation, chapter 2 set before us His humanity. Chapters 3 and 4 exhorted and warned those who had no heart desire to progress into a walk of faith. Chapters 5 and 6 exhorted and warned those who manifested a willingness to serve, but never brought forth fruit because they didn't let the Word exercise them "to discern both good and evil" (Hebrews 5:14). In chapters 7, 8, 9 and the first half of 10, God supplied us with detailed information about our Great High Priest needful for understanding His program and purposes on earth. Chapter 10 then exhorted and warned concerning willfully sinning after becoming a knowledgeable servant. Chapter 11 presented a roster of those who victoriously lived by faith in carrying out God's program on earth.

Now we hold the baton in God's great relay race. Those who have gone before us have a great interest in our performance (11:39-12:1). We must give heed to seven exhortations in 12:1-8:1. Let us rid ourselves of any encumbrance that would hinder our pace. 2. Let us be aware of sin (particularly the sin of unbelief) that would draw us aside. 3. Let us run with patient endurance. 4. Let us keep our eyes on Jesus who originated and will perfect our faith. 5. Let us carefully consider what He endured with joy because of His eternal perspective. 6. Let us not scorn or take lightly the Lord's chastening. 7. Let us remember that fatherly rebuke indicates love in the family relationship and is not a cause for fainting along the way.

Life **stEP** Jesus endured His sufferings on the cross because by faith He saw the ultimate joyful outcome. This type of sustaining joy is available to all who sufficiently value it.

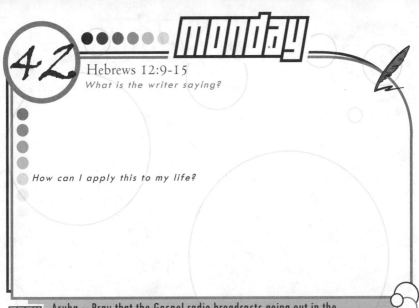

42.

Hebrews 12:9-15

What is the writer saying?

How can I apply this to my life?

PRAY Aruba — Pray that the Gospel radio broadcasts going out in the Papiamento language will yield fruit.

God desires "that we might be partakers of his holiness" (v. 10) so that our lives "yieldeth the peaceable fruit of righteousness" (v. 11). He wants us to walk in "straight paths" (v. 13) as we "follow peace with all men and holiness" (v. 14). We wouldn't need chastening if we always walked in straight paths. However, the prophet observes, "O LORD, I know that the way of man is not in himself: it is not in man that walketh to direct his steps" (Jeremiah 10:23). That is why the psalmist prayed, "Order my steps in thy word..." (Psalm 119:133) and declared, "Thy word is a lamp unto my feet, and a light unto my path" (Psalm 119:105). The Word discerns "the thoughts and intents of the heart" (Hebrews 4:12). When the Word shows us our sin, we should "come boldly unto the throne of grace" (Hebrews 4:16) and have our "senses exercised to discern both good and evil" (Hebrews 5:14). If we will not be exercised by the Word, then the chastening hand of our loving Father comes that we might be "exercised by it" (12:11).

Unfortunately, there are those children who refuse to be exercised by the Word or by the discipline of the Father. Some children resent chastening and become bitter. A root of bitterness springs up into a tree of bitterness that affects not only the resentful one but also those around him. When the cancer of bitterness spreads and impedes the Lord's work, He must take drastic measures. See 1 Corinthians 11:29-32 and 1 Timothy 1:19, 20 for what may be examples. "For the time is come that judgment must begin at the house of God..." (1 Peter 4:17). "The Lord shall judge his people" (Hebrews 10:30).

Let us abandon ourselves unreservedly to God's program for our lives. Then He will give us a hunger for His Word that will keep us on the right path.

Hebrews 12:16-24

What is the writer saying?

How can I apply this to my life?

pray Kenya — Believers willing to meet the spiritual and physical needs of the 2,100,000 living with AIDS and the 730,000 AIDS orphans.

Esau's error was two-fold. First, he chose the temporal at the expense of the eternal. Secondly, he forfeited a spiritual fortune for a material pittance. He was a spiritual fornicator because he esteemed bodily gratification over God's favor. His repentance came after he had already lost the blessing. He had to lie in the bed that he made for himself.

Verses 18-21 refer to Exodus 19:12-16 and 20:18, 19 when Moses received the law, which was the basis for the old covenant and is symbolized by Mt. Sinai. Verses 22-24 describe our entitlement under the new covenant made possible by the work of Christ on the cross and symbolized by Mt. Zion.

The city of verse 22 is the city prepared by God (Hebrews 11:16) for which Abraham looked (Hebrews 11:10) and for which the faithful Old Testament saints are still waiting (Hebrews 11:39). It is the same city for which we should be seeking (Hebrews 13:14). It is the prepared place of John 14:2 and is described more fully in Revelation 21 and 22. Three groups of created beings will inhabit the city with "... God the Judge of all ..." (v. 23) and "...Jesus the mediator of the new covenant..." (v. 24). The "innumerable company of angels" (v. 22) includes all unfallen angelic beings. The "church of the firstborn, which are written in heaven" (v. 23) refers to all who are indwelt by the Holy Spirit, from Pentecost until the rapture. "The spirits of just men made perfect (complete)" (v. 23) includes the Old Testament saints and the Tribulation saints.

"Eye hath not seen, nor ear heard, neither have entered into the heart of man, the things which God hath prepared for them that love Him" (1 Corinthians 2:9).

42

Hebrews 12:25-29

What is the writer saying?

How can I apply this to my life?

PRAY Dominican Republic — For church leaders and their congregation to be good witnesses in tense and inequitable situations.

It has been pointed out that Hebrews is a book of instructions, exhortations and warnings. The first warning (Hebrews 2:1-4) was against slipping (drifting) away by neglect of so great a salvation. Now we face the final warning of the book. It is against turning away after we have received all of the instructions and exhortations of the book. "…For unto whomsoever much is given, of him shall be much required…" (Luke 12:48). We are now fully aware of just who it is that is speaking to us from heaven! We must not lightly regard such a one.

When God gave the law to Moses, the voice from heaven shook the mountain and the people trembled (Exodus 19:16-19). Haggai 2:6, 7 prophesied of a time when both heaven and earth will be shaken. (See 2 Peter 3:10-12). The things that are shaken will be replaced by that which cannot be shaken. Our God, who is a consuming fire, has extended His grace to those who have heeded His voice and found refuge in a kingdom that will remain because it cannot be shaken. How fearsome is the future for those who refuse Him that speaketh! How incumbent it is upon us who have taken refuge to warn those who have not! "Let us have grace" (v. 28). To what purpose do we need His grace? "Serve God acceptably with reverence and godly fear" (v. 28).

Life stEP

"The Lord is … not willing that any should perish, but that all should come to repentance" (2 Peter 3:9). "God was in Christ, reconciling the world unto himself, not imputing their trespasses unto them; and hath committed unto us the word of reconciliation" (2 Corinthians 5:19). God's only plan for reaching our lost world is to extend His grace to those who have not only fled to Him for refuge, but also are willing to be His ambassadors (1 Corinthians 5:20).

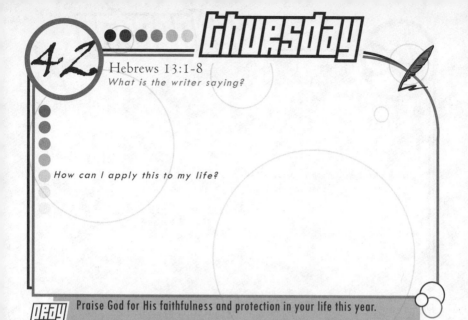

Hebrews 13:1-8

What is the writer saying?

How can I apply this to my life?

pray Praise God for His faithfulness and protection in your life this year.

The world detects true brotherly love (John 11:36; 13:35). Entertain strangers is the translation of one word in the original language which means love of strangers. The same word in Romans 12:13 is rendered given to hospitality. The strangers are brethren from elsewhere who very well may be in your midst as messengers from God as in 3 John 5-8. Abraham extended hospitality to three men who actually proved to be heavenly messengers from God (Genesis 18:2, 16; 19:1-12).

From the first century until now, there always have been Christians incarcerated for His name's sake and others like Onesiphorus who have ministered to them at great risk (2 Timothy 1:16-18).

Read verse 4 as an exhortation: let marriage be honored and highly esteemed for God will judge those who defile it by fornication or adultery.

"...Godliness with contentment is great gain" (1 Timothy 6:6). To be content and free from covetousness proves that one relies upon the promise. "I will never leave thee, nor forsake thee." That promise was given to Jacob (Genesis 28:15), to the people of Israel (Deuteronomy 31:6), to Joshua (Joshua 1:5), to Solomon (1 Chronicles 28:20), to the disciples (Matthew 28:20), and to you (Hebrews 13:5). You appropriate that promise when you say with the psalmist, "The LORD is on my side; I will not fear: what can man do unto me?" (Psalm 118:6). "Them which have the rule over you..." are your spiritual leaders. You should remember them (v. 7), obey them (v. 17), and salute them (v. 24).

Verse 8 is such a comforting truth! However, let us be careful how we apply it. Jesus doesn't change, but His ways of dealing with mankind do change. Therefore, just because Peter walked on water does not mean that we should be able to as well!

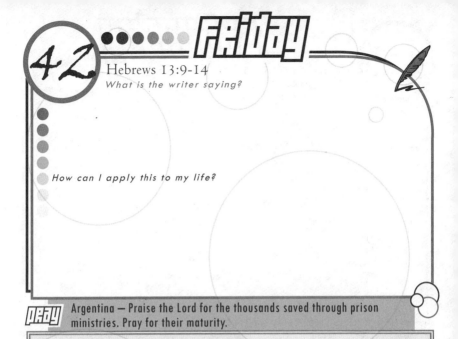

42 Friday

Hebrews 13:9-14

What is the writer saying?

How can I apply this to my life?

pray Argentina — Praise the Lord for the thousands saved through prison ministries. Pray for their maturity.

We learned from Hebrews 9:6-11 that the priestly procedures concerning the eating of or abstaining from certain foods were symbolic of that which was fulfilled in Christ. It does not now please God for us to be occupied with using foods as a means of gaining His favor (Colossians 2:16, 17). The Lord graciously has given to us His ordinance by which we commune in worship (1 Corinthians 11:23-28). Those priests had no opportunity to feast upon Christ (1 Corinthians 10:16) as is our privilege.

When the Old Testament priests were consecrated for service in the tabernacle (Exodus 29:10-14), they first put their hands on the head of the sacrificial bullock. This symbolized the transfer of their sins to the sinless one as the faithful Servant "obedient unto death, even the death of the cross" (Philippians 2:8). The blood was shed and applied at the altar representing the cross. Then the fat, which represented the ardent devotion of our Savior, was burned before the Lord on the altar (Leviticus 3:16). Finally, the sin laden bullock was taken outside the camp and burned.

The symbolism was fulfilled when Christ was taken outside the gates of Jerusalem to bear His reproach. We are sanctified (separated) unto Him when we go forth outside of the scope of religious procedures and place our trust solely in that which He suffered outside the city for us.

The religious leaders of that day considered the earthly city of Jerusalem as God's eternal abode on earth. In a few years, that city and its religious procedures were destroyed. Our continuing city is not here. It is where it cannot be destroyed.

Life stEP

The eye of faith sees beyond that which is visible. It comprehends that which is not available through reasoning. Faith trusts what God says.

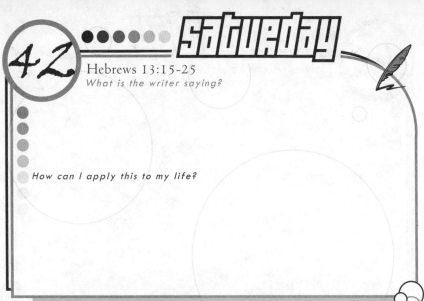

How can I apply this to my life?

pray   El Salvador — For their Christian Institutes and Media to continue the impact they have already brought to El Salvador.

"I will praise the name of God with a song, and will magnify him with thanksgiving. This also shall please the LORD better than an ox or bullock…" (Psalm 69:30, 31). Because the Lord Jesus Christ has offered for us the required blood sacrifice (Hebrews 9:22), we are privileged to offer that which pleases God best! Another pleasing and acceptable sacrifice is sharing our material goods (Philippians 4:18).

In John 10:11, Jesus designated Himself as the Good Shepherd who gave His life for the sheep. In Hebrews 13:20, He is the Great Shepherd who, as our Great High Priest, works in us and through us. In 1 Peter 5:4, He is the Chief Shepherd who will come for us. The Good Shepherd in the past did something for us that we might be free from the penalty of sin. The Great Shepherd in the present is doing something in us and through us that we might be free from the power of sin while being perfected unto every good work to do His will. These two aspects of our Shepherd are brought together in 1 Peter 2:24-25. He "bare our sins in his own body on the tree" that we who "were as sheep going astray" might now be shepherded by the overseer of our souls. Next, Peter speaks of the Chief Shepherd who will in the future come for us that we might be forever freed from the very presence of sin!

In verse 22, we are given the final exhortation of the book. It is a beseeching plea that we heed the word of exhortation presented throughout the epistle.

It is certainly true that the Hebrew's letter was originally fashioned by the Holy Spirit to meet the needs of a particular people at a particular place and time. You will miss the impact on your own life unless you also are confident that in His omniscience, the Holy Spirit had your spiritual progress in mind as He worded the message of this epistle.

lamentations

The author of Lamentations is Jeremiah; the "weeping prophet." His name means, Jehovah has appointed. He was of priestly stock. He never knew the joy of marriage, but engaged in pastoral prophetic work over the course of forty years under five kings of Judah, from 627 B.C. to beyond the destruction of Jerusalem in 586 B.C..

Jeremiah was considered a traitor by his own government for predicting the fall of Jerusalem to the Babylonians and his encouragement of the godly to submit to the decreed judgment. General Nebuchadnezzar led his father's armies to Nineveh and Carchemish, where, despite the help of the Egyptian army, the Assyrian empire was terminated. Nebuchadnezzar continued south to Jerusalem, securing its submission in 605 B.C.. The death of his father required a hasty departure.

Daniel and the three Hebrew youths were taken at this time. His succession to his father's throne secured and the Judean king plotting intrigue, Nebuchadnezzar returned in 597 B.C. in another show of strength. Ezekiel went in the ensuing deportation, resulting in three great prophets ministering at the same time in three strategic locales: a) Daniel in the capital city of Babylon, b) Ezekiel in the Babylonian countryside with his fellow Judeans and c) Jeremiah in Jerusalem.

Lamentations is one of six Old Testament books of poetry. Three are didactic (teaching): a) Proverbs teaching wisdom, b) Ecclesiastes teaching the futility of life apart from God and c) Job teaching patience under trials. The other three are devotional: a) Psalms on worship, b) Song of Solomon on love and c) Lamentations on judgment.

Lamentations means, to cry out loud. It contains five poems (each one constitutes a chapter). The meter of the poetry is melancholy, suitable for a solemn funeral procession. The first four poems are acrostics in that each verse (or in the case of poem three, each three verses) starts with a succeeding letter of the Hebrew alphabet. Furthermore, usually the same number of lines is used for each verse (three per verse in poems one and two, two per verse in poem four and one per verse in poems three and five).

Lamentations

For centuries, Jewish people have read Lamentations on the ninth day of the month of Av (Tisha B'Av) in remembrance of a number of national tragedies that took place on that day in the calendar in various years, including the destruction of the first and second temples in Jerusalem.

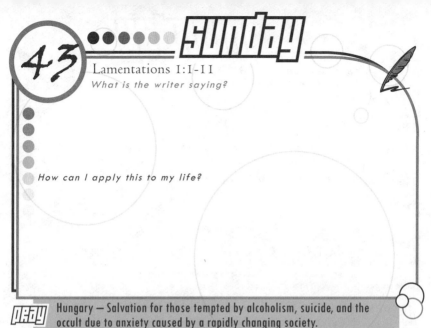

Lamentations 1:1-11

What is the writer saying?

How can I apply this to my life?

Jeremiah describes the destruction of Jerusalem. Chapter one contains the simplest vocabulary of the five chapters, indicating the prophet's struggle for words to express his grief. The vocabulary richness increases with each succeeding chapter, while the words for sorrow and mourning decrease as Jeremiah comes to grips with God's appropriate chastisement. Jerusalem is likened to an abandoned woman. She is a widow and a slave (v. 1). Her friends and lovers forsake her (v. 2). She is a captive (v. 3). Her children are gone (v. 5). She is homeless (v. 7). She is an adulteress (v. 9). She is violated (v. 10). The prophet identifies with his people in the confession, as do other great men of God as recorded in Ezra 9, Nehemiah 9, and Daniel 9. The great height from which Jerusalem fell is contrasted with the former fullness of the city (v. 1, the same word for both in Hebrew). At one time, Judah controlled Moab, Ammon, and Edom, nations related to her through Lot and Esau. Now they treacherously join with her enemy in the attack (v. 2). The dire straits of verse 3 are literal, a reference to the narrow mountain valleys leading away from Jerusalem where her enemies ambushed her. The princes of verse 6 could be the sons of King Zedekiah. The Babylonians murdered them in Zedekiah's sight before blinding him. Jeremiah said that he would be taken to Babylon (Jeremiah 32:5), but Ezekiel said that he would not see Babylon (Ezekiel 12:13). Jerusalem lost sight of her chosen-people responsibilities (v. 9). Within Israelite society, only the Levitical priests could enter the temple, but now Gentiles polluted it with their presence (v. 10).

Life st**EP**

It is a fearful thing to fall into the hands of God in judgment. His holiness does not allow Him to overlook willful sin.

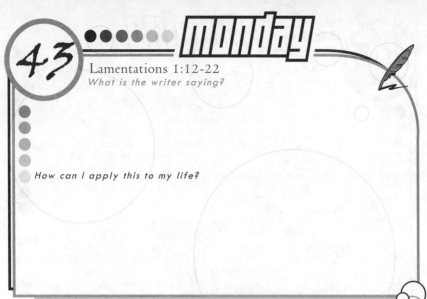

43 monday

Lamentations 1:12-22

What is the writer saying?

How can I apply this to my life?

pray Pray for those who teach in your church to be faithful to the word, enthusiastic in their presentation, and compassionate toward the lost.

In verses 1-11, Jeremiah speaks. In verses 12-22, the city speaks. She speaks of the horror of her judgment. She also acknowledges that her sin brought on the judgment (vv. 14, 18, 20, 22). Some of the terms that she uses to describe her horror are military concepts that the invading Babylonians would have literally used (nets v. 13, sword v. 20). While God used secondary means to punish her (the Babylonians), Jerusalem realizes that He was the prime mover. The Babylonians were merely a tool in the hand of God. The "winepress" (v. 15) is an impressive analogy that occurs several times in Scripture. In Revelation 14, the juice of the grapes is likened to the blood of humans destroyed at the Battle of Armageddon. Repetition is used for emphasis (v. 16). "Comforter" (v. 16) is the special name for the Holy Spirit in John

14. It is also the root idea of Nahum's name and of Barnabas' name. God wants us to experience spiritual and emotional comfort, but sin brings spiritual vertigo and we lose the "assurance" of our salvation. "Eternal security" is based on the fact that once we are saved we cannot lose that salvation, but "assurance" is an emotion that can be altered by our sin. The woman (v. 17) is ceremonially unclean and therefore not welcomed to enter the temple. She rails against her friends who not only did not help her in her time of trouble, but even rejoiced with her sorrows. She points out that judgment has already been decreed for them too (Jeremiah 50 & 51). She asks that God judge them as He had judged her (v. 22). The "many" of verse 22 harkens back to the "full" and "great" of verse 1. She used to be a large, prosperous, great city. Now she is great with sorrow.

Do not presume upon God. Jerusalem was chosen by God, but still received His chastisement for disobedience.

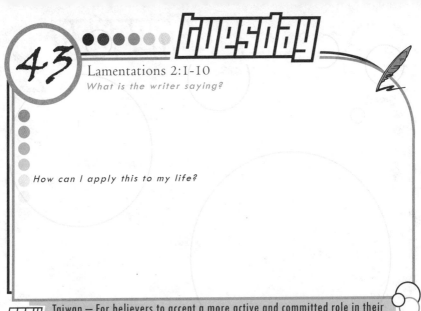

Lamentations 2:1-10

What is the writer saying?

How can I apply this to my life?

pray Taiwan — For believers to accept a more active and committed role in their local church bodies.

Zion (Citadel v. 1) originally was one of the seven hills of Jerusalem. Eventually it referred to the entire city. Daughter would refer to the human inhabitants of Zion. Israel means, he strives with God. Originally it referred to Jacob's wrestling match with God at Penuel (the face of God, Genesis 33). It then became a name for the entire nation. The feet are usually considered to be dirty and socially offensive. However, to be the footstool of the Creator of the universe was a compliment. In verse 2, Jacob is another designation for the nation. He was the father of the 12 tribes. Judah was the kingly tribe and also the name for the Southern Kingdom of Jeremiah's day. Horn (v. 3) is symbolic of strength. When a ram is charging you, you may intellectually know that it has ears, eyes, teeth and a tail, but all you see coming are those two dangerous horns. The right hand also speaks of strength (since most people are right handed). Verse 3 announces that God will not use His strong right hand to stop Israel's enemies. Verse 4 says He used His strong right hand to attack Israel. In her personal dwellings (tabernacle) where normally she would be secure, He killed her. In verse 5, God destroys her palaces, but in verse 6, His tabernacle. Ironically, in destroying Jerusalem He was destroying what actually belonged to Him. He judged the kings and the priests. He removed His dwelling place and therefore there was no place for worship (v. 6). The wall of verse 8 speaks of protection. Stretching out a line can be for the sake of building (Zechariah 2) or destruction (like in a fist fight where we might size up the opponent before beginning). The three divisions of Israelite government: prophet, priest, and king are all judged.

Life stEP

"God is not mocked: Whatsoever a man soweth, that shall he also reap" (Galatians 6:7).

Lamentations 2:11-22

What is the writer saying?

How can I apply this to my life?

pray Uganda — For new missionaries to adapt quickly, live the Word, and persevere amidst opposition.

Jeremiah speaks of his own grief (v. 11). The ancients located their emotions in the stomach area, here the bowels or liver. War affects the elderly, the young women (v. 10) and children (v. 11). Corn (v. 12) refers to the individual kernels of any agricultural product. Since sweet corn was not known in the ancient Middle East, this would refer to wheat or barley grain. The children cried for their daily bread and drink. He chides the false prophets for not identifying their sin as the cause of impending doom and even telling them that judgment would not fall. Sounds like some liberal preachers today. Rude noises and bodily gestures are regularly used by all human societies (v. 15). They are clearly for scorn as indicated in verse 16, but probably also as a good luck symbol to protect the viewer from the same fate. The gloating of the enemies added salt to the wound (v. 16). The people of Jerusalem have no one to blame but themselves. God had forewarned that He would destroy any generation that disobeyed Him (v. 17; Deuteronomy 28). He allowed their enemies to be strong while they were weak. Sorrow does not guarantee that true repentance is taking place, but it often does accompany true repentance. The prophet asks that the survivors cry out to God continuously to receive His forgiveness and reversal of the judgment (v. 19). What would they have to lose? To conclude the chapter, Jeremiah addresses the Lord directly. He calls upon the Lord's mercy and goodness. If God doesn't intervene, in desperation women will eat their children, even the smallest, most helpless babies (a span is only about nine inches long). Dead bodies desecrate the temple, God's own abode on earth (v. 20).

We should always pray and not faint.

How can I apply this to my life?

pray Guatemala — For medical ministries to reach the 55,000 war orphans and 5,000 street children.

In the first part of this chapter, Jeremiah pours out his personal anguish. We sometimes do not appreciate the emotions of such men. We assume that because God told them that such punishment was His plan and will, that they then somehow just accepted the fate of the judged. Jeremiah does not question God's doings, but he does express his intense sorrow at the damage done to his fellow countrymen and his country. The prophet then expresses his confidence in the Lord. He is merciful and compassionate (v. 22). He is consistently faithful (v. 23). In this verse, sleep is viewed as a mini-death that the prophet resurrects from every morning. Portion (v. 24) refers to what was given to the tribe of Levi when Israel entered the land. The other tribes received real estate. The Levites received cities to live in, but their primary focus was on serving the Lord in the tabernacle. When Hannah cried because she could not have any children, her husband said, "Am not I better to thee than ten sons?" (1 Samuel 1:8). Jeremiah's statement in effect was, "yes Lord, you are better than acres of real estate." Jeremiah counsels patience in the face of suffering. The Lord has His purposes and knows when they are complete, He will return to His faithful ones with blessing. The one who chaffs and complains under the trial is in danger of missing the greater blessing.

Maltbie D. Babcock said, "No affliction would trouble a child of God if he knew God's reasons for sending it. The tests of life are to make, not break us. Trouble may demolish a man's business but build up his character. The blow at the outward man may be the greatest blessing to the inner man. If God, then, puts or permits anything hard in our lives, be sure that the real peril, the real trouble, is that we shall lose if we flinch or rebel."

Friday

Lamentations 3:40-57

What is the writer saying?

How can I apply this to my life?

pray Angola – Pray for the provision of funds, buildings, and above all, godly teachers for leadership training.

Chapter 3 is the longest of the five chapters (triple the number of verses – three verses for each of the twenty-two letters in the Hebrew alphabet). Not only has the author organized the material with three verses for each letter of the alphabet, but he keeps the subject matter consistent to the three verses of each triplet. For instance, the study Bible I'm looking at divides the chapter by topic after verses 21, 39 and 51. All three are divisible by three indicating a change from one letter to the next. In verses 40-51 Jeremiah repeats the calamities that have befallen Jerusalem. He challenges his fellow citizens to examine their lives. In verse 42, he points out that while it was obvious that they had sinned, there was no evidence of repentance and therefore no indication that God was ready to forgive and relent in His judgments. In verse 47 fear and snare is a common doublet, the words sounding very similar in Hebrew: pahad and pahat. The words desolation and destruction also sound similar: hashet and hashaver. These powerful phrases really preach in Hebrew! In verses 52-57 Jeremiah relives the horrors of his own mistreatment at the hands of the kings of Judah. His ministry lasted for forty years. He preached that Judah deserved punishment and counseled the people to accept the attack by Babylon. If they resisted, they would die. If they surrendered, they would live. The kings and generals resented this teaching because they felt that it would ruin the will of the people to resist and fight. At one point King Jehoiakim cut up his writings and threw them into the fire (Jeremiah 36). Under King Zedekiah he was thrown into an abandoned well and sank into the mud at the bottom (Jeremiah 38).

"If I make my bed in hell, behold, thou art there." (Psalm 139:8). Jeremiah had a low down, dirty experience, but God was in the pit with him!

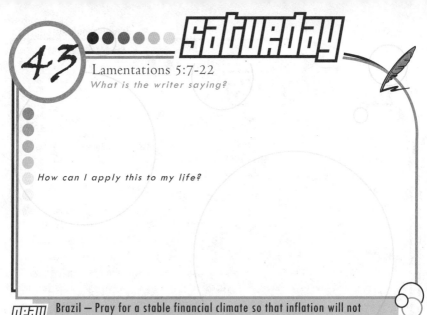

43

saturday

Lamentations 5:7-22

What is the writer saying?

How can I apply this to my life?

PRAY Brazil — Pray for a stable financial climate so that inflation will not diminish missionary support.

Their fathers sinned and have died. The children inherit the consequences of that sin. This does not mean, however, that the children are innocent. In Ezekiel, talking about this same time period, God says that He does not punish the children for the sins of their fathers, but that every man will be punished for his own sins (Ezekiel 18:1-9). As a result, they are ruled by inferior men (v. 8). They can find food to eat only by risking their lives in the sight of armed enemies (v. 9). Their bodies wasted away, overheating and discoloring in their hunger (v. 10). Their women (wives and daughters), their most intimate possessions, were violated in their sight (v. 11). Their elders were not honored (v. 12). The young men were forced into slavery. Even the children had to do hard labor (v. 13). The old men were missing from the gates (v. 14). This either means that they have died or that their influence has been ruined (the gates were the courtroom in Jewish cities where the elders sat to handle disputes and business transactions needing legal witnesses). There is no joy, no reason to dance (v. 15). Many modern Christians see dancing in the Old Testament and wonder why many conservative Christians refuse to dance. Biblical dancing as is practiced by orthodox Jewish people today was not a social event between the genders. Women danced with women and men with men, usually in separate places. The dance was more of a joyful skipping with a circle of people, arms interlinked. Foxes (v. 18) are symbolic of sly creatures and only appear where human habitation is reduced. Turned (v. 21) is the root idea of repentance. Jeremiah concludes with his hope for national repentance and the return of God's favor.

If God does not seem close any more, who moved?

1 CORINTHIANS

The book of 1 Corinthians is probably one of the more prominent books in the New Testament. It has the great love chapter, the chapters that deal with tongues, the resurrection chapter, the marriage chapter and the passage so often read at the Lord's Supper. We know so many of the components that we don't always see how they fit together.

The apostle Paul wrote the book from Ephesus on his third missionary journey. It is actually his second letter to this church. The first letter is lost. Paul describes this letter in 2 Corinthians as a sorrowful letter. He wrote it with a heavy heart because a disaster was taking place in the Corinthian Church. It was falling apart at the seams.

Founded on the second missionary journey, the church at Corinth was located in the most immoral city of the Roman Empire. In the world of that day, to call someone a Corinthian was to call them a pervert. It was located on the narrow section of land joining Achaia with the mainland. Thus, it was a bustling land route. There was also a set of tracks that were used to transport ships from the Aegean to the Adriatic Sea. Thus, it was a bustling seaport which made it an ideal location for prostitution and other such behavior.

In the church a number of problems had developed. In fact, the church was breaking down into cliques. Each group had their favorite leader. Things got so bad that a delegation was sent to Ephesus with a letter to meet with the apostle. 1 Corinthians is the response to that letter. The theme of the book is dealing with divisions within the church. A simple outline of the book might look something like this.

Introduction   1:1-9

I. The Root of Dissension 1:10-6:20

A. Man's Wisdom Versus God's Wisdom   1:10-2:16
B. Man's Wisdom Produces Rationalism   3:1-23
C. Man's Wisdom Produces Mysticism   4:1-21
D. Man's Wisdom Produces License   5:1-13
E. Man's Wisdom Produces Legalism   6:1-20

1 CORINTHIANS

I Corinthians 1:1-9

What is the writer saying?

How can I apply this to my life?

PRAY Portugal — For a mighty work of the Holy Spirit in the predominantly Catholic provinces of the north.

In writing to the church at Corinth, which was filled with problems, Paul first of all identifies them as saints (v. 2). The word means to be set apart. All Christians have been set apart from sin and unto God. Even if we are not living as we should, God is still in the process of making us holy. Paul then thanks the Lord for the church that was at Corinth. The church had many problems, as will be seen throughout the book, but there were still things for which Paul could thank God. He thanked God for the grace that he had shown to the Corinthians and that they were secure in their relationship with Christ. An interesting note is that although the Corinthians were immature, they all had spiritual gifts from the Lord. Spiritual gifts are given at salvation and have nothing to do with whether we are spiritual or not. The usage of spiritual gifts depends on one's walk with the Lord, but all who are saved have spiritual gifts, whether they are in fellowship or not. In verse 8, we see that God will bring the work of sanctification to fruition in the lives of all believers, and this was a great hope for Paul. Paul based this hope on the faithfulness and sovereignty of God (v. 9). What strikes us as we read this introduction to the book is the positive nature of the salutation. Here is a church torn with division and problems, yet Paul can find something in them for which to thank God!

Life stEP God desires that we are people who continually give Him praise. What are you thanking God for in your life? Who can you encourage with the truth that God is working in their lives? Are you resting in the faithfulness and sovereignty of God?

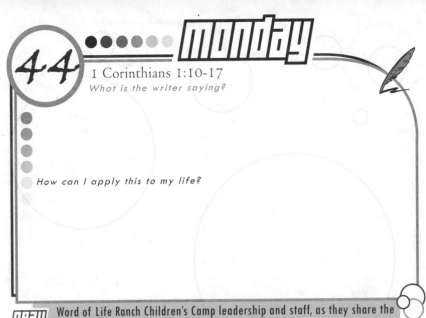

I Corinthians 1:10-17

What is the writer saying?

How can I apply this to my life?

PRAY Word of Life Ranch Children's Camp leadership and staff, as they share the Gospel with hundreds of children.

Paul quickly gets into the exhortation part of the epistle. In many of Paul's letters he starts out with a theological section and then makes application to a certain problem that the church is facing. In this epistle, Paul gets to the point quickly, for there are so many issues to deal with. The first one he wants to talk about is division in the church. The word translated division is the word we get schism from. There were inward divisions and outward splits. The word translated contentions (v. 11) means strife that is caused by rivalry. Paul's desire is that they would be perfectly joined together. This word was used of setting broken bones. They needed to get back together, yet they were divided into four camps. Most

likely, those following Peter were Jews who wanted to hold on to some of their Jewish traditions. Those who were following Apollos were Greeks who were impressed by his eloquence. Those who followed Paul were most likely the ones that he had led to the Lord and baptized (vv. 14-16), and the fourth group thought they were the most spiritual because they were of Christ (v. 12). That sounds spiritual at face value, but their attitude was probably one of pride thinking they didn't need a teacher. Paul rebuked them all and said they should be united for the cause of Christ.

Life stEP

We are to be sure that we are followers first and foremost of Jesus. Do you find yourself picking one teacher (or pastor) over another? Are you a person who causes unity or causes division? How are we to deal with people who cause division in the church? Let us commit to a person who causes unity in the body of Christ.

44 tuesday

I Corinthians 1:18-31

What is the writer saying?

How can I apply this to my life?

PRAY Czech Republic — Pray for the establishment and growth of Christian institutes and seminaries.

The preaching of the cross would be foolishness to the Greeks because they believed that their gods died and came back, but never would one of their gods die on a cross. The Jews saw death on the cross as shameful (Deuteronomy 21:23). Therefore, the cross made no sense to either group. The Gentiles wanted human reasoning (wisdom), and the Jews wanted miraculous signs, and neither understood the cross. However, to believers, the cross is what we glory in! Christians are saved by the preaching of the cross and it is the power of God to salvation (Romans 1:16-17). Those who are called by God are not called because of their abilities or their riches. God's call is always by grace. This is unmerited.

Grace has nothing to do with us; it has everything to do with God! God has chosen the insignificant and weak in order that He might get all of the glory. The believer has nothing to glory in, for the salvation that they enjoy is totally given to them by the grace of God. Many mysteries in the sovereign grace of God are hard to understand, but one can understand how God deserves the praise and the glory for He has made us righteous.

Life stEP

Why does God call the weak and the lowly ones? Why is the Gospel a stumbling block to the Jews? Why is it foolishness to the Gentiles? Are you glorifying God for your salvation daily? Go to the Lord now and thank Him for saving you by His grace and commit to give all glory and honor unto Him.

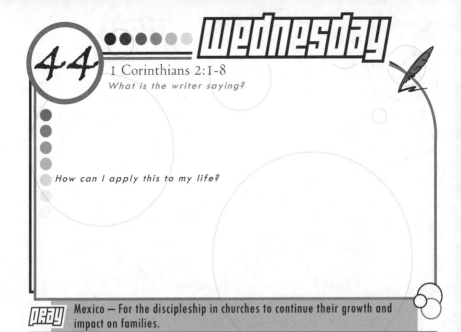

How can I apply this to my life?

PRAY Mexico — For the discipleship in churches to continue their growth and impact on families.

Paul reminds the Corinthians that they were saved as a result of Paul preaching the Gospel. Paul had the ability to speak in a philosophical way that would impress his hearers, but he did not succumb to that. He decided that he was going to stick to the Gospel, for God promises to bless His Word (Isaiah 55:10-11). The word translated determined means to resolve beforehand. Paul had determined to share the central truth of the Gospel, which is that Jesus died for our sins on the cross. The fear and trembling that Paul mentions here can be seen in Acts 18:1-11. It is hard for one to even imagine the great apostle being afraid, but he was. He had gone to Corinth alone, and seemed to have fear in his heart that was affecting his ministry. The Lord appeared to him in a dream to encourage him and as a result, he had a fruitful ministry in Corinth. The fruit of the ministry was a result of the power of the Gospel, not Paul's rhetorical skills. He wanted people to have their faith firmly placed in God and not on his personal abilities. He then assures them that there is wisdom in the Gospel of God, but it is not the wisdom of the world: it is far beyond that!

Are you determined to preach Christ crucified? Why would one want to try to use persuasive words instead of just sticking to the Gospel truth itself? Does your life reflect confidence in the Gospel? Ask God to help you stick to the Gospel when you are sharing with people who don't know the Lord.

I Corinthians 2:9-16

What is the writer saying?

How can I apply this to my life?

PRAY Slovakia — For a clear expounding of God's Word that results in obedience to His authority.

Paul quotes in verse 9 from Isaiah 64:4. At first glance, we might think that the emphasis is on heaven; however, the context in Isaiah that Paul quotes from has to do primarily with blessings here on earth. This emphasis is that God has great things prepared for those who love Him this side of glory as well! God reveals His will to the believer by the ministry of the Holy Spirit. Seeing that every believer has the Spirit living in him, every believer can discern the will of God. Paul says that Christians have been given the Spirit of God so that they might know all the wonderful things that God has blessed them with. The natural man that Paul mentions here is the unsaved man. The natural man is the foolish man, the unregenerate man. He not only does not understand the things of God, he CANNOT know them. The reason the unsaved man cannot understand the things of the Spirit is because he is spiritually dead (Ephesians 2:1-3). According to Romans 3:1-10, the unsaved man is running away from God and is not seeking God in and of his own will. However, when the Spirit of God draws one to Christ and one believes in Christ, hi is given the gift of the Spirit and then he has the great teacher who will lead him into truth. As a result, the believer can discern all things, that is, they can understand the Scriptures and apply them to life. That is what it means to have the mind of Christ.

Life stEP We should be seeking what God's will is for our lives. We should also realize that His plan for us is beyond what we could even imagine! Are you walking in the Spirit so that you can understand God's direction in your life today?

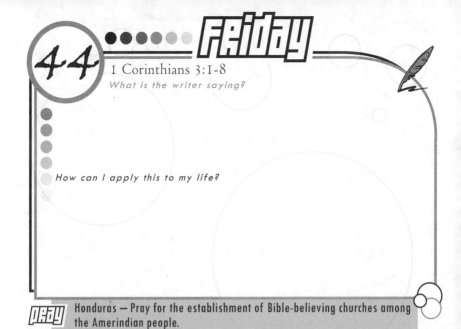

44

What is the writer saying?

How can I apply this to my life?

PRAY Honduras — Pray for the establishment of Bible-believing churches among the Amerindian people.

The apostle's desire was to talk to them as if they were spiritual, but he realized by their behavior that they were carnal. The word carnal means fleshly (a person is operating under the power of the flesh). What does it mean to be in the flesh? It is when we are living with unconfessed sin in our lives? As a result of living this way, we are controlled by our own fleshly desires instead of being controlled by the Spirit. As a result of living according to their flesh, the Corinthians had not grown spiritually and were still babes. Paul should be able to get into deeper truth with them by now, but he can't. The milk he talks about in verse 3 is the basic truths of the Christian life. He was saying, "When you were first saved, those were the things that I taught. But now you should be able to handle meat, that is, the deeper truths," but they were not. As a result of their carnality, they were divisive. Having a favorite Bible teacher is not wrong, but they were divided over who should be the ONLY teacher. Some said Paul and others said Apollos. Paul points out that they are all teachers. God is the one who brings forth salvation and growth, and He should get the glory. Teachers should not be exalted or glorified; they are only tools used by God to bring glory to Himself.

Are you growing in the Lord? If you have been saved for any period of time, you should be moving on to deeper things of the Word. Is the Spirit of God controlling your life? Stop right now and ask the Lord to search your heart and convict you of any sin you might have so that you can confess and get right with him!

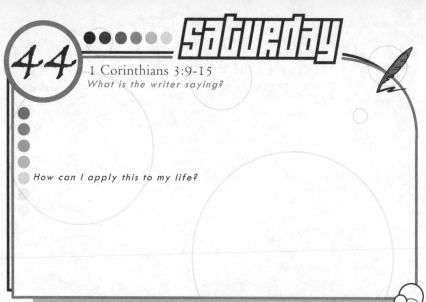

I Corinthians 3:9-15

What is the writer saying?

How can I apply this to my life?

All who serve the Lord are working together for the honor and glory of God. Paul likens the church to a cultivated field or to a building. He said that God is the one who brings forth fruit or, in the building illustration, God is the master builder. God uses the ministers of the Gospel as general contractors, but it is God who is the wise builder. The foundation upon which God builds the church is Jesus Christ. Every life is to be built on the foundation of Christ, and to grow up to represent Christ. The Bible is the blueprint for each believer, and we are to be careful how we build our lives. They should be built with gold, silver, and precious stones, not wood, hay, and stubble. When gold, silver, and precious stones are put into fire, they are purified. When wood, hay, and stubble are put in fire, they are burned up. All will stand before God someday and the fire of his glory and judgment will reveal whether a person has built wisely or unwisely. This is talking about the judgment for works, not for sin. All sin was already judged on the cross. The issue here is not our eternal destination, but our rewards in heaven. Paul said in Acts 20 that the Word of God is what builds us up. In Ephesians 4:11-14 he says that the church builds us up as well. Every church should be dedicated to teaching the Word so that people might grow.

Life stEP

We will all stand before God to give an account for our lives. Are you ready? Are you careful about how you are building your life, and what materials you are using to build it? It is the Bible and the church of God that builds you up. Be sure to make those a priority in your life.

45 SUNDAY

1 Corinthians 3:16-23

What is the writer saying?

How can I apply this to my life?

PRAY Spain — For an end to the government's selective restriction and closure of Christian radio stations.

The Holy Spirit of God indwells the life of every believer in the Lord Jesus Christ (Romans 8:9). Therefore, we as believers are the temples of God, and we are to be holy. In the Old Testament, when God dwelt in the temple, they were to keep very specific regulations as to purity so that God would be honored. The Christian needs to do the same thing now in his or her body, for God lives there. The person who believes in the Lord is to be wise according to the Bible, not according to the world. The wisdom of the world is foolish for it rejects the truth of God. The world says that our bodies belong to us and we can do whatever we want to. The world tells us that we can treat our bodies poorly and get away with it. God desires that we treat our bodies as the temples that they are. The primary concept is that we are to live so that we might reflect God, which is what it means to glorify Him. God's glory is who He is, and He is glorious. Each Christian is to radiate God's glory, which means to confront life in a biblical way. Many people today wear WWJD bracelets to help remind them of this great truth.

Life stEP When people watch you, do they see God's glory? Have you committed yourself as a temple to God? Are you allowing anything to come into your body that would offend the God who lives in you? Commit today to being a holy temple!

monday

45

1 Corinthians 4:1-13

What is the writer saying?

How can I apply this to my life?

pray United Kingdom — For revival in Strathclyde, Scotland's most densely populated, non-Protestant area.

Paul had a humble perspective of himself (v. 1). The word translated minister is a unique word. It is used of a lowly slave, which gives a perspective of what Paul thought of himself. He viewed himself as a steward of God's Word. In verse 2, he says that a steward of God's Word must first and foremost be faithful. Most people quote this verse with reference to giving money; however, it has nothing to do with that in context. Paul realized that he was to be judged by God so the judgment of men did not affect him. It seems that some people were judging him for his motives (vv. 4-5). Even though he did not think his motives were wrong, he knew that God was the One who really knew his heart. When God judges all will be known. The people that were attacking Paul, although bothersome, were not going to dissuade him from continuing to preach the Gospel. Some Corinthians were saying that they were wiser than the apostles (vv. 9-11) so Paul sarcastically speaks to them concerning this. There are times when the servants of Christ are ridiculed and abused for their service (vv. 11-13). Paul was willing to be seen as a fool for the glory of God.

Life stEP

Are there people in your life who think you are a fool for serving the Lord? Don't be tempted to soften your commitment to Jesus because you are being ridiculed for it. Remember, we will all stand before the Lord someday, and you will never regret then that you served Him while on this earth!

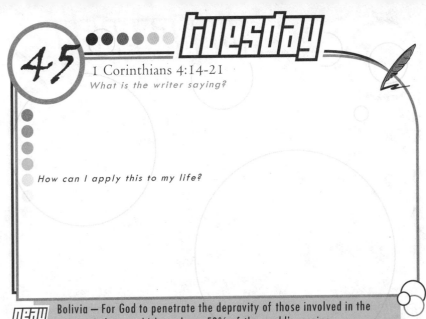

1 Corinthians 4:14-21

What is the writer saying?

How can I apply this to my life?

---

pray Bolivia — For God to penetrate the depravity of those involved in the cocaine industry which produces 50% of the world's cocaine.

The words that Paul was writing were hard, but he was writing out of love so that they might be changed (v. 14). There are many influences in our lives, but only a few who really build into our lives spiritually (v. 15). Paul refers to this with the brethren and reminds them that he poured his life into them and that they should follow him, not other teachers who have crept in since he left. The word follow in v. 16 is the Greek word we get mimic from. Paul is asking them to mimic him. Timothy was being sent to them to remind them of the basic truths that they were being tempted to forget. Paul would have loved to go himself, but he was not able. In verse 21, he asks if he did come now, would they want him to come meekly or with hard rebuke? There are times when both of those are necessary. Most of us, however, would want the meekness, not the rebuke. The point is that if they repented and started to act biblically, when he came, it would be in loving meekness. However, if they did not get things straight, he would have to come in harsh rebuke. In verse 20 he reminds them that the kingdom of God is not a matter of what we say, it is built on the power of God. God is building His church with His power; men do not build it.

Life **stEP** This was a hard rebuke from Paul. How do you take correction? Are you willing to change when confronted with sin? All of us have people who have really built into our lives. Take time this week to thank the people who have this role in your life.

I Corinthians 5:1-13

What is the writer saying?

How can I apply this to my life?

The Corinthian Church had received a letter from Paul previously in which he had told them that they should not have fellowship with people who were living in known sin, in particular, fornication (vv. 9-11). They had misunderstood him to mean that if a person is a believer and they are living like that, you are to accept them; but if they were unbelievers, then you were to withdraw from them. There was a man living with his stepmother in an illicit relationship (v. 1), and Paul rebukes the church for not confronting the couple in their sin. They seemed to have been rather proud of their willingness to accept people like that in the fellowship as opposed to being broken over their sin (v. 2). After confronting someone like this, if he is not willing to repent, we are to bring another witness with us and confront him again. If he refuses to repent, then we are to bring it to the church and the whole assembly is to confront the wayward believer in love. If he refuses to repent (Matthew 18), he is to be delivered over to Satan so that his flesh would be destroyed. This is the right thing to do, yet so many churches today refuse to exercise this kind of discipline. Paul points out that if discipline does not occur, the leaven of their sin will affect the whole congregation (vv. 7-8). If a person who calls himself or herself a Christian is living in unrepentant sin, we are not to have normal fellowship with him, even to the point of not sharing a meal. This may seem harsh, but it is this type of action that will help people consider the seriousness of sin. However, if an unbeliever is living like that, we are not to withdraw from him. He is simply doing what comes naturally, and we are to seek to reach him with the Gospel. God will judge the world when He returns; it is our responsibility to guard the integrity and holiness of the church.

Life stEP Our testimony affects the whole church, are you living holy? Is there someone you know who is living in sin that needs to be confronted? Our responsibility is to go to him personally, not to talk to others about it (Galatians 6:1).

I Corinthians 6:1-11

What is the writer saying?

How can I apply this to my life?

It is inevitable that there will be disagreements between brothers and sisters in Christ. How do we handle ones that have business implications? Are we to take them to court? Not according to Paul in this passage. If there is a legal matter that we have against a brother or sister in Christ that is not dealing with a criminal issue, we are to seek to get other Christians to arbitrate for us (vv. 1-4). If we take other Christians to court, it is a terrible testimony concerning the unity of the body of Christ, which is the church. This passage is dealing with civil issues. If a person has committed a crime, then we are to have the law deal with it. That is what they are there for (Romans 13). The discussion here involves a civil issue, dealing with business or disputes.

Before we would ever take it to court, we should be willing to take the wrong for the testimony of Christ (v. 7). Paul then reminds them that people who are living in continual sin will not go to heaven (vv. 9-11). Does this mean that we have to live without sinning in order to go to heaven? No, of course it does not. Paul means that if a person calls himself or herself a Christian, yet persists in a sinful lifestyle, they are lying, and are not really saved (1 John 2:1-6). He points out that the Corinthians used to live in sin like that, but now that they are saved they no longer live in such immoral conditions. When the Lord saves a person, He changes his life. A person who has been saved by the Lord is in the process of being changed to be like Him (Philippians 1:6; 2 Corinthians 5:17).

Are you willing to take a wrong so that God would be honored? Do you see God continually changing your life? Commit to God today to never take your complaints with another believer before others, but to deal with them face to face. If you have no satisfaction, then get some mature believers to help you solve the crisis.

45

Friday

1 Corinthians 6:12-20

What is the writer saying?

How can I apply this to my life?

pray Costa Rica — That the church's vitality will not be sapped by secularism, materialism, and the influence of the New Age mindset.

Paul states a principle of Christian liberty here that is vital for all to remember. In the gray areas of life, all things are lawful, but all things do not build a person up to be like Jesus. It seems that the Corinthians were treating sexual issues as if they were gray, and Paul points out here that they are not. Any sexual relationship outside the bonds of marriage is wrong. They had reasoned that sex was similar to food (v. 13) in that it was just a physical activity meant for the fulfillment of the body. As a result, they were engaging in sexual immorality with harlots (vv. 15-16) and justifying the activity as inconsequential. Paul shows that this reasoning is faulty and that the body is to be used as a vehicle to honor God and Him alone. We should never take that which is meant to glorify God and pollute it with a prostitute (vv. 16-18). The sin of fornication is a serious sin, for it defiles the temple in which God lives, which is our body. Paul encourages them to "flee fornication" (v. 18). The command here is in the present tense, which means that we are to go on continually fleeing. It is not a one-time thing, but a continual attitude that we are to cultivate in our hearts. The reason Paul gives here is powerful: God has bought us and we belong to Him, therefore we should use our bodies for His glory alone (vv. 19-20). To glorify God means to put Him on display in our lives. God is holy and pure, and to glorify Him with our bodies means to be holy and pure in our sexual lives.

What are you doing to maintain sexual purity? Are there things you watch that are sexually unclean? Does this help you in your quest for purity or hinder you? As you consider your relationships with someone of the opposite sex, be sure you stay as far away from situations that might lead to sexual temptation as you possibly can.

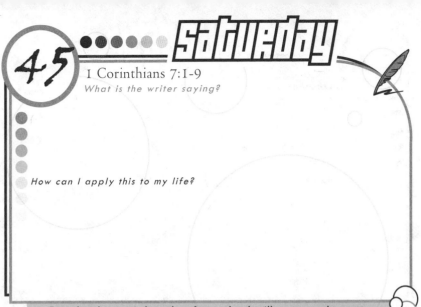

1 Corinthians 7:1-9

What is the writer saying?

How can I apply this to my life?

Pray that the married couples of your church will nurture and protect their relationships by a dependence upon God's Word.

In this chapter, Paul deals with celibacy. He points out that celibacy is good (v. 1); it is tempting (v. 2); it is wrong for married people (vv. 3-5); it is a gift from God (vv. 6-7); and, if it is too tempting, one should get married (vv. 8-9). In verse 1, Paul uses the word touch as a euphemism for sexual relationships. It is good for a man or woman not to have sexual relationships with one another. However, in order not to give into sexual impurity, God has ordained marriage. Marriage is the only context for sexual relationships that God blesses. The husband and wife are to meet each other's needs (vv. 3-4). The only exception to this is if they both consent to abstain temporarily for spiritual reasons (v. 5). Paul states that there are some that have the gift of singleness and some that do not. The gift of singleness is that of being single and loving it. God grants the gift of singleness to some, but not to many. The reality is that God intends most people to marry. However, there are some that have the gift of singleness, and Paul sees that as a great asset in the culture in which he lived at the time (v. 26). However, if you don't have the gift, it is not good to stay single for sexual temptation might overtake you.

Is it possible that you have the gift of celibacy (singleness)? If you are married, are you depriving your mate in this area? If you are dating, you need to be sure to stay pure until you are married. If the temptation becomes overwhelming, you should consider getting married if you know this is the person that God has for you (vv. 8-9).

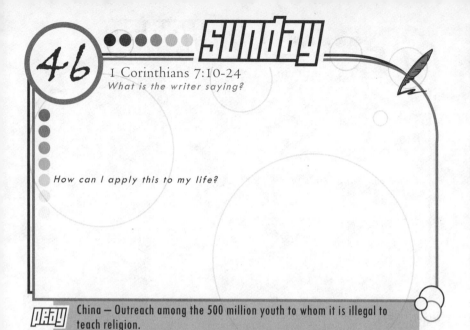

How can I apply this to my life?

pray China — Outreach among the 500 million youth to whom it is illegal to teach religion.

To understand this text, we must understand what was going on in this culture. These people were coming to know Christ. They viewed the marriage relationship to be spiritual and had many questions about what to do now that they were Christians. "Now that I am saved," they might have thought, "what do I do now? If I am saved, should I stay with my spouse even though they do not know the Lord? What if my spouse is unsaved and leaves me, what do I do then?" These are the questions that Paul answers in this passage. He first states that it would be wrong for a believer to ever divorce his spouse (vv. 10-11). Even if there is separation, there should not be divorce, (Paul is not condoning separation, he is just stating if there is separation, don't divorce the person.).

In verse 12, Paul says that there is no other revelation on this in the Bible, so he would comment on it himself. If you are married to a non-Christian, stay in the relationship with him (vv. 12-14). It is not a sinful relationship. God will use it to expose the spouse to the Gospel. Make sure that you live for the Lord and put Him first, and if your spouse can live with that, great. However, if the spouse cannot take the difference that Christ has made in your life and leaves, you are to let them go (v. 15). Another question might come up like, "What if I am saved and now married to my third wife? What should I do?" Paul answers this in verses 17-24. The principle he shares is simple: stay in the same marital situation you were in when you were saved.

If you are married to a non-believer, what are you doing to show your spouse the love of God? If you are single, don't ever consider marrying a non-believer, for it will dishonor God and make your life miserable. Commit to God today to be a godly spouse!

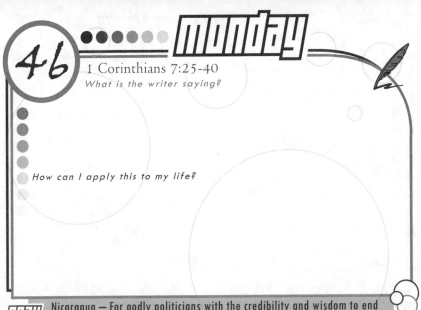

monday

1 Corinthians 7:25-40

What is the writer saying?

How can I apply this to my life?

pray Nicaragua — For godly politicians with the credibility and wisdom to end divisive disputes.

In this passage, Paul is sharing words of wisdom with those who are not married. There was some distress going on in this culture that caused Paul to say that if you were single it is probably better to stay so because of the situation. Some say that it was persecution, while others say that it was the poor view of marriage in Corinth. Whatever it was, Paul's encouragement was to stay single (v. 26). Nevertheless, if you do marry, you have not sinned. There are some advantages to being single. If you are married, you have to be concerned with meeting the material needs of another person; if single, you do not (v. 32). If you are married, you have to figure out how to meet the emotional needs of your spouse, and if you are single you can just concern yourself with what God wants. If you are married, before you make any decision, you have to make sure that your spouse is in agreement, working your way through many issues; if you are single, you do not (vv. 33-35). The last part of the passage is difficult to understand. Possibly Paul is talking to fathers of virgins, but more likely he is talking to men considering marriage. The Corinthians might be thinking, "What if a person is getting on in age and wants to be married?" Paul says to go ahead and get married; he is not forbidding that (v. 36). Moreover, if you decide not to marry, that is fine as well, (v. 37), as long as you know that when you marry it is for life (v. 39). People in our culture obviously have not taken this counsel to heart.

Have you considered singleness as an option for your future? Are you willing to pray about it? It is not the runner-up prize to be single. If you do not think you have the gift of celibacy, remember that marriage is for life!

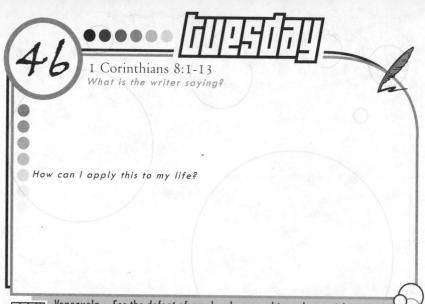

1 Corinthians 8:1-13

What is the writer saying?

How can I apply this to my life?

pray Venezuela — For the defeat of any legal proposal to end or restrict evangelism in any way.

In Chapters 8-10 Paul discusses gray issues. A gray issue is something that is not specifically addressed in the Bible such as clothing styles, music styles, what things you do on Sunday, and many others. These discussions can lead to angry arguments and divide churches. This is not new. There was an issue in Corinth that was affecting the church; that of eating meat offered to idols or that of eating in the temple restaurant. Animals were sacrificed to the gods in the pagan temples. Part of the meat was burned, part was served in the temple restaurant, and the rest sold in the temple market. People saved from this background were offended when they saw other Christians eating in the restaurant or serving meat that had been offered to the gods. They believed that demons attached themselves to that food and Christians should not eat it. Who was right? In the first six verses, Paul states that there is nothing wrong with the meat or with eating the meat. All things are clean and there is nothing wrong at all in eating the meat. Then was it okay to eat in the temple restaurant? Not necessarily, if eating in the temple or serving the meat at home would offend a weaker brother, then it should not be done (vv. 8-13). A weaker brother is someone whose faith has not been strengthened yet and who has not grown in biblical knowledge. They need to be loved, encouraged, and taught. If we exercise our liberty and it negatively affects them, then we sin against the Lord (v. 13). This is the principle of love: we are willing to not exercise our liberty because we love our brothers in Christ.

Are you willing to give up the right to do something that would negatively affect another Christian? If your music, or your dress, or anything else causes a weaker brother to stumble, you must be willing to not exercise that liberty around them.

wednesday

46

1 Corinthians 9:1-10

What is the writer saying?

How can I apply this to my life?

pray Slovakia — For the church planting to be successful in bringing the good news to many unbelievers.

In 9:1-18 Paul illustrates his willingness to give up his own liberty for the cause of Christ. In our passage today, he gives a number of reasons why he has the right to be paid for the Gospel ministry, and in tomorrow's passage he will give reasons why he gives up the right to a salary. First Paul argues that his apostolic office deserves payment for services rendered (vv. 1-6). The word apostle means to be sent. Paul was sent by the Lord Himself to the Gentiles to reach them with the Gospel. It seems some might have doubted his apostleship so he shares that he has the signs of being an apostle (v. 2). He had the right to take along a wife like Peter did, but he gave up that right to be more effective for Christ as described in chapter 7. Paul's second reason is that it is the usual custom to profit from your labor (v. 7). The third reason is that the Old Testament taught that laborers should be compensated for their labor (vv. 8-10). The point he is making here is that a person's sustenance should come from their work. In 2 Thessalonians 3:10 Paul says that if a man does not work, then he should not eat. If a person gives themselves to the Gospel ministry, then they should be taken care of by the people who are benefiting from the ministry. Could you imagine working and at the end of the week your boss coming to you and saying, "Well, I know you don't work for money, but for God's glory, so I am not going to pay you this week." What would your response be? We are to make sure that we are taking care of the men who preach the Word of God. They should be freed from the cares of this world so that they can concentrate on ministry for the honor and glory of God.

Pray for your church that they might generously take care of the needs of your pastors. Pray for those who are in ministry that their financial needs would be met so that they could give themselves wholly to the ministry of the Gospel.

1 Corinthians 9:11-18

What is the writer saying?

How can I apply this to my life?

PRAY South Africa — Medical ministry and Gospel outreach among the nearly 500,000 AIDS orphans.

In verses 11-14, Paul states that those who minister the Word of God should have their physical needs met by the people of God. This is how it was in the Old Testament (v. 13), and it is how it should be today. However, Paul says that as a missionary he gave up that right, so that people would not think that he was in ministry for the money (vv. 15-18). This is an illustration of being willing to give up a liberty for a higher good, which is the topic of Chapters 8-10. This is why we support missionaries from our local churches. We send them out with their financial needs met, so that when they preach in other countries, they are not asking for money. If they went and preached and then asked for money, the people would think that they are preaching for money. As they mature, they will realize that they are not doing it for the money, but that they do need to eat! However, so that the issue would not be confused, Paul did not take money from the people to whom he ministered when it was in a missionary setting. However, Paul did accept money from mature churches that knew that it was their responsibility to take care of the needs of missionaries. Then Paul makes a transitional statement in verse 16 that is stunning. He did not want glory for preaching the Gospel. One of the reasons he preached was that he realized that God would hold him responsible for being disobedient if he did not. Another motivation was that the Lord would reward him if he was faithful to the task (v. 17). Paul realized that the most important payday was the one coming when he stood before the Lord. Did he have the right to be paid for preaching to the lost? Yes, but he refused to exercise that right, and we should refuse to exercise rights that would not advance the Gospel of Jesus Christ.

Why do you share the Gospel? Why should you? Are you looking for creative ways to reach people for Christ? Here is a challenge. Get an index card and write the names of ten people that you want to be saved. Commit to pray for those people every day. Ask God to open opportunities for you to share Christ with these people. When one gets saved, add another to your list. Call it My Top Ten list.

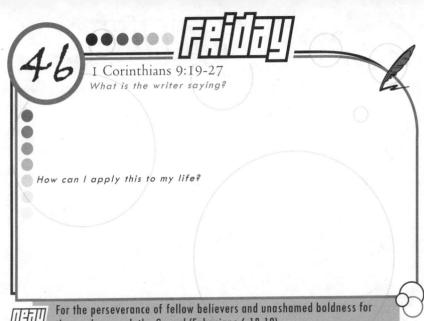

Friday

I Corinthians 9:19-27

What is the writer saying?

How can I apply this to my life?

pray For the perseverance of fellow believers and unashamed boldness for those who preach the Gospel (Ephesians 6:18-19).

There are two crucial principles Paul shares here that are vital in reaching people for Jesus Christ: self-denial and self-control. Although we are free from all extra-biblical rules in life, there are times when we should abide by some in order to reach people for Jesus. In verses 19-23, we are encouraged to exercise self-denial. We give up the right to do what we want in order to reach others. In verses 20-22 Paul says that he adapted to various people's customs in order to reach them. This is not talking about violating biblical principles. He would never do that. This is talking about condescending to others to reach them for Christ. If we are going to reach in-line skaters for Christ, we might have to buy some skates and go where they are to reach them. This is what Paul meant. He was willing to give up some of his comfortable ways in order to share the Gospel and that takes self-denial (v. 23). In verses 24-27, he shares that it takes self-control to be willing to lay aside your freedom to reach others. He illustrates with athletes. An athlete has the right to eat cake and cookies and wash them down with coke. Do they? No. They watch what they eat and drink. They train hard and long. They give up the freedom to hang out and rest. The great marathon runner Bill Rogers used to wake up at 2:00 AM to cook a meal to get his protein. He would run ten miles in the morning and ten again in the evening. Did he have to do that? No, only if he wanted to reach his goal. Do we have to give up our comforts? Only if we want to reach the goal of winning the lost to Christ! If an athlete is willing to do all that for temporal gains, what more should we be willing to do for the glory of God? In verse 27, Paul writes that the biggest enemy to being able to do this is US! We have to keep under our bodies, that means to beat them into submission. We are not to give into our fleshy desires, but to be committed to doing what is right and godly.

Remember the top ten list from yesterday? In what ways can you creatively reach those on that list for Christ? Are there things in your life that aren't necessarily wrong, but are hindering you from reaching others for Christ? What are you willing to give up to reach others for Christ?

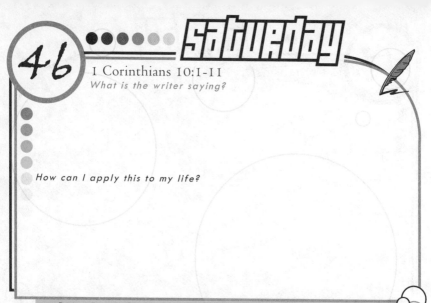

1 Corinthians 10:1-11

What is the writer saying?

How can I apply this to my life?

pray Peru — For a softening of hearts among the 700,000 unusually resistant, university students.

Paul talks about the danger of taking God for granted. The Israelites enjoyed the blessings of God. They had supernatural guidance from the Lord (v. 2). All of their needs were taken care of by the Lord in a miraculous way (vv. 3-4). Even though they had all those benefits, they did not walk with the Lord as they should. God gave them great blessings; yet instead of praising Him, they took Him for granted. Worse than that, they began to lust after evil things (v. 6). They got involved in idolatry, which, at its root, is to put anyone or anything in the place of God. In verse 7, it says that they got drunk and even were involved in sexual uncleanness (the meaning of play). This is recorded for us in Exodus 32. They put God to the test, and as a result, God judged them harshly. Two times in this text Paul says that these things are written for our benefit (vv. 6, 11). In times of blessing it is very easy to overlook the Lord and begin to get involved in evil. When we are in times of trouble we tend to look for the Lord, and in times of prosperity we tend to forget Him. The Israelites were well known as complainers (v. 10), and we need to be careful not to complain. When we complain, we are saying one of two things: either God is not in control or He is in control and we don't like what He is doing! There is a grave danger to spiritual privilege. Many who grow up in Christian homes and go to good churches and youth groups get so used to God's blessing, they take Him for granted. Then they complain, and eventually give themselves over to doing ungodly things. It's happened to others, and it can happen to us if we are not careful.

Life stEP Do you complain? About what? When you complain, what are you telling others about God? Go to God today and ask Him to help you to be content.

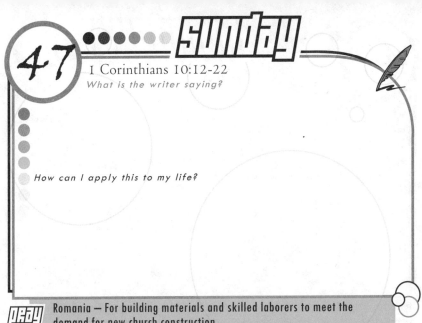

47 · SUNDAY

1 Corinthians 10:12-22

What is the writer saying?

How can I apply this to my life?

pray Romania — For building materials and skilled laborers to meet the demand for new church construction.

Paul evaluates the failure of Israel despite God's abundant blessing (vv. 1-11). First Paul mentions their over-confidence (v. 12). In other words, they were thinking, "that would never happen to me!" He says that we should take heed if we think that, for we could fall as well. The other attitude we might have is "well, what chance do I have? If it happened to them, it will happen to me." Flowing from that fear is one of the greatest promises in the Word of God (v. 13). The word temptation could be translated test. It is speaking of an external circumstance in our life. An external circumstance is simply a test; however, when we begin to lust, it then becomes a temptation. A friend leaving $100 on the table is an external circumstance or test. If we begin to lust and think of what we could do with a hundred bucks, then it has become a temptation. Well, in this text, Paul says that there is no circumstance that comes into your life that is unique to men. Moreover, with every circumstance in which you find yourself, you can trust that God is faithful to provide a way to handle it biblically. All you have to do is ask for the wisdom of God. One of the biggest temptations is to put something in the place of God (v. 14-15). Idolatry is all consuming. God will not tolerate any rivals in our lives, whether it is money or other people. We are to live for Him and for Him alone. Our fellowship with God is not right when we live for things. In verses 16-22, Paul talks about the fellowship of communion. If we are involved in idolatry, then we are not really having communion with God (v. 19). The Corinthians were involved in idolatry and at the same time were having communion services. This was an affront to God (vv. 21-22). God demands total holiness in worship. He wants us to be totally committed to Him.

Life stEP Paul defines covetousness as idolatry. That is when our desire for things is stronger than our desire for God. That puts it in a different light doesn't it? Ask God to help you put Him first!

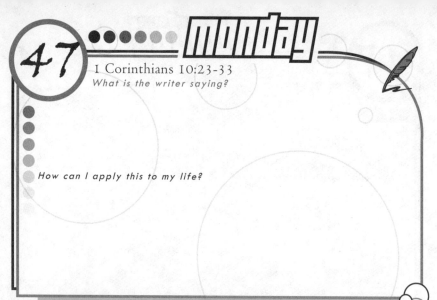

47 monday

1 Corinthians 10:23-33

What is the writer saying?

How can I apply this to my life?

pray Thailand — For believers to stand strong in a land where more people earn their living through crime than honest labor.

Paul wraps up his discussion of gray area issues. He again states that all things are lawful (v. 23). That means that all things that are not clearly forbidden in the Bible are lawful for us to do. Does that indicate that we should do them? Of course, it does not mean that. How can we cultivate conviction in these areas? That is exactly what Paul writes about here and he gives us some clear questions to ask that will help us cultivate our own personal convictions.

–Is this prohibited in the Scriptures? v. 23

–Will it build me up to be more like Christ? v. 23

–Will it help me build others to be like Christ? v. 23

–Am I doing this solely because I want to? v. 24

–Will it enhance or hinder my testimony to the lost? vv. 25-30

–Will it glorify God? v. 31

–Will it offend anyone? v. 32

From other chapters we could add:

–Would I want others to imitate me in this? 11:1

–Will it cause a young believer to stumble? 8:13

Paul was not willing to do anything that would make another Christian stumble or would hinder the Gospel in a lost person's life. Think of the above list. Now take an issue and process it through that list. For instance, the Bible does not explicitly forbid watching R-rated videos. Now ask each one of those questions about watching such a show. We are free, free to do what God wants us to do. Before we knew the Lord, we were not free to do what God wanted us to do because we were bound by our sin nature. But now that the Holy Spirit lives in us, we have the power to obey God and are free to do so!

What would Jesus do (WWJD) must be more than just a fad. Make it the determining factor in every decision you make.

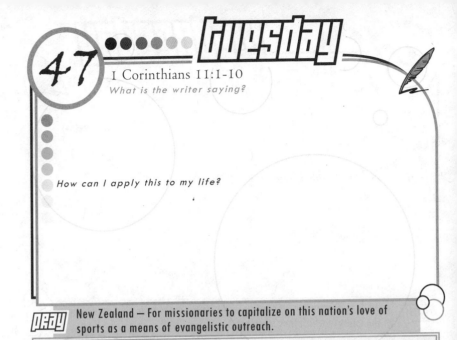

I Corinthians 11:1-10

What is the writer saying?

How can I apply this to my life?

pray New Zealand — For missionaries to capitalize on this nation's love of sports as a means of evangelistic outreach.

Paul discusses the chain of command in marriage. God has set the man to be the leader in the home (v. 3). In all relationships in life there has to be some type of submission. The authority of the man in the home has nothing to do with men being better than women; it has to do with the role that God has for us. For instance, if a policeman writes you a ticket, it does not mean he is better than you; it simply means that this is his role. We are all equal in essence, but we have different roles. God the Father and God the Son are equal in essence, but in verse 3 it says that the Father is the head over Christ. That is a great illustration. Men are the heads over women in the home, but they are equal in essence. In Greece at this time, there was a big women's liberation movement. The sign of submission in this culture for the woman was the wearing of veils. The veil was not a little piece of cloth on the head. It was a full head covering that went down around the face, and only the eyes were showing. The ladies were taking them off and, by doing so, were showing they were in rebellion against their husbands. Paul basically says, "Keep your veils on!" (vv. 5-10). The women were also shaving their heads (vv. 5-6) which was the hairstyle of prostitutes. Paul did not want them to be associated with prostitution. God created the woman for the man (v. 9). When women are fulfilling their God-ordained role, they will be fulfilled and God will be honored. This was not happening in Corinth. To apply this passage we must ask, "How does a Christian woman show her respect to her husband's leadership in the home?" It will be different from place to place, but we should be sensitive. God has made a clear distinction between the role of men and women.

Life stEP Ask God to give you wisdom concerning your unique role. Make a commitment to never rebel against how God ordained things to be in the family, but to gladly submit to His teachings!

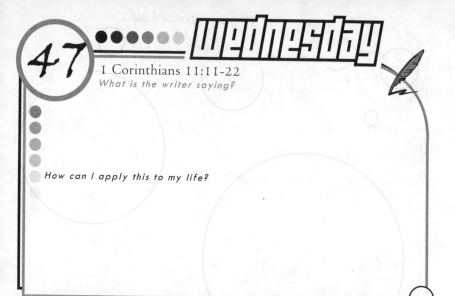

47

I Corinthians 11:11-22

What is the writer saying?

How can I apply this to my life?

PRAY Word of Life Open Air Evangelism — No interference from civil authorities in the cities in which they minister.

This passage continues the discussion on the role of men and women. God designed it that way for a purpose (v. 12). In the Corinthian culture, prostitutes shaved their heads, or wore the hair closely cropped. Therefore, if Christian women took off their veils and cut their hair short, they would be associated with the prostitutes. The conclusion is that a woman's hairstyle should be distinguishable from a prostitute's and also from a man's hairstyle. Paul then moves on into a discussion about some of their meetings. It seems that they were coming together for a potluck dinner, but people were not sharing. As a result, some people were going home hungry (v. 21). Others were getting drunk (v. 21). This was causing division in the church. God allows troubles in ministry at times so that the leaders will be made apparent (vv. 8, 19). Anyone can lead when things are going well, but you find the most qualified leaders by how people respond to adversity. In verse 22, Paul rebukes them and tells them to eat their meals at home, and not to despise fellow believers by coming together and not being willing to share.

What does our hairstyle and clothing style say about our walk with God? We should bring attention to God and His glory, not ourselves.

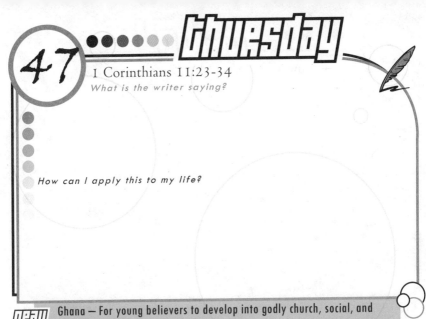

1 Corinthians 11:23-34

What is the writer saying?

How can I apply this to my life?

pray Ghana — For young believers to develop into godly church, social, and national leaders.

This passage describes the Lord's Supper. During the Passover meal, Jesus transformed that meal into the first Communion service (Matthew 26:26-28). The elements used are to stimulate us to remember Jesus; to have this memorial in remembrance of Him (vv. 24-25). The bread reminds us of the life of Jesus Christ. The bread was unleavened bread. Leaven is an illustration of sin in the Bible. Jesus was without sin. He was tempted in every way as we are, yet without sin. 2 Corinthians 5:21 says that Jesus knew no sin. Jesus is holy because He is God. The cup reminds us of the death of Jesus, as signified by the shedding of His blood. The cup represents the wrath of God for sin, and Jesus drank it for us! Jesus paid the price for our sins on the cross. The new covenant (promise) is based on the blood of Jesus Christ. Under this new covenant, we have a relationship with God through faith in Jesus Christ and Him alone as our Lord and Savior. We are to celebrate Communion to proclaim the Lord's death, and we are to do it until He comes again (v. 26). Before we partake of the Lord's Table, Paul instructs us to examine ourselves. As a matter of fact, if we go to the Lord's Table with unconfessed sin in our lives, we make a mockery of what we are doing. Is it right to celebrate Jesus dying for our sin while we are entertaining sin in our lives? It seems that the Corinthians were doing this, and as a result God was chastising them, some even to the point of death (v. 30). We are to examine ourselves and then to partake after we have confessed our sin to the Lord (v. 28). When God chastens us, He does so that we will be brought back in right relationship with Him. As a result, we will never experience the condemnation that the world has coming to them. God loves us enough to chasten us, not to hurt us, but to bring us back into a right relationship (v. 32). That is how much He loves us! That is our security!

Life stEP The next time you take Communion be sure to examine yourself and partake in a holy way!

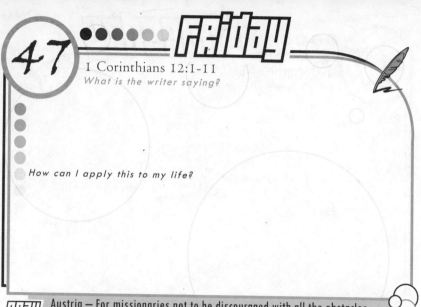

What is the writer saying?

How can I apply this to my life?

PRAY Austria — For missionaries not to be discouraged with all the obstacles they encounter.

This section introduces a discussion on spiritual gifts, which lasts for three chapters. It is obvious that the Corinthians were abusing spiritual gifts and Paul wanted to correct them. It seems that things had gotten so out of control in the church that someone had stood up in the assembly and said that Jesus was an anathema. In verse 3, Paul states that no man can say such a thing under the control of the Holy Spirit. The Corinthians had figured if it was wild and ecstatic, then that it was from God. This text corrects that misunderstanding of gifts. In verse 2, he states that when they were unsaved they acted out of control and wild, but that is not how the Spirit of God works. In verses 4-6 there are three terms used to describe gifts. In verse 4, the word is charismata, from which we get the word charismatic. It emphasizes that these are grace gifts from God. In verse 5, they are called administrations, which is the Greek word from which we get deacon. This emphasizes that gifts are given to minister. In verse 6 they are called operations, the word in the Greek from which we get energy. It emphasizes the fact that God gives the power for the usage of our gifts. Notice in verses 4-6 three times Paul states that there are differences...but the same. This shows the great truth that unity comes from diversity. We are all given different gifts, with different ministries, with different amounts of power to minister for God's glory. However, we are all ministering for the same purpose, to bring glory to God. In verse 11, we see that the same Spirit directs all of the gifts. Moreover, it is the Spirit of God that has given the gifts according to His will. We do not pray to get certain gifts; it is the Spirit's call. Notice He gives gifts to everyman. You have gifts from God.

Life stEP

Do you know what gifts God has given you? Are you using those gifts for His glory? Today thank God for the unique way that He has gifted you.

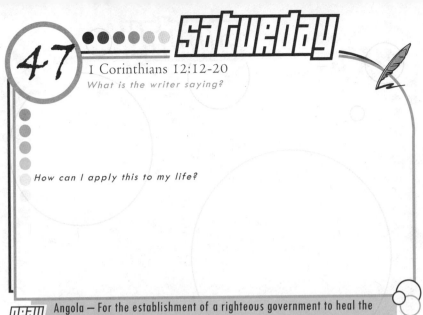

1 Corinthians 12:12-20

What is the writer saying?

How can I apply this to my life?

pray Angola — For the establishment of a righteous government to heal the despair caused by war, famine, and religious persecution.

The illustration of the body is used here to show the interdependence all believers have on one another. In the first part of the passage he stresses the unity that we have in Christ. In verse 13, he states that the Holy Spirit has baptized us all. This concept has been misunderstood by many. Notice it says that we have all been baptized into the body of Christ. The word baptize simply means to dip, or to place into. In water baptism, we are placed into the water and taken back up out of the water to signify that we are identifying with the death, burial, and resurrection of Jesus Christ. Spirit baptism occurs at salvation when the Spirit places us into the body of Jesus Christ. This is not an experience; it is something the Spirit does at salvation. That is why there is no place in the Bible where we are commanded to be baptized by the Spirit because it happens at salvation. We know this because it says that all are baptized, not just the ones who received a second blessing as some teach. Not only does the Spirit of God place us in the body, He places us exactly where he wants to place us. It is that He designs us to be the part of the body that He wants us to be. God is the One who sets the members in their place (v. 18). We are all different by design and we are all needed. In the physical body, all the members are needed to function effectively, and all cannot be the same body part, or there would be no effective function. So it is in the body of Christ; we are all different (vv. 4-6), and we are all needed.

Life stEP You are needed in the body of Christ. Are you functioning the way you should? Imagine what it would be like if your legs decided not to work. What kind of effect would that have on you? Don't be a non-functioning member of the body.

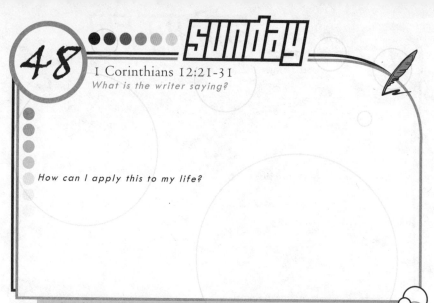

1 Corinthians 12:21-31

What is the writer saying?

How can I apply this to my life?

PRAY Brazil — For godly government officials who will put an end to corruption and discrimination.

There is a tendency to think that certain people are more important in the church than others. It would be very easy to think that the youth leaders are more important than the members of the youth group, but is that true? Paul says here that every member of the body is equally important. Even those parts of the body that we think are not as presentable, we spend time on them. For instance, take our toes. They are not the best looking part of the body. What do we do? If you are a girl you pedicure them, paint the toenails, and do whatever you can to make them presentable. What is the point? We are to spend time with all parts of the body (vv. 23-26). Each part is vital to the church being successful in glorifying God. As in the physical body, when one member of the body hurts, it affects the whole body. Have you ever hit your thumb with a hammer? Does it affect your whole body? We are to be sensitive to every member of the body of Christ, not just the pastor, elders, deacons, youth leaders, or the most popular. We are all needed in the fellowship of the saints. In addition, we are all made differently by God (vv. 28-30). We are not all the same and that is by God's design. According to verse 28, God is the one who has set us in the body with the gifts that we have.

Life stEP

Do you have a tendency to look at others in the church and wish you had their gifts? Do you look down on others in the body because they are not like you are? God is the one who made people the way they are, and we are to appreciate each person in the body and to love them equally. Ask God for help today to love those who are a bit different from you.

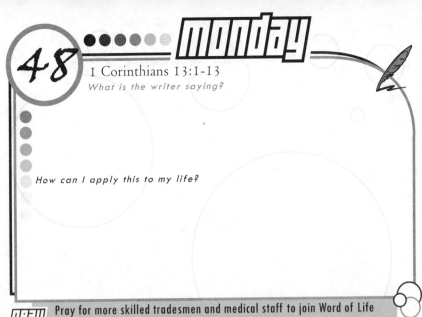

I Corinthians 13:1-13

What is the writer saying?

How can I apply this to my life?

PRAY Pray for more skilled tradesmen and medical staff to join Word of Life Nehemiah Network ministry teams.

This chapter is known as the love chapter. In context, Paul is showing that all spiritual gifts need to operate in the context of love (vv. 1-3). No matter how wonderful our gifts are, if they are not operated in the attitude of love, then they matter little (vv. 1-3). Love is not defined here as much as it is described. We are shown here how love acts in a practical manner. There are sixteen statements made here about love. The emphasis on these is how we treat people. Love is patient with people (v. 4). Love does not try to exalt self, but others (vv. 4-5). Love does not get easily upset because it is primarily concerned with others, not with its own feelings (v. 5). The point is that love is others oriented. Love is concerned with the other person, not with self. As a result, it is positive and encouraging (v. 7). Love is enduring. For all of eternity we will love God and love others. The spiritual gifts that the Corinthian people were giving all of their attention to will one day pass away, but love will never pass away. As vital as gifts are, love is much more vital for it is eternal. In verses 10-13, Paul states that when we get to heaven there will be no more need for those spiritual gifts that we hold so dear now, so we need to keep them in their proper perspective. There are three virtues that he exalts in verse 13. Faith is vital; it is by faith we have been saved. Hope is important, for we have a confident expectation that Jesus is coming back. As important as those two are, love is the greatest for love exemplifies the character of God (1 John 4:18).

Write down the sixteen characteristics of love from this chapter, and ask God to help you love others in that manner.

1 Corinthians 14:1-9

What is the writer saying?

How can I apply this to my life?

PRAY Spain — For missionaries to be humble, loving, and culturally sensitive as they seek to minister.

The Corinthian Church had exalted the gift of tongues above all other gifts. The gift of tongues is the ability to speak in an unlearned foreign language. Some people today teach that speaking in tongues is angel talk or ecstatic utterance. However, the Bible clearly teaches that it is simply being able to speak in a language you did not previously learn (Acts 2:1-21). Because it was a showy gift, and mysterious as well, it seems that many wanted to be able to do it. Now we saw earlier that not all people have the same gifts. Some teach all should speak in tongues, but that principle contradicts what Paul taught in chapter 12. Paul states here that speaking in tongues has its place, but prophecy is more needed. Prophecy is speaking forth God's Word to edify, exhort, and encourage (v. 4). Tongues will not edify the whole body if there is not an interpreter, and it seems that this is how they were using it (vv. 5-6, 9). In verse 6, Paul states that if he came speaking in tongues, it would not benefit the body for they would not understand what he said. But if he comes speaking God's Word clearly, all will understand and be built up. The goal of spiritual gifts is to build up the whole body, and tongues cannot do that if they are not used correctly, which they weren't in this assembly. The key in public ministry is seen in verse 9, that what is spoken should be able to be understood by all who are there.

Life stEP

Ask God to help you clearly share His message. Make a commitment to know the Word of God so that you can share it with others.

48 ••••••• wednesday

I Corinthians 14:10-17

What is the writer saying?

How can I apply this to my life?

PRAY **Italy — Outreach among the 31,000 communities without a Gospel witness.**

There are many people making noise in the world (v. 10), yet they do not make sense if I don't know what they are saying (v. 11). If you exalt spiritual gifts, exalt the ones that edify the body (v. 12). The word edify is a building word. It was used of building a home or a temple. We are to be sure that the gifts we have are building the body, not tearing it apart. Some have so exalted the gift of tongues, it has torn churches apart instead of building them up. Could speaking in tongues build up? Yes, but only if there was an interpreter (v. 13). What about praying in tongues? In verse 15, Paul says it makes no sense at all to pray in a language that you do not know or to worship in a language you do not know.

This is instructive, because many say that they are able to worship and pray in tongues, and it is the best worship and prayer that they have known. Paul states just the opposite of that here. God is most honored when we worship Him according to knowledge. It is fine to pray in the Spirit, and if we do that, it will be with understanding as well (v. 15). God wants both, not one over the other. There was a time and place for tongues along with some strict rules for using them (which we will see in the next passage). The Corinthians were misusing the gift of tongues, and they had exalted this above all other gifts. Unfortunately, the same error is taking place today in some churches.

One doesn't have to speak or sing in tongues for you not to understand what is being said. We should speak and sing to God with full understanding of what we are communicating. Do you sing in church knowing what you are really singing about? Try it this week!

393

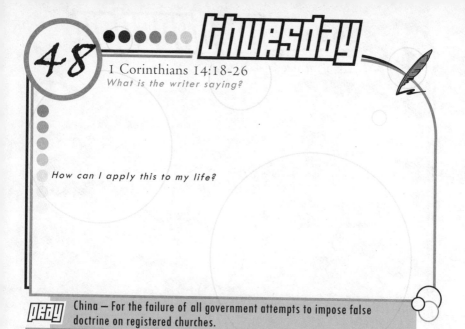

1 Corinthians 14:18-26

What is the writer saying?

How can I apply this to my life?

pray China — For the failure of all government attempts to impose false doctrine on registered churches.

In verse 19, Paul states that he would rather speak five words in the church that people could understand than to be able to speak 10,000 words in tongues. The emphasis should be on how gifts are used, not on how mysterious they seem to be. This seems to have been the Corinthians major problem. We see here in this text the main reason why tongues have passed off the scene today. According to verses 21-22, tongues were a sign to the Jews. What was this sign about? Paul quotes from Isaiah 28:11-12. Tongues were to be a sign of the impending judgment of God on Israel for their rejection of Him. In verse 21 God says that He would speak to Israel with people of other nationalities, yet they would still not listen. In verse 22, he then states that tongues are a sign not to believers, but to those who do not believe. What is the major reason for tongues? A sign of judgment to unsaved Jews that God was about to judge them. Did this come to pass? Yes, in A.D. 70 Titus of Rome attacked Jerusalem and wiped it out. Once the judgment came, the sign warning of the judgment was no longer needed. This is true now; however, in Paul's day, the gift was still functioning and he was trying to get them to use it in a biblical way. Tongues could never help the lost come to Christ (v. 23). As a matter of fact, those without Christ will think people are nuts who speak in tongues without an interpreter. It is much more effective to speak forth (prophesy) the Word of God, and God will use that to win the lost (vv. 24-26).

When you are sharing with the lost, be sure to stick to the Word of God. It is the most effective tool we have in evangelism.

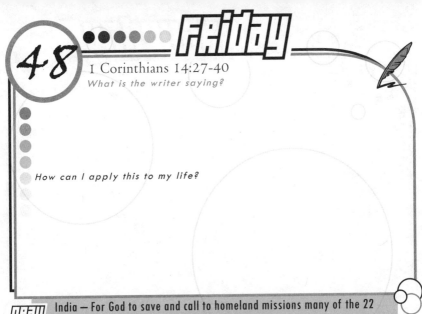

1 Corinthians 14:27-40

What is the writer saying?

How can I apply this to my life?

PRay India – For God to save and call to homeland missions many of the 22 million Indians living abroad.

Tongues were given to the church by God and were to be used according to God's principles. Paul closes the chapter by guidelines for the use of tongues in the body. We saw yesterday that tongues are no longer in use today, but when they were, there were some important limitations. First, because tongues were a sign to unsaved Jews of God's impending judgment, there should be unsaved Jews present in the assembly. Second, no more than three people should speak in tongues at any given service (v. 27). Third, there had to be an interpreter present (v. 28) and if there was not, then the tongue speakers should be silent. This is interesting, for each must have known their gifts and others as well. If the people who had the gift of interpretation were not there, then tongues could not be used. The fourth limitation is that women were not to speak in tongues in the assembly (v. 34). The last guideline is that if the other four principles were kept, then they were not to forbid tongues in the service. As we compare this to today, we see a big gap. In many churches that practice tongues speaking, women are the major speakers, which violates this passage. Another problem is that at times hundreds will speak in tongues at the same time, with no interpreters, another violation. The main point for the use of tongues is that it was to be done in order that people would clearly understand what was occurring. Unless a spiritual gift is being used to build up the body, it is not being used correctly.

Life st**EP**

Are you using your spiritual gifts to build others up in the Lord? Are you helping others realize what their gifts are so that they can know the fulfillment of using them?

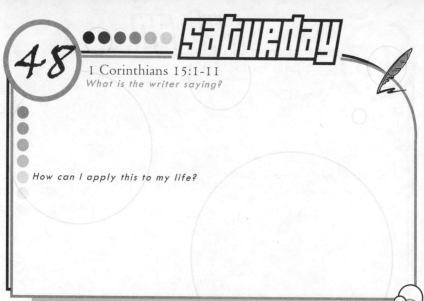

1 Corinthians 15:1-11

What is the writer saying?

How can I apply this to my life?

PRAY Thank the Lord for his all-encompassing forgiveness and compassion (Psalm 103:10-13).

In this chapter, Paul clearly teaches the truth of the resurrection of Jesus Christ from the dead. Some were teaching that Christ did not rise bodily from the dead. One must believe that Jesus has risen from the dead to be saved (vv. 3-4). In verse 1, Paul says that he had preached to them the Gospel when he was with them. He defines the central truths of the Gospel in verses 3-4. The word gospel means good news. What are the central truths of the Gospel? Christ died for our sins, He was buried, and He rose again. Paul points this out to show that the resurrection is a vital part of what we must believe in order to be saved from our sin. In the Old Testament, in order for a truth to be established, you needed two witnesses. Paul, in verses 5-8, goes far beyond that. He states that Peter, the other apostles, over 500 believers, His brother James, and even he saw Jesus. Paul defines himself in verse 9 as the least of all the apostles. He was amazed that God had called one who previously had devoted his life to persecuting the church. As a result Paul realized that he was who he was totally and only by the grace of God. Grace is God's unmerited favor. It is God giving us what we do not deserve. Paul realized he did not deserve salvation, let alone the privilege to preach the Gospel. He was so thankful, that he ministered as hard as he could for the glory of God (vv. 10-11).

When you share the Gospel, make sure that you include the teaching about Jesus rising from the dead. Along with Paul, we can say that we are who we are by the grace of God. Thank God for saving you today even though you deserve hell!

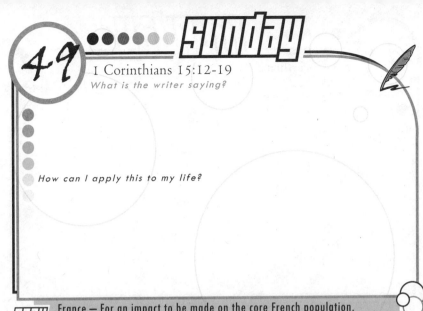

1 Corinthians 15:12-19

What is the writer saying?

How can I apply this to my life?

PRAY France — For an impact to be made on the core French population.

To argue for the truth of the resurrection, Paul starts out by showing what happens if there is no resurrection from the dead (v. 12). If there is no resurrection, then Jesus is not risen from the dead, and if He is not risen from the dead, then Paul was lying, and the Gospel was not true (vv. 12-14). If it is not true, then Paul is a false witness and is worthy of death. If the dead do not rise, then Christ did not rise. If that is true, there is no good reason to believe in Jesus. If salvation is by faith, then that faith is in vain, therefore to no avail. If that is true, then we have not been saved from our sin and are still dead spiritually and on our way to hell (vv. 16-18). If Christ is not raised and there is no resurrection, then all of the people who have died previously have perished and will never be heard from again. If all this is true, then we are to be pitied above all people, for we have lived a lie (v. 19). As a matter of fact, we should be miserable. The point he is making is that the resurrection is not just a secondary teaching of Christianity—it is a fundamental teaching of the faith. If you do not believe in that, then you are not saved. You cannot be a Christian and deny the resurrection. It is the bedrock of our faith. If Jesus is not alive, then we do not have salvation in Him.

Life stEP

When was the last time you thanked Jesus for rising from the dead? Why does the church meet on Sunday? It is to remember that Jesus rose again on the first day of the week. Do not allow a Sunday to go by in church where you forget to praise the RISEN SAVIOR.

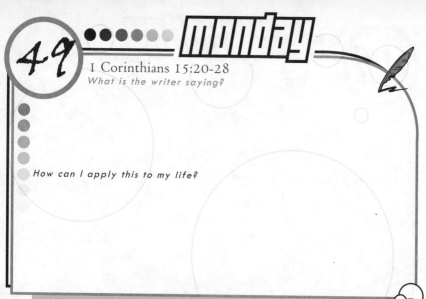

I Corinthians 15:20-28

What is the writer saying?

How can I apply this to my life?

PRAY Nicaragua — For unity among the communities so the government can make the changes that are needed.

In verse 20, we have one of the most victorious statements in the entire Bible, "Now is Christ risen from the dead." In the Greek, it can be translated that "Christ is risen from among the dead ones." Jesus was buried with the dead ones, but unlike them, He rose from the grave! Seeing that Christ is risen from the dead, Paul goes on to state the implications of that. All who are born are born dead (in Adam), but all who are in Christ are alive. Why? Because Jesus is alive (v. 22)! If Christ rose again, so shall we rise someday. Jesus will reign and so shall we because we are in Him (vv. 24-26). Because Jesus is alive, the last enemy is doomed, which is death. The point of all redemptive history is that God might be honored and glorified (v. 28). God is glorified in the resurrection of Jesus Christ. Jesus said we live because He lives! The guarantee we have that we will rise again is that Jesus rose again. There was a time in our lives when we were dead in our trespasses and in our sins, and God made us alive. Once we are made alive, we will never die spiritually. The assurance that all of this is true is based on the truth of the resurrection of Jesus Christ. Because He is alive, He is the eternal ruler. How could Jesus be King of kings and Lord of lords if He had not risen from the dead? But He has and we thank God!

Life stEP

Just as surely as Jesus rose and went to heaven, so you too will rise and go to heaven. If you are a believer, you are in Christ, and He is alive, so you will be alive forever and ever! Thank God today.

I Corinthians 15:29-38

What is the writer saying?

How can I apply this to my life?

PRAY God to prosper our Needy Camper fund so that more youth can be given scholarships to attend camp.

The baptism for the dead in verse 29 means those who are being saved now and being baptized are taking the place of those who used to be alive serving the Lord. In other words, if there is no resurrection, then what good is it to be baptized like those before us, if they are dead forever. Then when we die, we will be dead forever like them. Another argument for the resurrection is that Paul and the other apostles continually were persecuted for their faith, and if there is no raising from the dead, then that suffering is in vain as well (v. 30). Paul encourages them not to spend time with those who are rejecting the resurrection (vv. 33-34). The bad company that they were spending time with was corrupting them. In verse 34, we see that bad theology leads to bad living. They had started being open to the teaching that there was no resurrection and that led them to a sinful lifestyle (v. 34). When you spend vast amounts of time with people who reject the truth of Christianity, it won't be long before you start to live like them. We are to get to know people in the world in order to reach them for Christ, but we are not to have them as our closest friends, for eventually they will corrupt our morals (v. 33). Paul says that there will be some who will reject the resurrection because the body dies, and if it dies it is corrupted. However, that is not even true in natural life. Unless a plant falls into the ground and dies, it does not bring forth fruit. So, our bodies will go in the ground at death, but will be raised by the Lord (vv. 35-37). On top of that, God is all-powerful and He is able to give us a new body ready for eternity when our time to go home to glory comes (v. 38).

Life stEP

Who do you spend time with? Are you affecting them for Christ more than they are affecting you for the world? Choose wisely those whom you will allow to have input into your life.

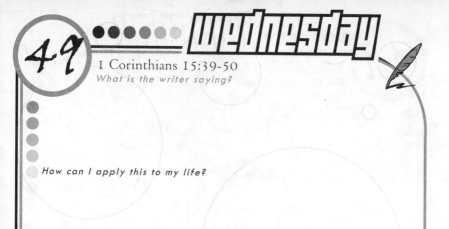

49

WEDNESDAY

1 Corinthians 15:39-50

What is the writer saying?

How can I apply this to my life?

PRAY Costa Rica — For spiritual and cultural barriers to be broken down so churches can multiply.

In verses 39-41, Paul reasons that there are many different kinds of bodies. Men have one kind of body; animals have another kind of body, just as true bodies in heaven are different from bodies on the earth. He likens that to the difference between the moon and the sun. They are both different kinds of heavenly bodies. So, it is true of our bodies. The body that we live in now, that will be put into the grave someday, is perishable. In some miraculous way, God will take it and raise it powerfully and change it to be a heavenly body (vv. 41-44). We now live in a natural body, but we will be given an eternal spiritual body. We come from Adam, and Adam was made of a physical body and then God breathed into him spiritual life (vv. 45-50). The same is true with us. We were born physically alive, but spiritually dead. When we were saved, God made us spiritually alive in Christ. Jesus, however, was different. He was alive before He had a body, and a body was made for Him. When we die physically, we are alive spiritually, and God will make a body for us that will be eternal. God will take the elements of our earthly body and make a heavenly body for us! The heavenly body is changed so that it is not made out of flesh and blood, for that kind of body cannot live in heaven (v. 50). The next body we get will be an eternal body; the one we will have forever!

When you get tired and sick, remember that God is going to give you a body someday that will never tire, and never get sick. When you are not on top of it physically, let it cause you to focus more on heaven.

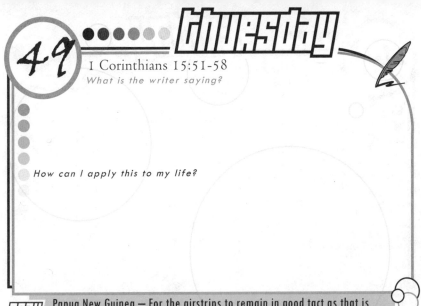

I Corinthians 15:51-58

What is the writer saying?

How can I apply this to my life?

PRAY Papua New Guinea — For the airstrips to remain in good tact as that is their source of supplies.

The question that must have been on the readers' minds by now would be "What about those who are alive when the Lord returns? What will happen to their bodies?" Paul answers that in this section. A mystery (v. 51) is something that had been previously hidden, but is now divinely revealed. Our bodies will be changed. We get the English word metamorphism from the Greek word Paul uses here. It means to totally change form. It will happen quickly, as quickly as we can blink our eyes (v. 52). The body we presently have will be changed to a body that is ready for heaven. Our present bodies are mortal bodies, but we will get immortal bodies - that is, they will last forever. What bodies they will be! The result of having an immortal body is that they will never die. Death will have been totally defeated and life will win. We will never fear death again (v. 55). All of the thanks and glory goes to the Lord for giving us the victory (v. 57). As a result of this great truth, we should stand firm in the faith. That is what the word steadfast means in verse 58. The word immovable means to refuse to let anything at all move you from your objective. In light of the reality that we will spend eternity with the Lord, we should not be swayed from serving the Lord with all of our hearts while on this earth. Paul encourages us to always give ourselves to serving the Lord, for we know that He will reward us when we go home to be with Him. The labor we do for Christ is not in vain (v. 58). That means that it is not empty or useless.

All of the above will happen when the Lord Jesus returns. That could happen at any time. Are you ready for the Lord to come back? Is there anything in your life that would embarrass you if the Lord came back right now? If so, repent and get right with the Lord today!

How can I apply this to my life?

Paul gives some closing instructions at the end of this letter. First, he talks about a special offering for the church in Jerusalem (v. 3). He tells them to take the offering on the first day of the week (v. 2). Why should they give on the first day of the week? Because the early church met for worship then. The sum that they should give is not specified here. All Paul says is that we should give that which is in keeping with our income. To some people ten percent might be a big sacrifice; to others fifty percent wouldn't even be a hardship. We should give as the Lord has moved us in our hearts. Our primary giving should go to our local church, but it is advisable to give to other worthy ministries as the Lord moves our hearts. In verse 5, Paul says that he will come to them after he goes through Macedonia. That area is what we know today as Greece. He hopes that he can stay the winter there. This shows that the apostle had a special link with these people. He has spent eighteen months there before and would love to be able to renew his relationships with the people. He gives some instructions concerning a potential visit by Timothy (vv. 10-11). Paul wants them to receive Timothy and to treat him well. He then tells them that Apollos was encouraged by Paul to go to Corinth now, but Apollos did not think it was the right time. He would come at a later date.

Life **stEP** Are you giving faithfully to the work of the Lord? Maybe you feel you do not have a lot of money. Give of what you have. Don't wait until you can afford it to give to the Lord. Be faithful in your giving to the Lord in the present time. If you are, it will be easier to be faithful in the future!

1 Corinthians 16:13-24

What is the writer saying?

How can I apply this to my life?

PRAY Bermuda — Pray that believers would have their hearts renewed with passion to follow Christ.

In this last section of the book, Paul gives some general exhortations and some greetings. In verses 13-14 he reminds them of five basic principles. First, he encourages them to be on their guard, to watch out for evil teaching and evil people. Secondly, he tells them to be steadfast, or firm in their faith. It means not to waver, but to hold to the fundamentals of the faith with all of their might. Third, he instructs them to be courageous (quit you like men). This reminds us of the words of the Lord to Joshua in Joshua 1:6-9. We need people of courage who are willing to stand firm in a day of wickedness. The fourth thing Paul encourages them with is the concept of being strong. It takes strength to stand firm for the Lord. The fifth and last in these two verses is to make sure that all of this is done in an attitude of love. Be sure to put other people's needs before our own. He then encourages the people to support Stephanas in the work of the ministry there. It is most likely that he was a pastor there or that the church met in his home. Paul sends them greetings (vv. 19-20) from the churches in Asia and from the people that were ministering with Paul. Paul always remembered people. He realized that true effective ministry is all about people. He was never too busy or too big for people. He then closes the letter with a warning and a loving farewell.

Life stEP

In this epistle, we see that Paul loved people enough to tell them the truth. We need to follow that example. At times, we are tempted to tell people what they want to hear as opposed to what they need to hear. Commit yourself today to be willing to tell people what they need to hear from the Word of God. Thank God today for the example of the Apostle Paul.

2 Timothy

Second Timothy is one of three books known as the Pastoral Epistles, the other two being 1 Timothy and Titus. They were written by the older Apostle Paul (in his 60's) to two younger men, Timothy and Titus (probably in their 30's). These young men were serving in pastoral-like roles, Timothy in Ephesus and Titus in Crete. Paul wanted tell them how to "behave" themselves "in the house of God the church of the living God" (1 Timothy 3:15).

Helpful to the understanding of the books individually is to take them collectively. Three themes resonate throughout all three: (1) church organization, (2) sound doctrine, and (3) consistent Christian living. While all three books touch on all three themes, each book has its particular emphasis, and those three themes follow the order in which they have been placed in most Bibles (though not written in that order). 1 Timothy emphasizes church organization; 2 Timothy, sound doctrine; and Titus, consistent Christian living. Charles Erdman, in writing of these three books early in the twentieth century, offered this summation of these three themes: "Church government is not an end in itself; it is of value only as it secures sound doctrine; and doctrine is of value only as it applies to real life." The point is this: you organize (1 Timothy) so that you can teach sound doctrine (2 Timothy), and you teach sound doctrine so that consistent Christian living (Titus) can result.

As Paul writes, Timothy is serving as his representative to the church in Ephesus. During Paul's first missionary journey (Acts 13-14), he and Barnabas preached the Gospel in the cities of Lystra and Derbe (Acts 14:1-20). Timothy, who had a Greek father and Jewish mother, responded to the message, leading Paul to address him as "my son in the faith" – my own "born-one in the faith" (1 Timothy 1:2; 2 Timothy 1:2). The book of Acts, as well as Paul's own letters, makes it clear that Timothy was a capable, trustworthy individual. He could be sent ahead or left behind to carry on the apostle's work (19:22; 20:4).

As to personality, there is some indication that he was somewhat timid in nature (2 Timothy 1:6-7), easily discouraged or frightened (1 Corinthians 16:10-11; 2 Timothy 1:8), and prone to sickness (1 Timothy 5:23).Yet, with all that being said, there is

2 timothy

no question that Paul placed great trust in him. His recommendation to the Philippian Church makes that crystal clear: "I have no man likeminded" (Philippians 2:20).

As to 2 Timothy itself, it is written from prison where Paul is awaiting execution. It is the last known writing we have from the great apostle's pen, and in effect it is his last will and testament, the most personal of all his letters (with the possible exception of the short letter written to Philemon). It is believed by many that Paul was arrested and placed in prison when Nero began his campaign of persecution shortly after Rome burned down in A.D. 64. Nero blamed the Christians for starting the fire. (After all, had they not predicted the world would come to an end in a great fire?) He also executed many of them in extremely cruel fashion, including Peter, who, according to one of the early church fathers, was crucified upside down. As Paul authors this second letter to his son-in-the-faith, Timothy, he was very much aware of his apparently soon-to-come death (by beheading).

This letter, as well as the other Pastoral Epistles, but even more so, is marked by the open sharing of feelings and thoughts. The major emphases of the book would include:

(1) Encouragement to be faithful... Timothy was somewhat timid and Paul, reminded of his tears (1:4), and used this letter to challenge him to hang in there. Paul was well aware that the Christian life is not played out on a ball field, but lived out on a battlefield, and that one of the essential characteristics of a faithful servant of Jesus Christ would be endurance in the midst of difficulties.

(2) To turn over leadership to Timothy... generations come and go, and knowing his time was short Paul wanted to be sure that leadership for the next generation was in place. Jack Wyrtzen, founder of Word of Life Fellowship, often remarked, "It is the responsibility of each generation to reach its generation for Christ."

(3) Paul's final and definitive testimony...a reminder to Timothy that he (Paul) had finished well, and an underlying, not-so-gentle hint that he (Timothy) too, should he desire a similar finish.

2 Timothy

Major theological emphases would include: (1) the coming apostasy of the last days, detailed in chapter 3. Paul warns Timothy that there will be difficult days ahead for believers, and so he passes on instruction as to how Christians are to behave and respond. Jesus had predicted such times would come (John 15:18-25; 16:33; 17:15-18). Paul himself had written earlier of those coming days (1 Thessalonians 3:1-8), and warned the Ephesian elders of them (Acts 10:29).

(2) The importance, value and application of Scripture, scattered throughout the book, including 1:13; 2:2,15; 3:14-17; 4:2-4. Paul was encouraging Timothy not only to pass on the truths of Scripture to the generations that follow, but also to pass on the basis of those truths, the inspired (God-breathed) Word of God. It is, as many conservative local church constitutions state: "The final authority (the supreme standard) for all faith (what we believe) and practice (how we behave)."

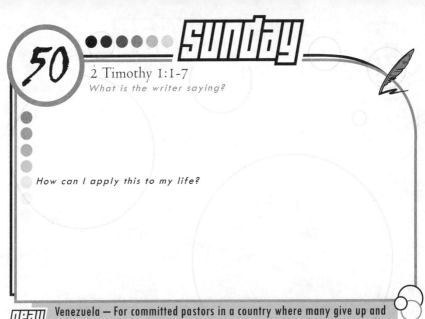

How can I apply this to my life?

PRAY   Venezuela — For committed pastors in a country where many give up and return to secular jobs.

Paul, as in his earlier letter to Timothy, introduces himself as an apostle of Jesus Christ, a title unnecessary if this letter was for Timothy's eyes only, for Timothy certainly knew Paul's position. Nevertheless, as in his other pastorals, Paul was providing Timothy with the credentials necessary to carry out his task of leading the church of Ephesus. While some might choose to downplay the words of their young pastor, they could hardly do the same with the words of one who was clearly recognized as one sent from God, with a message to deliver. Adding the words by the will of God, Paul makes it clear that he understood his apostleship was an assignment from God. This letter, with the possible exception of Philemon, is the most personal of all that Paul wrote. Written from a Roman dungeon, it is often looked upon as Paul's last will and testament, and was the final book from his pen. He addresses Timothy as his dearly beloved son (or his own born-one), and in that designation makes it clear that he and Timothy had a very special relationship, that of father and son in the faith (see 1 Timothy 1:2). The relationship engendered both deep concern as well as thanksgiving in Paul's heart for his young protégé (vv. 3-4).

Concerned that Timothy's apparently timid nature could curtail his ministry (see tears, v. 4), Paul reminded him of his faith (found first in his mother and grandmother, v. 5) and of his gifting (v. 6). That gifting was the enabling resource that Timothy was to use to carry out his ministry; it was already present, not something to be added to his character, and was to be rekindled. Broadening the thought of gifting Paul challenges Timothy to remember that neither he nor Paul (us in verse 7) had been given "the spirit of fear; but of power... love, and of a sound mind" (v. 7).

Life stEP

Timothy had Paul's letters; we have much more, the entire Word of God. He was gifted; so are we. Let us see to it that we use what we have been given (and it is not fear) to perform our service for the Lord.

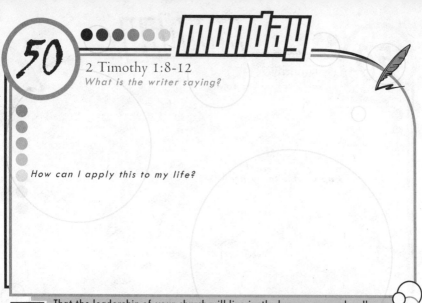
How can I apply this to my life?

pray That the leadership of your church will live justly, love mercy, and walk humbly with God (Micah 6:8).

Aware that Timothy's timidity could cause enough shame for him to back away from an effective ministry, as well as from Paul (as a prisoner) himself, the apostle encourages his young follower to be a "partaker of the afflictions of the gospel" (v. 8). Suffering is part of the believer's calling and when it comes, should be accepted as part of God's will. Furthermore, when it comes, it will be accompanied by the power of God, always available for encouragement and strength.

Verse 8, which ends with God, is followed by the work of God in salvation, ("hath saved... and called us"). He does so "not according to our works, but according to his own purpose and grace (v. 9). That purpose, once hidden, is now revealed through Paul. God did not eliminate death through the cross, but He did disarm it. For the believer, its sting is gone (cp. 1 Corinthians 15:55-57) and Christ has brought "life and immortality" (v. 10)...the condition of never dying to

light (they were in the shadows in the Old Testament).

The believer is called to holiness (v. 9; 1 Peter 1:15-16). Writing to persecuted believers, Peter advocated holy living... lives consecrated to God, and lives befitting our true identity and position in Christ (1 Peter 2:10-11). Paul's challenge to Timothy is similar, using himself as an example. He had suffered many things for the cause of the Gospel (vv. 11-12) but was never ashamed. Why? Because: "I know whom I have believed (a continuing attitude of belief with trust), and am persuaded that he is able to keep that which I have committed unto him" (his very being) (v. 12)...and that which God committed to both he and Timothy, (v. 14), God had committed the Gospel to Paul (1 Timothy 1:11); he was passing it on to Timothy (1 Timothy 6:20; 2 Timothy 4:7), who was to pass it on to faithful men...(and) others also (2 Timothy 2:2).

The believer has a choice when suffering comes: to back away in shame from his commitment to Christ hoping to avoid pain; or to accept it as part of God's purpose in his life and meet it head on with the provided power of God.

2 Timothy 1:13-18

What is the writer saying?

How can I apply this to my life?

---

pray
Word of Life Island Teen Camp leadership and staff, as they minister in camper's lives this summer.

In verse 12, we found Paul using himself as one who steadfastly remained faithful to his commitment. In verses 13-14, Timothy is exhorted to maintain a similar commitment. He is to "hold fast the form of sound words." Form can mean example or pattern (1 Timothy 1:16). Paul both preached and lived the Gospel, establishing a pattern for others to follow (1 Corinthians 11:1). Sound comes from a Greek word that gives us our English word hygiene, meaning healthy. Words means teaching (in Titus 1:9 it is "sound doctrine," also 1 Timothy 1:10). Taken together the challenge is to provide healthy teaching, for the opposite (cp. 2 Timothy, 2:17) could result in a crippling disease.

"That good thing that was committed unto thee" (v. 14), is a clear reference to the Gospel (1 Timothy 6:20). Having received it, Timothy was to keep it, and was reminded that only by the power of the Spirit could he do so. Keep means to guard, and coupled with 1 Timothy 6:20 ("keep that which is committed to thy trust") means the Gospel has been placed on deposit with Timothy (a banking analogy). It is to be guarded, kept, and available for use on demand.

Remember, this letter is being written from a prison dungeon where Paul awaits trial and subsequent beheading. Circumstances are dire. Desertion among believers has escalated. The some of 1 Timothy (1:6; 1:19; 5:15; 6:10; 6:21) have become the hyperbolic "all" of 2 Timothy (1:15; 4:16), many being led by two deserters named Phygellus and Hermogenes. Yet even in troubled times God provides relief, and He does so here in the person of Onesiphorus (one who brings profit or benefit) This godly man was probably a deacon in Ephesus when Paul was there, for verse 18 can be translated: "…and in how many things he fully played the deacon…" He came to Rome, searched hard for Paul, found him and served him without fear or shame (v. 16).

Life stEP

Onesiphorus was unashamed to serve Christ and his fellow believers. We should do likewise.

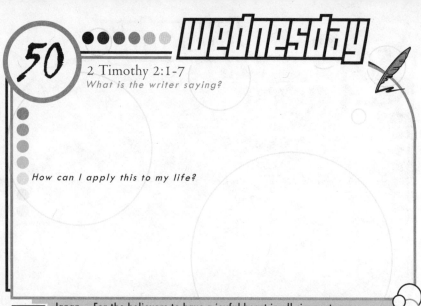

2 Timothy 2:1-7

What is the writer saying?

How can I apply this to my life?

PRAY | Japan — For the believers to have a joyful heart in all circumstances.

"Thou therefore, my son (an expression of strong affection), be strong in the grace (undeserved divine help) that is in Christ Jesus" (v. 1). With these words Paul both exhorts and challenges Timothy to be faithful to his calling, while at the same time drawing a contrast between that which he desires for his young son-in-the-faith, and the defectors of the previous chapter (1:15). They had turned their backs upon Paul and the Gospel ministry, but by depending on the grace that is in Christ Jesus and its accompanying power, and not upon his own, Timothy would not have to repeat their error nor experience their fate.

After that begins a series of pictures demonstrating the characteristics of a faithful servant of Jesus Christ. He is to first be faithful as a teacher (v. 2). That which he has heard he is to pass on to others. In fact, Timothy is to be part of an endless chain of passing on truth to succeeding generations

(i.e., God to Paul to Timothy to faithful men to others also). This is the same procedure laid out by Christ in the Great Commission (Matthew 28:19-20), that of making disciples (discipleship).

In vv. 3-6 Paul gives three additional illustrations of faithfulness to demonstrate to Timothy the seriousness of his task. The first is that of a soldier, and as such he is to (a) endure hardness; (b) not entangle himself with the affairs of this life (not that they are wrong — just don't get caught up in them); and (c) seek to please his commander, and for the believer that is Jesus Christ. The second illustration is that of an athlete. He is to "strive for masteries" (contend in the games), but to do so lawfully. To receive the victor's crown, his life and ministry must follow biblical directives. The third illustration is that of a hardworking farmer. Only through strenuous, diligent effort will a bountiful harvest result.

Life stEP

We should follow Paul's example and ask the Lord to give us understanding to please Him.

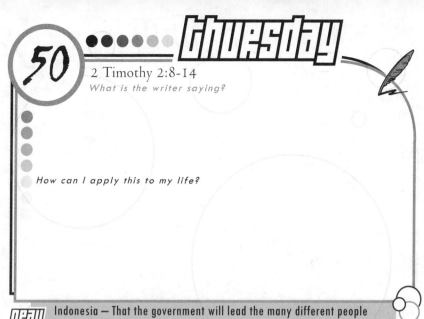

2 Timothy 2:8-14

What is the writer saying?

How can I apply this to my life?

PRAY Indonesia — That the government will lead the many different people groups wisely and fairly.

Here Paul directs the readers' thoughts, as well as ours, to Jesus Christ and His resurrection. Of the seed of David points to His humanity and the fulfillment of the promises God made to David (cp. 2 Samuel 7:16). Raised from the dead focuses attention on the deity of Christ, and the power of God demonstrated in the resurrection (cp. Romans 1:1-4). To Paul, the paramount truth of the Gospel (he called it my Gospel – Romans 2:16; 16:25; 1 Corinthians 15:1), was the resurrection. That Gospel of his (v. 8) is what brought about his present distress (v. 9). He is chained like a common criminal, because he preached it. Yet "the Word of God is not bound" (v. 9). In fact, in prison he could still preach the Word. In fact, as many have pointed out, he often had a captive audience, the Roman soldiers to whom he was chained. That being the case, he was able to "endure all the things for the elect's sake."

He wanted to see the salvation resulting in these who believed, culminating in eternal glory, salvation's final state (v. 10).

In verses 11-13 we have the longest of the five faithful sayings contained in the pastorals (1 Timothy 1:15; 3:1; 4:9; 2 Timothy 2:11-13; Titus 3:8). Thought to be prophetic sayings by the New Testament prophets in the early church, they summarized their beliefs in a pre-canon age. The theme here is Christ's death and resurrection, and our union with Christ in those significant historical events (v. 11). "If we suffer (better: endure), we shall also reign with him," but, "if we deny (fail to endure) him, he also will deny us (the reign or reward that could have been)" (v. 12). Then comes a contrast of God's faithfulness versus man's unfaithfulness (v. 13). The latter can never abrogate the former. For Christ to abandon His own would be contrary to His nature (cp. John 10:27-30; Hebrews 10:23; 13:5).

Life stEP

God faithfully fulfilled His promise by sending the Redeemer. Pause now to thank Him for His faithfulness and recommit yourself to be faithful to Him.

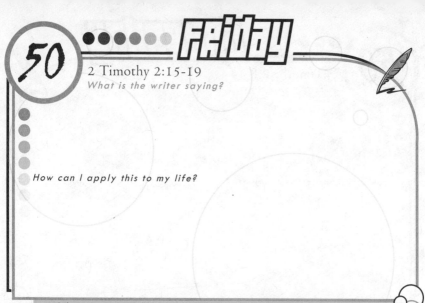

2 Timothy 2:15-19

What is the writer saying?

How can I apply this to my life?

PRAY Cuba — For more Bibles, books, and teachers to train the leaders and pastors.

Paul's charge to Timothy continues, "Don't get caught up in fighting over words!" The result is no profit and the subverting (turning upside down) of the hearers. Positively, however, (v. 15) "study (be eager, zealous, diligent) to shew (present oneself for service) thyself approved (accepted after testing) unto God, a workman that needeth not to be ashamed, rightly dividing (cutting straight) the word of truth." Proper preaching, says Paul, goes straight ahead, never veering left or right, always correctly handling the Word, never twisting or changing the truth.

Having been attacked by false teachers, Timothy was warned to: (a) Stick to the essentials. Don't argue over empty words and philosophies (v. 16) (b) Rightly divide the Word. Failing to do so gives room to false teachers to promote false doctrines which, unchecked, eats like a gangrene (Greek- gangraina, i.e., a malignant sore that eats away healthy tissue) (v. 17). These false teachers (two are named) erred (wandered away) concerning the truth (v. 18), probably teaching there was no bodily resurrection, that the resurrection of believers had already occurred. Early Gnosticism emphasized a spiritual resurrection over a future bodily resurrection. Unchecked, this sort of spiritualization will destroy weaker believers, because the resurrection is central to the Gospel, hence the need for proper exegesis. "Nevertheless" (v. 19)…in spite of the efforts of the false teachers…"the foundation of God standeth sure." Exchanging his negative tone for a note of encouragement, Paul…based on the tense of the verb…indicates that he saw the truth of God standing firm, not only in the past, but also in the present (cp. Isaiah 40:8). Armed with that truth, and knowing to whom we belong, the challenge is to live a life of purity.

Life stEP

Pray for those whose job it is to preach the Word of God. The souls of their listeners may be dependent upon their rightly dividing the Word of Truth.

How can I apply this to my life?

PRAY For the missionaries from your church to find favor with the governments of the foreign countries in which they serve.

Verse 20 employs the phrase *a great house*. A reference to the church, the household of God (1 Timothy 3:15), in which are two general types of vessels: those of honor and much value (gold and silver), and those of dishonor and little value (wood and earth – pottery). The emphasis is not on the usefulness of the vessels (for the latter are probably more useful than the former that are saved for special occasions) but the value or quality of the vessel. Wood and pottery will eventually chip and break and must be replaced (a picture of false teachers whose worthlessness is recognized and leads to removal). This is not true with gold or silver. Their value is retained.

The honored vessel is to purge himself from those who are dishonored (v. 21). Contamination must be avoided. The results of doing so: (1) he is sanctified – set apart for a holy purpose; (2) he is meet – profitable for the master's use (master – Greek despot – strong term denoting God's total authority);

and (3) prepared (ready) for every good work. Having avoided contamination, the honored vessel is to maintain his value by staying clean. This is a two-step process. Negatively – Flee: avoid, shun youthful lusts (more than simply sexual, but also pride, ego, power, love of money, etc.) Positively – Follow: pursue after, righteousness, faith, charity, peace (1 Timothy 6:11). Both steps are vital. To fail in either will render one's ministry valueless.

Paul then cautions Timothy to avoid "foolish and unlearned (stupid) questions (arguments)...they do gender (breed) strifes (quarrels)." He had given similar instructions earlier (1 Timothy 1:4,7; 4:7; 6:20; 2 Timothy 2:16). He then calls Timothy the servant (doulos) of the Lord, and as such he has no will of his own. He is to be governed by his master in every respect. The chapter's latter verses (vv. 23-26) explain how to deal with problems in God's house so that strife and contention are avoided.

Let us also flee, follow, and avoid.

Life stEP

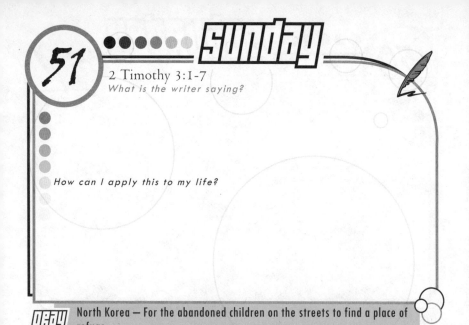

2 Timothy 3:1-7
What is the writer saying?

How can I apply this to my life?

pray North Korea — For the abandoned children on the streets to find a place of refuge.

Here we see the necessity of chapter two's exhortation. The theme is "the last days" (v. 1) and the character of men in those days. Those last days began with the life and ministry of Christ (Hebrews 1:2), and will continue until Christ returns. They will be difficult days marked by apostasy (a falling away – the act of professed Christians who deliberately reject the revealed truth of the deity of Christ and the effectiveness of His cross work). As Christ's return draws closer, man's evil characteristics (vv. 2-5, 18) will intensify (v. 13). Civilized behavior will completely break down.

Numbered among those characteristics are lovers of their own selves and covetous, the twin sins from which all the others flow. That such is the case can be seen in such characteristics as unthankful, unholy, high-minded (conceited) and lovers of pleasure more than lovers of God. Without natural affection and disobedient to parents suggest the breaking up of society as God intended it to be. Striking one's father was as bad as murder in Roman law; abusing a parent in Greek culture caused disinheritance; and honoring parents was the fifth of the Jews' Ten Commandments. Today's divorce statistics show how rapidly we are moving away from God's standards and how rapidly we seem to be moving to the end of the age. All of the age-end characteristics can be found on the pages of today's newspapers, further indication that Christ's return is drawing near.

Accompanying all of the above is a form of godliness, but that is all that it is…a form… for the true power of godliness is denied. The apostate religionists of the last days go through the motions and maintain their external forms, but they have not experienced the dynamic power of true Christianity that results in changed lives. From such, turn away.

The dark days in which we live have only one remedy: the Gospel of Jesus Christ.

51 MONDAY

2 Timothy 3:8-12

What is the writer saying?

How can I apply this to my life?

PRAY — Ghana — Pray for God to send laborers to the 15,000 villages with no bodies of believers.

Paul uses Jannes and Jambres (not mentioned in the Old Testament, but found in Jewish tradition opposing Moses) as examples of men in the past that resisted God's truth. They were men of corrupt minds, similar to the apostates of Paul's day (and ours) who cannot understand truth (cp. Romans 1:21, 22; Ephesians 4:17, 18; 1 Timothy 6:5), and reprobate concerning the faith (v. 8). Like Jannes and Jambres, this new group of truth-deniers will not get very far for "their folly shall be manifest unto all" (v. 9). Truth always triumphs in the end.

Verse 10 begins a new section of what can be considered Paul's final advice to Timothy. To encourage him to hang in there, he gives a strong word of personal testimony. He begins with "But thou...," demonstrating the difference between Timothy and the men Paul just referenced and continues: "hast fully known (you've observed)"...and notes that which his observation revealed: a life-style (that of Paul's) worth emulating. It begins with doctrine (teaching), goes on to manner of life (conduct), purpose (chief aim), and faith (the Gospel). To underscore that none of the above came easily, he mentions some personal characteristics that are vital when persecution comes to those who desire to live godly lives (v. 12): "longsuffering, charity, patience (endurance)." He reminds Timothy that he had endured numerous persecutions, but out of them all, the Lord delivered him (v. 11; cp. Acts 14:19, 20; Psalm 34:17).

Paul moves from his own experiences to a word of encouragement by noting that persecution, in some sense at least, is the lot of all non-compromising believers. God does not always deliver His children from persecution but, as Paul has demonstrated and as Scripture testifies, He promises to be with them as they go through it (Matthew 28:20b).

Endurance demonstrates the seriousness of our commitment to Christ. Keep on keeping on!

415

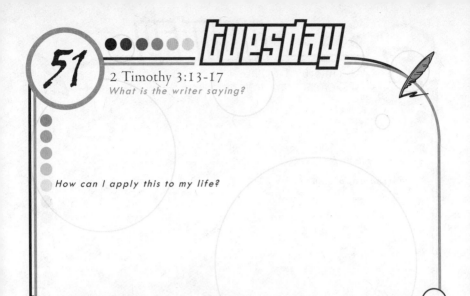

51 — tuesday

2 Timothy 3:13-17

What is the writer saying?

How can I apply this to my life?

PRAY Netherlands Antilles — For the Papiamento Bible that was published in 1997 to be an impact on those who use it.

Verse 13 is a transitional verse linking Paul's charge to Timothy (v. 14), and the importance behind it to the offenders described earlier in the chapter. "Therefore, Timothy, remember what you've learned, and who taught you" (your mother, grandmother and Paul). The ladies taught him the Old Testament and pointed him to the Messiah. Paul comes along and provides the information that Christ indeed was the Messiah, and Timothy responded in faith.

Verses 14-17 are the key verses in 2 Timothy, demonstrating the unparalleled value of the Scriptures. Its words bring about salvation (v. 15) and equip us for productive Christian living (v. 17). Its effectiveness is because "all Scripture is given by inspiration of God" (one word in the Greek: God-breathed). Inspiration... the out-breathing of God...was the process that produced the product: the Word of God. Because it is God's Word, it is profitable (v. 16). It takes the believer and guides all his footsteps, from start to finish. One writer (Guy King) describes those steps this way: (1) FORWARD STEPS – doctrine, teaching. How to move ahead in the Christian life. (2) FALSE STEPS – reproof. The pointing out of one's faults. (3) FALTERING STEPS – correction. Learning not only how we have gone wrong, but how to get right. (Cp. Psalm 119:9; John 7:17). (4) FIRST STEPS – instruction. This is a word that would be used for the training of a child. That training is to be in righteousness. For all these purposes, the Holy Scriptures are both highly profitable and highly effective. By faith Timothy became a child (teknon – born one) of God (1 Timothy 1:2). Now, by utilizing the Scriptures, he has grown into a man of God. "The result is good works" (v. 17).

Life stEP

The title man of God usually reserved for prophets in the Old Testament can today belong to all believers. Let's live up to it!

2 Timothy 4:1-4

What is the writer saying?

How can I apply this to my life?

pray Panama — For this nation of diversity and potential to be used to bless the world.

Be reminded as we work our way through this fourth and final chapter of the book that this is the last chapter we have from the pen of the Apostle Paul. As he begins to bring this letter to a close, Paul's appeal to Timothy to hang in there comes into clear focus. To support his appeal he reminds Timothy that Jesus will one day return in judgment (v. 1) and he is answerable to the Lord as to how he carries out his ministry. This idea of judgment is a primary theme of the apostle, especially as it relates to the life and ministry of believers (1 Corinthians 3:11-17; 5:10).

The ministry Timothy is to have is spelled out in verse 2 where five exhortations are given. The final four flow quite naturally out of the first, which is: (1) "Preach the Word," for the Word is the foundation of any ministry. It is to be done (2) with urgency: "instant in season, out of season..." Whether the time is convenient or inconvenient, or circumstances favorable or unfavorable...just do it!

(3) Included should be reproof (to correct, convince) – show them how they have done wrong. (4) Rebuke- show them how wrong they were to do wrong. Finally, (5) exhort – show them that they must right the wrong and not repeat it. There is an implication in this Preach the Word command. It is not preach about the Word, or even from the Word, but preach the Word, which implies knowledge. This makes study (remember 2:15) of the Word vital. All of these exhortations are to be accompanied with long-suffering (great patience) and doctrine (careful instruction) (v. 2).

Why the command? Because the time will come (v. 3) when men will not want the Word. They will want to hear what makes them feel good, (having itching ears). Given time those itching ears, that are satisfied with shallow religious entertainment, will soon become deaf ears, as they turn away from the truth to man-made fables (v. 4).

Life stEP

Preach the Word. The instruction is to Timothy, but applies to us as well. Faithfully pass on the Word of God.

2 Timothy 4:5-8

What is the writer saying?

How can I apply this to my life?

PRAY Word of Life Area Missionaries and Local Church Ministries staff to be encouraged.

Earlier (v. 1) Timothy is told to "preach the Word." Why? "…the time will come" when men will not want "sound doctrine" (v. 3) or "truth," but will turn to "fables" (v. 4). In light of that, Timothy is given four instructions in verse 5: "Watch" - be sober in judgment. "Endure afflictions" – the work of the ministry in not without its price. "Do the work of an evangelist" – remember to evangelize the lost (a difficult, but still required, task for someone timid). "Make full proof of thy ministry" – accomplish the purpose to which you've been called. Those instructions are valid not only for Timothy, but for all of God's children.

In verses 6-8, Paul makes it clear it is time for him to move on and pass the torch to others. His reflective words form perhaps the greatest exit testimony ever recorded. He has come to the end of his life with no regrets. He goes on (v. 6) to illustrate in two ways his victorious view of death. First,

"I am now ready to be offered" (poured out like a drink offering). He considered his life and ministry an offering to God (Romans 15:16; Philippians 2:17). Second, "the time of my departure is at hand." It is time to set sail, take down the tent and move on (2 Peter 1:14-15).

He then uses three illustrations (v. 7) that demonstrate his finishing well. "I have fought a good fight," i.e., the act of a soldier (2:3-4). "I have finished my course," i.e., the goal of an athlete (2:5). "I have kept the faith," i.e., the responsibility of a steward of the Gospel. Having done so (1 Timothy 1:11), Paul expects the same from Timothy (1 Timothy 6:20, 2 Timothy 1:14).

"Henceforth," (v. 8) a reward is waiting, the end result of a lifetime of faithful service to Christ the righteous judge, who when He returns, would bring with Him rewards for those who served God faithfully during their earthly sojourn (Matthew 5:10-12).

Life stEP What a joy to have no regrets and to know that you have done what God asks of you. Follow Paul's example!

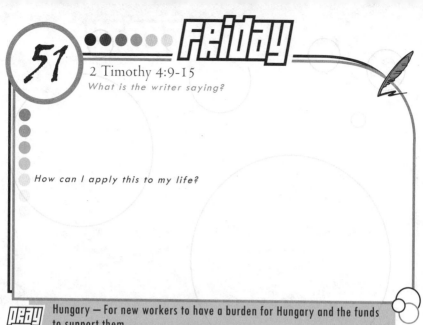

51

FRIDAY

2 Timothy 4:9-15

What is the writer saying?

How can I apply this to my life?

PRAY Hungary — For new workers to have a burden for Hungary and the funds to support them.

Following his exit testimony (vv. 6-8), Paul requests Timothy to: "come shortly unto me (v. 9)," and "come before winter" (v. 21) implying that when winter comes, travel will be more difficult, so an early arrival would be preferable. "The cloak that I left at Troas with Carpus, when thou comest, bring with thee" (v. 13), for it will provide some comfort in the cold surroundings of his prison cell.

Paul then begins to list some of his co-workers (he always recognized their importance and was grateful for their assistance). The first one mentioned, however; triggered unpleasant memories. Demas, who at one time had been one of Paul's trusted co-workers (cp. Colossians 4:14; Philemon 24), had deserted him for what the world had to offer (v. 10) and, apparently when he was most needed. Crescens was off to Galatia on ministry and Titus to Dalmatia as Paul's emissary. "Only Luke is with me" (v. 11), but for one afflicted with some physical problem as was Paul (2 Corinthians 12:7-9), who better to have as a companion than a medical doctor? "And bring John Mark." This was the young man who had earlier deserted Paul but had since proved himself (Colossians 4:10). He was now profitable for the ministry (v. 11).

Besides the cloak, Paul requests his books and parchments. The books may have been some of Paul's own writings, and parchments Paul's personal copies of Old Testament Scriptures. In verses 14-15 Paul refers to an Alexander, who in some way did Paul evil. Regardless of how it was done, Paul shows no bitterness or get-even attitude. At the same time, Paul cautions Timothy to be on guard against him.

Life **stEP**

The ministry of one's co-workers can make or break the ministry being performed. Thank God for those who serve faithfully with you, and pray that like John Mark, you also will be ministry-profitable.

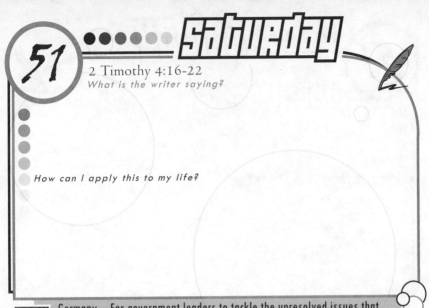

2 Timothy 4:16-22

What is the writer saying?

How can I apply this to my life?

PRAY Germany — For government leaders to tackle the unresolved issues that face them.

In this passage, the forgiving attitude of Christ is seen in Paul. Although many had abandoned him, he asked the Lord not to hold them accountable for their actions (v. 16). He writes, "At my first answer" (defense) – the preliminary hearing prior to trial – "no man stood with me." No one appeared to serve as defense attorney, though that was a common practice. Furthermore, "all men forsook me." Those who could have testified for him were also absent. Yet Paul, in spite of their abandonment, like Christ (Luke 23:34) and Stephen (Acts 7:60) before him, exhibits the grace of God he himself had experienced (1 Timothy 1:12-15).

Left alone (but not alone – "the Lord stood with me," v. 17), Paul conducted his own defense and took the opportunity to preach the Gospel… "that by me the preaching might be fully known." He left nothing out. Even as he said to the Ephesian elders in Acts 20:27, "I… declare unto you all the counsel of God," he used this opportunity to preach the complete Gospel about which he had written (1 Corinthians 15:1-4). His defense was unusual; it said little about him, but much about the Lord, "that all the Gentiles might hear." The Lord again (2 Corinthians 11:16-33), delivered him "out of the mouth of the lion," a metaphoric expression in Paul's day to express deliverance from extreme danger and a biblical image Paul was familiar with (Psalm 22:21; Daniel 6:22).

Paul extends final greetings (vv. 19-22), naming nine of his co-workers. His benediction (v. 22) is two-fold. Personal to Timothy: "The Lord Christ Jesus be with thy spirit." Corporately to all believers: "Grace be with you (all). Amen.

Life stEP Grace… the watchword of Paul's life. He had experienced it, and he passed it along to others. May the forgiving Spirit that prevailed in him permeate our lives as well.

The prophet's name means comfort. The name for the city of Capernaum on the northern shore of the Sea of Galilee translates, village of Nahum. He wrote around 620 B.C. and condemned Assyria, the nation who deported the ten northern tribes in 722 B.C. and attacked Judea in 701 B.C. The great Assyrian king, Ashurbanipal, ruled for forty-two years (669-627 B.C.) but Nineveh fell just fourteen years later! Nahum foretells the destruction of the capital of Assyria, Nineveh, which was fulfilled in 612 B.C. when Nebuchadnezzar's father Nabopolassar (a Babylonian) and Cyaxares (a Mede) defeat it. As predicted in Nahum 2:6, a flood helped wash away part of the wall. It was so utterly destroyed that the site was lost to history until found by archaeologists in the 19th century. Nahum also mentions the fall of Thebes in Egypt, which happened in 663 B.C. (Nahum 3:8). An outline for this short book:

God's Might	1
Nineveh Judged	2
Nineveh Condemned	3

In Christ's day, the Pharisees rather sarcastically asked if any prophet comes from Galilee, because in their day the Galilean region was considered backward. Not one, but two important prophets actually did come from the Galilee – Nahum and Jonah.

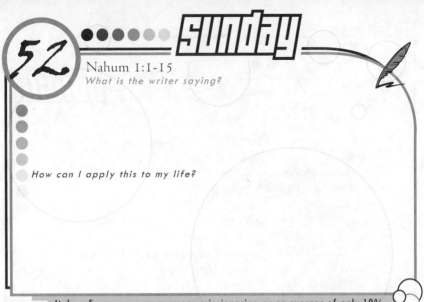

sunday

Nahum 1:1-15

What is the writer saying?

How can I apply this to my life?

PRAY Italy — For perseverance among missionaries, as an average of only 10% return for a second term.

The word burden can also be translated oracle. It is a heavy prophecy, fraught with gloom and doom. Nineveh was the capital of Assyria, situated on the Tigris River. Assyria was the most ferocious empire in the ancient world, piling up human heads and impaling the citizens of conquered cities alive on wooden stakes. Jonah was dispatched to evangelize Nineveh, much to his chagrin. Amazingly, the people of his day, including the king, repented and judgment was temporarily averted. Unfortunately, the revival did not last and by Nahum's day, 100 years later, God announces that the judgment will fall. It didn't fall for another 100 years, but fall eventually it did. Nahum is called an Elkoshite which refers to his hometown. Unfortunately, no one knows where it was located. The strongest tradition places Elkosh in the extreme southern portion of Judea in the territory of the tribe of Simeon. Verse 4 refers to places normally known for their beautiful vegetation. Bashan was located on the high plateau of what today is called the Golan Heights. It was famous for its good grazing lands and luxurious cattle (Amos 4:1). Carmel (orchard) was famous for its olive trees. It is the mountainous ridge overlooking the Valley of Armageddon. Elijah challenged Baal (the agricultural god) on Carmel. Lebanon (white mountain) was well-watered and in addition to the flowers mentioned, was also famous for the beautiful cedars of Lebanon. The Tigris River flooded and broke down her walls enabling her quick defeat (v. 8). Verse 11 refers to the wicked exploits of Sennacherib (who attacked King Hezekiah in 701 B.C.).

Life stEP

Verse 15 contrasts Nineveh's destruction with the salvation God offers to Jerusalem. Paul quotes it in Romans and applies it to our spiritual salvation.

The author of the Book of Malachi (the great Italian prophet!?!) is called Malachi which means, the messenger of Jehovah. Either this was the man's given name or it is the title for an unnamed prophet who is functioning as God's messenger. The book is dated to the period of 450-400 B.C. Ezra's revival (Ezra 7) is dated 458 B.C. Nehemiah ministered 445-433 B.C. and ???-425 BC. Since Nehemiah 5, 10, and 13 have similar themes; it is felt that Malachi also ministered at this time. Notice: 1) Criticism of the laxity of the priests (1:6); 2) Mixed marriages (2:10) and 3); Neglected tithes (3). Malachi is distinguished by the following features:

1) It has been about 100 years since the return of some of the Jews from the Babylonian captivity. Things have not gone as planned. To begin with, only a small percentage of the Jews returned from Babylon (perhaps less than five percent!) In Ezra 1-6, Haggai, and Zechariah, we see the struggles they experienced getting the temple built and their Jewish national life re-established. As time passed, few Jews joined them and the exciting prophecies of the coming Messiah in Zechariah did not materialize, perhaps discouragement and spiritual apathy set in.

2) This is the last prophetic voice from heaven for the 400 years leading up to the actual birth of Messiah. God has always provided adequate information for His people to be without excuse for not obeying and believing that all He has promised will come to pass. On the other hand, it is only normal for humans to prefer a current supernatural communication as opposed to reading information given centuries earlier.

We have no real knowledge of time spans between supernatural communication prior to Abraham. Starting with Abraham, we see thirteen years of silence between God's first and second communication with Abraham. God spoke with the other patriarchs, but then the heavens were silent for the 400 years of enslavement in Egypt. Now the heavens would fall silent again for another 400 years. This does not mean that nothing significant took place on earth. Actually, great political and military activity took place that set the stage for the coming of Christ under the great Roman Empire in the fullness of time as Galatians 4:4 says! Even while Paul was enjoying supernatural revelation, he anticipated another silence (1 Corinthians 13:8).

malachi

Here we are in the transition from the Twentieth to the Twenty-First Century (since Christ!). We too have experienced silence, but we too wait for the heavens to open once again!

3) Malachi is in the form of twenty-three questions. Each question is preceded by an affirmation by Jehovah of a particular wrong behavior followed by Israel's hypothetical protesting question. The defensive question is then refuted by Jehovah. (cf. 1:2).

4) Malachi criticizes ritualistic/ hypocritical worship. Therefore, the theme of the book could be called challenge to true worship.

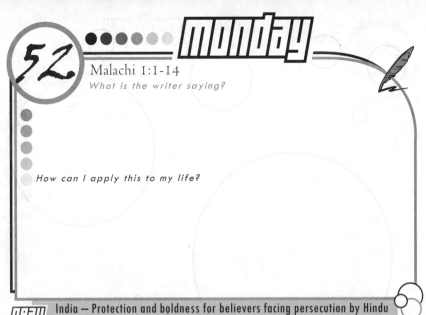

Malachi 1:1-14

What is the writer saying?

How can I apply this to my life?

pray India — Protection and boldness for believers facing persecution by Hindu extremists.

The Lord affirms His love, but the Israelites of Malachi's day question it. The Lord answers with an explanation of His elective choice of Jacob over his older twin brother Esau. His hate of Esau's descendants is in the sense that they are not the chosen people. Individuals from that line, however, can experience God's love in salvation and in fact, unbelievers among the chosen people will also experience God's wrath. Amalek was a grandson of Esau and the Amalekites were Israel's first enemy as they came out of Egypt. The descendants of Esau became the nation of Edom (red in honor of Esau.). They frequently caused Israel trouble, especially harassing her when attacked by other enemies. They were displaced from their territory by the Nabateans around 400 B.C. The last known Edomites in history were the Idumeans from which the family of the Herods came. Lord of hosts (Jehovah Sabaoth) occurs twenty times in Malachi. After a brief statement about Jehovah's love for Israel, Malachi launches into a long section describing Israel's contempt for God (1:6 3:15). Certainly all the people are guilty, but notice that the religious leaders (the priests) are rebuked! Polluted (1:7) occurs just eleven times in the Old Testament, but three of those occurrences are here in the little book of Malachi. It is used in Daniel 1:8 to refer to Nebuchadnezzar's pagan food. They had profaned the Lord's Table. Profane means to treat as common. The root of the word refers to a doorstep that everyone entering the room steps on. In English, the word vulgar carries the same connotation. The law required and unblemished male animal, these people were bringing damaged female animals (v. 14, in Hebrew).

No matter how dark the hour, the proper response is to trust the Lord and demonstrate that trust by continued obedience!

Malachi 2:1-9

What is the writer saying?

How can I apply this to my life?

pray Pray for the salvation and protection of the emergency service workers in your community.

One of the chief functions of the priest was to be a pastor to the people. They were to help the people confess and make atonement for sin. They were to lead them in worship. They were to bless them, both in the general performing of these duties and in a verbal blessing similar to our practice of closing a worship service with a benediction. The curse that God would send would most likely be agricultural since that was one of the main reasons the people sought the Lord's favor and the priests lived off of the food they brought as offerings. Having successful descendants to carry on the family name in honor was important. The innards of the sacrificial animals, including the manure, were to be burned outside of the camp (Exodus 29:14). Instead, God says he will smear the refuse on these hypocritical priests and they will be carried outside the camp of Israel! In verse 4, God refers to a covenant with Levi. This was not with the man Levi but the tribe (Exodus 29:9). In Numbers 25, a Levite by the name of Phinehas defended God's honor by killing an Israelite who grossly sinned against God. God responds by promising Phinehas that his descendants would enjoy a perpetual priesthood. Eventually his family line became the high priestly line and in fact in Ezekiel that same line is promised the priesthood in the Messianic Temple. Therefore Levi here refers to his descendants and in particular, his illustrious descendant, Phinehas. Instruction in the law was one of the responsibilities of the priests. These had miserably failed and would be judged. Contemptible (2:9) is the same word they used to despise the Lord's Table (1:7). They would be treated as they had treated the Lord.

If we expect God's blessings then we should do things His way.

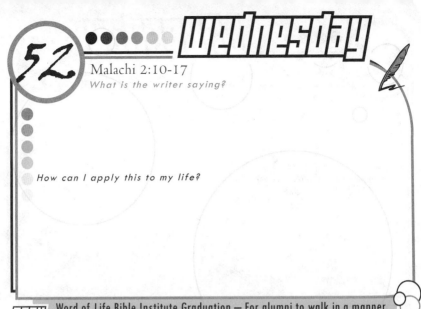

Malachi 2:10-17

What is the writer saying?

How can I apply this to my life?

PRAY Word of Life Bible Institute Graduation — For alumni to walk in a manner worthy of the Lord (Colossians 1:10).

Verse 10 establishes the principle of loyalty to the community of the chosen people. The Israelites had one father, Abraham. By definition, they also were to have one God, the God of Abraham. By marrying foreign wives, they were violating this brotherhood both biologically and religiously (as the foreign wives worshipped other gods). This phenomenon can be stated: "Marry me; marry my religion." It is the covenant of our fathers (plural) in the sense that it takes faithfulness down through the generations to maintain the spiritual purity. Deuteronomy 7 lists the nations with which the Israelites were not to establish marriage contracts. The only exceptions were in situations where the pagan women converted to Jehovah (like Ruth). Dealt treacherously (2:11) occurs five times in 2:10-16. It usually is used of adultery. Israel was already married to Jehovah. By marrying pagan women and worshipping their gods, they were committing spiritual adultery. Ironically, the Hebrew word for married is the word Baal – the same word as the pagan god of agriculture! God also condemns Israel for her contempt of Him as demonstrated in divorce (2:13 16) and then in impiety (2:17). Verse 16 implies that these Jewish men were divorcing their older Jewish wives in order to marry younger pagans. Verse 13 indicates that these carnal men were so dull that it didn't occur to them that their treacherous treatment of their wives had any affect on their relationship with God. Ignorantly they plead with Him to bless their crops not realizing that He had withdrawn His pleasure from them because of their sinful behavior. The original purpose for the chosen people was to remain spiritually dedicated to Jehovah (v. 15).

Life **stEP**

Love transcends physical beauty. Love is a command, not an emotion.

52 ● ● ● ● ● ● thursday

Malachi 3:1-6

What is the writer saying?

How can I apply this to my life?

PRAY Mexico – That the Mexicans find their identity in a personal faith in Christ.

My Messenger is Malaki in Hebrew (Malachi v. 1). It applies to the forerunner of the Messiah who by Jewish and Christian tradition is the prophet Elijah. In Christ's first coming, the role of the forerunner was played by John the Baptist. While John came in the spirit and power of Elijah he was not Elijah. (Matthew 11:14 "If you will receive it, this is Elijah ..." 17:11 "Elijah shall come." 17:12 "Elijah came and they didn't recognize him."). God in His sovereignty knew that the Jews would reject Christ and so John was not Elijah. When Christ comes the second time it would seem that the real Elijah will return, perhaps as one of the two witnesses of Revelation 11. Verse 2 speaks of the forerunner's purifying effect on the world. In ancient cities the launderers' guild had their shops downwind from the towns because of the smelly animal fats and urine (for uric acid) used in launderer's soap making it a potent bleach. God would bring the sinful chosen people through the refining fires and bring forth people worthy of worshipping His great name. Sorcery is just one of the forbidden skills used to contact the spirit world. Deuteronomy forbids any contact with the spirit world and then concludes on the positive note that God would send another prophet like Moses to give people more information. Ultimately this other prophet was/is Messiah. The first three sins are normally considered rather perverse and wicked (sorcery, adultery and lying under oath). Notice that not treating those around us fairly is in the same category. Oppressing the poor, widows, orphans and strangers is condemned in several of the Minor Prophets. Verse 6 abruptly changes from judgment to an explanation that God has promised (unconditionally) to eventually bless them.

Chastisement is not pleasant, but it yields eternal benefit, if we respond.

52 ●●●●●● Friday

Malachi 3:7-15

What is the writer saying?

How can I apply this to my life?

PRAY New Zealand — To see many won to Christ through church-run food banks and counseling ministries.

Tithe means ten percent. The Israelites were required to give ten percent of all they earned each year as a tax for God's rule over them (the theocracy, which was religious and governmental). Offerings were above the tithe and were freewill. In failing to provide the tax and love offerings, they were snubbing God. The word for nation in verse 9 is the Hebrew word for Gentile nation (goy). The storehouse was part of the temple complex. The Old Testament economy had one theocratic capital, one temple, and one place of worship through giving. Since we live under a different system, there is no New Testament tithe (tax) mandated, nor a New Testament storehouse. The Greek grammar of 1 Corinthians 16:2 speaks of regular but private (at home) storage of offerings from which discretionary giving can take place when needs arise. New Testament giving is to be done out of a heart of gratitude as God has blessed each one. In their spiritual dullness, they had concluded that there was no profit in serving God and flagrantly rebelled against Him. Compare William Henley's famous Invictus: "Out of the night that surrounds me, black as the pit from pole to pole, I thank whatever Gods there be for my unconquerable soul. It matters not how straight the gate, how charged with punishments the scroll! I'm the master of my fate; I'm the captain of my soul!"

Life stEP

Those of us who love the Lord and know better can calmly reply in the words of Dorthea Day: "Out of the light that dazzles me, bright as the noonday sun from pole to pole, I thank the God I know to be for Jesus the lover of my soul. It matters not how straight the gate, He cleared from punishment the scroll! Christ's the master of my fate; Christ is the captain of my soul!"

Malachi 3:16-4:6

What is the writer saying?

How can I apply this to my life?

pray   China — For the effective use of radio and the Internet in reaching and discipling the Chinese.

The two types of people are listed in 3:16 18. Malachi watches as the angels bring a special book and the names of the righteous are written in the book for special care and blessing. Chapter 4 describes the nature of the coming judgment. It is the fiery day of the Lord"(4:1). Sinners get away with murder for the time being, but all the while they are losing all of their moisture and one day they will go up in flames like a month old Christmas tree. Verse 2 introduces the gracious Savior. Christ is spoken of as the S-U-N of Righteousness (The SON is the SUN). Wings refer to the rays of the sun. We know now that there is literally healing in the rays of the sun as the ultraviolet light kills germs and promotes the healing of wounds. Warmed by the rays of that life-giving orb, saints will skip through life like calves released on a spring day after a long, harsh, confining winter. Verse 3 explains why we don't have to envy the wicked. We should just consider their ends. The Israelites are told to remember the Law of Moses given on Mt. Horeb (Sinai) (4:4) and to look for Elijah, the forerunner of the Messiah (4:5 and 6). Both men made trips to Mt. Horeb (Exodus 19 and 1 Kings 19) and both appeared on the Mount of Transfiguration with Jesus before His crucifixion. Some feel that these two men are good candidates for the two witnesses of Revelation 11. Both had strange circumstances surrounding their departure from this life (Moses' body was buried by God Himself and Elijah went up in the fiery chariot). At least the two witnesses of Revelation 11 will function in the spirit and power of Moses and Elijah.

Life stEP   Genesis tells how a curse fell on the whole human race. The last words of the Old Testament indicate that the curse is still there. The first book of the New Testament introduces Him who came to remove the curse!